Economic Voting

Economic voting is a phenomenon that political scientists and economists can hardly overlook. There is ample evidence for a strong link between economic conditions and government popularity. However, not everything is that simple and this edited collection focuses on "the comparative puzzle" of economic voting. It has proven nearly impossible to identify stable vote or popularity functions in cross-country research or even within a country over time. Recent trends in economic voting research concentrate on the role played by institutions and structural factors in the relationship between economic fluctuations and voting behavior.

Economic Voting suggests a new approach. The theoretical and empirical assessment of economic voting needs to account for the contextual effects of political institutions and voter heterogeneity. It emphasizes the importance of comparative research design and argues that the psychology of the economic voter model needs to be developed further. Questions discussed include:

- Why are economic vote and popularity functions so unstable?
- What is the level of sophistication of the economic voter?
- How do political institutions affect economic voting?
- Can economic voting be explained with fundamental psychological variables, such as risk aversion, limited rationality or emotional response?
- Why did Al Gore lose the 2000 US Presidential Election while the economy was doing so well?
- What is the relationship between economic voting and the cost of ruling?

Han Dorussen is Lecturer in the Department of Government at the University of Essex. His main areas of research are comparative and international political economy and international relations.

Michaell Taylor is Senior Economist in the REIS Economics Research Group, New York. His main areas of research are comparative political behavior, comparative political economy and institutions.

Routledge/ECPR Studies in European Political Science

Edited by Jan W. van Deth, *University of Mannheim, Germany on behalf of the European Consortium for Political Research*

ecpr

The Routledge/ECPR Studies in European Political Science series is published in association with the European Consortium for Political Research – the leading organization concerned with the growth and development of political science in Europe. The series presents high-quality edited volumes on topics at the leading edge of current interest in political science and related fields, with contributions from European scholars and others who have presented work at ECPR workshops or research groups.

Economic Voting

Edited by Han Dorussen and
Michaell Taylor

London and New York

First published 2002
by Routledge
2 Park Square, Milton Park, Abingdon, Oxon, OX14 4RN

Simultaneously published in the USA and Canada
by Routledge
270 Madison Ave, New York NY 10016

Routledge is an imprint of the Taylor & Francis Group

Transferred to Digital Printing 2007

Typeset in Baskerville by
Integra Software Services Pvt. Ltd, Pondicherry, India

British Library Cataloguing in Publication Data
A catalogue record for this book is available from the British Library

Library of Congress Cataloging in Publication Data
Economic voting / edited by Han Dorussen and Michaell Taylor.
    p. cm.
  Includes bibliographical references and index.
  1. Voting—Economic aspects. 2. Economic policy—Public opinion.
  3. Rational choice theory—Political aspects. 4. Social choice—Political
aspects. I. Dorussen, Han, 1962– II. Taylor, Michaell.
JF1001 .E28 2002
324.9—dc21

                                       2002069952

ISBN10: 0–415–25433–7 (hbk)
ISBN10: 0–415–45974–5 (pbk)

ISBN13: 978–0–415–25433–5 (hbk)
ISBN13: 978–0–415–45974–7 (pbk)

Contents

Figures

Tables

Contributors

Paolo Bellucci is Associate Prof. of Political Science at the Università del Molise and Visiting Professor at the University of Siena. His research interests include comparative political behavior, public policy and elites. He is co-founder and member of the Board of the Italian National Election Study. He serves on the editorial committee of *Polis* and *La rivista trimestrale di scienza dell' amministrazione*.

Sean Carey is a Research Fellow at the Harvard-MIT Data Center and a Ph.D. Candidate in the Department of Government, University of Essex. His doctoral dissertation examines the impact of political parties on public support for European integration.

Harold D. Clarke is Ashbel Smith Prof., School of Social Sciences, University of Texas at Dallas. He is Editor-In-Chief of *Electoral Studies* and Joint Editor of *Political Research Quarterly*. His research focuses on voting, elections, and the political economy of party support in Anglo-American democracies. His articles have appeared in the *American Political Science Review*, the *American Journal of Political Science*, the *British Journal of Political Science*, the *Journal of Politics*, and other journals.

Aida Díaz is a Ph.D. Candidate in the Department de Ciència Política i de Dret Públic at the Universitat Autònoma de Barcelona.

Han Dorussen is Lecturer in the Department of Government at the University of Essex. His main areas of research are applications of game theory, comparative and international political economy, and international relations. Current research focuses on the political economy of voting and the use of economic instruments in international politics. He has published in *Public Choice, Electoral Studies*, the *Journal of Peace Research*, and the *Journal of Conflict Resolution*. He serves as Associate Editor of the *Journal of Peace Research*.

Raymond M. Duch is Prof. in Political Science at the University of Houston. He is the author of *Privatizing the Economy* (Michigan,

1994). He has also authored numerous articles, which have appeared in the *American Political Science Review*, the *American Journal of Political Science*, the *Journal of Politics*, and other journals. Currently, he is conducting two major research projects. The first project develops a set of formal explanations for democratic failure, supported with empirical analysis. The second project examines the micro-foundations for the successful adoption of market economies in the post-communist regimes. He currently serves on the editorial board of the *American Journal of Political Science*.

Marta Fraile is a Doctor member of the Juan March Institute (Madrid). She is Lecturer in the Department of Political Science at the Pompeu Fabra University in Barcelona. She specializes in electoral behavior, public opinion on social policies, statistics and methodology of the social sciences.

Peter Nannestad is Prof. in Public Politics, Department of Political Science, Aarhus University since 1991, and was the Head of Department from 1998 until 2001. He specializes in rational-choice theory, economic voting and economic policy. He has (co)authored of five books and numerous articles.

Helmut Norpoth is Prof. of Political Science at the State University of New York, Stony Brook. He is co-editor of *Economics and Politics: The Calculus of Consent*, and author of *Confidence Regained: Economics, Mrs Thatcher, and the British Voter*. His work on American electoral politics has been published in the *American Political Science Review, American Journal of Political Science*, and the *Journal of Politics*, among others. He regularly assists the *New York Times* with Election Day analyzes, and currently serves as director of studies at the Foreign Policies Association.

Martin Paldam is Prof. of Economics, University of Aarhus and was Chairman of the Economics Department, Aarhus, 1982/84. Approximately 160 articles published, of which fifty articles published in international journals, such as *Scandinavian Economic Journal, European Economic Review, Public Choice, Industrial & Labor Relations Review*, etc., thirty chapters in edited volumes from North-Holland, Cambridge University Press, etc. Publications further include three books (in Danish) and three edited books. President of the European Public Choice Society 1983/84, co-editor of the *Scandinavian Economic Journal* 1985/95 and the *European Journal of Political Economy*.

Harvey D. Palmer is Assistant Prof. at the Department of Political Science at the University of Mississippi. He specializes in voting behavior, public opinion, and political methodology. He has published in the *American Journal of Political Science, European Journal of Political*

Research, the *British Journal of Political Science, Electoral Studies, Journal of Politics*, and other journals.

Clara Riba is member of the Departament d'Economia i Empresa at the Universitat Pompeu Fabra in Barcelona. She teaches statistics and methods to Political Science students. Her main fields of research are political behavior and education and she has also performed some studies about evaluation of public policies. She has published in the *European Journal of Political Research, Evaluation and Program Planning* and other journals.

David Sanders is Prof. at the University of Essex. Author of *Patterns of Political Instability, Lawmaking and Co-operation in International Politics*, and *Losing an Empire, Finding A Role: British Foreign Policy Since 1945*, and numerous articles. Current research interests include international relations theory, British foreign policy, electoral behavior and election forecasting. Co-editor of the *British Journal of Political Science*.

Randolph T. Stevenson is the Albert Thomas Assistant Prof. of Political Science at the Department of Political Science at Rice University. He specializes in comparative democratic government and political methodology. He has published in the *American Political Science Review, American Journal of Political Science, Public Choice*, the *British Journal of Political Science*, and other journals.

Marianne C. Stewart is Prof. of Government, Politics and Political Economy in the School of Social Sciences at the University of Texas at Dallas. Her research focuses on elections and electoral choice, and democracy and political participation. She has published in the *American Political Science Review*, the *American Journal of Political Science*, the *European Journal of Political Research*, the *Journal of Politics*, and other journals. At present, she is co-investigator of The 2001 British Election Study and at work on *Political Choice in Britain* to be published by Oxford University Press (with Harold Clarke, David Sanders and Paul Whiteley).

Michaell Taylor is Senior Economist, Economics Research Group, REIS, New York. Main areas of research are comparative political behavior, comparative political economy, and institutions. Current research focuses on the political economy of voting, political participation, and system support in subelectorates and the mediating effects of institutions in political economics. He has published in the *European Journal of Political Research, Political Behavior, Electoral Studies*, and the *American Journal of Political Science*, among others.

Paul F. Whiteley is Prof. in Government at the University of Essex. Research interests are in the comparative study of political participation and citizenship, modeling the relationship between political support and the economy, investigating the links between social capital and political development and understanding British political parties. Publications include six books and numerous articles in academic journals including the *American Political Science Review*, the *British Journal of Political Science, the Journal of Politics*, and *the European Journal of Political Research*.

Guy D. Whitten is Associate Prof. of Political Science at Texas A&M University. He specializes in comparative politics and political methodology. He has published in the *American Journal of Politics*, the *British Journal of Political Science, Electoral Studies*, and other journals.

Series editor's preface

Marxists, presidential advisers, and many other people agree that the economy affects politics. In fact, this idea seems rather trivial and one does not have to become a Marxist or a political consultant to accept its accuracy. Yet empirical research in this area in the last decades resulted in a few nasty complications. Economic circumstances and developments – especially unemployment, inflation, and economic growth – do have an impact on the decision to vote for a party, but corroborations are mainly based on analyses of aggregate data and macro-level studies. Relying on data from individual voters it appears to be much more difficult to demonstrate a direct link between economic conditions and prospects on the one hand, and actual political decisions of voters on the other. Apparently, voters do care about the economic situation and they do hold politicians responsible for economic success and decline, but much remains ambiguous and unclear if we review the empirical evidence available.

Despite the impressive amount of work on "economic voting" in the last decades, several white spots still exist. Many analyses focussed on the relationships between objective economic indicators, subjective interpretations and economic expectations, and voting decisions. However, in attempts to apply general theories about the calculus that drives economic voting, the specific *political* aspects of elections seem to be neglected. The contributors to this volume all accept the idea that the cognitive processes of economic voting varies with the political context. They differ clearly in their research interests, study designs, selected material, and the scope of their analyses, but they all cope with the impact of specific political and economic circumstances on voting decisions. The three major parts of this volume address the central questions of this project: the relevance of political institutions, the differences between distinct groups, and the changes in economic voting.

Before specific treatments of these three themes are presented, Han Dorussen and Harvey Palmer offer an overview of the main approaches and contested conclusions in this area (Chapter 1). Subsequently, they arrange the various contributions to this volume according to the research design applied and the main research topics selected (groups/ institutions and prospective/retrospective approaches). The first part consists of five contributions addressed to the impact of political institutions. In a straightforward analysis Peter Nannestad and Martin Paldam show that ruling implies costs in terms of the share of votes government parties have to "pay" if they are re-elected (Chapter 2). Randolph Stevenson argues that economic changes, which occur in different economic contexts, have different political consequences (Chapter 3), whereas Harvey Palmer and Guy Whitten explore the limits of voter sophistication under different political and economic circumstances (Chapter 4). On the basis of a comparison of Dutch and German experiences with multi-party systems Han Dorussen and Michaell Taylor show that economic subgroups offer a more appropriate level of analysis than individual or national levels do (Chapter 5). Helmut Norpoth presents a highly interesting explanation of the puzzle about the 2000 US-presidential election by introducing term limits as a relevant factor (Chapter 6). The next three contributions focus on the heterogeneity of voters. Raymond Duch and Harvey Palmer start this part with the idea that voters' evaluations of the economic conditions are not idiosyncratic but form an important part of the effects of individual characteristics (Chapter 7). Using a Catalonian case study Clara Riba and Aida Díaz show that not only national governments are the object of the economic voting calculus of citizens (Chapter 8). David Sanders and Sean Carey present findings of cross-national analyses indicating the existence of temporal variations in economic voting within countries (Chapter 9). The third part of the volume continues this debate by focussing on the changes in economic voting. Harold Clarke, Marianne Stewart and Paul Whiteley argue that emotional reactions to economic conditions play a significant role in British elections (Chapter 10). The necessity to study specific circumstances and contexts in order to understand the way economic voting actually functions is demonstrated for Italy by Paolo Belluci (Chapter 11) and for Spain by Marta Fraile (Chapter 12). Finally, Han Dorussen returns to the major problems and prospects of economic voting in his concluding chapter by underlining the need for comparative studies and for a further development of more sophisticated psychological models of economic voting than offered by conventional rational-actor theories (Chapter 13).

With the continuing emancipation of mass electorates in the near future traditional ties and influences will be replaced gradually by more policy-oriented attitudes. This does not mean that more and more voters in different countries simply become more and more similar in the way they decide to vote. On the contrary, as the empirical analyses presented in this volume show, economic voting depends highly on the specific economic and political conditions. Combining the attempts to develop a general cognitive theory about the calculus of economic voting on the hand, and taking into account evident contextual differences on the other, is an exciting challenge for anybody interested in the way modern democracies function.

Jan W. van Deth
Mannheim, January 2002

Preface

Economic voting is one of the enduring themes of Political Science. There are probably two main reasons for its attractiveness. First, there is ample evidence for a relatively strong link between economic conditions and government popularity. Economic voting is a phenomenon that political scientists and economists can hardly overlook. Politicians are also acutely aware of the fact that economics matters, which gives the research clear policy relevance. The second reason may very well be that plenty of questions and unresolved debates remain. In other words, there is still enough work left to do. The chapters in this volume focus predominantly on an issue that has become increasingly important, namely the instability problem or the comparative puzzle. So far, it has proven impossible to identify stable vote or popularity functions in cross-country research or even within a country over time. Although the papers do not provide a direct solution to the problem, together they do suggest an approach that may prove fruitful. First of all, the importance of comparative research is emphasized. Second, it is argued that the psychology of the economic-voter model needs further development. In particular, it is important to identify fundamental parameters that help us understand how voters deal with the complexity of their political and economic circumstances. To put it more simply: we need to know how a rational economic voter reasons.

The project got its start at the ECPR 1999 Joint Sessions which were held in Mannheim, Germany. We had organized a workshop on political institutions as intermediaries between economics and politics. The workshop provided a forum for lively discussions that were, in everybody's opinion, extremely constructive. Clearly, the research community on economic voting benefits from a shared understanding of the main issues and the qualities and pitfalls of various research designs. And fortunately, enough room for idiosyncrasy is left. As discussions progressed, our original notion about the relevance of political institutions had to compete with ideas about voter heterogeneity, especially pertaining to levels of information and sophistication, as possible explanation for the instability problem. The quality of the meeting provided an encouragement to reconvene the participants and to try to collect their papers.

Most participants of the original workshop met again in the spring of 2000 in Trondheim, Norway. At that time, earlier versions of the articles assembled here were presented, and a real effort was made to distill a common perspective. To a large extent, the book represents the outcome of those discussions. A consensus emerged that the instability problem is more apparent than inherent. The comparative enterprise remains crucial to advance our knowledge of economic voting. However, there remains a clear need for better theory, research design, and data. All of this requires a proper understanding of economic voting with a heightened awareness of its underlying socio-psychological factors. To put it slightly differently, economic voting is a theory about *applied* rational, that is *reasoning*, behavior.

Acknowledgments

Economic Voting is first of all the result of two weeklong meetings. Moreover, the chapters all benefited from external review. As a result, we are indebted to a large number of people. In Mannheim, the staff of the ECPR and the department of Political Science got us started right; special thanks to Jan W. van Deth. The meetings in Trondheim received generous financial support from the Norwegian Research Council (NFR 134517/530), the School of Social Science and Technology Management, and the Department of Sociology and Political Science of the Norwegian University of Science and Technology. Mary Prestløkken, the secretary of the Department of Sociology and Political Science, and Ragnhild Thorin were extremely helpful in helping to organize the meetings in Trondheim.

The book got additional financial support from the Norwegian Research Council (NFR 144306/530). We would like to thank Tåle Baadsvik for compiling the index and the lists of tables and figures. We are especially thankful to Marian de Vooght for her work as language editor and editorial assistant. We also gratefully acknowledge the permission of Elsevier Publishers to reprint Table 1.1: The main stylized facts about the VP function, by Martin Paldam and Michael Lewis-Beck (2000) "Economic Voting: An Introduction," *Electoral Studies*, 19, 2/3: 114.

The following persons helped with their participation in the discussions and/or reviews of earlier versions of the chapters: Toke S. Aidt, Glenn Alcoe, Christopher J. Anderson, Nathaniel Beck, Ton Bertrand, Fredrik Carlsen, Eduardo Feldman, Jan Fidrmuc, Linda Gonçalves Veiga, Bruno Jerôme, Marc Hetherington, Tse-min Lin, Ola Listhaug, Michael Lewis-Beck, Ole Nørgaard, and Gerrit de Vries.

1 The context of economic voting

An introduction

Han Dorussen and Harvey D. Palmer

Research in economic voting has become increasingly comparative by nature. The most likely reason is the persistence of the comparative puzzle, which can be succinctly put as: Given the finding of temporal and spatial instability of vote and popularity functions (VP functions), what, if any, is the foundation of economic voting? The chapters in this volume argue that a foundation is to be found in "deep" socio-psychological factors. Economic voting is a theory about applied rational, i.e. *reasoning*, behavior. Rationality provides only a baseline (ideal) model. The application of such a baseline model requires an understanding of the "real" psychological environment in which thinking about the economy and using these thoughts to make voting decisions takes place. Three sets of variables are of special interest. Previous research suggests that people are generally risk averse. Further, investigation of socio-psychological factors calls for modest expectations about and a realistic assessment of the level of voter sophistication. Finally, emotional or affective factors may matter. Moreover, the impact of these factors need not be constant across political institutions and, perhaps even more obviously, personal contexts. With respect to the latter, a better understanding of voter heterogeneity expands knowledge of group differences in the applied reasoning that underlies economic-voting behavior. Thus, further theoretical development and empirical evaluation of the economic-voting paradigm need to account for these contextual effects.

1.1 ECONOMIC VOTING AS POLICY VOTING

Economic voting is an instrumental act. Ideally, the electorate expresses at the ballot its preferences about proper management of the economy, arguably the most important area of domestic politics. Somewhat less ambitiously, voters evaluate the incumbent government on the basis of economic policy outcomes – inflation, unemployment, growth, value of national currency, development of stock prices, etc. Politicians who fail to heed the policy goals of the public, or who show a lack of competence in "managing" the economy, are turned out of office. Economic voting thus constitutes a mechanism of democratic accountability.

In its ideal form, the theory of economic voting is a special case of the rational-choice perspective on electoral behavior. Economic voting enables the electorate to maximize individual utility or welfare. Office-seeking politicians offer policy packages that maximize their likelihood of winning elections and thereby obtaining a role in government. So far, the only restrictive or "empirical" assumption is that economic policy dominates the utility functions of – at least a sufficiently large part of – the electorate. Much of the early research on economic voting demonstrated the validity of this "empirical" assumption, i.e. that economic policy, or at least economic performance, had enough salience among the electorate to significantly influence election outcomes. The explosive growth of the economic-voting literature, though, has largely been due to the emergence of numerous controversies surrounding the nature of the economic-voting calculus. Exactly which economic policies matter most to voters? Is the electorate generally concerned about personal financial circumstances or about national economic conditions? Does the salience of economic policy vary in meaningful ways across groups of voters, electoral contexts, and political systems?

Political reality does not necessarily match the ideal of democratic accountability. Voters may fail to recognize the relevant policy outcomes or to accurately attribute policy-making responsibility for them. Such failures undermine the electoral incentives that governments have to pursue the public's policy goals. Poorly informed voters might reward or punish incumbent governments at the polls based on erroneous assessment of policy outcomes. They may also identify the policy outcomes correctly but misperceive who is responsible for them. Consequently, they might punish or reward the "wrong" politicians. In the case of complete failure, the electoral process might make politicians attentive to swings in public opinion but would not shape government policy making. Consequently, in the case of complete policy ignorance, finding a statistical relationship between economic perceptions (emotions) and voting behavior would not constitute evidence of policy representation.

This scenario of policy-ignorant economic voting is the antithesis of the characterization presented earlier of highly informed, policy-oriented economic voters. Most scholars would agree that the political reality of economic voting is located somewhere between the ideal of policy voting and the cynical view of largely unpredictable swings in public opinion. The main point is that the limits of voter sophistication constrain economic voting as a mechanism of democratic accountability. Evidence of economic voting only demonstrates that elections ensure representative government if the electorate to some degree approaches the ideal of the rational voter. The extent to which the voter actually engages in applied reasoning on economic policy is still an issue of considerable debate.

Survey research generally shows low levels of political sophistication, i.e. typical voters lack much knowledge and interest in politics (Iyengar, 1987; Suzuki, 1991). According to this perspective, the state of the economy serves as an information shortcut that simplifies voting decisions for the largely uninformed and uninterested public. Voters are myopic and retrospective, deciding whether to reward or punish the incumbent based on national economic conditions (performance) (Aidt, 2000; Paldam and Nannestad, 2000). Voters rely on this retrospective evaluation without any consideration of what possible implications the election outcome might have for future government policy and their own financial well-being. MacKuen *et al.* (1992) refer to such economic voters as "peasants."

In contrast to survey research, macro-level studies consistently find a strong relationship between macroeconomic conditions and government popularity and political support. These findings suggest that voters are – or at least in the aggregate behave as if they were – relatively sophisticated, conforming to rational expectations or at least limited rationality. According to this perspective, voters are policy-oriented and prospective, making election decisions on the basis of the future implications that the candidates' or parties' policy positions have for the national economy and their own personal welfare. These sophisticated economic voters not only employ past economic conditions and performance as information-economizing devices, but also incorporate current information when forming expectations about the incumbent's future policy performance. MacKuen *et al.* (1992) find evidence for the existence of such economic voters, to whom they refer as "bankers."

The question about whether economic voters are "peasants" or "bankers" reflects a broader scholarly interest in the exact nature of the decision calculus that drives economic voting. In a recent survey essay, Lewis-Beck and Paldam (2000) summarize the main findings of the burgeoning literature on economic voting. Their findings are reproduced in Table 1.1, and identify two notable gaps in the current literature: instability problems, also known as the comparative puzzle (IX), and the lack of understanding of the cognitive reality of economic voting (VIII). Both of these gaps in the literature relate to the issue of whether contextual factors shape the applied reasoning underlying economic voting. Macro-level research has successfully identified several vote and popularity functions (henceforth VP functions), just to find that these VP functions disappear when empirical models are extended to more countries or even more time points in the same country. At worst, this instability indicates that efforts to validate the VP function have been frustrated by low voter sophistication and hence any evidence of economic voting will be only haphazard by nature. At best, the comparative puzzle suggests that we are overlooking something important – perhaps that the cognitive process of economic voting varies with the political

Table 1.1 The main stylized facts about the vote and popularity function

I	VP functions are basically similar, but the fit of popularity functions is better
II	*E-fraction*: economic change explains about one-third of the change in the vote
III	*The big two*: the vote reacts to a few macroeconomic variables – mainly unemployment and inflation
IV	Voters are myopic and hence make decisions with a short-time horizon
V	*Retrospective/prospective controversy*: voters react to past (retrospective) events more than to expected (prospective) ones, but the difference is small
VI	*Sociotropic/egotropic controversy*: sociotropic (national) economic voting is generally stronger than egotropic (personal) economic voting; however, there are some notable country exceptions
VII	*The grievance asymmetry*: voters may react more to negative changes than to corresponding positive ones
VIII	Little is known about the macroeconomic knowledge of voters and how it is obtained
IX	*The instability problem*: the main problem in the literature is that the VP function lacks stability, both in cross-country studies and in the same country over time

Notes
Reprinted from Lewis-Beck and Paldam (2000) Economic Voting: an introduction. *Electoral Stud.*, **19**(2/3), 114. Copyright 2000, with permission from Elsevier Science.

context. The chapters in this volume pursue this more optimistic implication of the comparative puzzle by investigating whether electoral circumstances, institutions, and socio-psychological factors condition the VP function in theoretically meaningful ways.

In their seminal work, Powell and Whitten (1993) identified the political context as one factor generally overlooked by previous research on economic voting. The political and economic institutions in which public policy is made serve as a lens that adjusts our perception of government responsibility. The clarity-of-responsibility hypothesis states that economic voting, as an effective mechanism of government accountability, is conditional on the political context – increasing in strength when responsibility is clear and decreasing in strength when it is not. Hence, Powell and Whitten demonstrated that political institutions condition the VP function (also see Anderson, 1995, 2000; Pacek and Radcliff, 1995; Whitten and Palmer, 1999; Nadeau *et al.*, 2002).

Even earlier, several researchers had also observed variation in the personal context of economic voting – the issue of voter heterogeneity (Weatherford, 1978; Hibbs, 1982a–1982c; Krause, 1997). Information about and interest in economics and politics varies from country to country, from one socioeconomic group to another, and even over time. Analogous to the responsibility hypothesis, the salience hypothesis asserts that economic voting is conditional on personal context – increasing in strength when and for whom political-economic factors are salient and decreasing in strength when and for whom they are not. Without properly accounting for the political, economic, and sociological contexts of economic voting, we should not expect to find stable VP functions.

Even though a careful identification of the context of economic voting is indispensable, we do not consider this to be a panacea for all our problems. More fundamentally, the rationality of the economic voter is better seen as reasoning behavior. Rationality provides only a baseline or ideal model. Economic voting is an application of the baseline model and requires an understanding of the "real" cognitive environment of the voter. The central question is to determine how voters think about the economy and how they use these thoughts to choose among parties/candidates at the polls. The mass political behavior modeled in VP functions is inextricably connected with the cognitive environment. By necessity, we measure and thus aim to explain *reasoned* instead of *rational* behavior.

1.2 PATHS AND PITFALLS OF ECONOMIC VOTING

Economic voting is often presented as a black box: changes in economic conditions provide the input, producing changes in vote share, and/or popularity as the output. The causal chain, however, consists of several possible links. In Figure 1.1, we open the lid of the box to identify the main elements and to further detail the processes that translate changes in economic conditions into swings in voting/popularity. This schematic representation allows us to distinguish various paths from economics to

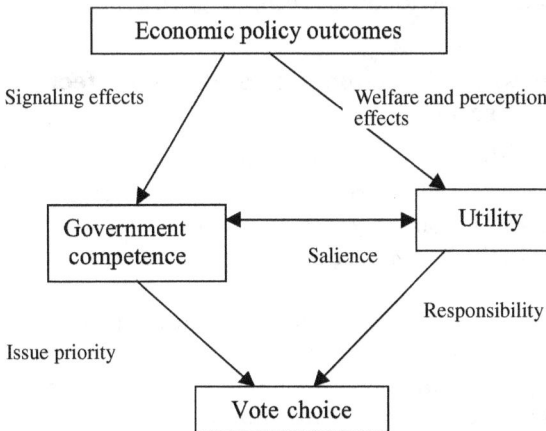

Figure 1.1 Schematic representation of economic voting.

voting, for example, by way of welfare effects and attribution of policy responsibility. It follows directly that the causal chain might contain weak links: either voters may fail to perceive the effect of economic conditions on their personal welfare, or they may fail to properly attribute responsibility for economic policy outcomes. The existence of such weak links, regardless of their exact nature, obscures the evidence of economic voting (at least along a particular causal path).

For economic voting to work as an effective mechanism of democratic accountability, the causal chain connecting economic policy outcomes to vote choice must be complete. This imposes two requirements on the voters' decision calculus. First, it requires that either the welfare/perception effects or signaling effects, or both in tandem, are strong enough to influence citizens' perceptions of government economic performance. Second, perceptions of performance must consistently shape voting behavior. This requires that attribution of responsibility and/or issue-priority effects are sufficiently strong that politicians respond to economic voting as a manifestation of voters' demands about how to manage the economy.

Thus, the rational economic voter has to make a complete, comprehensive evaluation of economic circumstances and to find answers to the following kind of questions. What do economic indicators tell me about the government's management of the economy? To what extent is my personal welfare (which is likely to be influenced by the state of the national economy) affected by these conditions? Does the state of the economy provide a reliable indication of government competence in general? Do economic conditions give me reason to care at all? Should the current government be held responsible for these conditions? If so, is there a viable alternative to the current government? What kind of policies would I want a future government to pursue? All these questions raise important issues for research on economic voting. We consider these issues in more detail in the following, using Figure 1.1 as a compass.

1.2.1 Welfare: how/when do economic conditions affect the utility/welfare of the electorate?

It is commonly assumed that economic conditions affect the welfare (and thus the utility) of the electorate in a direct and obvious manner. Moreover, governments would have little ability to influence this link. However, several enduring controversies in the literature concentrate exactly on this link.

- How accurate are citizens' perceptions of economic conditions? Especially, are there systematic biases in these perceptions? For example, are supporters of the governing parties more likely to perceive the economy as being in better shape?
- Is it more appropriate to use actual economic indicators or perceptions of these indicators? In case we use objective indicators, should

they be measured in real or nominal terms (i.e. are we looking for income effects or not)?

- We may observe asymmetries in reactions to economic indicators. The grievance-asymmetry hypothesis states that voters react more to negative changes than to positive ones. People do not necessarily react in the same way to similar economic conditions. Not all people are equally vulnerable to unemployment, sensitive to price increases, or likely to benefit from economic upswings.
- *A priori*, we should not equate utility with personal prosperity. The controversy about the relative importance of personal and more general (national) economic conditions is well known. Utility effects, however, should also encompass affective reactions to economy conditions.
- It is not necessary that governments remain passive. Instead, they can try to influence the welfare/utility effects of economic conditions. Business-cycle arguments are clearly relevant in this respect, but also questions about what motivates governments to provide safety nets or other forms of subsidies protecting certain groups from the negative effects of economic fluctuation.

A lot of these issues point at voter heterogeneity as a possible source of systematic bias in the link between economics and voting. The final argument, however, suggests that institutions may also matter: not all political institutions allow for similar techniques to manipulate the economy or to shield groups from economic downturns. In sum, the context of voting potentially shapes how and when economic conditions affect the personal welfare of the electorate.

1.2.2 Signaling: economic conditions as a signal of competence?

Economic conditions also provide information about political actors that is useful for the electorate. To a certain extent, we can distinguish these informational effects from direct effects on the personal welfare of the electorate. Yet, the proposition that economic conditions signal government competence is not far removed from traditional conceptions of economic voting. The classic reward–punishment hypothesis implies a basic form of signaling. This model of economic voting assumes that past indicators are useful directives for future behavior and that good times ask for stability and bad times for change. The implication is that voters care about the competency of the incumbent. Rational-expectations models assign an even more prominent role to signaling or information effects and present arguments that go considerably beyond the rather simplistic reward–punishment hypothesis. The distinction raises several issues.

- Economic conditions provide only a signal about competency when they are *separating*. In other words, the electorate should care only about the extent to which economic conditions differ from what a competent government could have achieved. In practice, this means that the electorate should pay attention only to the unexpected components of inflation and economic growth.
- The signal should not indicate only the state of competency but, preferably, should differentiate between levels of competency as well. When all parties are equally (in)competent in handling the economy, it is inconsequential which party is actually in government. Moreover, voters might expect parties to vary in their competency in handling different dimensions of the economy. The evaluation of (in)competency is thus related to the stated issue priority of a party.

Clearly, rational-expectations models assume high levels of voter sophistication. Voter heterogeneity matters in that we may only be able to actually observe strong signaling effects for those people for whom this assumption is appropriate. For example, signaling effects are relevant only for those segments of the population that have a cognitive advantage or a special interest in paying close attention to the economy, the so-called informational elites. However, we could perhaps observe similar effects indirectly in mass political behavior, which is generally characterized by rational ignorance.

1.2.3   Responsibility: when can politicians take credit for a strong economy, or escape responsibility for a bad one?

Even if voters notice that economic conditions have an effect on their lives, this need not lead them to assign credit or blame to politicians. Weatherford (1983) suggests that the politicization of economic conditions is inversely related to an ethic of self-reliance. More generally, the willingness to attribute responsibility to economic conditions is likely to vary across socioeconomic groups.

Political institutions also play a role in conditioning the attribution of responsibility for economic policy outcomes, as Powell and Whitten's (1993) research clearly demonstrates. The clarity-of-responsibility hypothesis posits that the mix of political institutions and electoral circumstances in a country shape citizens' perceptions of government responsibility for policy making and economic management. The list of potentially relevant factors here is long and there remains uncertainty about which ones matter most. Researchers have considered the effects of bi- or unicameralism, divided government, electoral rules, number of parties, party fractionalization, majority versus minority governments, single-party versus coalition governments, and the fractionalization of coalition government.

But even this long list does not exhaust the set of possible factors. The attribution of responsibility in federal systems might vary depending on the level of government under consideration. Independence of the executive (e.g. central bank independence) might enable politicians to avoid responsibility for certain economic conditions. Globalization might even allow them to characterize economics as a force of nature. Then again, the limits of voter sophistication suggest that the electorate does not particularly care about such subtleties. Concern with economic conditions makes the electorate eager to administer "vengeance or reward" at the polls, but their target might be the one clearest in sight rather than most deserving.

1.2.4 Issue priority: "The best (wo)man for the job?"

By definition, voting is a prospective act: parties are going to benefit or suffer in the future from the aggregated decisions of voters in the present. Nevertheless, the vote choice is often portrayed in exclusive retrospective terms: reward/punishment for past performance. A vote is only an instrumentally rational act if it makes a difference in the election outcome. This requirement rests on the existence of two conditions.

First, a voter (or a group of them) should feel pivotal in the relationship between economics and future government. To the extent that economic conditions influence the personal welfare of specific groups in society, they should matter only if their vote is of importance to the creation of future governments. A viable alternative to the incumbent government should actually be available. This latter condition is sometimes referred to as the clarity-of-opposition hypothesis. Many of the political factors identified above in the context of the clarity-of-responsibility hypothesis also have relevance for the clarity-of-opposition hypothesis. Moreover, it is reasonable to expect that their conditioning role is even more significant here because voters have to evaluate the implication of their votes on the composition of the future government, mitigated through the maze of more or less complex institutions.

Second, the implication of a future government for economic policy has to be evaluated. Party ideology determines for a large part the extent to which parties feel justified to intervene in the economy. Thus, it should be much more important for a leftwing government to demonstrate competency in handling the economy than for a rightwing government. The evaluation of competency also varies depending on the professed priorities of a given party. Evaluation is made relative to expectations. A conservative party is expected to control inflation and limit fluctuations in the value of the national currency. In contrast, a labor government is expected to produce decent unemployment statistics. These expectations are held by the core supporters of the left- and rightwing parties if not by the electorate in general. Given these expectations, the target(s) of economic voting should vary with the relative salience of different issues. Yet, the opposition might hardly represent a credible alternative to the government in handling the most salient economic issues. Consequently, a trade-off between issue priority and competency exists: a slightly less competent government but one that places more emphasis on a given policy area might occasionally be preferable.

1.2.5   Salience: "When the going gets tough,…"

Concerns about management of the economy are not always equally important. The salience hypothesis asserts that welfare and/or signaling effects need to be sufficiently strong before economic conditions will actually affect the voting decision by way of responsibility or issue-priority attribution. Economic voting is conditional on the psycho-sociological context that makes economic conditions salient. The grievance-asymmetry hypothesis provides a particular application of salience effects. It states that voters are particularly attuned to economic troubles, because they are averse to risk. In economic crises, feelings of uncertainty or even fear may also come to dominate, thereby augmenting the impact of economic conditions on voting behavior. On the other hand, during good times, voters might take the economy for granted and shift their attention to other issues. Moreover, economics may have relatively low priority in countries that have recently gone through major political or institutional upheaval.

The scheme in Figure 1.1 can also be read in a slightly different way. Two dimensions (or controversies) dominate the research on economic voting presented in this volume. The first dimension distinguishes the level of assumed voter sophistication. The first path from economic conditions to the vote decision goes by way of signaling as evaluation of competency. Thus voters act more in response to expected (prospective) events. This model of economic voting assumes relatively high levels of voter sophistication. In contrast, welfare and responsibility effects constitute a reaction to past (retrospective) events, and the model assumes a lower level of voter sophistication. The second dimension distinguishes between institutions and voter heterogeneity as the main contextual factors. This dimension distinguishes signaling and welfare effects from issue-priority and responsibility effects, where the former are mainly concerned with voter heterogeneity and the latter with institutional variation.

1.3   AN OUTLINE OF WHAT FOLLOWS

The chapters in Part I, focus on the context provided by political institutions. In various ways, they extend the insight of Powell and Whitten (1993) that we should not expect to find stable vote or popularity functions without considering the institutional differences in which economic voting takes place. However, to trace the effects, if any, of these institutional differences, they need to be placed in a wider context. Chapter 2 thus provides an important cornerstone to the remainder of the volume, because Nannestad and Paldam convincingly demonstrate the existence of a political phenomenon, the cost of ruling, that is extremely stable across a wide variety of political institutions and even across divergent economic circumstances. The electorate reacts to incumbency in a predictable way. The stability is best explained by a "deep" socio-psychological factor: framing effects or risk aversion.

The other chapters in the first part of the volume focus on how the institutional context affects the "reasoning" of economic voting. In doing so, they emphasize various links between economic conditions and voting. Stevenson emphasizes the path from welfare effects to issue-priority voting. Palmer and Whitten focus on the signaling effect of economic conditions and its impact by way of responsibility. Dorussen and Taylor link welfare and perception effects to the assignment of responsibility. Norpoth considers the attribution of responsibility under a specific institutional feature of American presidential elections. He demonstrates that term limits impinge on the basic model of economic voting.

Voter heterogeneity – the main topic of Part II – resembles institutional variation in that both require a comparative approach and, theoretically, suggest a need to find a common foundation in the cognitive reality of economic voting. Social institutions (i.e. those that account for voter heterogeneity) provide differences in the context of economic voting. Duch and Palmer argue that voter heterogeneity, especially with respect to proclivity to seek and process information, causes systematic bias in aggregate economic evaluations. Institutional features provide, moreover, possible explanations for cross-national variations in the magnitude of these biases. Riba and Díaz examine economic voting in the context of multilevel government. Their argument emphasizes individual and contextual factors in the causal links between evaluation, approval, and vote intention. They find that even institutions without explicit responsibility for macroeconomic policy are still held responsible by the electorate. They also find support for the grievance-asymmetry hypothesis. Sanders and Carey demonstrate that social institutions are a logical corollary to political institutions. Moreover, they suggest that cross-national variation in the strength of the clarity-of-responsibility effect is due to variation in voters' risk

Table 1.2 Survey of featured studies

Author(s)	First dimension		Second dimension	
	Voter heterogeneity	Institutional variation	Low sophistication	High sophistication
Paldam and Nannestad	Comparative	Constant cost of ruling	Loss aversion	NI
Stevenson	Comparative	Economic conditions	NI	Luxury goods
Palmer and Whitten	Comparative	Clarity of responsibility, unemployment benefits	NI	Unexpected inflation and growth
Dorussen and Taylor	Comparative (Netherlands, Germany) — Group economic voting	Coalition complexity	Loyalty	Coalition formation heuristic
Norpoth	US	Term limits	Incumbent-oriented voting	NI
Duch and Palmer	Comparative — Information differences and subjective considerations	Partisan cues and media influence	Retrospective voting similar	Prospective voting similar
Riba and Díaz	Spain (Catalonia) — Grievance asymmetry	Multilevel government	Retrospective voting	NI
Sanders and Carey	Comparative	Temporal variation of feel-good factor (risk orientation)	NI	NI
Clarke, Stewart and Whiteley	UK — Interaction between affective and cognitive response	NI	Retrospection	Expectations
Bellucci	Italy — Classes	Party programs	Retrospective voting	NI
Fraile	Spain	Credibility of opposition	Retrospective voting stronger	Prospective voting smaller

Note
NI: not investigated.

orientations. Thus, all these chapters link responsibility effects to variation in welfare and perception effects.

Changes in economic-voting behavior are the main concern of Part III. Under normal circumstances, the political and social context of economic voting only exhibits minor changes over time, which explains the relative stability of country-specific VP functions. All countries, however, occasionally experience economic and/or political crises. These crises are likely to lead to a "changing economic voter." The three final chapters of this volume examine the impact of system shocks on economic voting, reiterating the importance of the themes presented earlier. Clarke, Stewart and Whiteley focus on the interactive effect of economic crises and voter heterogeneity. They evaluate the importance of emotional reactions to national and personal economic conditions. In "normal" times, perception and evaluation follow object-ive indicators closely. But following a crisis, affective factors, like feel-ings of insecurity or even fear, intervene in the causal linkage and create grievance asymmetry. Bellucci traces changes from class-based voting to economic voting, which suggests how different mixes of institutional and sociological factors may limit or heighten the import-ance of economic voters. Finally, Fraile examines the return to "normality" of economic voting in Spain. Following a profound institu-tional shock (the end of the Franco dictatorship), it took nearly two decades for the opposition to gain credibility. This was a necessary condition for the retrospective economic voter to emerge.

Table 1.2 presents a summary guide through the chapters that follow. It identifies the area of application and the comparative method used. Additionally, we characterize each study along the voter heterogeneity/institutional dimension, and the prospective/retrospective dimension (or the assumption of either high or low sophistication). Finally, we provide keywords to summarize the argument used by the authors to explain why the sociological and/or political factors that they analyze have relevance as conditioning variables in the economic-voting model.

The contributions to this book share a concern for the proper identi-fication and measurement of the context of economic voting. The fea-tured studies are all comparative, many applying pooled time-series analysis, that combine the comparison of countries and time periods. Several studies also include comparisons within countries, e.g. between levels of government or socioeconomic groups. Any effort to find stable results without controlling for context would thus be idle hope. Most importantly, however, the studies are also united in their search for a common foundation in the psychological context of economic voting. Some studies explicitly include emotional or affective factors. Collectively, however, the studies demonstrate a preference for either risk aversion or voter sophistication as important candidates for "deep" parameters of human behavior in economic voting.

14   *Han Dorussen and Harvey D. Palmer*

REFERENCES

Aidt, T.S. (2000) Economic voting and information. *Electoral Stud.*, **19**(2/3), 346–362.

Anderson, C.J. (1995) *Blaming the Government: Citizens and the Economy in Five European Democracies*. Armonk, NY: Sharpe.

Anderson, C.J. (2000) Economic voting and political context: a comparative context. *Electoral Stud.*, **19**, 151–170.

Hibbs Jr., D.A. (1982a) The dynamics of political support for American Presidents among occupational and partisan groups. *Am. J. Political Sci.*, **26**, 312–332.

Hibbs Jr., D.A. (1982b) Economic outcomes and political support for British Governments among occupational classes: a dynamic analysis. *Am. Political Sci. Rev.*, **76**, 259–279.

Hibbs Jr., D.A. (1982c) On the demand for economic outcomes: macroeconomic performance and mass political support in the United States, Great Britain, and Germany. *J. Politics*, **44**, 426–462.

Iyengar, S. (1987) Television news and citizens' expectations of national affairs. *Am. Political Sci. Rev.*, **81**, 815–832.

Krause, G.A. (1997) Voters, information heterogeneity, and the dynamics of aggregate economic expectations. *Am. J. Political Sci.*, **41**, 1170–1200.

Lewis-Beck, M.S. and Paldam, M. (2000) Economic voting: an introduction. *Electoral Stud.*, **19**(2/3), 113–123.

MacKuen, M.B., Erikson, R.S. and Stimson, J.A. (1992) Peasants or bankers? The American electorate and the US economy. *Am. Political Sci. Rev.*, **86**, 597–611.

Nadeau, R., Niemi, R.G. and Yoshinaka, A. (2002) A cross-national analysis of economic voting: taking account of the political context across time and nations. *Electoral Stud.*, **21**, in press.

Pacek, A.C. and Radcliff, B. (1995) Economic voting and the welfare state: a cross-national analysis. *J. Politics*, **57**, 44–61.

Paldam, M. and Nannestad, P. (2000) What do voters know about the economy? A study of Danish data, 1990–1993. *Electoral Stud.*, **19**(2/3), 363–391.

Powell, G.B. and Whitten, G.D. (1993) A cross-national analysis of economic voting: taking account of political context. *Am. J. Political Sci.*, **37**, 391–414.

Suzuki, M. (1991) Rationality of economic voting. *Am. J. Political Sci.*, **35**, 624–642.

Weatherford, M.S. (1978) Economic conditions and electoral outcomes: class differences in the political response to recession. *Am. J. Political Sci.*, **22**, 917–938.

Weatherford, M.S. (1983) Economic voting and the symbolic politics argument: a reinterpretation and synthesis. *Am. Political Sci. Rev.*, **77**, 158–174.

Whitten, G.D. and Palmer, H.D. (1999) Cross-national analyses of economic voting. *Electoral Stud.*, **18**, 49–67.

Part I

Political institutions and economic voting

2 The cost of ruling

A foundation stone for two theories

Peter Nannestad and Martin Paldam

2.1 INTRODUCING AN UNDERUTILIZED FACT

Few facts are so robust – and so little discussed – in political economy as the one that it costs votes to rule. Table 2.1 defines the outcome C_e of election e as the government's gain in the share of votes. The average gain is negative and hence a cost. Section 2.1.1 shows that the cost of ruling is $\lambda \approx 2.5$ percent.[1]

This is a puzzling fact. The ability and luck of governments vary, but – by definition – the average government must rule exactly as the rational voter expects. Therefore, the voters should vote as before. Consequently election outcomes should vary, but have no systematic component, i.e. there should be no cost of ruling, $\lambda = 0$. Clearly an explanation is needed.[2] Three explanations are available, of which two are shown to integrate well into other theories. Our main aim is to show that the cost of ruling provides a solid stone in the foundation of two alternative theoretical complexes in modern political economy.

Table 2.1 Definition of terms used in cost-of-ruling models

e	Time of election considered; the election is at $t = e$
e − 1	Time of last election; G may be installed just after e − 1 or later
G_e	Government ruling up to e; G may be one or more parties
L_{e-1}	The vote (in % of the votes cast) for (the parties of) G_e at election e − 1
V_e	The vote (in % of the votes cast) for (the parties of) G_e at election e
C_e	$= V_e - L_{e-1}$ is the election outcome, measured as the change in the vote for G_e
η	Operator for expectation; it may be assessed as the average of the past, i.e. $\eta(x) = \text{Avr}(x)$
λ	cost of ruling: minus the expected (or average past) election outcome $\lambda = -\eta(C_e) \approx -\text{Avr}(C_e)$
$v = s^2$	variation and standard deviations of C_e, i.e. $v = \eta(C_t + \lambda)^2 = \text{Var}(C_e)$

Notes
$L_{e-1} = V_{e-1}$ if G ruled before last election (e − 1), while $L_{e-1} \neq V_{e-1}$ if G changed between e − 1 and e.

The introduction has two subsections. The first defines the concepts discussed and shows how the cost of ruling relates to the vote function.[3] The second gives a brief overview of the rest of the chapter.

2.1.1   Basic definitions and the relation to the VP function

The two key concepts discussed are: (1) The election outcome, C_e. It sees elections as a referendum on the pre-election government. (2) The cost of ruling, λ, is the expected election outcome for the government before it starts ruling $\lambda = -\eta_{e-1}(C_e)$.[4] It is estimated as the average C_e, and so $\lambda \approx -\text{Avr}(C_e)$. The definitions of the two variables are further elaborated in Table 2.1.

The election outcome is explained by a vote function of the following type:

$$C_e = \lambda + F^e \text{ (economic change)} + F^p \text{ (political change)} + u \qquad (2.1a)$$

where F^e and F^p are calibrated so that the expectations

$$\eta(F^e) = \eta(F^p) = 0 \qquad\qquad\qquad\qquad\qquad\qquad (2.1b)$$

Here F^e and F^p are the economic and political parts of the function. At present F^e and F^p are not discussed. Model 1 is calibrated so that these terms have zero average for the average government. That is, the VP function is taken to be normalized so that the cost of ruling λ is the constant in the VP function. This allows us to say that the variation around the average is due to economic and political changes as assessed by the voters. This raises two problems.

Firstly, most VP function estimates are not calibrated as required by (1), and so the constant estimated contains λ + the calibration fault. This should be kept in mind, when the reader looks at his favorite VP function estimates and finds that the constant deviates from our estimate of $\lambda = 2\frac{1}{2}$.

Secondly, λ is supposedly accumulating over time. It has been claimed that λ is cyclical during the election period. The following section on the election cycle discusses this possibility. When not explicitly stated, the cost of ruling is taken to deal with an election period of "normal" duration of about three and three-quarter years.

2.1.2   Contents: a brief reader's guide

This section is an analysis of the cost of ruling for 19 established democracies over the last 50 years, generating 19 national λ_i's. The empirics of the cost of ruling were the subject of Paldam (1986, 1991),

Table 2.2 The empirical cost-of-ruling result

R1	The average government in an established democracy, ruling a normal election period, suffers a loss of $2\frac{1}{2}\%$ of the votes
R2	The standard deviation is $4\frac{1}{2}\%$ under parliamentary systems and twice as much in presidential systems

and so the present discussion is brief. The variation of election outcomes is large, and so the λ_i data can be generated by many processes. Consequently, the principle of Occam's Razor is applied. It asks: What is the simplest process that can generate these data?

It proves that the λ_i data are consistent with the simplest possible hypothesis. With a few easily explained exceptions, they can be generated by the same distribution, as listed in Table 2.2. Our key empirical claim is that λ does not depend upon the election system, the party structure, or the size of the country.

The exceptions mentioned under (R1) are:

(E1) λ is larger in very small countries (see the first part of the following section).

(E2) λ is different for governments ruling briefly.[5]

(E3) For newly established democracies it may take half a dozen elections for the party system to stabilize. While this happens C_e is likely to be unusually variable (see Fidrmuc, 2000).

(E4) In countries with large economic variability, C_e also becomes more volatile, and λ becomes larger. Compare here the findings of Gavin and Hausmann (1998) showing that economic volatility is relatively large in Latin America, with the large numbers for λ in the Latin American countries found in Remmer (1991).[6]

However, λ is remarkably constant in established democracies with a stable economy. (R1) and (R2) will be used to argue two theoretical points (T1) and (T2):

(T1) The cost of ruling has much greater explanatory power than hitherto recognized.

(T2) As the cost of ruling is an unusually stable constant, it should be explained by something going beyond institutions, i.e. by a "deep parameter" of human behavior.

Three theories try to explain the cost of ruling: Ex1, the coalition of minorities theory; Ex2, the median gap theory; Ex3, the grievance-asymmetry theory. Section 2.3 presents these theories and argues that Ex2 and Ex3 are the most convincing in the sense that they are integrated into two theoretical complexes: the median voter complex and the loss aversion complex, respectively.

Section 2.4 further discusses the loss aversion complex in a broader setting that also includes the grievance asymmetry. The loss (or risk) aversion of the average individual is the "deep parameter" explaining the cost of ruling in this complex. Section 2.5 shows that the cost of ruling simplifies political business cycle theory and makes the observed facts of a partisan cycle easier to understand. Section 2.6 turns to the alternative: the median voter complex. It also shows that the loss aversion complex provides an alternative explanation of most of the facts normally explained by the median voter theorem and the minimum winning coalition theory. The loss aversion explanation is thus shown to have the advantage of parsimony. By Occam's Razor it is a superior explanation. Section 2.7 asks if we have made extravagant claims, but concludes by making an even stronger claim.

2.2   A LOOK AT THE FACTS: THE DISTRIBUTION OF ELECTION OUTCOMES

The statistics for election outcomes in nineteen developed democracies for the last 50 years are compared in Section 2.2.1. For each country, the election outcomes are a sample of 8–21 observations. The standard deviations of the country samples are about twice the mean. This variation is large relative to the sample sizes, giving considerable variation in the calculated mean and standard variation.

Section 2.2.2 shows that the appropriate tests are unable to reject that most samples are random draws from the same general distribution. This section takes a further look at the distributions of election outcomes. Section 2.2.3 considers the development of λ over time. Once more λ turns out to be (almost) constant, though with a highly significant drop in the 1990s. Section 2.2.4 looks at λ for governments ruling shorter than a normal election period.

2.2.1   A look at data for nineteen countries: are election outcomes drawn from the same distribution?

The extreme right-hand column in Table 2.3 tests for normality. It appears that normality of the election outcomes can be rejected for none of the countries, though it gets close in a few cases. One should reject normality in one to two cases when performing nineteen (seemingly independent) tests at the 5 percent level, the distributions are so "normal" that the standard tests based on normality can be used.

Figure 2.1 displays the averages and standard deviations for the nineteen countries of Table 2.3. This figure suggests that election outcomes have much the same mean and variance for a main group of countries (as is

Table 2.3 Descriptive statistics of the elections tested on the cost of ruling ($N = 283$)

Country	Type of election	N	Statutory period	Average period	Average C_e	Standard deviation	Normality P-value (%)
Australia	House of Representatives	21	36	30.2	-1.95	4.38	71
Austria	Nationalrat	15	48	39.1	-1.71	5.22	8
Belgium	Chambre des Représentants	15	48	29.3	-3.7	4.47	14
Canada	House of Commons	16	60	38.1	-4.02	9.78	33
Denmark	Folketinget	21	48	25.5	-0.77	4.98	21
Finland	Eduskunta	14	48	17.4	-3.1	3.68	27
France	Assemblée Nationale	14	60	25.3	-3.27	8.87	6
Germany	Bundestag	13	48d	41.7	0.67	5.06	59
Iceland	Alting	15	48	34.6	-4.95	4.72	83
Ireland	Dáil Eirann	15	48	37	-3.73	4.37	7
Italy	Camara dei Deputati	12	60	19.8	-1.88	5.41	10
Japan	House of Representatives	17	48	26.9	-2.65	5.23	19
Luxembourg	Chambre des Députés	8	60	59.1	-5.39	3.37	29
Netherlands	Tweede Kamer	15	48	34.8	-2.46	6.9	6
New Zealand	House of Representatives	16	36	33.6	-3.8	5.14	73
Norway	Stortinget	13	48 ND	39.4	-0.42	3.72	83
Sweden	Andra Kammaren	17	48/36/48	32.7	-2.12	3.08	52
UK	House of Commons	14	60	42.9	-1.91	4.2	34
USA	President	12	48 ND	46 (48)	-2.5	10.99	76
All governments		283		33.5	-2.54	5.97	0.00
Governments lasting less than 1 year		37			-0.95	6.33	
Governments lasting between 1 and 2 years		37			-0.88	4.89	
Governments lasting between 2 and 3 years		68			-2.5	4.08	
Governments lasting between 3 and 4 years		97			-2.49	6.23	
Governments lasting more than 4 years		43			-6.12	7.21	

Notes

Statutory and average periods are given in months. Jarque-Berra test (skewness/kurtosis) is used for testing normality. Note that the averages – both for all 283 election outcomes and the 97 lasting a *normal election period* of 3–4 years are very close to $\lambda = 2\frac{1}{2}\%$.

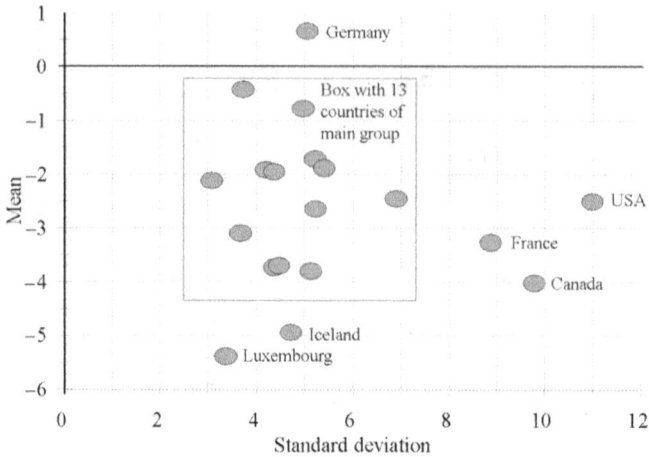

Figure 2.1 The means and standard deviations of the cost of ruling for the nineteen countries of Table 2.3.

proved in Table 2.4). The thirteen countries of the main group are placed in a box in the middle of the picture. The figure points to some exceptions:

(e1) The average deviates in three cases. It is high (positive) in Germany and low in Iceland and Luxembourg. These deviations are insignificant in Table 2.4.

(e2) The variance is larger in the United States, Canada, and France. This is significant in Table 2.4.

Table 2.4 performs the standard test for homogeneity of the country samples. For the thirteen countries in the main group, the tests do not reject that the observations are from the same distribution. The two tests are quite powerful with more than 200 observations; so it is an amazing result considering that the group contains countries as different as Sweden, Japan, UK, and the Netherlands. When the three countries with deviating means are added, the tests still do not reject that the distribution is the same. However, variance homogeneity is rejected for all nineteen countries, but the test does not reject that the means are the same. Thus, we have been unable to reject that the cost of ruling is the same in all nineteen countries.

The empirical cost of ruling result given in Table 2.2 has thus been confirmed. These are remarkable results when considering the differences between the countries in size, in election systems, party systems, etc. Clearly, the cost of ruling is a *basic fact*.

Table 2.4 Tests for homogeneity of mean and variance of the cost of ruling

Countries	Group	N	Same variance			Same mean		
			χ^2	*(df)*	*P-value (%)*	*F*	*(df$_1$, df$_2$)*	*P-value (%)*
13	Main group	204	13.9	12	30	0.73	(12, 192)	72
16	Main + dev avr	240	15.1	15	44	1.40	(15, 225)	14
19	All countries	283	64.4	18	0.0	0.92	(18, 263)	55
19	All countries		Kruskal–Wallis test			$\chi^2(18) = 20.7$		29

Notes
The country groups follow Figure 2.1, and the abbreviation + dev avr means: plus the three countries with deviating averages (Germany, Iceland, and Luxembourg). The variance homogeneity test is the Bartlett test, while the mean homogeneity test is the classical *F*-test. Strictly speaking, the classical *F*-test cannot test for mean homogeneity when variance homogeneity is rejected. This problem occurs for all nineteen countries; so the results for mean homogeneity are here given in italics. However, an alternative test is added in this case. It still refuses to reject that the means are the same.

2.2.2   The distribution of election outcomes

To further study the distribution of election results, the 19 samples and the joint distribution of all 283 election results have been graphically analyzed by probit diagrams.

Figure 2.2 shows typical probit graphs for four countries in the main group. They are chosen to be the most "different" based on *a priori* knowledge. Nevertheless, the probit graphs for the four countries intersect many times. It is no wonder that the tests in Table 2.4 point to no difference in the four distributions.

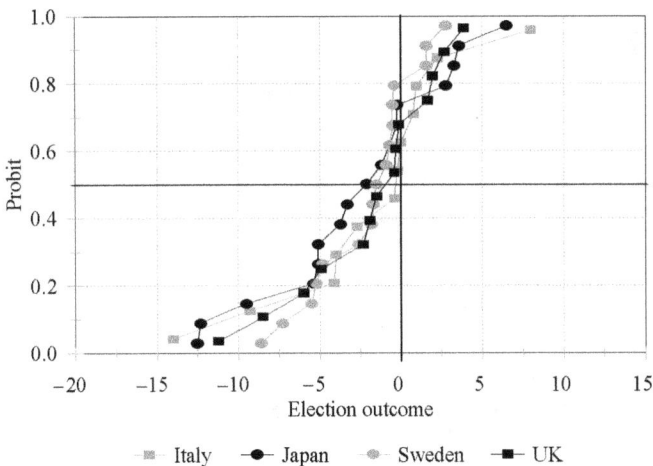

Figure 2.2 Four typical cases of the cost of ruling: Italy, Japan, Sweden and UK.

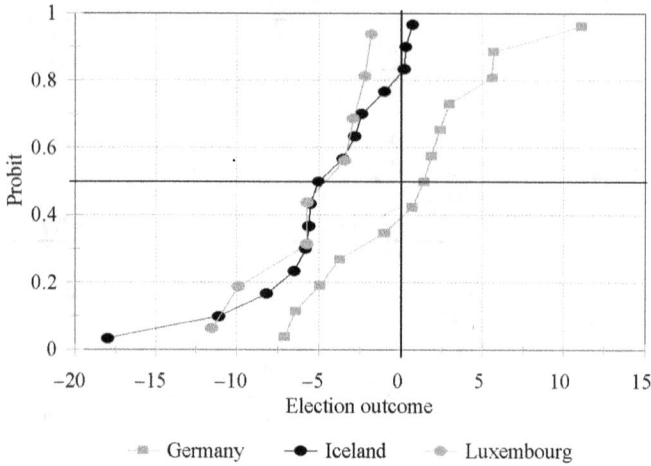

Figure 2.3 The three countries with large and small means in the cost of ruling: Iceland, Luxembourg and Germany.

Figure 2.3 shows the three countries with the most deviant averages (e1). It is clear that the variances (slopes) of the three country lines are the same as the one of the countries in the main group; however, the tests of Table 2.4 are needed to know that the means are no more different than they should be by random draws.

Figure 2.4 shows (e2) the three high-variance countries (note change of scale). They appear to have the same average (i.e. intersection with

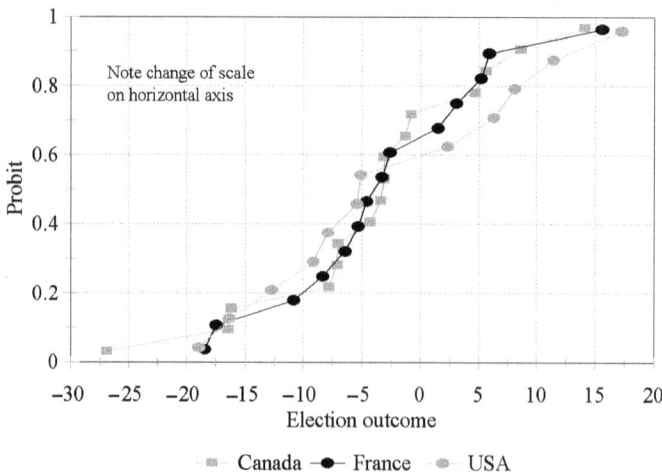

Figure 2.4 The three countries with large variance in the cost of ruling: Canada, France and USA.

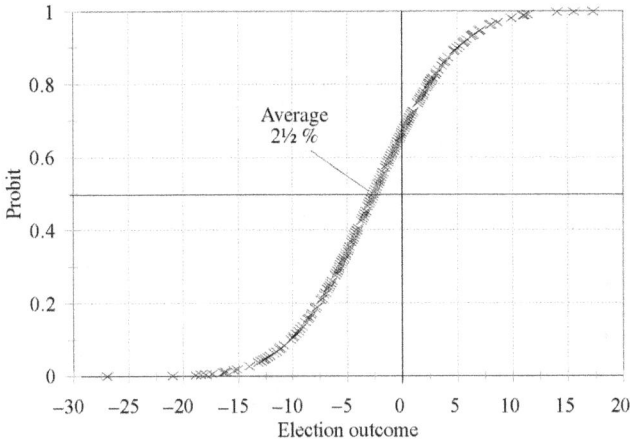

Figure 2.5 Distribution of the cost of ruling of the 283 election outcomes.

the bold 0.5-line) as the countries in the main group. It appears that Canada has a section in the middle with the standard slope, and so maybe Canada is the least deviant of the three countries; however, Canada has experienced the most extreme of all 283 elections considered.

When all the 19 countries are considered, it appears that a few extreme elections occur in most countries. This suggests that the high-variance countries may only differ by having relatively many extreme elections. All 283 election outcomes have therefore been arranged in one string and the joint distribution is analyzed in Figure 2.5.

It shows why the 283 observations strongly reject normality in Table 2.3. The probit graph looks perfectly linear in the middle part of the distribution, i.e. in the interval $C_t \in [-2.5 \pm 4]$. However, the (symmetrical) tails of the distribution show strong non-normality. In fact, the tails are quadratically normal as demonstrated in Paldam (1986). This observation is interpreted by a two-type theory of elections:

i   Most elections are normal elections, determined by a sum of many issues. It is hence reasonable that these elections are normally distributed, and follow the same normal distribution.

ii A few elections are extreme elections, dominated by one issue, where the outcome is quadratically normal.

We have looked at some of the extreme elections and think that the two-type theory is basically true. However, it is not central to our main argument, and so it will not be further discussed.

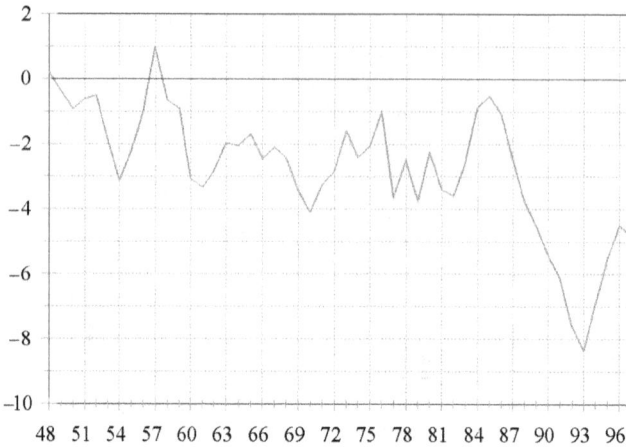

Figure 2.6 The time path of the cross-country cost of ruling (λ).
Note: Each point is average over three years (see text); points are placed above the mid-internal.

2.2.3   How stable is C_t over time?

Once it is known that election outcomes are stable across countries, all elections can be merged in the same time series and its stability over time can be studied.[7] The yearly average number of elections is six in the nineteen country sample. Figure 2.6 shows how the cross-country average Acc(C_t) has evolved from 1948 to 1997. The bold line shows the three-year moving average:

$$\text{Mcc}(C_t) = \frac{1}{3}\left(\text{Acc}(C_{t-1}) + \text{Acc}(C_t) + \text{Acc}(C_{t+1})\right)$$

The curve seems trendless from the start till the late 1980s. Then it moves downward. While the cost of ruling used to be around −2 per cent, it is now around −5 per cent. Parts of this change appear to be due to a few spectacular losses, but the trend is visible in the data from nearly all 19 countries. It is likely that the change is connected to the economic changes in the 1990s, but at present we do not attempt to explain the downward shift in the cost of ruling in the last decade.

2.2.4   The election cycle in C_t over the election period

The bottom section of Table 2.3 shows that a great many governments last less than a full election period. In some cases because the government acquiring power after an election has such a small majority that it calls a snap election, in other cases the government falls due to internal strife.

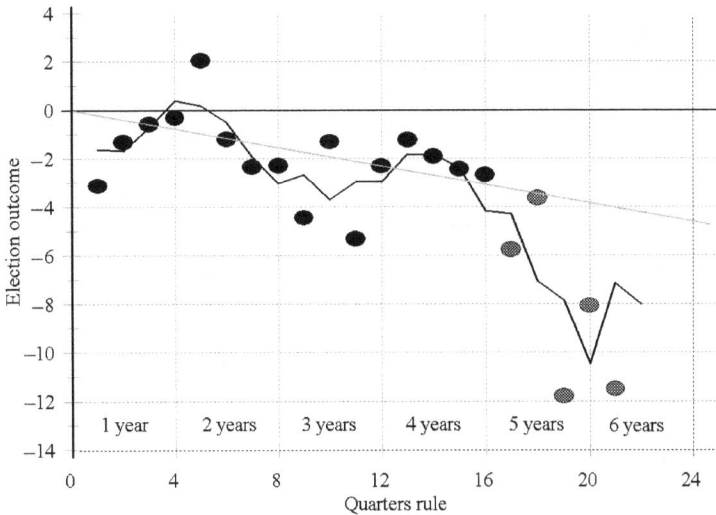

Figure 2.7 The path of election outcome, measured as the change in the vote for the government, during the election period.

Notes: The round points are the average observations, and the solid curve is a moving average line (for three points at a time). We have also included a straight line assuming a constant loss per quarter. Note that a few of the cistitutions only allows governments to rule more than four years, and so the last five points to the right are based on much fewer observations than the other points.

Finally, some governments came into power late in the election period after a resignation of the old government, and have to call an election after a brief period of rule.

Figure 2.7 shows the path of C_t during the election period based upon how long governments rule before the election. The figure shows considerable variation, but there are some signs of a "honeymoon" effect for a new government. Normally it is said to be the first 100 days, but in our data it rather comes after six months. Also, the few governments lasting more than four years – in the few countries where this is possible – have unusually large losses.

The average straight line through the points is drawn to assess the annual slope (i.e. the annual cost of ruling). It is about 0.75 percent, but a little less – about 0.66 percent – if only "normal" elections in the countries of the main group are considered. For a standard election period of three and three-quarter years, 0.66 percent per year adds up to 2.5 percent.

The figure is based upon the data in Table 2.3, but they are further subdivided. Note that data might contain a counter-causality bias. When governments have a choice, they are most likely to call an early election if they stand well in the polls. However, at the statutory limit governments have to call an election irrespective of their standing in the polls. The counter-causality bias will thus increase C_t early in the period and decrease C_t late in the period, making the cyclicality larger.

Also, the graph is calculated including the extreme elections; so, for the 3–4 years of a normal government period, the average is a bit larger than in our conclusion (R1).

2.3 THREE EXPLANATIONS OF THE COST OF RULING – LOOKING FOR THE DEEP PARAMETER

Three theories have been made to explain the cost of ruling: Ex1, the coalition of minorities theory; Ex2, the median gap theory; Ex3, the grievance-asymmetry theory. As λ was found to be unusually constant, it must be explained by something that is likely to be unusually stable as well. Preferably, the theory should build upon the "rock" of a deep parameter in human behavior.

2.3.1 Ex1, the coalition of minorities theory: a constant "sucker-fraction"

The theory was sketched in a short paragraph in Mueller (1970) in the article presenting the first popularity function.[8] To our knowledge it has never been fully developed, but has remained a loose idea.

The idea is that an opposition party can forge a coalition of enough groups to reach a majority by making inconsistent promises. When the opposition gains power, it has to make actual choices. Decisions have to be more consistent than promises. Hereby the true preferences of the party are gradually revealed. One group after the other becomes disappointed, and turns to the opposition that is busy building an alternative coalition.

A complex theory is implied in this argument. The theory builds upon two ideas: (a) the group idea, (b) the idea that over-promises are revealed by ruling. The theory only needs (b), while (a) is an extra idea. The group idea (a) implies some kind of lumpiness in the loss of ruling. It generalizes across countries only if the structure of the relevant groups is the same across countries and over time. The idea (a) therefore appears far fetched.

Idea (b) that over-promises are revealed by ruling is more substantial and complex. Four variables are needed to discuss this idea: Popularity Π, perceptions Φ, policies P, and economic outcomes Z. A party has a declared policy P, but its true policy is revealed, when it actually rules. People are known to be mostly interested in outcomes. They know the outcome from the declared policies P, and from experience Z_L, where L is a lag, showing how recent the experience is. Popularity is a function of the perceived outcome, $\Phi(Z) = \Phi(Z_L, P)$:

$$\prod = \prod(\Phi(Z_L, P)) \tag{2.2}$$

The true policy Z is the smallest in the sense of popularity Π, thus $\Pi(P) > \Pi(Z)$. All parties try to declare policies with large $\Pi(P)$'s, to obtain a $\Phi(Z) > Z$. Election promises are made if an "area" Ω for P exists "above" Z where

$$\prod(\Phi(Z_L, P)) > \prod(Z) \quad \text{for} \quad P \in \Omega \tag{2.3}$$

Voters try to see through P to the true Z. When parties rule, Z_L converges toward Z, but when they are in opposition, Z becomes distant, and voters have only P to consider. Voters have rational expectations if

$$Z^* = \Phi(Z_L, P) = Z + \varepsilon \tag{2.4}$$

where ε is white noise. The longer a party has been in opposition, the more uncertain is the assessment ($\partial|\varepsilon|/\partial L > 0$), but it is not obvious that the central assessment should change ($\partial Z^*/\partial L = 0$). The idea (b) that over-promises are revealed by ruling consequently turns into the claim that voters are too easily deceived by promises.

The constant "sucker-fraction" theory

$$\frac{\partial Z^*}{\partial L} = \mu > 0 \tag{2.5}$$

The constancy of λ here means that μ is the deep parameter of human behavior: *a constant fraction of all populations is gullible*. You cannot fool all the people all the time, but you can fool 2.5 percent of the people every fourth year. This is almost rationality: 97.5 percent of people remains undeceived.

It is surely politically correct to assume that "naivety" is evenly distributed across all countries. However, no other finding suggests a constant "sucker-fraction" across countries and time. If this is really such an important constant, it is strange that it has not emerged before.

2.3.2 Ex2, the median gap theory: center voters get their preferred policy by government changes

This theory is worked out in Paldam and Skott (1997) and Stevenson (n.d.). It considers a country with a one-dimensional issue space from left to right. It has two parties Left and Right. The median voter has the position M in the issue space. This assumption is a little – but not very – unrealistic. Nannestad (1989) analyzes the issue space in the complex Danish party system. Even here voters do order issues and parties on a Left–Right scale to a surprising extent, and parties and journalists all tend to recognize this order.

Hotelling (1929) shows that with such a set-up, Left and Right come to fight over the vote of the median voter. They hence reach the same policy M – the choice of the median voter. Hereby hangs a paradox: Why would anybody vote, if the two parties have exactly the same policy? In order to be distinguishable there must be a certain visibility gap, γ, between the parties. Party Left, converges to policy $M - \gamma/2$, while Right converges to policy $M + \gamma/2$. The two policy points divide the voters in three groups: left voters – L percent – prefer policies in the interval $[-\infty, M - \gamma/2]$ center voters – Γ per cent – prefer policies in the "median gap" $]M - \gamma/2, M + \gamma/2[$, and right voters – R percent – prefer policies in the interval $[M + \gamma/2, \infty]$.

Left voters can do no better than to vote for Left, and right voters can, likewise, only vote for Right. These voters do not get their desired policy, but they obtain a "gain γ" in their direction if their preferred party wins. If γ is large enough, they bother to vote.

However, center voters have a problem. They want a mixture of the policies proposed by both parties. They may get their desired policy outcome – on an average – if the two parties alternate in power. If policies change gradually over an election period in a known way, one can solve the model and calculate the number of swing voters who optimize the policy outcome by changing between the parties at each election, and hence the cost of ruling.

In Paldam and Skott (1997), the model is solved for several cases that appear as reasonable as possible. The middle case is summarized in Table 2.5. It is shown that one-third of the center voters (i.e. $\Gamma/3$ per cent of the voters) should change between the parties at each election, given the usual rationality assumptions. They change away from the government and are hence a cost of ruling.

The cross-country constancy of λ must mean that a constant fraction of the voters lies in the median gap. The key constancy thus boils down to

Table 2.5 Orders of magnitudes in the median gap model – a case

Center voters	In interval	Fraction
Stick to L-party	$]M - \gamma/2, M - \gamma/6]$	$\Gamma/3$
Change at every election	$]M - \gamma/6, M + \gamma/6[$	$\Gamma/3$
Stick to R-party	$[M + \gamma/6, M + \gamma/2[$	$\Gamma/3$

Notes
The case is covered in Paldam and Skott (1997), together with other cases. Assumptions:
(1) Policy outcome changes linearly between the L-outcome and the R-outcome over election period. (2) Distribution of voters is flat in median gap – used only to calculate fraction.

$\Gamma = \Gamma(\gamma)$ being constant. It is likely that the flatter the distribution is, the larger the median gap (γ) has to be visible. So, it is conceivable that Γ is similar in different countries, but it is surely not a proven fact.

The Γ-group is clearly smaller than the other two groups, but the distribution is likely to be fat around the median, and so it may hold 5–10 percent – say 7.5 percent – of the voters. The numbers from the case in Table 2.5 suggest that $\Gamma/3 = 2.5$ per cent will change at every election. Clearly, the model is easy to calibrate to explain the observed cost of ruling. Furthermore, the model demands no irrationality to work.

The model also explains how the cost of ruling evolves over the election period as analyzed empirically in Section 2.4. It is possible to calibrate the model to explain a broad range of developments in λ over the period, as shown by Stevenson (n.d.).

2.3.3   Ex3, the grievance-asymmetry theory

Consider the effect on the popularity of the government of a symmetrical change up and down of an economic variable. A grievance asymmetry means that the effect of the positive change is smaller than the one of the negative change. The mechanics of the grievance asymmetry, ρ, is given in Table 2.6.

Most researches in the VP function disregard the possibility of a grievance asymmetry. That is, it estimates case (1) but not (2) of the table. However, nearly all studies which have looked at the possibility (since Mueller, 1970) have found it. Recent large-scale micro-based studies (Price and Sanders, 1994; Nannestad and Paldam, 1997) found a large asymmetry (see, however, Lewis-Beck, 1988). In the terms of Table 2.6 the typical finding is that $\rho = \frac{1}{3}$; so the effect of an economic improvement is only one-third of the effect of the corresponding deterioration.

When the average government rules as expected, some variables improve and some deteriorate. If the government tries to maximize the

Table 2.6 The mechanics of the grievance asymmetry

α	Effect of economic variable E	$\alpha = (\alpha_i + \alpha_d)/2$	Provided $z = 0$
α_i	Effect of improvement E_i	$\alpha_i = 2\alpha\rho/(1+\rho)$	α_i calculated from α and ρ
α_d	Effect of deterioration E_d	$\alpha_d = 2\alpha(1+\rho)$	α_d calculated from α and ρ
ρ	$= \alpha_i/\alpha_d$ grievance asymmetry	$0 < \rho < 1$	The ρ interval considered

Notes

If E is not a first difference series and z is not zero, a few trivial amendments have to be made to the formulas at the bottom right cell of the table. We disregard the possibilities that $\rho < 0$ or $\rho > 1$.

(1) $C_t = a + \alpha E_t + \cdots$ is a vote function used for estimating the effect of the economic variable E_t on changes in government popularity C_t. Normally E is in first difference. Split E_t into an improvement, E_{it}, and a deterioration, E_{dt}, using z as the splitting criterion. Normally $z = 0$. $E_{it} = E_t$ if $E_t > z$ and $E_{it} = z$ if $E_t \le z$. $E_{dt} = E_t$ if $E_t < z$ and $E_{dt} = z$ if $E_t \ge z$.

(2) $C_t = a + \alpha_i E_{it} + \alpha_d E_{dt} + \cdots$ is the split version of the vote function.

Table 2.7 An example of the cost of ruling showing some orders of magnitudes of grievance asymmetry

---

The true vote function is: $\Delta V = 0.67[\Delta x_1 + \Delta x_2 + \Delta x_3 + \Delta x_4]$ so that $\alpha = \frac{2}{3}$. The x's are the economic variables

The grievance asymmetry is $\rho = \frac{1}{3}$: $\alpha = \frac{2}{3}$ splits into $\alpha_i = \frac{1}{3}$ for an improvement and $\alpha_d = 1$ for a deterioration

The two first variables improve 2% points and the last two deteriorate correspondingly: the effect is $\Delta V = +\frac{1}{3}[2\% + 2\%] + [-2\% - 2\%] = -2\frac{2}{3}\%$

Notes

The VP function in this table is not calibrated as per Eqs (2.1a) and (2.1b). When so calibrated λ will appear as the constant. However, with the grievance asymmetry integrated, the formal theory becomes a bit complicated.

welfare of the voters and hence the vote function, the variables improving should have the same average weight in the function as the variables deteriorating. If the vote function was symmetric, the government would receive exactly the same vote as last time, but with a grievance asymmetry the government loses.

The true vote function has proved elusive, but some orders of magnitudes have been found allowing us to make a few "guesstimates". Table 2.7 gives an example assuming a simple linear vote function with reasonable orders of magnitudes. It appears that it can produce an average cost of ruling as observed. So the grievance-asymmetry theory can be operationalized and calibrated to explain the observed fact of the cost of ruling. The example also shows that the asymmetry has to be substantial to generate a cost of ruling as observed. The main problem with this model is that the robustness of the empirical cost of ruling depends upon the stability of the vote function.

Section 2.4 argues that the grievance asymmetry is the logical consequence of the well-known – and theoretically well-integrated – fact that the average voter has a certain loss/risk aversion. We will argue that a lot of evidence and theory point to loss/risk aversion as a deep parameter in human behavior.

2.3.4   Summary of the three theories

Our discussion so far has shown that all the three theories have weaknesses and strengths. The main arguments are summarized in the three columns Ex1 to Ex3 in Table 2.8. In our opinion, especially Ex1, but also Ex2, suffer from the main problem that the "deep parameter" necessary to create the empirically observed stability of λ seems to be too weak to carry such a burden. Only Ex3 builds upon a suitable deep parameter at our present stage of knowledge. Furthermore, Ex3 is linked to a complex of other theories and findings.

Table 2.8 Strengths and weaknesses of the coalition of minorities theory, the median gap theory, and the grievance-asymmetry theory

Theory	Ex1, coalition of minorities	Ex2, median gap	Ex3, grievance asymmetry
Deep parameter	Sucker-fraction	Median gap fraction	Loss aversion
Status	Unconfirmed, unlikely	Unconfirmed, likely	Confirmed
Other strengths	Election promises are common	Consistency, elegance	Links to other theories
Other weaknesses	Demands (small) irrationality, under-theorized	Needs pre-RE economics and one-dimensional issue space	Needs stable VP function
Exclusivity	Might work with Ex2 or Ex3	Not Ex3	Not Ex2

Notes
The *deep parameter* should be a constant as explained in the text. The term *status* is used to indicate if independent evidence exists to make it likely that the said parameter could be constant.

The bottom row of the table previews results discussed in Sections 2.5 and 2.6. It will be shown that theories Ex2 and Ex3 are mutually exclusive, while Ex1 may be true alongside either Ex2 or Ex3.

2.4   ECONOMICS: THE GRIEVANCE ASYMMETRY AND LOSS/RISK AVERSION COMPLEX

One of the controversies in the literature on the VP function deals with the question: Do people react to past losses and gains or to expected future ones? This is only one part in the discussion on loss aversion (for past events) versus risk aversion (for expected future ones). Table 2.9 defines a relevant terminology as regards risk aversion for the political scientist. Section 2.4.1 looks at the general literature, Section 2.4.2 returns to the grievance asymmetry, and Section 2.4.3 tries to pull the whole section together.

Table 2.9 The concept and terminology of risk aversion

Agent A receives an income flow, $y(t)$, where the average $a = \eta(y) \approx \mathrm{Avr}(y)$ and the variance $v = s^2 = \eta(y - \eta(y))^2 \approx \mathrm{Var}(y_t)$. The agent obtains utility $U_A(y_t)$ from the flow
We consider two marginal utilities $U_a = \partial U_A / \partial a$ and $U_v = \partial U_A / \partial v$
$U_a > 0$, true per definition
$U_v < 0$, *risk aversion*; normal situation with a trade-off between a and v
$U_v = 0$, *risk neutrality*; people care about a only
$U_v > 0$, *risk loving*; people are willing to pay for risk; known to afflict a small minority

2.4.1   Loss aversion or risk aversion – general

Risk aversion is a widespread concept in economic theory, but estimates are not so common. This section poses two questions: (q1) does the empirical literature suggest that loss/risk is a deep parameter of human behavior and (q2) do the estimates suggest that the effect is so large as demanded to explain the cost of ruling? For space reasons, only a few remarks can be made on the four most relevant empirical literatures: (L1)–(L4). One deals with loss aversion and three with risk aversion:

(L1)   *The experimental literature* looks at loss aversion, by comparing people's reaction to gains and losses in various situations. See here the survey by Kahneman (1994) and for alternative evidence Dunn (1996). Large asymmetries are found, much in line with our results.[9]

   When we turn from the past to the future, the main empirical claim is that the average human has risk aversion as regards most of his/her income, even when many people like to run a big risk with a tiny fraction of the income by purchasing lottery tickets, etc.

(L2)   The key observation supporting the claim is that risk pooling is a large sector in the economy. People are willing to pay, e.g. insurance companies to get "security", in a wide range of circumstances. When the ratio between the premium paid and the expected gains from the insurance is calculated, it appears that most people must have considerable risk aversion.[10]

   While (L2) has generated many casual observations, of which some point to a large size of the aversion, it is difficult to summarize the observations to a number. However, the last two empirical literatures have allowed systematic estimates. Unfortunately they reach embarrassingly different results.[11] They are contrasted in the classical article by Mehra and Prescott (1985).

(L3)   *The growth literature* defines risk aversion as a curvature coefficient for the utility function. It can be estimated indirectly by calibration experiments with long-run growth models. The main results found are that the risk aversion is small, even though it is significant (see Lucas, 1987 for a discussion).

(L4)   In *the financial literature*, it is well known that the average yield on (risky) equity shares has been found to consistently exceed the yield on (secure) government bonds, by perhaps 50 percent in real terms; so here a rather large risk premium appears (see Kocher-lakota, 1996 for a new survey).

   This section started with two questions. They can now be answered: (q1) loss/risk aversion is a deep parameter in human behavior – it appears in many different fields. However, (q2) while most of the evidence suggests that it is a large effect, all findings are not in agreement.

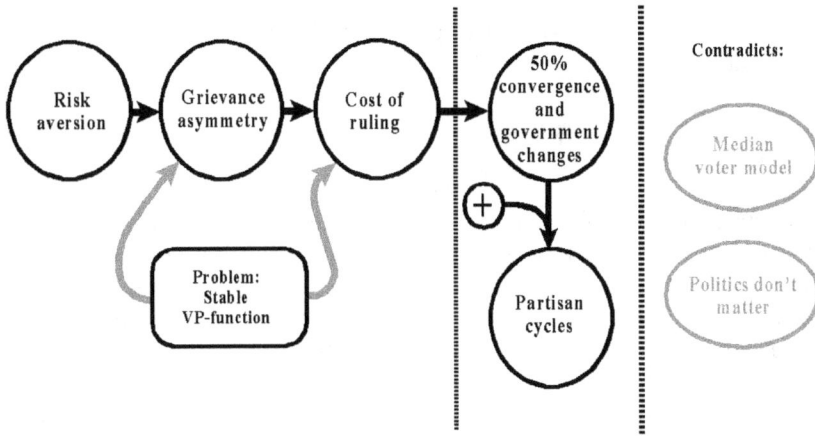

Figure 2.8 The logical structure of the loss-aversion complex.

2.4.2   The grievance asymmetry and loss aversion

The literature on VP functions has (as mentioned) tried to determine if voters are retrospective or prospective. We know of about 50 studies – including several of our own – which have found data allowing them to distinguish.[12] Most of these attempts have concluded that voters are retrospective, but the difference is typically small, as voters form largely static expectations. If this is the case, risk and loss aversions are the same.

The theory discussed has the logical structure given in Figure 2.8, where the part to the right of the dotted line is discussed in Section 2.5. A VP function with loss/risk aversion causes a grievance asymmetry, and a grievance asymmetry causes a cost of ruling. The cost of ruling becomes stable given that the VP function is sufficiently stable. Note that the logic of this whole theoretical structure depends neither upon the election system nor upon the party structure.

The only weak part of the complex is the VP function (the rectangular box). It is dubious that it is sufficiently stable to give the necessary stability in λ. However, the theory does not demand that the VP functions are very stable. If the reader goes through the above argument, it is clear that the theory demands that the amount of economic voting is approximately constant. In terms of Equation 2.1a, the F^e term should explain a constant fraction of the variance.

All arrows go toward the right on the figure as the cost of ruling can be explained by other explanations than the grievance asymmetry. However, if a grievance asymmetry is found, this is a clear indication of loss/risk aversion.

2.4.3   Returning to the evidence

If the above theory is true, the grievance asymmetry must grow with economic variability:

$$\frac{\partial \lambda}{\partial \text{Var}(\text{economy})} > 0 \tag{2.6}$$

A constant cost of ruling must therefore mean that the variance in the economy is much the same across the developed economies, as is actually the case. However, three pieces of evidence were found above.

First, it is well known that very small economies are relatively more volatile, and it appears that they have higher λ's than other countries.[13] Second, economic variability varies over time in our country sample, and as shown in Figure 2.6 λ rises when variability does. Third, evidence was cited in Section 2.1.2 that λ is (much) higher in countries – as the Latin American ones – where economic variability is (much) higher. All three pieces of evidence corroborate Eq (2.6) and the loss aversion theory.

2.5   POLITICAL ECONOMY: EXPLAINING PARTISAN CYCLES

It has often been claimed that there is a political business cycle (PBC). Different authors have pointed to different cycles. The two main types are: *election cycles* generated by governments manipulating the economy to maximize re-election chances, and *partisan cycles* generated by changing governments pursuing different goals. Paldam (1997) surveys the many theoretical claims and empirical studies and concludes that even though the empirical evidence is somewhat underwhelming, it is most supportive for the partisan model of the PBC. In fact, the support for the election cycle is rather flimsy.

2.5.1   The conditions for getting partisan cycles

Partisan cycles occur if the three conditions (Pc1)–(Pc3) listed in Table 2.10 are fulfilled:

Item (Pc2) of the table immediately takes us to the core of the big discussion about RE (rational expectations) that was central to macroeconomics from the mid-to-late 1970s and for almost two decades: are economic policies efficient? The big – seemingly paradoxical – claim of the RE school was that given all agents had perfectly RE, all predictable policies become ineffective.

Table 2.10 The three conditions for Partisan cycles to occur

(Pc1) Partisanship: different governments systematically pursue different goals, determined by party ideologies, and hence different policies (see Section 2.6)

(Pc2) Policy efficiency: different policies lead to different outcomes (see Section 5.1)

(Pc3) Governments change: this happens once there is a cost of ruling (see Section 5.2)

---

i   In pre-RE theory policies were taken to be effective so that in Hibbs' partisan cycle theory the different policies led to different trends in the policy interesting variables.

ii   In RE theory policies can only have *transitory* effects on economic outcomes so that in Alesina's partisan cycle theory the different goals lead to post-election blips in the policy interesting variables.[14]

iii A great deal of post-RE economic theories is now available. A main finding is that most policies do have non-transitory effects. This is now causing the emergence of hybrid partisan cycles looking like a mixture of Hibbs' and Alesina's models.

2.5.2   The change of government condition (Pc3) and the 50 percent convergence

Item (iii) in the list is where the cost of ruling comes in. It causes governments to change frequently, and is therefore a key condition for partisan cycles to occur. It replaces the more tortuous theories that have been proposed.

The cost of ruling also acts as an effective device hindering governments in pursuing election cycles. Golen and Poterba (1980) tried to calculate the maximum gain governments can obtain from pursuing the path that maximizes re-election chances. It appears small relative to the cost of ruling. Hence once governments recognize the size of λ, the better course for a new government is simply to pursue its ideological goals.

If governments pursue ideological goals and there is a cost of ruling, one is likely to get something looking like (irregular) partisan cycles. Under these circumstances one should not observe the "politics does not matter result" as some authors claim to have found. Policy outcomes should be different under parties of different political observation.

The cost of ruling causes government parties to decrease. In a two-party system both governing parties must eventually fall below 50 percent, and then the opposition party becomes the government and

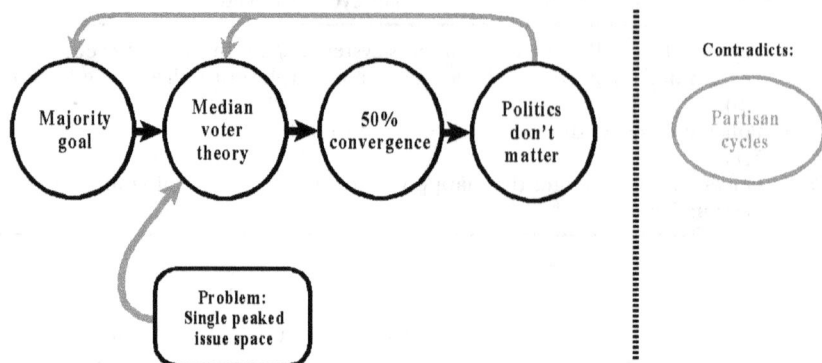

Figure 2.9 The logical structure of the original median voter complex.

starts to fall.[15] Both the government and the opposition must therefore converge to steady-state vote shares of 50 percent as is actually observed in most countries with two-party systems.

Note that the 50 percent convergence is reached with no reference to the median voter theorem and no use of the minimum winning coalition idea.

2.6   POLITICS: THE MEDIAN VOTER COMPLEX

However, if the cost of ruling is explained by the median gap theory, we are back into the median voter and minimum winning coalition framework, though with a few interesting twists.

2.6.1   The static median voter model: no cost of ruling

Figure 2.9 shows the good old median voter theory. It shows the influence of the wish to be re-elected on policy making in a two-party country. Given the minimum winning coalition theory, the two parties want to win and not to be too large, and so they end up fighting for the median voter.

The strict conditions for obtaining the median voter result are: (a) the majority goal, and (b) a one-dimensional issue space. The result can also be reached if the conditions are relaxed a little, but not very much. The median voter model produces two observable results: (M1) the party system converges to two parties having 50 percent of the vote each, and (M2) since the two parties come to adopt the policy preferred by the median voter, they come to have the same policy. The two results (M1) and (M2) emerge from exactly the same mechanisms.

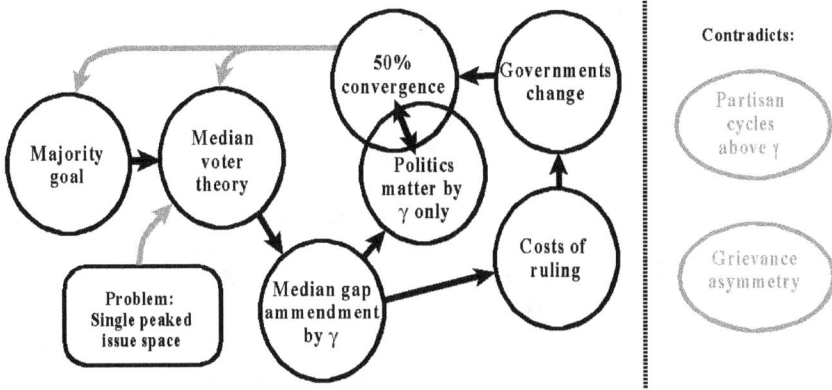

Figure 2.10 The logical structure of the full median voter complex.

The logical structure of the model is simple as shown in Figure 2.9. It is sometimes alleged that one actually observes (M2). This observation is then taken as proof that the theory is confirmed, as drawn by the gray arrow. As the parties reach the same policy, the theory explicitly rejects the possibility of partisan cycles. Furthermore, no explanation of the cost of ruling is provided. Also, it is not explained why governments change. The theory is static.

2.6.2   The median voter complex with the median gap amendment

Figure 2.10 shows the full median voter complex: the majority goal is still the goal of the parties. This leads to the median voter theorem as before, but now the theory is amended with the median gap theory described in Section 2.2. The policies of the parties differ by the (small) "visibility gap" of γ around the position of the median voter. This introduces some dynamics and allows us to account for the cost of ruling.

Two observable results are (still) reached: (M1) the 50 percent convergence, and (M2) that policies do not matter (they matter by γ only), but now they are reached differently. So they are drawn as overlapping in Figure 2.10. For readability, the overlapping is limited in the drawing.

The model takes observations looking like (M1) and (M2) as indications that the logic is coherent, but they are still not sufficient conditions, and so the "return arrows" are gray as before. If this theory is true, it allows only very small partisan cycles, and no grievance asymmetry, etc. In effect, the support for the whole of the loss aversion complex vanishes.

2.6.3   The alternative explanation of the 50 percent convergence

Both the loss aversion theory of Figure 2.8 and the median voter theory of Figures 2.9 and 2.10 explain the 50 percent convergence, but do so in two different ways. In the median voter theory it is caused by the pull from the median voter, while in the loss aversion theory it is caused exclusively by the cost of ruling. The key theoretical problem for the median voter complex is that it needs a (near) linear issue space.

The median gap theory leaves a marginal role only for politics. Policies in a two-party country can differ by γ only, while politics can be quite different in the loss aversion model. If the reader agrees that non-negligible partisan cycles exist, the medium gap theory has a problem. We conclude that the loss aversion explanation has an edge. It is a little simpler and builds upon more basic behavior.

2.7   EXTRAVAGANT CLAIMS?

The cost of ruling is a well-known effect which is normally treated as a small sideshow – often relegated to a footnote. However, it is not generally known how robust the fact actually is, and few attempts have been made to provide an explanation, and to see how it fits into a broader range of theories. Our chapter has tried to move the sideshow to center stage.

The argument starts with the empirical result that the cost of ruling is almost constant in all stable, developed democracies. The constancy applies both across countries and over time. Only a few small deviations from perfect constancy were found – most notably a large increase in the costs during the early 1990s. When more data are analyzed, and new techniques are trained at them, other small deviations from perfect constancy may be found. However, the deviations from strict constancy will probably remain remarkably small.

We are thus dealing with an unusually strong fact. It is worth contemplating how much it can explain. Two complexes have been considered. (i) The *loss/risk aversion complex* that appears to hang well together, and to have a deep parameter of human behavior in its center. (ii) The *median voter complex*. The two complexes are largely alternative. However, the loss aversion complex explains more, and does so in a simpler way.

Even if these complexes are not fully explored, it is clear that they both provide a coherent framework for understanding a range of political and economic phenomena, notably the 50 percent convergence in two-party systems and the political business cycle. These are strong claims, but hopefully the reader has been convinced that they are not extravagant.

In the end, we therefore want to make an even stronger claim. It builds upon the old observation that it is crucial for democracy that governments change. Without government changes, oppositions would have no legal ways to gain power, and hence they would be forced to use illegal means. The cost of ruling is one of the underlying reasons why governments change. Therefore, it is important for keeping democracy viable.

ACKNOWLEDGMENT

We thank Randy Stevenson for a fine comment extending the median gap model, and other discussants at workshop 12 at the 27th ECPR Joint Sessions of Workshops in Mannheim, and in Trondheim. We are also grateful to the referee and three economists Torben M. Andersen, Peter Raahauge and Peter Skott for discussions especially on the complex issue of loss/risk aversion. Viggo Høst has helped with the tests of Table 2.4. Maja Annette Hansen was research assistant on the project.

NOTES

1 For brevity two shortcuts are used: Sizes of political groups and parties are always measured in *percent of the votes cast*, even if it is not explicitly stated. The term *"two-party systems"* also includes *two-party group systems*.
2 This article generalizes work we have been doing for some time – both jointly and with others. It hence builds upon Paldam (1986, 1991), Paldam and Skott (1997) and in particular Nannestad and Paldam (1997). An alternative approach describes the dynamics of government popularity by hazard functions, using event histories for each country (see, for example, Warwick, 1992). One may interpret the cost of ruling as a basic property of the hazard function, and start theorizing from there. This approach demands much data, and so a simpler approach is used.
3 We build upon the theory on VP functions (vote and popularity functions). The literature on this approach is surveyed in Paldam (1981), Lewis-Beck (1988), and Nannestad and Paldam (1994), while the newest research is covered in Lewis-Beck and Paldam (2000).
4 Two points should be made. (1) Many governments are coalition governments. It is not discussed how parties in a coalition share the costs. (2) As governments rule they acquire a record changing the expected outcome.
5 Several other small qualifications also exist. Under "big coalitions" of (nearly) all parties, the voters can go nowhere else so λ declines. Some governments have – more or less formal – coalition partners, who are not members of the government. Here the distinction between governments and opposition blurs.
6 Some of the results listed under (E4) might be due to (E3). Some Latin American countries have experienced frequent switches between democracy and dictatorship. So perhaps their party systems are less established. However, it is (often) interesting to note how quickly the old party system re-emerges after a period of military rule.

7 This section builds upon Høst and Paldam (1990) searching for international "political Right/Left waves". That is, casual observers (journalistic) often claim that sometimes voters throughout the West all turn to the Left and sometimes to the Right. The article makes a test for this possibility based on a merged time series for seventeen countries, where the governments were classified into Left and Right. No systematic shifts in political orientation were found.

8 The theory goes back to Downs (1957, Ch. 4.II.B). Downs' theory is a bit different as it serves another purpose. It is thus a theory that can be developed in several directions. We shall develop it in the direction making it stand out as much as possible from the other two theories.

9 An interesting consequence of these results is that people's assessments of a change from situation A to another situation B come to depend upon the path followed by the movement from A to B – a property known as "framing". It is not only the result that matters, the "variability" of the way by which it is reached also matters.

10 Financial intermediaries like banks and insurance companies produce 3–4 percent of GDP. That is, people are willing to pay that amount for risk pooling and other services.

11 The main deviations from risk aversion are: (1) Many people like to run risks with a small fraction of their income, so nearly all countries have lotteries with very negative sums where people can run a high risk for a small part of their income. (2) Many of the most famous business people have had a period of their life where they played at a high stake to build up their "business", but they have later consolidated their holdings. (3) People, who throughout their lives love risk, are known as compulsive gamblers. It is a well-known mental problem afflicting a small minority.

12 The most direct test available is perhaps Nannestad and Paldam (1994). In Lewis-Beck and Paldam (2000), 10 of the 18 studies look at this problem – reaching mixed results.

13 The variability of the economy decreases with country size, though the decrease is very small for the range above a couple of million inhabitants. However, the effect is clear for very small economies, and so this explains why λ is larger in very small countries.

14 The Hibbs model was first described in Hibbs (1977) and reprinted in Hibbs (1987). The Alesina model is presented in a whole set of papers since 1987, all surveyed in Alesina and Roubini (1997). Many other writers have participated in the development, recent surveys are Paldam (1997) and Frey (1997), containing also a reprint of the key papers in the PBC literature.

15 Most election systems have a small (or large) disproportionality in the system of representations (Z percent) so that the party favored by the system needs only $(50 - Z)$ percent to rule and the least favored party needs $(50 + Z)$ percent to rule. They converge to these points.

REFERENCES

Alesina, A. and Roubini, N. (1997) *Political Cycles and the Macroeconomy*. Cambridge, MA: MIT Press.

Downs, A. (1957) *An Economic Theory of Democracy*. New York: Harper & Row.

Dunn, L.F. (1996) Loss aversion and adaptation in the labor market: empirical indifference functions and labor supply. *Rev. Economics Statist.*, **78**, 441–450.

Fidrmuc, J. (2000) Economics of voting in post-communist countries. In M.S. Lewis-Beck and M. Paldam (eds), Economic Voting. *Electoral Stud.*, **29**, 113–440 [Special Issue on Economics and Elections].

Frey, B.S. (ed.) (1997) *Political Business Cycles*. The International Library of Critical Writings in Economics 79, Cheltenham: Edward Elgar.

Gavin, M. and Hausmann, R. (1998) Macroeconomic volatility and economic development. In S. Borner and M. Paldam (eds), *The Political Dimension of Economic Growth*. London: Macmillan.

Golen, D.G. and Poterba, J.M. (1980) The price of popularity: the political business cycle reexamined. *Am. J. Political Sci.*, **24**, 696–714.

Hibbs, D.A. (1977) Political parties and macroeconomic policy. *Am. Political Sci. Rev.*, **71**, 1467–1487.

Hibbs, D.A. (1987) *The Political Economy of Industrial Democracies*. Cambridge, MA: Harvard University Press.

Hotelling, H. (1929) Stability in competition. *Economic J.*, **39**, 41–57.

Høst, V. and Paldam, M. (1990) An international element in the vote? A comparative study of 17 OECD countries 1946–1985. *Eur. J. Political Res.*, **18**, 221–239.

Kahneman, D. (1994) New Challenges to the Rationality Assumption. *J. Inst. Theoret. Economics*, **150**(1), 18–36.

Kocherlakota, N.R. (1996) The equity premium: it's still a puzzle. *J. Economic Literature*, **36**, 42–71.

Lewis-Beck, M.S. (1988) *Economics and Elections: The Major Western Democracies*. Ann Arbor, MI: Michigan University Press.

Lewis-Beck, M.S. and Paldam, M. (2000) Introduction. In M.S. Lewis-Beck and M. Paldam (eds), Economic Voting. *Electoral Stud.*, **29**, 113–440 [Special Issue on Economics and Elections].

Lucas, R.E. (1987) *Models of Business Cycles*. Oxford: Basil Blackwell.

Mehra, R. and Prescott, E.C. (1985) The equity premium: a puzzle. *J. Monetary Economics*, **15**, 145–161.

Mueller, J.E. (1970) Presidential popularity from Truman to Johnson. *Am. Political Sci. Rev.*, **64**, 18–34.

Nannestad, P. (1989) *Reactive Voting in Danish General Elections, 1971–1979*. Aarhus: Aarhus University Press.

Nannestad, P. and Paldam, M. (1994) The VP function: a survey of the literature on vote and popularity functions after 25 years. *Public Choice*, **79**(3–4), 213–245.

Nannestad, P. and Paldam, M. (1997) The grievance asymmetry revisited: a micro-study of economic voting in Denmark, 1986–1992. *Eur. J. Political Economy*, **13**(1), 81–99.

Paldam, M. (1981) A preliminary survey of the theories and findings on vote and popularity functions. *Eur. J. Political Res.*, **9**, 181–99 [Special Issue on Economic Approaches to Politics].

Paldam, M. (1986) The distribution of election results and the two explanations of the cost of ruling. *Eur. J. Political Economy*, **2**, 5–24.

Paldam, M. (1991) How robust is the vote function? A study of 17 countries over four decades. In H. Norpoth, M.S. Lewis-Beck and J.-D. Lafay (eds), *Economics and Politics: The Calculus of Support*. Ann Arbor, MI: Michigan University Press.

Paldam, M. (1997) Political business cycles. In D.C. Mueller (ed.), *Perspectives on Public Choice. A Handbook*. Cambridge, MA: Cambridge University Press.

Paldam, M. and Skott, P. (1997) A rational-voter explanation of the cost of ruling. *Public Choice*, **83**, 159–172.

Price, S. and Sanders, D. (1994) Party support and economic perceptions in the UK: a two-level approach. In D. Broughton, *et al.* (eds), *British Elections and Parties Yearbook*. London: Frank Cass.

Remmer, K.L. (1991) The political impact of economic crisis in Latin America in the 1980s. *American Political Science Review*, **85**, 777–799.

Stevenson, R.T. (n.d.) The cost of ruling, cabinet duration, and the median-gap model. *Public Choice*, in press.

Warwick, P.V. (1992) Rising hazards: an underlying dynamic of parliamentary government. *Am. J. Political Sci.*, **36**, 857–876.

3 The economy as context
Indirect links between the economy and voters

Randolph T. Stevenson

In recent years, a number of scholars have begun to explore how the differences in the context in which an election is held can affect the extent and nature of economic voting. Most of these scholars have focused on aspects of context having to do with institutional or party system differences across countries. For example, Powell and Whitten (1993) and Anderson (1995) have suggested that economic voting is strongest when policy responsibility is clearly attributable to incumbents – the so-called clarity-of-responsibility hypothesis. Similarly, Stevenson and Vavreck (2000) show that the length of the campaign preceding the election impacts how much economic voting is empirically detectable.

One aspect of the electoral context that has remained mostly unexplored, however, is the economic context itself. Since "economic voting" is simply an empirical relationship between changes in the economy (or in individual perceptions of the economy) and the electoral support of parties (or individual vote choice), it need not be the same for economic changes that occur in different economic contexts. For example, if the impact of economic change on the electoral support of incumbent parties is different when the change occurs in a recession than when the same change occurs during an expansion, then the economy is itself an important contextual variable to consider.

In this chapter, I first discuss several theoretical perspectives on how the economy can condition economic voting, deriving from each, the specific empirical hypotheses that stem from the theoretical argument. Next, I subject these hypotheses to data on the aggregate economic and electoral performance of countries and parties in the postwar period.

3.1 THE ECONOMY AS CONTEXT: ASYMMETRY HYPOTHESES

In their review of the literature, Nannestad and Paldam (1994) point out that despite the fact that almost all the empirical literatures do so, there is no reason to assume, *a priori*, that voters treat positive and negative changes in the economy similarly. This reminder echoes the many studies by psychologists that show that in various choice situations, individuals are sensitive to perceived asymmetries in the options among which they choose, even when these asymmetries are not substantive but only affect the frame in which the voter perceives the situation (Kahneman and Tversky, 1979). Bloom and Price (1975) were early proponents of asymmetry in economic voting. Specifically, based on aggregate data for the United States case, they argued that parties are punished for economic downturns but are not rewarded for improvements (Claggett, 1986 is another example). The result has been harder to find in microlevel data, however. Kiewiet (1983) fails to find this asymmetry at the individual level for American voters, Lewis-Beck (1990) replicates Kiewiet's non-finding for Britain, France, Germany, and Italy, and Nannestad and Paldam (1993) for the Danish case. In this volume, Paldam and Nannestad refer to this kind of asymmetry as a grievance asymmetry and relate it to the well-known fact that incumbent cabinets tend to lose votes in parliamentary democracies.

A related argument is simply, that bigger changes in the economy will produce disproportionately large effects on the vote (either positive or negative). The idea here is that when the economy is changing slowly (say unemployment increases by 1 percent over a year), it will not be an important issue to many voters, i.e. the economy will have low salience in the election. It is only when change is larger that the media begin to focus on the economy, people begin to notice that things are getting better or worse, and, consequently, they put more weight on the economy in their voting calculus. Again, however, microlevel support for this hypothesis has not been forthcoming.

Despite these negative results at the microlevel, however, it is worth including an analysis of asymmetry in this study for two reasons. First there is the simple fact that there has not yet been a systematic test of the asymmetry hypothesis on a large sample of countries over time using aggregate data. Such a test should be done, however, as one may find that asymmetries only come out when elections with very different economic contexts are analyzed together.

Second, the asymmetry hypotheses have always been tested in isolation from other possible contextual effects that may mask asymmetries. These include differences in contextual factors like clarity of responsibility as well as differences in the partisanship of the incumbent (an important distinction that I will elaborate below). We do not know, then, if accounting for other contextual difference will reveal asymmetries that have not been observed previously.

For these reasons, then, I include an examination of two asymmetry hypotheses in what follows. Both are cast, as are all the hypotheses in this chapter, at the aggregate level.

(H1) The impact of economic change on the electoral performance of incumbents will be greater for negative changes than for positive changes.

(H2) The impact of economic change on the electoral performance of incumbents will be greater for larger changes.

3.2 THE ECONOMY AS CONTEXT: HOW ECONOMIC PERFORMANCE AFFECTS POLICY VOTING

A second way in which the economic context can condition the extent of economic voting comes from a model of economic voting in which voters are assumed to be policy-oriented: voting for the party that advocates the policy package with which they most agree. Specifically, if policy voters condition their preferences for policies on the state of the economy, then an indirect, "contextual" effect of the economy on voting is achieved. This logic is quite different from the asymmetry hypotheses discussed above, since it does not rest on the standard reward/punishment story that has usually been used to provide a theoretical underpinning for economic voting.

Further, this idea is very different from how most scholars have explored the effect of the economy in policy-oriented models of voting. These scholars have usually sought a direct connection between the economy and the vote by suggesting that since all voters prefer a good economy to a bad one, they will try to use their vote to achieve this outcome (i.e. by choosing parties that are more competent in handling the economy or whose economic polices are judged to be more effective at producing growth). Ostensibly, voters make judgments of which party is likely to produce a good economy based on observed economic performance during the tenure of the incumbent administration. Thus, like the standard reward/punishment logic, such "issue-competency" models imply that voters will vote against incumbents that preside over a poor economy.

Various problems with this logic have been suggested in the literature: the implicit assumption that voters believe governments can control the economy is quite strong; and the main empirical implication (i.e. that incumbents lose votes in a poor economy) is indistinguishable from the simple reward/punishment model. It is not my purpose to evaluate these critiques in this chapter; however, it is worth pointing out that in the model proposed here, the economy only indirectly impacts the vote and so neither of these criticisms apply. Depending on exactly how one thinks the economy affects peoples' general policy preferences (two possibilities are discussed below), the model produces empirical implications that are not identical to those produced by the reward/punishment logic. Further, in this framework an empirical connection between changes in economic performance and changes in vote choice is possible even if voters know nothing about economic policy or policy making, and attribute no responsibility for economic performance to the policies or competence of incumbent governments. Neither, however, does it rule out such connections. Instead, it shifts the focus of policy-oriented voting away from "economic" policy *per se* and back to a more general characterization of the policies that voters may care about.

More specifically, below I suggest that voters evaluate parties based on their understanding of the parties' long-term policy commitments. To give some structure to these evaluations, I focus on the distinction between leftist and rightist policy packages and suggest that voters can (and do) evaluate parties relative to one another based on differences in these policy packages.

The connection to economic performance then comes not (necessarily) from a direct preference for certain kinds of economic policies,[1] but from an indirect link in which voters systematically prefer different Left/Right policy packages in different economic contexts. Depending on which policy packages one assumes voters prefer in specific economic circumstances, different empirical connections between the economy and the policy-oriented vote will be obtained.

The distinction I am making between "economic" policies and general Left/Right policies is worth emphasizing. There is no assumption in my formulation that the policies on which the voters base their voting decision are "economic policies," like specific monetary or tax regimes. Instead, the crucial policies upon which they vote may be anything on which the different parties in the election are likely to differ and for which the voter's preferences are conditional on the state of the economy. For example, in the "luxury-goods" model discussed below, the Left could be proposing a system of national daycare centers that the voter would be happy to support in a good economy, but would reject when the economy is in trouble. The point is that the determination of one's preferences for general kinds of policy might be dependent on the expected state of the economy when those policies go into effect or, more importantly, when they have to be paid for.[2]

Below, I discuss two assumptions that lead to empirically testable implications that are distinct from each other as well as from the predictions of the reward/punishment or competency models of economic voting.

3.3   THE LUXURY-GOODS MODEL OF ECONOMIC VOTING

The underlying idea of this model is quite intuitive: voters will be more willing to pay for social "luxuries" like social welfare, expanded health programs, and unemployment insurance (the traditional leftist policy agenda) when they feel the nation can afford it, i.e. during good economic

times. Conversely, when the economy is contracting they are not interested in getting these "luxuries" but want government to be more fiscally
conservative (the traditional priorities of Liberal, Conservative, and
Christian Democratic parties).

While part of the appeal of this idea is that it is simple, there are some
subtleties that deserve attention. Specifically, it is important to understand that the model is not simply saying that, because the leftist policy
agenda is more expensive than that of the Right, voters reject it during
economic downturns. Rather, the analogy of thinking of leftist policy as
consisting of "luxury goods" is important to the logical consistency of the
model. Formally, a luxury good is one for which consumption increases
as income increases. In contrast, an inferior good is one for which consumption decreases as income increases (like potatoes) and a necessary
good is one in which consumption of the good is the same at different
income levels (Kreps, 1990).

The reason this distinction is important is that leftist policy agendas are
not always more expensive than those of the Right (e.g. the Reagan
defense build up in the United States). If, however, those policies purchase goods that are seen as national necessities, the connection with
national income (i.e. economic performance) is broken. In this theory,
then it is only those policies that purchase "luxury" goods that voters shy
away from in economic downturns. If we assume that voters identify the
Left and Right with specific policy packages and that these packages
produce different mixes of "luxury" and "necessary" public policies, it
follows that they will treat the parties differently in any given economic
situation. Since the Left's agenda has traditionally been composed of
more "luxury-goods" policies, the expectation is that leftist parties will
be turned out of office in economic downturns, but rightist parties will
not. Further, to the extent that rightist parties do not deliver enough
"luxury goods" in economic expansions, they will be turned out as well.[3]

(H3) *Luxury-goods hypothesis.* Good economic performance leads to a gain
in votes for leftist parties, while rightist parties lose votes; and poor
economic performance leads to a loss in votes for leftist parties,
while rightist parties gain votes.

Some evidence that argues for this view of economic voting can be
found in Durr's (1992, 1993) work that examines changes in "policy
mood" among voters in the United States. Looking at thousands of
survey questions in hundreds of polls and surveys, over several decades,
Stimson (1991) developed a measure of the degree to which voters favor
a "liberal" or "conservative" policy agenda at any point in time. Durr then
used this measure in a sophisticated empirical analysis to show that as the
economy improves, there is a significant leftward shift in the policy preferences of Americans. This result is fully consistent with the theoretical

story given here and provides an almost direct test of its chief underlying assumption.

In a recent paper, Stevenson (2001) has confirmed Durr's result in a large sample of the developed democracies. I show that there is a remarkably robust relationship between change in the economy and the aggregate policy preferences of the electorate that applies regardless of country. This conclusion should lend considerable support, then, to the plausibility of the luxury-goods model.

In addition to this evidence, if one goes back to Lewis-Beck's (1990) individual level analysis of economic voting in Britain, France, Germany, and Italy, and looks for the kind of voting described here, there exist results that are again consistent with the luxury-good story. In Tables 4.2 and 4.3 of Lewis-Beck (1990, pp. 60–61), we find that cases with leftist or "mixed" incumbent cabinets (his dependent variable was incumbent vote choice) show significant positive effects of perceptions of national economic performance on the vote. In the other cases, of rightist incumbents, the effects are small and statistically insignificant.

A final reason, and perhaps the most compelling one, to entertain the luxury-good model as a description of the way that voters evaluate policy agendas relative to the economy, is that it has an obvious analogy in the everyday decisions that voters make about their personal "policy agendas." That is, for most people, the time to take a vacation, buy a new car, or contribute to charity, is when their personal economic fortunes are rising, not when they expect a decline. They intuitively understand and act on a luxury-good model in their own lives and so we need not assume, in this model, that they have a sophisticated understanding of the workings of the economy.[4]

3.4   A "KEYNESIAN" AND/OR SAFETY-NET MODEL OF ECONOMIC VOTING

The luxury-good model described above is clearly dependent on a particular view about the kinds of policies that voters find appropriate during economic downturns, i.e. voters prefer economic conservatism during downturns and are willing to "buy" more public services during economic good times. Other assumptions that are consistent with policy-oriented economic voting are also possible. In this section, I discuss two such assumptions that lead to an empirical conclusion that is the exact opposite of the one that comes out of the luxury-good model. The first assumption relies on the economic ideas of Keynesianism, which was the dominant economic paradigm used by many governments for many years of the twentieth century. Its prescriptions are well known – that during recession governments should borrow and spend in order to boost aggregate demand and during expansions should check the economy via spending cuts. What if voters are Keynesian? One answer is that they should prefer a leftist policy agenda during economic downturns. Unlike the luxury-goods model, however, this conclusion depends on the assumption that votes think the Left will borrow and spend more freely than the Right. If this is the case, then Keynesian voters can be sure that if the Left is elected during an economic decline, it will pursue a policy agenda in which there will be relatively more spending than if the Right is in power.

I find the theoretical arguments for this model to be less compelling than that for the luxury-goods model for three reasons. First, it seems to me unlikely that many voters understand Keynesian demand management sufficiently to apply it in their voting decision. Indeed, the kind of economic knowledge required to apply Keynesianism is exactly the sort of thing that voters have traditionally not been able to articulate to researchers. Second, even if voters were Keynesian once, it is not likely they are still Keynesian, given the widespread rejection of the theory after the economic crises of the 1970s. Indeed, in Europe, where the example of Germany looms large, and the final fate of "Keynesianism in one country" was decided in France with the debacle of the early Mitterand years, the conversion from demand management to fiscal conservatism and austerity as the leading cure for economic ills has been dramatic.[5] Finally, in order to have a systematic relationship between voting for the Left and Right and economic performance under this model, the Left must borrow and spend consistently more than the Right. As pointed out above, however, this is not always the case, since the difference between the Left and Right is often not how much is spent but what is purchased.

A more likely logic that supports the same conclusion as the Keynesian model (i.e. that the Left will do well in poor economic times) but that does not suffer from its drawbacks, might be called the "safety-net" model. It simply suggests that voters are more likely to be concerned about unemployment insurance, guaranteed healthcare, pensions, and welfare (the leftist agenda) when they expect economic decline is in the offing. Consequently, they may want the Left to be in power to assure that these kinds of policies are not degraded just when they are needed most. Like the luxury-goods model, this model requires little sophistication on the part of voters, and distinguishes clearly between the Right and the Left in terms of the kinds of policies they pursue rather than their overall price tag.

While I think the safety-net logic is more compelling than the Keynesian story, the observable implications of the two models are the same. Specifically:

(H4) *Keynesian/safety-net hypothesis.* Good economic performance leads to a gain in votes for rightist parties, while leftist parties lose votes; and poor economic performance leads to a loss in votes for rightist parties, while leftist parties gain votes.

To sum, the traditional view of economic voting has been one of reward and punishment, with some scholars suggesting that punishment is greater for incumbents when they fail on the policy that is of most concern to "their" constituents (Hibbs, 1982; Powell and Whitten, 1993). A policy-oriented view, however, leads to two new hypotheses in which the economy acts as a context that may modify the voters' preferences over the traditional policy packages of the Left and the Right. Unlike the reward/punishment models, these theories have no requirement that voters should be incumbency-oriented in their economic voting; rather, voters should be more sensitive to partisan differences in the parties than to incumbency status. Ultimately, the question of which (if any) model voters use to map economic performance to the appropriate policy responses is an empirical one. Consequently, the empirical analysis below is designed to confront these models (reward/punishment, L/R policy-oriented luxury goods, L/R policy-oriented Keynesian/safety-net) with data in a way that will either discriminate between them or show that none are particularly useful.

3.5   DATA AND METHODS

The data I use in this project consist of observations on the electoral performance of parties in each election for which economic data are available for the following countries: Australia, Austria, Belgium, Canada, Denmark, Germany, Italy, Luxembourg, Norway, the Netherlands, Sweden, and UK. The yearly coverage varies due to missing data for some economic series. In general, I have at least some economic data for all elections after 1950.

In all the analyses that follow, I present results of the effects of changes in economic variables on changes in the electoral performance of individual parties. The economic measures I use are *changes in the unemployment rate* and *inflation* (which is by definition a change variable). I present the analyses in terms of changes because this is the clearest measure by which to test the hypothesis that voters are less likely to reward incumbents for positive changes in the economy than they punish them for negative changes. These data were collected and used in two forms. In one set of analyses, I use a mixture of monthly and quarterly data (interpolated to monthly figures) to calculate the average of the economic variables over the six-month period previous to the month of the election. This measure then captures economic performance directly proximate to the election. This time period corresponds to the period in which voters are thought to begin paying attention to an upcoming election (Gelman and King, 1993; Stevenson and Vavreck, 2000). To examine long-term effects, however, I also measure the economy using annual data. In a case in which an election occurred in the second half of the year, I use the data for the year in which the election occurred. If, however, it occurred in the first half of the year, I use the previous year's data.

3.5.1   The unit of analysis

Most aggregate studies of economic voting use the electoral performance of the incumbent cabinet as a whole as the dependent variable. In this study, however, I focus on individual parties rather than the entire cabinet. Specifically, I estimate models of how the economy changes the vote shares of three different sets of parties: single-party prime ministers, prime ministers of coalition cabinets, and cabinet partners other than the PM.

I adopt this strategy primarily because of the compelling evidence that indicates that voters treat parties differently depending on the role that they play in the political system. Most parties do not experience a significant "economic vote", i.e. their vote shares do not vary significantly with the economy. This appears to be the case for most opposition parties as well as cabinet parties that do not have a significant share of the authority in the cabinet (Powell and Whitten, 1993; Anderson, 1995). The particular distinction I make between cabinet partners and the two kinds of prime ministers comes from my previous work in which I have shown that economic voting (when not accounting for some of the asymmetries introduced here) most clearly accrues to single-party prime ministers and not other kinds of cabinet parties (Stevenson, 1997, 1999).

3.5.2   Specification of the statistical models

The analysis in this chapter departs from much of the literature on economic voting in that it begins with a nonparametric approach to examining the relationships suggested by the theoretical discussion. This is advisable for a number of reasons. First, it has been my experience (Stevenson, 1999), and the experience of other scholars examining aggregate economic/electoral data (such as Paldam, 1991), that estimates of the relationship between the economy and the vote in large samples of countries are quite sensitive to issues of model specification. As a result, a particular parameterization that would impose (possibly arbitrary) structures on the form of the relationships leads to an "overfitting" of the data and to results determined more by the parametric assumptions than by any underlying structure in the data.

Besides this worry, the very nature of the first two hypotheses discussed above argues for flexibility in the specification of the functional relationship between changes in the economy and changes in the vote. Specifically, the whole point of (H1) and (H2) is that the functional form

Hypothesis 1

Hypothesis 2

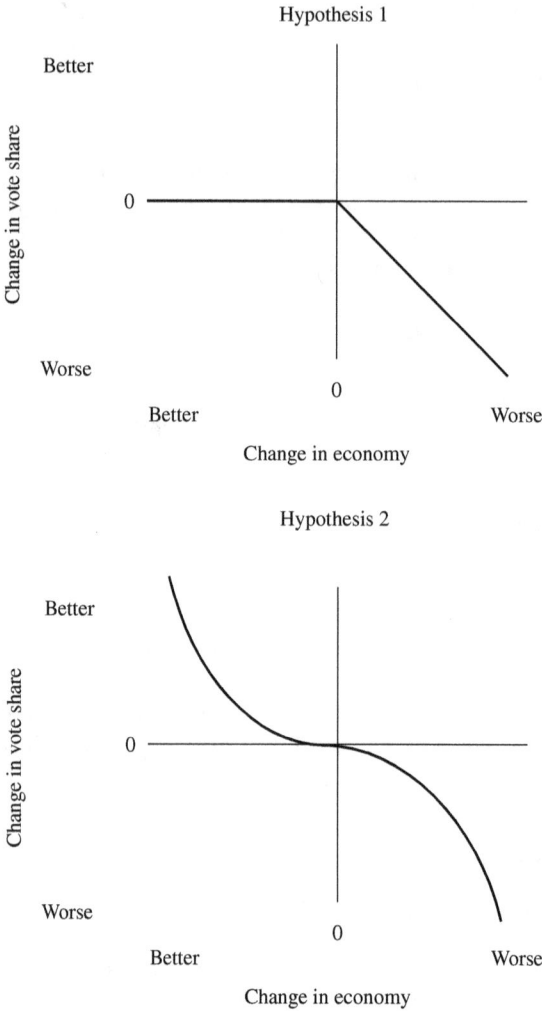

Figure 3.1 Asymmetry hypotheses for economic change on change in vote share.

of the relationship between changes in the economy and changes in the vote shares of parties should be nonlinear. Figure 3.1 gives a graphical representation of what each hypothesis implies about how the relationship between changes in the economy and the electoral performance of incumbents should look.

Given this hypothesized nonlinearity, the standard linear regression model cannot be used without adding some transformations that allow for the possibility of nonlinearity in the mean function. The parametric way to do this would be to transform the economic change variables in the model with a cubic function. This is a flexible form that includes the linear model as a special case, but also the forms implied in Figure 3.1.

I report some estimates from this cubic model below but there are drawbacks to such a parametric test. First, modeling nonlinearity in the mean function through the use of higher-order polynomial functions often produces a high degree of multicollinearity and an instability in the effect of parameter estimates and their variances. The severity of the problem depends on the particular data. In my estimates, discussed below, the problem was mild for the unemployment data but severe for the inflation data. Indeed, in this case the problem was so pronounced, that it produced negative variance estimates over meaningful ranges of the covariates and so made a useful analysis impossible (VIF statistics were in the hundreds).[6] As a result of this and the other reasons suggested above, I focus on nonparametric techniques for most of the chapter. Fortunately, the nonparametric analysis is fairly clear on the question of whether (H1)–(H4) are supported in the data, and so it is likely that we would gain little from models with more assumed structures, even if they could be estimated precisely.

The specific nonparametric procedures that I use here have been called generalized additive models (GAMs). These models have been used extensively in other disciplines and have been advocated recently in political science by Beck and Jackman (1998). This technique allows the data to determine the relationship between x and y at each value of x. This is done, for each value of x, by estimating a bivariate linear regression on a sample of observations centered on that value and including a specified percentage of the available cases (called the band-width) around the point. The slope coefficient from this regression is then used as the estimate of the slope of the partial mean function at the given value of x. A bandwidth of 0.5, for example, would use the half-sample centered on a given value of x to estimate the slope of the function relating x to y at that point (an uncentered subsample is used for endpoints). In addition to this, each observation in the subsample of the data that are used in each regression is weighted by its distance from the central point in the subsample. Consequently, the data closest to the point count more in the determination of the slope than observations further away. This "local regression" is a good way to pick up nonlinearity that is local to specific regions of the data. This contrasts with parametric specifications that impose global conditions on the functional relationship between the variables. If we find evidence of the nonlinearity implied by (H1) and (H2) in the GAM estimation, it will be a particularly strong result, since with small enough bandwidths little in the estimation method, except the data themselves, is informing us about the functional form of the relationship.[7]

3.6 RESULTS AND CONCLUSIONS

3.6.1 Nonparametric models

Since the GAM estimates produce a slope coefficient for x at each of its realized values, one does not obtain a table of coefficients, but rather a graph of the estimated relationship at various values of x. Consequently, the results of the nonparametric analysis are presented in Figures 3.2–3.7. The middle line in each graph represents (via its slope) the estimated effect of a particular economic variable on the change in vote share for an incumbent party. The upper and lower lines are 95 percent confidence bounds for this effect. Results based on both annual and quarterly/monthly data are provided.

Looking at Figures 3.2–3.7 together, one can quickly identify several general conclusions. First, there is absolutely no indication that there is any relationship between changes in the economy and changes in electoral performance for parties not in sole control of the prime ministry. The lines in Figures 3.4–3.7 are all flat. This accords well with the literature suggesting that only parties that hold the primary responsibility (and accountability) for policy making will be rewarded

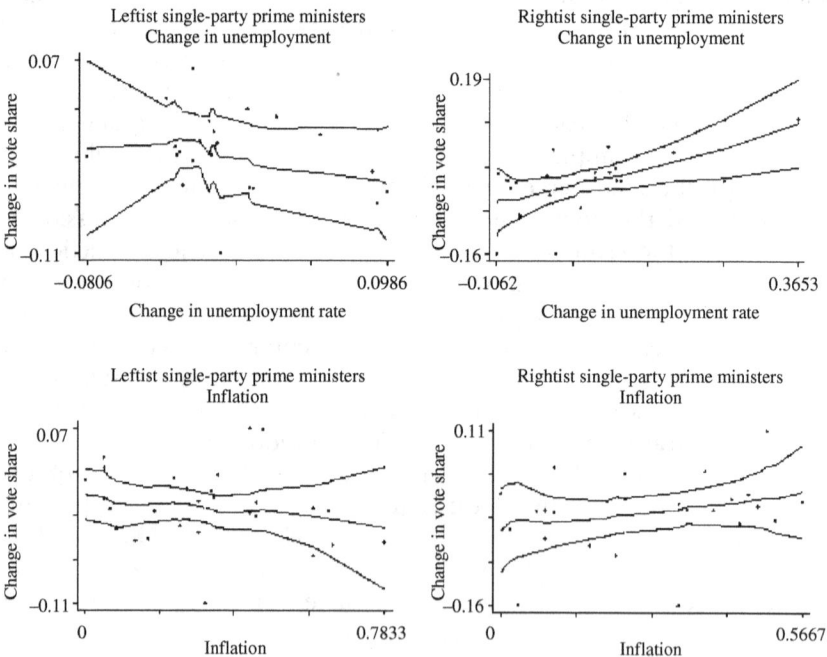

Figure 3.2 Change in vote share for single-party prime ministers: quarterly/ monthly economic data.

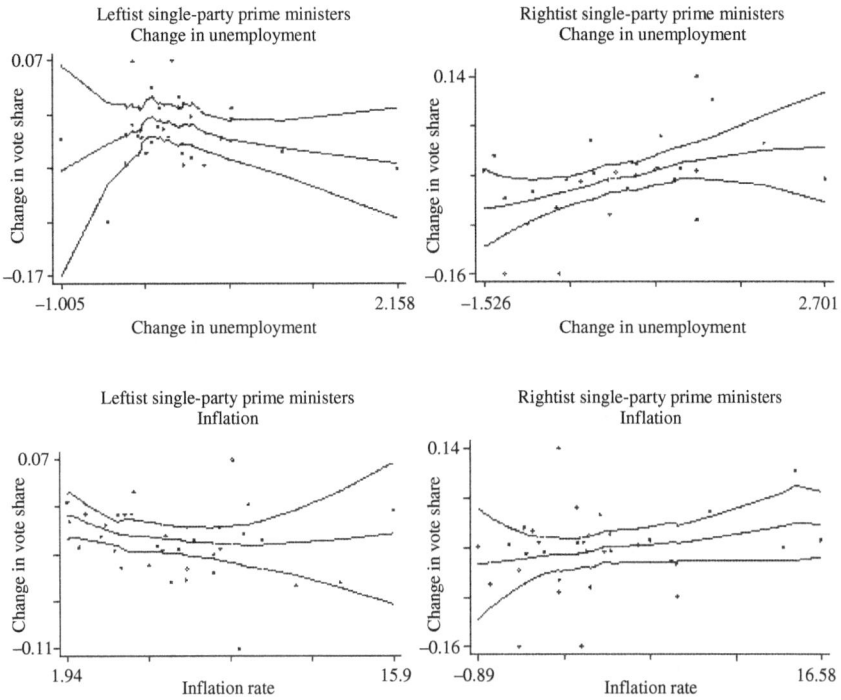

Figure 3.3 Change in vote share for single-party prime ministers: annual economic data.

or punished for a good or bad economy. It is especially supportive of Anderson's (1995) notion that only parties holding a large share of the cabinet posts will be held accountable, since, by definition, single-party prime ministers hold a 100 percent of the cabinet posts. Of course, this result should not be taken as an indirect confirmation of the reward/punishment view of economic voting (upon which the account-ability/clarity of responsibility thesis has been built) since the result also makes sense in terms of the luxury-good and Keynesian/safety-net hypotheses suggested above. Specifically, if policy voters (whose pre-ferences have been shaped by the economy) want to bring a party to power to pursue policies commiserative with those preferences, they should vote for (or against) those parties that will be most able to effect policy change when they come to (or give up) power. In another work, Stevenson (1999) has traced out these incentives and shown that this kind of economic voting should be concentrated on parties that are in contention to gain the prime ministry and that can change policy effectively when they get there.

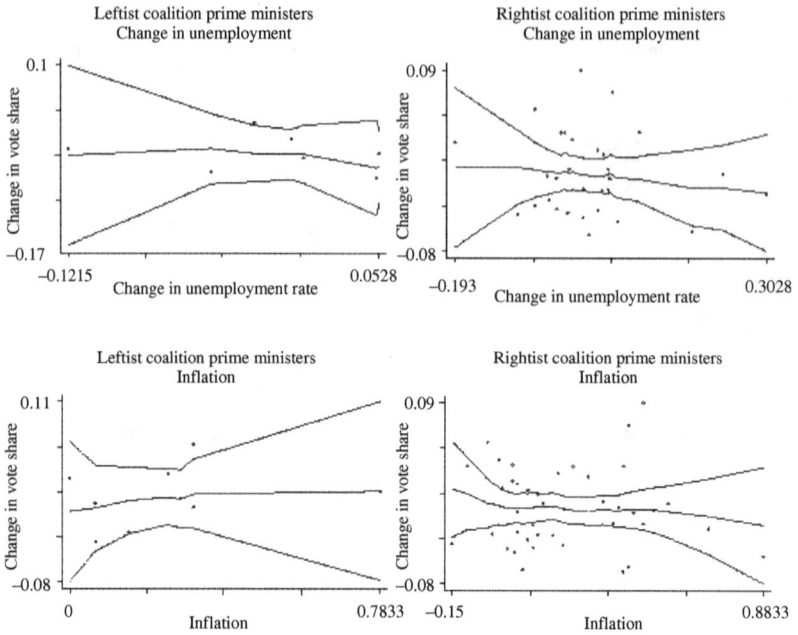

Figure 3.4 Change in vote share for coalition prime ministers: quarterly/monthly economic data.

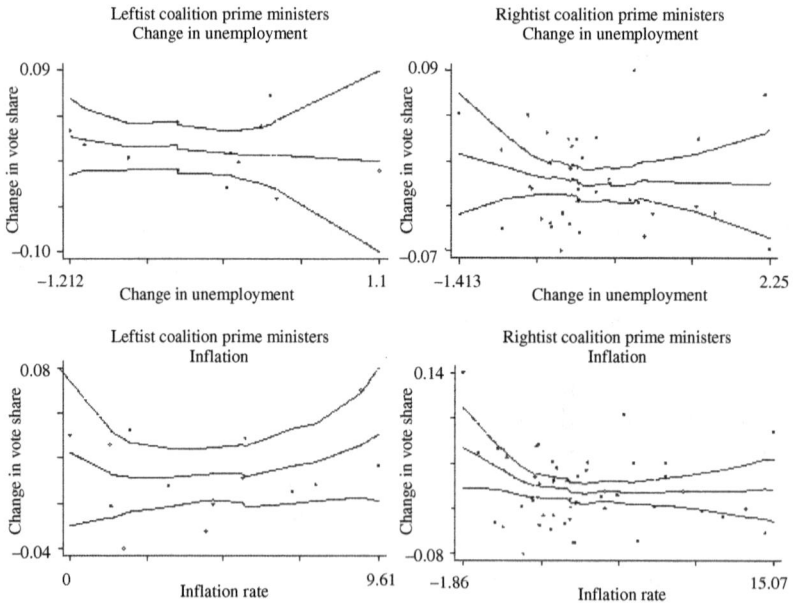

Figure 3.5 Change in vote share for coalition prime ministers: annual economic data.

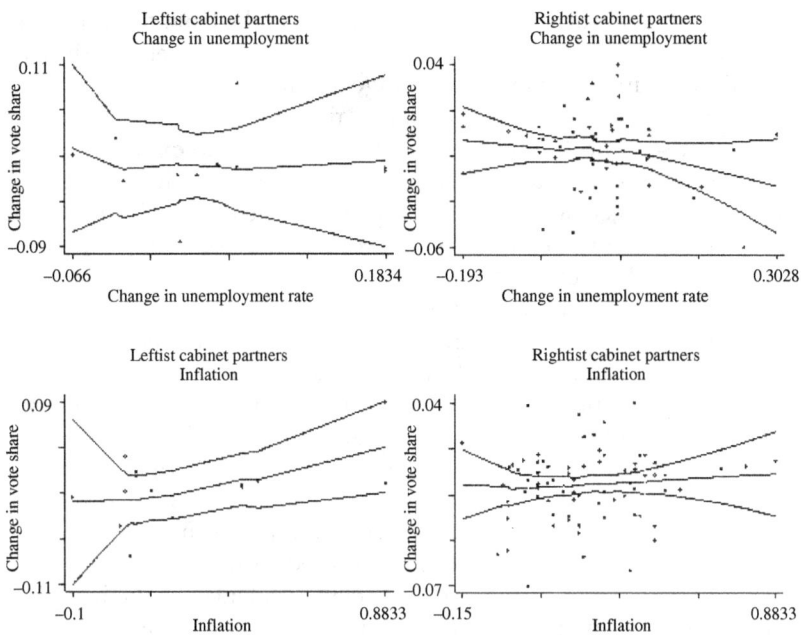

Figure 3.6 Change in vote share for coalition partners (other than the PM): quarterly/monthly economic data.

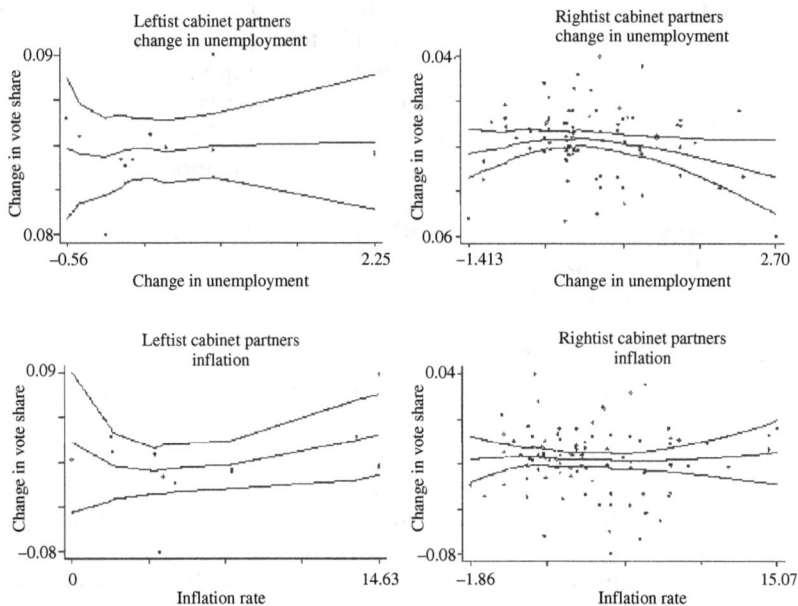

Figure 3.7 Change in vote share for coalition partners (other than the PM) annual economic data.

The second general conclusion that one can make from the evidence in Figures 3.2–3.7 is that unemployment has more of a relationship with electoral performance than does change in inflation. This mirrors some other results from large cross-country, time-series studies (Stevenson, 1997; Stevenson and Vavreck, 2000) that have tried to explain the result with reference to Iyengar and Kinder's (1987) notion that inflation is a more difficult subject for the media to prime in the minds of voters than is unemployment, and so its effects on vote choice (or public opinion in general) will be harder to find.

Looking more closely at how the results bear on the hypotheses elaborated above, the graphs for single-party prime ministers are clear. First, there is little indication of significant nonlinearity in the estimates and so (H1) and (H2) are not supported. Only in the northwest panel of Figure 3.3 (leftist, unemployment) is there any indication of nonlinearity. Specifically, the left side of the line is constrained by its upper confidence bound to flatten out the otherwise negative slope. This result is in accordance with the idea that poor economic performance is punished but good economic performance is not rewarded. However, it is quite a weak result and could not be considered compelling evidence for the hypothesis.

(H3) and (H4) suggest that the electoral effects of economic change should differ between the Left and the Right. This idea is supported more clearly than the asymmetry hypotheses, but again is not overwhelming and demonstrates the tenuousness with which the relationship exists in the aggregate data. Nonetheless, there is something there. Specifically, in Figures 3.2 and 3.3 the electoral performance of rightist single-party prime ministers is significantly helped by increases in unemployment. This clearly supports the luxury-good hypothesis (H3) and weighs against the Keynesian/safety-net hypothesis (H4), as well as against the traditional reward/punishment model of economic voting.

With respect to the Left, the results are more ambiguous, but weakly in line with the expectations of the luxury-good model. While one cannot reject the hypothesis of no relationship between unemployment change and the electoral support of leftist single-party prime ministers (in Figures 3.3 and 3.4 one could draw a horizontal line and remain in the confidence interval), the relationship is close to significantly negative over the ranges of the graphs with the most data. Turning to the results for inflation, one can find a negative slope for leftist parties and a slight positive slope for rightists (as the luxury model predicts), but these effects are quite modest except in the case of leftist parties using annual data. In this case, the negative slope on the left side of the figure is at least as strong as the unemployment effects.

What can we conclude from these plots, then? I think it is safe to say that, in so far as there is any evidence for an effect of economics on the electoral performance of parties in these data, this effect seems to confirm the luxury-good hypothesis. The relationship, however, is not striking. It is there, but only weakly.

3.6.2 Parametric models

Given the relationships identified in the nonparametric specification, it may be useful to examine more parameterized models using the same data (at least for single-party prime ministers). Do the relationships in the raw data come out more clearly when we are willing to gain estimation efficiency by making assumptions about the functional form of the relationship? Below, I present two sets of parametric results. In the first, I model the conditional mean function of vote change as a cubic function of changes in the economy. This allows the model to capture any of the

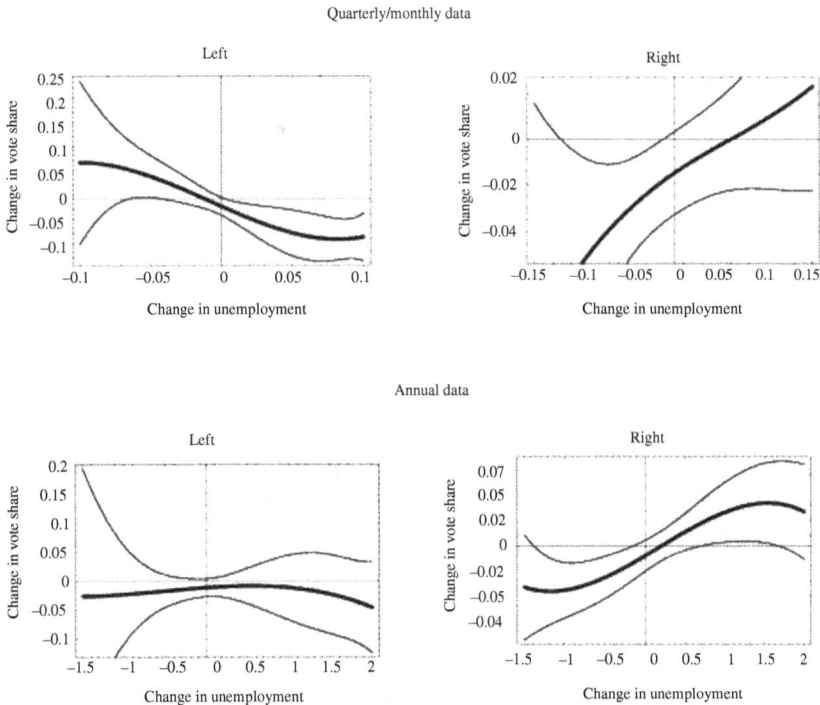

Estimated equations are of the form:

$$\Delta y_t = \alpha + \gamma y_{t-1} + \beta_1 \Delta X_t + \beta_2 (\Delta X_t * \text{left}) + \beta_3 \Delta X_t^2 + \beta_4 (\Delta X_t * \text{left})^2 + \beta_5 \Delta X_t^3 + \beta_6 (\Delta X_t * \text{left})^3$$

where ΔX_t = change in unemployment or inflation.

Figure 3.8 Change in vote share for single-party prime ministers: flexible parameters specifications.

asymmetries pictured in Figure 3.1 as well as any symmetric relationships that might exist. Differences in the relationship between the Left and the Right are captured with interactions terms and because the interpretations of these interactions are not intuitive by looking at coefficients, I do not report them. Instead, I simply graph, in Figure 3.8, the relevant relationships, along with 95 percent confidence intervals. As noted above, one drawback of the cubic specification is that it can suffer from multicollinearity. Indeed, this problem prevented me from getting reliable estimates for models with inflation. Consequently, only estimates for the effects of changes in unemployment are reported.

Examining Figure 3.8, one finds that the basic conclusions of the previous analyses come out, i.e. the luxury-good hypothesis remains the only theoretical proposition consistent with the data. Further, despite using a specification that is amenable to finding asymmetries like those indicated in (H1) and (H2), none appear. Indeed, given the fact that there seem to be no asymmetries, a cubic parameterization may be an overfitting of the data. Consequently, I do not think it is wise to put too much confidence in this particular specification or to overinterpret the differences between these graphs and the nonparametric estimates provided earlier.

In the absence of evidence for asymmetry, however, it may be advisable to explore a simple linear specification. Estimates from such models are provided in Table 3.1.[8]

Again, the result of this analysis is in accordance with the nonparametric estimates, except that the insignificance of inflation comes out more

Table 3.1 Change in vote share for single-party prime ministers, (OLS regression)

Variable	Monthly data	Annual data	Monthly data	Annual data
Previous vote share	−0.11	−0.11	−0.16	−0.15
	(−1.53)	(−1.86)	(−2.46)	(−2.21)
Change in unemployment	0.24	0.02	–	–
	(2.56)	(2.56)	–	–
Change in unemployment × Left	−0.28	−0.03	–	–
	(−1.27)	(−1.67)	–	–
Inflation	–	–	0.005	0.0002
	–	–	(0.11)	(0.09)
Inflation × Left	–	–	0.007	0.0005
	–	–	(0.19)	(0.316)
Constant	0.03	0.03	0.05	0.05
	(0.83)	(1.29)	(1.53)	(1.47)
N	48	61	54	67
Adj. R^2	0.19	0.15	0.07	0.05

Note
OLS estimates, numbers in parentheses are *t*-ratios.

strongly in comparison with the result for unemployment. Ultimately, then, the conclusion of the study should be, like Paldam's (1991) attempt at a similar analysis, that it is difficult to find strong evidence of economic voting in these aggregate economic data. Where evidence of a relationship is apparent, however, it supports the luxury-good model.

Based on this, it seems reasonable to assert that the idea of the economy as a context in which voters form their preferences for Left/Right policies deserves consideration as a serious theoretical model. At the same time, however, the results clearly suggest that aggregate data will be of limited usefulness in testing the model or in empirically investigating any of its subtleties. While stronger parameterizations may well produce apparent relationships, we know that these are based on very little real covariation in the actual aggregate data. It seems to me, then, that the way forward is to abandon aggregate analysis altogether and, instead, pursue these hypotheses in individual level survey data.

NOTES

1 Such policies are only likely to change slowly over the long-term and so, if voters are assessing parties' policy commitments in a general way and weighing the long-term record of policy over campaign promises, then their preferences for different policies would likely be more stable than an empirical theory of economic voting would allow.
2 Clearly, not all policies should have even this indirect connection with the economy. Specifically, voters' preferences for some policies, e.g. public morality issues, probably are not conditional on the expected state of the economy. Preferences for policy that will require a significant amount of public expenditure, however, may all be conditional on expected economic performance (as outlined below). Since these kinds of policies make up much of what we think of as the differences in the Left and the Right policy agendas, I specifically call my policy-oriented economic voters Left/Right policy-oriented.
3 I have not found any policies for which I can convincingly argue that they concern inferior goods; so I do not discuss them here. The logic possibility of extending the analogy to policies that produce inferior goods remains.
4 It is also worth noting that although this theory explicitly has voters looking ahead to what parties will do when they come into office and whether these policies will be the best given the economic future that they expect, this does not mean that voters may not be relying on retrospective information about the economy to make their judgment about future economic performance. Specifically, I assume that voters use their current information about the state of the economy, including retrospective information, to forecast the economic future. Consequently, retrospective measures of national economic performance are used in the empirical model to measure voters' expectations of the likely economic future.
5 The "conversion criteria" for entrance into the European monetary union and the requirements of the stability compact are witness to this.
6 The VIF or variance inflation factor is a standard measure of the extent of multicollinearity in the data (Green, 2000).

7 GAMs are quite flexible and may be estimated for models in which some variables enter the mean function parametrically, while others are determined nonparametrically. In this chapter, I only report the bivariate results since few important control variables have been identified for aggregate economic-voting models.
8 For consistency with the analyses in Figures 3.2–3.7, I do not include inflation and unemployment in the same equations. Doing so does not destroy the relationships reported, although they make them somewhat harder to detect statistically.

REFERENCES

Anderson, C.J. (1995) *Blaming the Government: Citizens and the Economy in Five European Democracies*. London: Sharpe.

Beck, N. and Jackman, S. (1998) Beyond linearity by default: generalized additive models. *Am. J. Political Sci.*, **42**, 596–627.

Bloom, H. and Price, D. (1975) Voter response to short-run economic conditions: the asymmetric effect of prosperity and recession. *Am. Political Sci. Rev.*, **69**, 1240–1254.

Claggett, W. (1986) A re-examination of the asymmetry hypothesis: economic expansions, contractions, and congressional elections. *Western Political Quart.*, **39**, 623–633.

Durr, R. (1992) An essay on co-integration and error correction models. *Political Anal.*, **4**, 185–228.

Durr, R. (1993) What moves policy sentiment? *Am. Political Sci. Rev.*, **87**, 158–170.

Gelman, A. and King, G. (1993) Why are American presidential polls so variable when election outcomes are so predictable? *Brit. J. Political Sci.*, **23**, 409–451.

Green, W. (2000) *Econometric Analysis*, 4th edn. Englewood Cliffs, NJ: Prentice-Hall.

Hibbs, D. (1982) On the demand for economic outcomes: macroeconomic performance and mass political support in the United States, Great Britain, and Germany. *J. Politics*, **44**, 426–462.

Iyengar, S. and Kinder D. (1987) *News that Matters: Agenda-Setting and Priming in a Television Age*. Chicago, IL: University of Chicago Press.

Kahneman, D. and Tversky, A. (1979) Prospect theory: an analysis of decision under risk. *Econometrica*, **47**, 263–291.

Kiewiet, R. (1983) *Macroeconomics and Micropolitics: The Electoral Effects of Economic Issues*. Chicago, IL: University of Chicago Press.

Kreps, D. (1990) *A Course in Microeconomic Theory*. Princeton, NJ: Princeton University Press.

Lewis-Beck, M.S. (1990) *Economics and Elections: The Major European Democracies*. Ann Arbor, MI: University of Michigan Press.

Nannestad, P. and Paldam, M. (1993) *The egotropic welfare man: a Microstudy of Danish economic voting*. Working paper. Aarhus University.

Nannestad, P. and Paldam, M. (1994) The VP function: a survey of the literature on vote and popularity functions after 25 years. *Public Choice*, **79**, 213–245.

Paldam, M. (1991) How robust is the vote function? A study of 17 nations over four decades. In H. Norpoth, M.S. Lewis-Beck and J.-D. Lafay (eds), *Economics and Politics: The Calculus of Support*. Ann Arbor, MI: The University of Michigan Press.

Powell, G.B. and Whitten, G.D. (1993) A cross-national analysis of economic voting: taking account of the political context. *Am. J. Political Sci.*, **37**, 391–414.

Stevenson, R.T. (1997) *How parties compete: electoral performance and cabinet participation in parliamentary democracies.* Ph.D. Dissertation. University of Rochester.

Stevenson, R.T. (1999) *Contextual effects in policy-oriented models of economic voting.* Paper presented at the European consortium for political science research, Joint Sessions, Mannheim, Germany.

Stevenson, R.T. (2001) The economy and policy preference: a fundamental dynamic of democratic politics. *Am. J. Political Sci.*, **45**, 620–633.

Stevenson, R.T. and Vavreck, L. (2000) Do campaigns matter? Testing for cross-national effects. *Brit. J. Political Sci.*, **30**, 217–235.

Stimson, J.A. (1991) *Public Opinion in America: Moods, Cycles, and Swings.* Boulder, CO: Westview.

4 Economics, politics, and the cost of ruling in advanced industrial democracies

How much does context matter?

Harvey D. Palmer and Guy D. Whitten

4.1 INTRODUCTION

Economic voting is a form of policy voting. According to this paradigm, voters evaluate the incumbent government on the basis of national economic policy outcomes – growth, inflation, and unemployment. Economic voting constitutes a mechanism of electoral accountability that spurs governments to meet the policy goals of the public. Citizens in aggregate apply the "reins" of elections to control the policy direction taken by the government.

Political reality does not necessarily match this ideal of democratic accountability. This ideal requires that voters recognize the relevant policy outcomes and then accurately attribute policy-making responsibility for them. Failure to meet these requirements would undermine the electoral incentives that governments have to pursue the public's policy goals. If voters persistently fail to recognize the relevant policy outcomes, they might punish or reward the incumbent at the polls for erroneous policy outcomes. Or if they identify the correct policy outcomes but misperceive who is most responsible for them, they might apply the electoral "reins" inappropriately.

In the case of a complete failure, incumbents would view economic voters as fickle and unpredictable. The electoral process would make politicians attentive to swings in public opinion but would not shape government policy making. To the extent that the electorate was unable to accurately connect policy cause and effect, elected officials would have little reason to represent the policy preferences of the mass public. Economic voting, as a mechanism of democratic accountability, would be an empty construct where evidence of a statistical relationship between economic outcomes and voting behavior would not constitute evidence of policy representation. Any representation would be coincidental rather than a product of, the electoral process.

The political reality of economic voting is somewhere between the ideal of democratic accountability and a complete failure of the electoral process on informational grounds. The larger point, though, is that economic voting as a mechanism of democratic accountability is constrained by the limits of voter sophistication. To the extent that voters can recognize economic policy outcomes and correctly attribute policy-making responsibility, economic voting is an effective mechanism for democratic representation. To the extent that most citizens lack the necessary sophistication, evidence of economic voting does not demonstrate that elections ensure representative government.

In this chapter, we explore the limits of voter sophistication by investigating how economic voters behave under different political and economic contexts. The political and economic context in which public policy is made serves as a lens that adjusts our perception of government responsibility.[1] Hence, if economic voting is an effective mechanism of democratic accountability, it must be conditioned on the context – increasing in strength when responsibility is clear and decreasing in strength when it is not. Evidence that economic voters respond differently depending on the political and economic contexts would suggest rather sophisticated behavior. But if economic voters evaluate elected officials in the same manner regardless of context, it is doubtful whether economic voting provides precise enough accountability to control policy.

We propose and evaluate several hypotheses regarding the role of political and economic institutions in economic voting. Our central hypothesis states that voters are primarily concerned with unexpected growth and unexpected inflation since unexpected economic changes have real income effects and serve as more reliable indicators of government competence (Palmer and Whitten, 1999). Thus, we posit that unexpected components of growth and inflation affect public support for incumbent policy makers more strongly than the expected ones. This perspective is inherently prospective since the expected component is a weighted sum of past performance while the unexpected component is an "innovation" or "shock" unique to the current period, which thus represents the only non-retrospective information in the current period on which expectations about future performance are formed.

We also investigate whether other aspects of political and economic contexts condition policy voting in a sophisticated manner. First, we consider whether the increase in electoral volatility during the 1990s was associated with an increase in economic voting. If economic voting is actually policy voting, the electoral importance of national economic outcomes should have increased over time with the decline of class voting, expansion of mass media coverage, and theorized rise in issue voting (e.g. Inglehart, 1977; Flanagan, 1987; Dalton, 1988; Palmer, 1995).

Second, we investigate whether political and economic contexts influence the "cost of ruling" or decline in the incumbent parties' vote share from the previous election. If voters are sophisticated, the cost of ruling should reflect policy concerns and hence vary with national economic outcomes and the clarity of government responsibility. More specifically, we posit that the cost of ruling should be greater when national economic performance is poorer – lower unexpected economic growth, higher unexpected inflation, and higher unemployment. Similarly, we posit that the cost of ruling should be greater when government responsibility is clearer owing to longer government duration, fewer government parties, and the presence of political institutions that concentrate control over policy making into the hands of the incumbent parties. Finally, we investigate whether the effect of unemployment on the cost of ruling varies with the generosity of the country's unemployment benefits.

To investigate our hypotheses regarding political and economic contexts, we estimated various regression models of incumbent vote and incumbent vote swing using economic and political data from 1970 to 1998 pooled across 19 industrialized countries. These models were estimated using least-squares (LS) with panel-robust coefficient standard errors. As expected, our empirical analysis revealed stronger electoral effects for the unexpected components of growth and inflation than for their overall levels. We also found stronger evidence of economic voting in elections during 1980–1998 than during 1970–1989 consistent with the expectation that policy voting has increased over time. Finally, our analysis provides empirical support for our hypotheses regarding the effect of clarity of government responsibility on the cost of ruling and reveals that the electoral impact of unemployment varies with the country's policy stance on unemployment insurance.

4.2   ELECTORAL IMPORTANCE OF UNEXPECTED INFLATION AND UNEXPECTED GROWTH

The central hypothesis of this chapter is that voters care more about unexpected changes than expected ones in national output and consumer prices, and hence adjust their support more dramatically in response to such changes for incumbent policy makers. With respect to inflation, expected and unexpected price changes clearly have different implications for personal finances. Collective bargaining agreements, pension plans, and other long-term economic contracts are negotiated and devised keeping in mind the expected level of inflation. If economic actors engage in rational expectations, so that labor and financial markets are efficient, expected inflation should not have real effects on output and personal income. Thus, we should expect voters to discount expected changes and hence not punish (reward) government parties for expected increases (decreases) in prices. In contrast, unexpected inflation produces real negative income consequences by eroding the value of liquid assets and contract salaries (at least those that do not include automatic standard-of-living increases pegged to inflation).

On the basis of this theoretical argument, we expect to find a negative relationship between unexpected inflation and the vote share for parties that compose the government. Also, we expect the unexpected component of inflation to have a greater impact on election outcomes than overall inflation (or its expected component). Based on a different theoretical argument, Chappell and Keech (1985) predict a similar relationship for unexpected inflation. They posit that voters interpret unexpected inflation as a signal of whether the incumbent administration's macroeconomic policy was too "loose", resulting in endogenous inflation, for which it is punished at the polls, or "tight" enough to produce lower than expected inflation, for which it is rewarded at the polls.

Reasonable arguments exist for why voters might hold governments accountable for both expected and unexpected components of economic growth. Higher overall rates of growth, whether expected or not, should produce greater public satisfaction with incumbent policy makers. Whether that public satisfaction translates into stronger electoral support depends on the sophistication of voters, at least according to the voter rationality debate.[2] Sophisticated voters, however, may attribute temporal trends in economic growth, at least in part, to movements in the world economy or business cycle rather than the policies of their domestic government. In other words, they might take the current economic context into account. Consequently, they might discount this expected component of growth when evaluating incumbent policy makers.[3]

Additionally, voters might use unexpected economic growth as an indicator of government competence. Unexpectedly high (low) rates of growth represent improvements (declines) over recent trends that voters could logically attribute to effective (detrimental) government macroeconomic policies. Recent formal models of the political economy have adopted a similar perspective on the unexpected (or error) component of growth and how it affects public support for the incumbent government. Alesina *et al.* (1993, p. 15) model the unexpected component of growth as being composed of a supply or technology shock and administration "competence." They interpret the competence term as the "administration's ability to avoid inefficiency and, generally speaking, to create an environment conducive to growth without inflation." In their political-economy model, the competence term influences support for the incumbent president's party in US national elections.[4] Consistent with their model, we believe that the unexpected component of growth, as a proxy for competence, affects public support for the incumbent in a prospective fashion by influencing expectations about future growth if the incumbent government is returned to office.

For unemployment, we expect voters to care about the overall rate and not distinguish between expected and unexpected changes. We hold this expectation for two reasons. First, the families of the unemployed represent a voting bloc whose members are more likely to be dissatisfied with the macroeconomic performance of the incumbent government. Unlike with expected inflation, those who lose their jobs cannot protect themselves from the real income consequences of expected unemployment. As the unemployment rate increases, the size of this voting bloc increases with negative electoral implications for the government. Whether the higher unemployment rate is due to unexpected or expected changes does not alter the discontent of the newly unemployed, so there is no theoretical reason to assume that these two components of unemployment have different impacts on voting behavior.

Second, employed workers may react negatively to the unemployment rate owing to greater job insecurity (i.e. concerns about losing their jobs in the future). Even if the unemployment rate does not change, the group of unemployed workers changes over time as some of the unemployed find jobs while some of the employed lose their jobs. This cycling of workers, in and out of the unemployment ranks, creates anxiety about job loss, particularly among citizens who possess little human capital, have job skills that are industry-specific, and are employed in non-unionized occupations. The higher the unemployment rate, the greater is the probability of job loss. If this occurs, we have no theoretical reason to posit that the employed react differently toward unexpected and expected unemployment since both pose the same threat to their future employment status.[5]

Our theory concerning the differential effects of unexpected and expected inflation and growth also stems from our suspicion that cross-national differences in expected growth and expected inflation are potentially meaningless in comparative voting models. This supposition is based on two observations. First, substantial long-term differences exist in the economic performances of industrialized countries, particularly with respect to inflation. Second, economic interdependence produces temporal fluctuations in the economic performance of all industrial nations, even though this effect is stronger for those nations with smaller domestic markets and greater reliance on international trade. Thus, in comparative voting models, cross-national and temporal differences in the overall rates of growth and inflation may not explain the variations in public support for the incumbent government. From a theoretical perspective, this implies that voters' evaluations of government performance depend on the economic and political contexts in which they live. In other words, we should not expect French voters in 1973 to have evaluated their government's economic performance in the same way as Australian voters did in 1987.

Like Powell and Whitten (1993), our conceptualization of the comparative economic-voting relationship presumes a greater level of voter rationality than assumed in a pure retrospective sociotropic specification. The supposition that voters, on an average, react more strongly to unexpected components of growth and inflation assumes that citizens, at least in general, are sophisticated enough to put current economic performance in the context of past trends and thereby distinguish among the unexpected and expected components. Moreover, we contend that the strength of unexpected inflation's impact on government support varies with individuals' exposure to the real income effects of unexpected changes in consumer prices. Similarly, we also hypothesize that the unemployment's effect upon public support for incumbent policy makers varies with individuals' job security owing to seniority, human capital, and non-industry-specific work skills. In sum, our specification of the economic-voting relationship assumes a considerable level of sophistication on the part of the public. Like MacKuen *et al.* (1992), the public in our model behaves more as "bankers" than as "peasants."

In the context of the debate about voter rationality, our specification of the economic-voting relationship has two unique aspects. First, it includes unemployment in the economic-voting model. To the authors' knowledge, previous research on voter rationality has ignored unemployment. Suzuki (1991) justifies the exclusion of unemployment from his analysis on the grounds that unemployment and growth are highly collinear and previous research has found real output growth rather than unemployment to have a significant effect on voting behavior. We believe, however, that unemployment independently influences voters' assessments of government performance and hence should not be excluded from the analysis.

Second, our conception of voter rationality is less ambitious than that assumed in most other theoretical models containing rational voters. Peltzman (1990), Alesina and Rosenthal (1989), Suzuki (1991), and Suzuki and Chappell (1996) contend that voters respond to permanent rather than cyclical changes in income. Such a specification assumes that voters can forecast how current government policies will affect income far into the future. Alesina *et al.* (1993) also posit that rational voters focus on permanent income growth but limit the effect of competency on permanent income to one period into the future. Yet, their model assumes that voters can effectively distinguish between administration competence and supply shocks. In sum, all these models assume that voters are forward-looking and make political decisions in accordance with rational expectations.

Our conception of voter sophistication is consistent with limited information rationality (Popkin, 1991). We believe that the average voter does not have sufficient incentive to thoroughly analyze the sources of macroeconomic performance, and hence evaluates the incumbent government on the basis of information received from the mass media and opinion leaders.[6] Recent research has demonstrated that the media influences political discussion, public opinion, and voting behavior (Bartels, 1993; Hetherington, 1996), and that uninformed voters can behave in a sophisticated manner using voting cues from informed voters (Lupia, 1994). We do not believe, however, that information obtained from the media and opinion leaders is sufficient to enable voters to act politically in accordance with rational expectations. Our specification of the economic-voting hypotheses and the autoregressive models used to derive the expected components of inflation and growth (discussed below) reflect the limited nature of our conception of voter rationality.[7]

4.3   ADDITIONAL EXPECTATIONS REGARDING POLITICAL AND ECONOMIC CONTEXT

As stated above, our analysis also considers several additional hypotheses regarding the impact of political and economic contexts on the strength of the economic-voting relationship and the cost of ruling. The first of these hypotheses focuses on change in the importance of economic voting over time. The remaining hypotheses consider how factors that influence the clarity of government responsibility might alter the cost of ruling.

4.3.1   Temporal change in economic voting

Political context might adjust the economic-voting model indirectly through changes over time in the structure and nature of politics in advanced industrial democracies. Lipset and Rokkan's (1967) characterization of democratic politics as being firmly structured by class differences and, in certain countries, by religious and ethnic cleavages has gradually been replaced by a more pluralistic characterization. Studies of comparative political behavior have claimed that there has been a decline in the "old politics" over the period covered by our study owing to the growing salience of non-economic issues (see, e.g. Inglehart, 1977; Dalton *et al.*, 1984; Flanagan, 1987; Dalton, 1988; Palmer, 1995).

Under the so-called "old-politics" system, voters decided how to vote on the basis of a combination of traditional cleavage structures and retrospective evaluations of incumbent performances. Some scholars speculate that voting behavior has become more volatile in terms of "old-politics" affiliations, with more issues playing a role in determining how citizens of industrial democracies vote. If this is true, the strength of economic-voting relationships should increase over time. In addition, greater electoral volatility should cause the variance of economic-voting models to increase over time. In previous research (Palmer and Whitten, 1999), we have presented evidence consistent with the latter expectation. In the analysis presented below, we also consider whether the electoral importance of national economic performance has increased over time.

4.3.2 Cost of ruling and macroeconomic performance

Incumbent governments generally lose support in the next election – approximately 2 percentage points of their vote share in the previous election (Paldam, 1986; Powell and Whitten, 1993; Nannestad and Paldam, 1994). This widely recognized empirical regularity has been labeled the "cost of ruling." Paldam and Skott (1995) propose a policy explanation for this vote loss based on the median voter theorem and the failure of parties to fully converge to the policy ideal point of the median voter. Stevenson (n.d.) generalizes Paldam and Skott's theoretical model to distinguish among governments in terms of their length of tenure. Stevenson theorizes that the cost of ruling increases with government duration.

In sum, one possible explanation for the cost of ruling is that the government loses its electoral support as a result of political compromises made during the formulation and enactment of public policy. If this explanation is valid, the cost of ruling should vary in sensible ways with macroeconomic performance and factors that obscure or clarify government responsibility. As with incumbent vote, we expect incumbent vote swing to be positively related to unexpected economic growth and negatively related to unemployment and unexpected inflation.

Additionally, we expect cross-national differences to exist in the way that voters react to unemployment owing to differences in unemployment insurance schemes. In nations with higher benefit levels, unemployment should have a smaller negative effect on support for incumbent political parties since the more generous "safety net" reduces the risks and costs of becoming unemployed. On the other hand, the level of unemployment benefits in a nation might be endogenous. Politicians might be responding to their citizens' likely reactions to unemployment when they set the levels of benefits and the length of time over which unemployed individuals can draw such benefits. In this case, unemployment would have a larger negative effect on incumbent voting owing to the more generous "safety net" reflecting the greater issue salience of unemployment in national politics. Our analysis provides an empirical basis for choosing between these competing hypotheses.

Table 4.1 presents a nation-by-nation description of the data that we obtained on unemployment benefits. These data are estimated replacement rates, or the percentage of an unemployed person's wages before they became unemployed that they are paid as unemployment benefits. Greater replacement rates represent a more generous "safety net" for the unemployed. A key issue here is whether voters recognize that their country has a generous or austere "safety net" relative to other countries and hence adjust their calculus for evaluating government economic policy. Evidence that the effect of unemployment varies with these replacement rates would bolster the argument that voters have the

Table 4.1 Unemployment benefits in OECD countries, 1970–1995

Country	Mean benefits	Standard deviation	Minimum (year)	Maximum (year)
Australia	23.7	2.9	15.4 (1970)	26.7 (1995)
Austria	32.2	2.3	26.7 (1970)	35.0 (1985)
Belgium	49.6	2.6	46.2 (1995)	54.8 (1975)
Canada	56.9	1.5	51.5 (1970)	58.6 (1975)
Denmark	60.5	6.9	41.6 (1970)	68.5 (1980)
Finland	46.5	13.7	27.4 (1970)	64.9 (1995)
France	57.9	2.6	51.2 (1970)	61.8 (1980)
Germany	38.2	1.2	36.3 (1995)	40.2 (1970)
Ireland	41.1	7.7	24.8 (1970)	52.2 (1980)
Italy	15.0	15.5	1.9 (1980)	43.4 (1995)
Japan	30.6	2.9	26.6 (1980)	39.8 (1970)
Netherlands	67.8	2.3	65.0 (1970)	70.0 (1995)
New Zealand	28.4	1.5	26.4 (1995)	31.2 (1985)
Norway	48.4	16.4	14.3 (1970)	61.5 (1995)
Spain	65.9	8.1	41.8 (1970)	75.5 (1980)
Sweden	69.8	14.7	24.4 (1970)	80.3 (1990)
Switzerland	48.8	22.5	2.7 (1970)	69.5 (1995)
UK	27.0	5.2	21.6 (1995)	35.1 (1970)
USA	27.6	2.1	23.7 (1970)	32.0 (1980)

Notes
Benefits are an estimate of the amount of previous wages that are replaced for the unemployed under each nation's welfare system. These data were calculated by Olivier Blanchard (i.e. Blanchard and Wolfers, 2000) following OECD procedures that adjust for family types, length of unemployment spells, previous income levels of the unemployed, partial coverage schemes, and data discontinuities.

necessary sophistication to truly hold governments accountable for economic policy rather than simply responding in an emotional fashion to shifts in the economy.

4.3.3 Cost of ruling and clarity of government responsibility

Across a wide range of model specifications and operationalizations, scholars have found that clarity of responsibility matters (Powell and Whitten, 1993; Anderson, 1995, 2000; Whitten and Palmer, 1999; Nadeau *et al.*, 2002). Defined by institutional arrangements and political circumstances, clarity of responsibility proves to be an important intervening variable in the relationship between economic circumstances and support for incumbent politicians. We posit here that the cost of ruling is greater when responsibility for public policy is clearer.

We explore several factors theorized to influence the clarity of responsibility. First, we investigate whether the cost of ruling is greater in countries with political institutions that provide the government with broader and more exclusive control over the policy-making process. Second, we consider whether the cost of ruling increases with government duration. The longer that incumbent parties control policy making, the more likely that peripheral party supporters will become alienated enough by policy decisions to abandon the government in the next election. This hypothesis is generally consistent with Stevenson's (n.d.) model. However, we view elections as an opportunity for the public to evaluate the incumbent government's policies and hence treat all governments as ending with the next election even if the incumbent parties do not change. Finally, we investigate whether the cost of ruling decreases with the number of government parties based on the belief that policy responsibility becomes less clear as the number of government parties increases.

4.4 DATA AND METHODOLOGY

The empirical analysis presented below uses pooled time-series cross-sectional data. Beck and Katz (1995) and Greene (1997) provide thorough discussions of the econometric methods for analyzing such data. Our pooled data set, though, is somewhat atypical. Our data set pools 116 quarters from 1970 to 1998 across 19 countries. The 19 countries are Australia, Austria, Belgium, Canada, Denmark, Finland, France, West Germany, Ireland, Italy, Japan, Netherlands, New Zealand, Norway, Spain, Sweden, Switzerland, United Kingdom, and United States. In most of these quarters, only one national parliamentary election occurred, and so our data set includes just 156 elections and most of the 2204 observations contain missing data. Table 4.1A of Appendix A lists the elections by quarter and country. The inclusion of missing-data observations gives our data set a balanced structure to facilitate estimation of Beck–Katz panel-robust standard errors. However, the subsample of observations containing non-missing data (i.e. the 156 elections) represents a pooled set of non-continuous times series that are unbalanced and contain very few quarters in common (i.e. quarters in which more than one country held a parliamentary election). This subsample of 156 election observations was used to estimate the LS regression models of incumbent vote presented below. The larger data set of 2,204 observations with missing-value observations filled with zeros was used to derive the Beck–Katz robust standard errors for evaluating the LS coefficients.

Our analysis employs two dependent variables: *incumbent vote* is the percentage of votes received by the political parties that compose the government at the time of the election, and *incumbent vote swing* is the change in the governing parties' vote share between the current and previous elections. For each election, we constructed a set of political variables: *previous vote, number of government parties, clear government responsibility*, and *government duration*. *Previous vote* is the vote share received by the current government party or parties in the previous election. In models of *incumbent vote*, the closer the positive coefficient on *previous vote* is to zero, the less stable is electoral support for the government parties. In models of *incumbent vote swing*, a negative coefficient on *previous vote* reflects greater electoral volatility in that governing parties suffer an automatic decay in their electoral support and benefit less from a strong performance in the previous election. This negative relationship is consistent with the "regression-to-the-mean" hypothesis that government parties with stronger (short-run) support in the previous election lose more of their vote share as the electorate shifts back to normal (long-run) voting patterns.

Our analysis includes several variables that influence the clarity of government responsibility for public policy. We expect a positive relationship to exist between *incumbent vote* and *number of government parties* since an increase in the number of government parties increases the likelihood that dissatisfied voters shift their support to another party in the government rather than to an opposition party. Similarly, we expect an increase in the number of government parties to decrease the clarity of government responsibility and thereby decrease the cost of ruling.

Clear government responsibility is a dummy variable denoting the "most clear" category of an index constructed by adding four dummy variables for minority government, bicameral opposition, weak political parties, and opposition committee chairs. More specifically, elections are coded as "most clear" when the governing parties controlled a majority of the seats in the legislature, while the opposition did not control a politically significant upper house and influential committee chairs within the legislature, and internal party cohesion was strong. These characteristics obscure responsibility for actions taken by the legislature, thereby making it more difficult for voters to assess credit or blame for policy outcomes. Additionally, countries with these legislative characteristics might place greater value on government "checks and balances" and be less deferent to political authority. We theorize that electoral volatility is greater for governments in the "most clear" category of policy responsibility. Hence, we expect the positive coefficient on *previous vote* in *incumbent vote* models to be closer to zero and the cost of ruling to be greater for governments in the "most clear" category.

Government duration is the number of quarters since the last election. This definition treats each government as unique even if the election outcome does not change the parties that compose the government. Hence, our focus is on the length of time since the electorate last had an opportunity to hold the governing parties accountable for policy decisions rather than the length of time (perhaps across multiple governments) that those parties had control over policy making. We theorize that the clarity of government responsibility increases with the length of time since the last election and hence expect *government duration* to have a negative effect on *incumbent vote swing*.

For each election, we also constructed measures of economic growth, unexpected economic growth, inflation, unexpected inflation, and unemployment.[8] Using an expanded set of quarterly economic data from 1967 to 1998, we estimated autoregressive models of growth, inflation, and unemployment. The authors gathered these economic data from Organization of Economic Cooperation and Development (OECD) and International Labor Organization (ILO) sources. A separate set of regressions was estimated for each country. The following autoregressive specification was adopted for all three economic variables:

$$Y_{i,t} = \gamma_1 + \gamma_2 Y_{i,t-1} + \gamma_3\left(Y_{i,t-1} - Y_{i,t-5}\right) + \delta_1 Q_{2i,t} + \delta_2 Q_{3i,t} + \delta_3 Q_{4i,t} + \varepsilon_{i,t}$$

where $Y_{i,t}$ is the economic measure for country i at time t, Q_2, Q_3, and Q_4 are dummy variables for the second, third and fourth quarters, respectively the γ's and δ's are unknown parameters to be estimated, and $\varepsilon_{i,t}$ is a white noise error process. The quarter dummy variables control for seasonal trends. The second regressor, $Y_{i,t-1} - Y_{i,t-5}$, accounts for business cycle trends. A positive lagged annual difference in growth (inflation and unemployment) indicates upward movement out of a business cycle trough, while a negative lagged annual difference suggests downward movement from a peak. Thus, we expect current growth, inflation, and unemployment to vary positively with their lagged annual differences (i.e. $\gamma_3 > 0$). To improve the overall fit, each model also included one-quarter lags of the other two economic indicators (e.g. the growth model included lags of inflation and unemployment).[9]

In total, we estimated 19 sets of three auxiliary regressions; each set corresponding to a separate country in our incumbent voting data set. These auxiliary regressions served two purposes. First, we used the growth and inflation regressions to calculate election-specific residuals. These residuals were then included in our incumbent vote models as measures of unexpected growth and inflation. Since the fitted values from these regressions represent a weighted average of all values from prior quarters, the residuals for a particular country represent changes from expectations derived on the basis of time series of past values in that country. We contend that this simple and purely autoregressive specification approximates the process by which individuals form expectations about future economic conditions. As with Powell and Whitten's comparative measures, our measures of unexpected growth and inflation standardize performance according to the economic context in which it occurred, thereby making them comparable across countries and over time.

Second, we used the auxiliary regressions to eliminate seasonal differences in our economic measures. For most countries, the raw measures of growth, inflation, and unemployment (i.e. those collected from OECD and ILO sources) were already seasonally adjusted. To ensure, however, that the economic measures for all countries did not contain seasonal

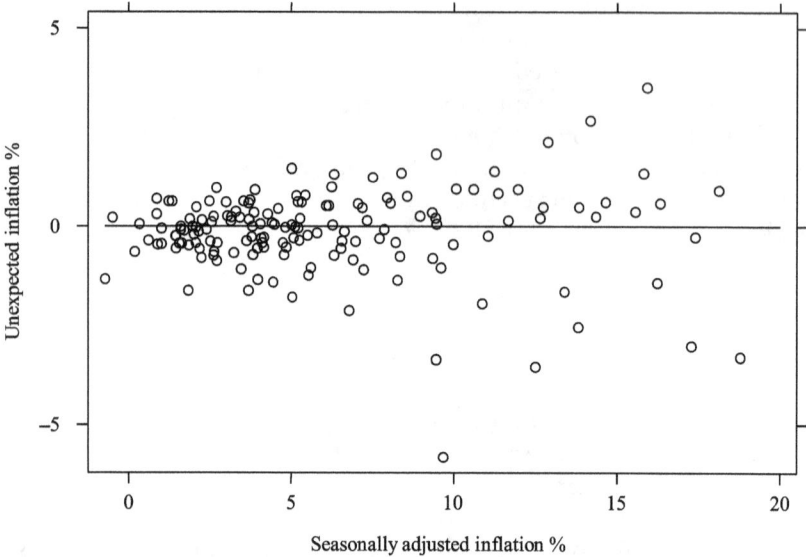

Figure 4.1 Plot of unexpected components versus seasonally adjusted measures for inflation in 156 election quarters.

patterns, we used the coefficients on the quarter dummy variables to purge the raw measures.

Figures 4.1 and 4.2 plot the values of the unexpected components versus seasonally adjusted measures for inflation and growth respectively, for the 156 election quarters in our data set. Both figures show the relatively strong fit of the models described above. The patterns of unexpected components are fairly constant across the range of values except for the extremely high values. For growth, however, the largest unexpected components occur at both extremely low and high values.[10]

Using the 156 election observations, we estimated regression models of *incumbent vote* and *incumbent vote swing*. As demonstrated by Beck and Katz (1995), LS estimation with pooled data produces incorrect coefficient standard errors. Therefore, we evaluate the LS coefficients with panel-robust standard errors. Adapting Greene's (1997, p. 653) notation, we use the following asymptotic covariance matrix:

$$Est.\ Var[b] = \left(\sum \mathbf{X}_i'\mathbf{X}_i\right)^{-1} \left(\sum_i \sum_j \left(\frac{e_i'e_j}{T_{ij}}\right)\mathbf{X}_i'\mathbf{X}_j\right) \left(\sum \mathbf{X}_i'\mathbf{X}_i\right)^{-1}$$

where e_i and e_j are the LS residual vectors, $\mathbf{X}_i$ and $\mathbf{X}_j$ are the regressor matrices for countries i and j, and T_{ij} is the number of common election (i.e. non-missing) observations for countries i and j. The panel-robust

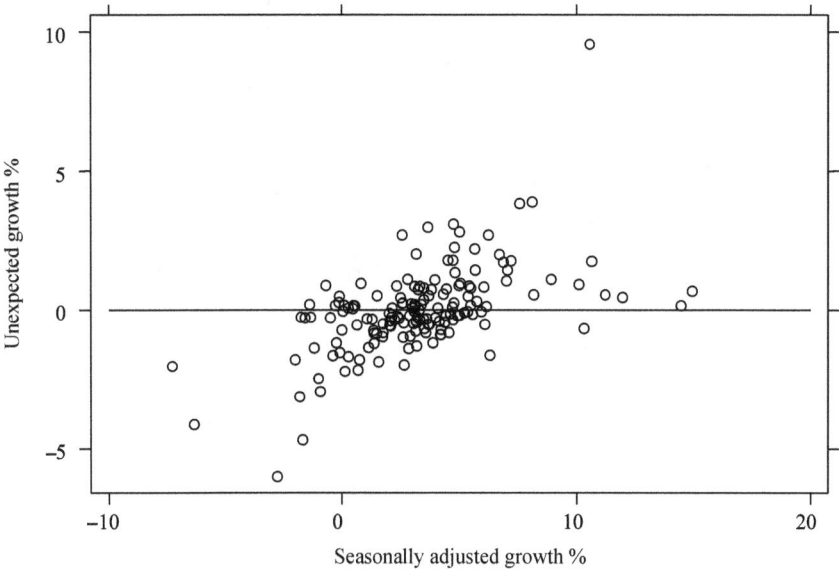

Figure 4.2 Plot of unexpected components versus seasonally adjusted measures for growth in 156 election quarters.

coefficient standard errors are derived by taking the square roots of the diagonal elements in Est. Var[*b*]. We also used the panel-robust covariance matrices to derive *F*-statistics for the overall model, which test the joint null hypothesis that all the non-constant parameters equal zero.

4.5   EMPIRICAL RESULTS

To begin our analyses, we estimated two models of *incumbent vote* with specifications very close to the models that produced the main results in our earlier paper on the effects of *unexpected growth* and *unexpected inflation* (Palmer and Whitten, 1999). These models, estimated with 22 additional cases, are reported in Table 4.2. As we found previously, when we specify the model with seasonally adjusted indicators of *growth* and *inflation*, the results are not supportive of established economic voting hypotheses. In Model 1, the parameter estimate for *growth* is positive, as expected, but smaller than its standard error. The predicted effect of *inflation* is statistically significant but positive, which contradicts the expectation of the economic-voting paradigm. When we re-specify the model with *unexpected growth* and *unexpected inflation*, the regression produces estimates in the expected direction that prove statistically significant at conventionally accepted levels. Although our specification of *unemployment* does not change from Model 1 to Model 2, the

Table 4.2 Incumbent vote regression models with alternative specifications of growth and inflation

Variable	Model 1	Model 2
Previous vote	0.877***	0.844***
	(0.047)	(0.047)
Clear government responsibility × previous vote	−0.088***	−0.086***
	(0.019)	(0.019)
Unexpected growth	–	0.439**
		(0.213)
Growth	0.127	–
	(0.142)	
Unexpected inflation	–	−0.829**
		(0.364)
Inflation	0.285***	–
	(0.091)	
Unemployment	−0.136	−0.239**
	(0.083)	(0.093)
Number of government parties	1.089***	1.061***
	(0.413)	(0.400)
Constant	0.530	4.900
	(2.249)	(2.131)
Adjusted R^2	0.820	0.819
F-statistic for overall model	150.3***	152.0***
Number of observations	156	156

Notes
Dependent variable is the percentage of votes received by the governing parties. Panel-robust standard errors are given in parentheses below the least-squares coefficients.
* $p < 0.10$ (two-tailed t-tests).
** $p < 0.05$ (two-tailed t-tests).
*** $p < 0.01$ (two-tailed t-tests).

re-specification of the other two economic variables leads to an increase in the magnitude and statistical significance of the estimated effect of unemployment on the incumbent government's vote share.

The results in Table 4.2 also have interesting implications for the role of political context in economic-voting models. *Previous vote* is the vote share received by the governing parties in the previous election. We also interacted this lagged dependent variable with *clear government responsibility* – a dummy variable that identifies governments for which policy-making responsibility was most clear. Model 2 estimates that governing parties, on an average, retain 84.4 percent of their vote share from the previous election. Incumbent parties in "most clear" governments, however, retain only 75.8 percent of their vote share from the previous election. This difference is consistent with our proposition that electoral volatility increases with clarity of government responsibility and that

Table 4.3 Political and economic volatility by decade, 1970–1990s

	1970s	*1980s*	*1990s*
Incumbent vote swing	−1.95	−2.63	−6.12
	(5.00)	(4.04)	(7.42)
Unexpected growth	0.09	−0.04	−0.05
	(2.04)	(1.19)	(1.36)
Unexpected inflation	0.05	−0.28	−0.16
	(1.26)	(1.20)	(0.59)
Unemployment	3.70	8.14	8.44
	(2.62)	(4.50)	(4.60)
Number of observations	55	56	45

Notes
Mean value for the variable appears above the standard deviation in parentheses. Cases for the 1990s do not include 1999 cases (Austria, Belgium, Finland, New Zealand, Switzerland) for which we are still collecting economic data.

governing parties in "most clear" policy-making contexts depend more on favorable policy outcomes to retain their electoral support.

We also find that governments with more political parties retain more votes. As discussed elsewhere (see Whitten and Palmer, 1999), we believe that there are several reasons for such an effect. The more the parties in a government coalition, the more likely it is that disgruntled voters will switch from one party of the government to another instead of supporting a party from the opposition. This effect is also perhaps due to the tendency of each party to have a core of supporters who are unlikely to vote against the party, regardless of how they have performed in office. Finally, we believe clarity of government responsibility decreases with the number of governing parties since partisan control over policy making becomes less centralized.

Next we turn to the question of whether electoral volatility and economic voting have increased over time. Table 4.3 presents decade-specific means and standard deviations of *incumbent vote swing*, *unexpected growth*, *unexpected inflation*, and *unemployment* for the three decades covered by our analyses. Clearly electoral volatility has increased over time as *incumbent vote swing* has increased from −1.95 in the 1970s to −2.63 in the 1980s to −6.12 in the 1990s. Similar evidence does not exist, however, that variation in macroeconomic performance measures has also increased over this period. Only the standard deviation of *unemployment* has increased over time and this increase largely occurred between the 1970s and 1980s.

Table 4.4 considers this question more directly and rigorously by estimating subsample regressions of *incumbent vote* for 1970–1989 and 1980–1998.[11] As in Table 4.3, the regression results indicate that electoral volatility has increased over time. During 1970–1989, governing parties, on an average, retained 86.2 percent of their vote share from the

Table 4.4 Temporal change in economic voting (subsample regressions of Model 2 for 1970–1989 and 1980–1998)

Variable	1970–1989	1980–1998
Previous vote	0.862***	0.839***
	(0.041)	(0.060)
Clear government responsibility × Previous vote	−0.087***	− 0.086***
	(0.015)	(0.029)
Unexpected growth	0.303*	0.706*
	(0.179)	(0.383)
Unexpected inflation	−0.883***	−1.018**
	(0.291)	(0.496)
Unemployment	−0.127	−0.183
	(0.088)	(0.117)
Number of government parties	0.949***	1.082**
	(0.358)	(0.453)
Constant	4.567**	4.029
	(1.776)	(2.896)
Adjusted R^2	0.893	0.753
F-statistic for overall model	188.9***	97.2***
Number of observations	111	101

Notes
Dependent variable is the percentage of votes received by the governing parties. Panel-robust standard errors are given in parentheses below the least-squares coefficients.
* $p < 0.10$ (two-tailed *t*-tests).
** $p < 0.05$ (two-tailed *t*-tests).
*** $p < 0.01$ (two-tailed *t*-tests).

previous election (77.5 percent if government responsibility was "most clear"). In contrast, governing parties in elections during 1980–1998 retained 83.9 percent of their vote share from the previous election (75.3 percent if government responsibility was "most clear").

But did economic voting increase along with electoral volatility? Yes, according to the regression results in Table 4.4. All the macroeconomic performance measures have stronger marginal effects in the 1980–1998 regression than in the 1970–1989 regression. The most striking difference is for *unexpected growth*. For example, suppose that actual GDP growth is 5 percent when expectations based on past macroeconomic performance are that GDP growth should be only 2 percent, i.e. *unexpected growth* is 3 percent. The 1970–1989 regression estimates that this, rather than expected economic growth, would have increased the governing parties' vote share by 0.91 percentage points, but the 1980–1998 regression predicts an increase of 2.12 percentage points.

Table 4.5 shifts our focus to the cost of ruling. Regression results are presented for three different model specifications. Models 4 and 5 build upon Model 3 by adding factors theorized to alter the political and eco-

Table 4.5 Economic voting regression models of the cost of ruling (Incumbent vote swing) with controls for clarity of responsibility

Variable	Model 3	Model 4	Model 5
Previous vote	−0.161***	−0.137***	−0.149***
	(0.047)	(0.043)	(0.043)
Unexpected growth	0.450**	0.454**	0.393*
	(0.217)	(0.221)	(0.213)
Unexpected inflation	−0.826**	−0.662*	−0.675*
	(0.371)	(0.391)	(0.393)
Unemployment	−0.231**	−0.232**	−0.154*
	(0.095)	(0.092)	(0.093)
Unemployment benefits × unemployment	–	–	−0.143**
			(0.069)
Clear government responsibility	−4.040***	−3.227***	−3.283***
	(0.978)	(0.947)	(0.945)
Number of government parties	0.978**	1.006**	1.141***
	(0.398)	(0.391)	(0.380)
Government duration	–	−0.319***	−0.324***
		(0.109)	(0.105)
Constant	5.257**	8.051***	7.994***
	(2.156)	(2.445)	(2.398)
Adjusted R^2	0.182	0.222	0.242
F-statistic for overall model	6.40***	6.58***	6.14***
Number of observations	156	156	156

Notes
Dependent variable is the change in governing parties' vote share between the current and previous elections. Panel-robust standard errors are given in parentheses below the least-squares coefficients.
* $p < 0.10$ (two-tailed *t*-tests).
** $p < 0.05$ (two-tailed *t*-tests).
*** $p < 0.01$ (two-tailed *t*-tests).

nomic context in meaningful ways – *government duration* and *unemployment benefits*. As stated above, *government duration* is the number of quarters since the last election. *Unemployment benefits* is a three-category measure ranging from −1 for contexts in which government unemployment benefits provide the lowest rates of wage replacement to 1 for contexts in which unemployment benefits provide the highest rates of wage replacement.[12]

As expected, the cost of ruling varies with macroeconomic performance in a manner consistent with the economic-voting paradigm. Across all three model specifications, *unexpected growth* has a statistically significant positive impact on *incumbent vote swing*. Similarly, *unemployment* and *unexpected inflation* have negative effects on the cost of ruling that achieves statistical significance at the 10 percent level or better.

Table 4.5 also demonstrates that the cost of ruling increases as responsibility for public policy becomes clearer. According to Model 4,

Table 4.6 Cost-of-ruling estimators (Incumbent vote swing) under different political contexts

Previous vote (%)	Number of government parties and government duration								
	Single-party government			Two-party coalition government			Four-party coalition government		
	8 qtrs	12 qtrs	16 qtrs	8 qtrs	12 qtrs	16 qtrs	8 qtrs	12 qtrs	16 qtrs
20	2.31	1.03	−0.25	3.31	2.04	0.76	5.32	4.05	2.77
30	0.94	−0.34	−1.62	1.94	0.67	−0.61	3.95	2.68	1.40
40	−0.43	−1.71	−2.99	0.57	−0.70	−1.98	2.58	1.31	0.03
50	−1.80	−3.08	−4.36	−0.80	−2.07	−3.35	1.21	−0.06	−1.34
60	−3.17	−4.45	−5.73	−2.17	−3.44	−4.72	−0.16	−1.43	−2.71
70	−4.54	−5.82	−7.10	−3.54	−4.81	−6.09	−1.53	−2.80	−4.08
80	−5.91	−7.19	− 8.47	−4.91	−6.18	−7.46	−2.90	−4.17	−5.45

Notes
Cell entries are predicted values of *incumbent vote swing* derived using the Model 4 coefficients in Table 4.5. *Clear government responsibility* equals 0 (modal category) while the other explanatory variables were set to their sample means.

the cost of ruling increases by 3.2 percentage points when political institutions create a context in which policy-making responsibility is "most clear" but decreases by 1.0 percentage point for each additional party in the government coalition. Similarly, Model 4 estimates that the cost of ruling increases by 1.3 percentage points for each four-quarter increase in the current government's tenure. Additionally, the cost of ruling increases with the government's vote share in the previous election, consistent with the "regression to the mean" hypothesis. According to Model 4, the cost of ruling is 1.4 percentage points higher for each 10 percentage points increase in the government's vote share in the previous election. Table 4.6 further illustrates how the predicted cost of ruling varies with *previous vote, number of government parties*, and *government duration*.

Model 5 in Table 4.5 considers how public policy on unemployment insurance conditions the electorate's response to unemployment. As stated above, there are two plausible conflicting theories about how unemployment benefits affect the relationship between unemployment and the governing parties' vote share. On the one hand, in societies with higher benefit levels, unemployment insurance might mitigate the pain of unemployment thereby causing the electorate to hold the government less accountable for unemployment. On the other hand, the level of unemployment benefits might reflect incumbent politicians' expectation that voters are particularly sensitive to changes in unemployment. Thus, the level of benefits might capture the electoral salience of unemployment as a policy outcome and hence the effect of unemployment on incumbent vote would be greater in contexts with higher benefit levels.

Model 5 in Table 4.5 reports that the parameter estimate for *unemployment benefits × unemployment* is negative and statistically significant at the five-per cent level. This result indicates that *unemployment* has no impact on the cost of ruling when *unemployment benefits* equals −1 but increases the cost of ruling by 0.3 percentage points for each 1 percentage point increase in *unemployment* when *unemployment benefits* equals 1. In other words, unemployment ranges from being irrelevant for electoral contexts in which unemployment insurance is a low policy priority to increasing the cost of ruling by as much as other macroeconomic performance indicators for electoral contexts in which unemployment insurance is a high priority.[13]

4.6   DISCUSSION

The purpose of this chapter is to investigate whether the political and economic contexts in which elections are held conditions the comparative economic-voting model. Our empirical analyses demonstrate that the political and economic contexts do matter, playing a crucial role in shaping the nature of policy voting. When context is ignored, the economic-voting paradigm appears to have little value in explaining cross-national variation in election outcomes. But when macroeconomic performance is placed within the proper economic and political context (so that elections in different countries are truly comparable), the economic-voting paradigm is strongly confirmed.

Our analyses also reveal that the strength of economic-voting relationships changes with the political and economic context. The electoral importance of macroeconomic performance, as a specific form of policy voting, has increased over time along with electoral volatility. Similarly, the electoral importance of unemployment is greater in political systems in which unemployment insurance is a policy priority. Finally, we find that the political context strongly influences the cost of ruling. The cost of ruling is higher when government responsibility is clearer due to fewer government parties, longer government duration, and political institutions that centralize partisan control over policy making.

The larger theoretical question that motivated our research is whether the effectiveness of elections as a mechanism of democratic accountability is constrained by the limits of voter sophistication. The scope of this question is obviously too broad to adequately answer in a single study. However, the empirical results reported in this chapter do provide a preliminary though qualified answer. Our analyses indicate that the political and economic context conditions economic voting in a rather sophisticated manner. More generally, policy voting appears to vary across political and economic contexts in a way that is consistent with the accountability model of democracy – having greater importance when government responsibility for policy outcomes is clearer.

However, our analyses only consider the electorate in aggregate. The fact that election outcomes respond in a sophisticated way to changes in policy outcomes does not necessarily imply that voters in general are sophisticated and attentive enough to conform to the requirements of the accountability model of democracy. It is possible that only a small segment of the electorate truly engages in economic voting while other voters evaluate economic policy outcomes in a biased manner inconsistent with the accountability model (Duch *et al.*, 2000). In summary, larger theoretical questions about the precise nature of economic voting remain unanswered.

APPENDIX A

Table 4.A1 Parliamentary elections in advanced-industrial-democracies dataset, 1970–1998

Quarter	Countries
70.00	2, 6
70.25	20
70.50	18
71.00	13
71.50	5
71.75	2, 3, 19
72.00	6
72.25	11
72.75	1, 4, 8, 12, 13, 14, 21
73.00	7, 10
73.50	18
73.75	5
74.00	3, 20
74.25	1
74.50	4
74.75	20
75.00	5
75.50	6
75.75	1, 2, 14, 19
76.25	11
76.50	18
76.75	8, 12, 21
77.00	5
77.25	10, 13
77.50	15
77.75	1
78.75	3, 14
79.00	6, 17
79.25	2, 4, 11, 20
79.50	18
79.75	5, 12, 19

80.00	4
80.25	12
80.75	1, 8, 21
81.25	7, 10, 13
81.50	15
81.75	3, 5, 14
82.00	10
82.50	13, 18
82.75	10
83.00	1, 6, 8, 12
83.25	2, 11, 20
83.75	19
84.00	5
84.50	4
84.75	1, 14, 21
85.50	15, 18
85.75	3
86.00	7
86.25	12, 13, 17
86.75	2
87.00	6, 8, 10
87.25	11, 20
87.50	1, 5
87.75	3, 14, 19
88.25	5, 7
88.50	18
88.75	4, 21
89.25	10
89.50	13, 15
89.75	17
90.00	1, 12
90.75	2, 5, 8, 14
91.00	6
91.50	18
91.75	3, 19
92.75	11, 20
92.75	10, 21
93.00	1, 7
93.25	17
93.50	12, 15
93.75	4, 14
94.25	13
94.50	5, 8, 18
94.75	2
95.00	6
95.25	3
95.75	2, 19
96.00	1, 17
96.75	12, 14, 21
97.25	4, 7, 10, 20
97.50	15

Table 4.A1 (Continued)

Quarter	Countries
98.00	5
98.25	13
98.50	8, 18
98.75	1

Notes

Legend to country codes (total number of elections): 1 – Australia;
(12); 2 – Austria (9); 3 – Belgium (8); 4 – Canada (8); 5 – Denmark
(12); 6 – Finland (8); 7 – France (6); 8 – Germany (8); 10 – Ireland
(9); 11 – Italy (6); 12 – Japan (9); 13 – Netherlands (9); 14 – New
Zealand (9); 15 – Norway (6); 17 – Spain (5); 18 – Sweden (10);
19 – Switzerland (7); 20 – United Kingdom (8); 21 – United States (7).

Table 4.A2 Descriptive statistics for variables used in economic-voting and cost-of-ruling models

Variable	Mean	Standard deviation	Minimum	Maximum
Previous vote	49.1	11.6	11.1	84.4
Clear government responsibility × previous vote	13.7	21.9	0	78.2
Unexpected growth	0.002	1.58	−6.00	9.56
Growth	3.27	3.25	−7.28	14.92
Unexpected inflation	−0.13	1.09	−5.80	3.52
Inflation	6.08	4.40	−0.74	18.76
Unemployment	6.66	4.52	0.001	22.60
Unemployment benefits × unemployment	0.58	6.84	−12.49	22.60
Clear government responsibility	0.289	–	0	1
Number of government parties	1.90	1.25	1	5
Government duration	13.24	4.02	2	20

ACKNOWLEDGMENT

We thank Olivier Blanchard for providing us with his data on unemployment benefits. Robert Bohrer, George Hwang and Edward Yang provided valuable research assistance in the collection of our economic and political data.

NOTES

1 Hibbs *et al.* (1982) conducted some excellent work on how the effect of economic measures on public support for governing parties varies across time and national contexts.
2 There is substantial evidence of rationality on the part of mass publics with respect to economic indicators. Hibbs (1979) is one of the earliest works

to show that mass publics respond rationally to fluctuations in inflation and unemployment.

3 This argument may hold with greater validity for voters in small European countries, such as Belgium, which maintain open economies and frequently champion liberal international trade. Political leaders and voters in these countries are more willing to accept as normal rates of economic change and dislocation that their counterparts in large advanced industrial countries view as intolerably high (Katzenstein, 1985). Thus, voter indifference toward expected growth, at least in small European countries, may be a natural consequence of public attitudes toward economic liberalism.

4 Alesina *et al.* (1993) model also incorporates unexpected inflation but treats it as a partisan effect due to differences in the inflationary nature of Republican and Democratic policies. Hence, it produces a partisan election cycle in growth rates but does not influence voting behavior as a government competence factor.

5 At least superficially, our unemployment hypothesis conforms to a traditional retrospective sociotropic perspective. Our theoretical argument, however, for why employed workers may react negatively to higher unemployment rates suggests a prospective perspective, as well. The claim that higher unemployment reduces job security by increasing the likelihood that employed workers will lose their jobs in the future, implies a prospective evaluation on the part of employed workers.

6 MacKuen *et al.* (1992) make a similar argument. For a critique of this argument, see Clarke and Stewart (1994) and Norpoth (1996).

7 Moreover, we do not believe that voters or even "experts" form expectations about growth and inflation in the same manner or with the same accuracy (see Nadeau *et al.*, 1999, 2000). The autoregressive models used to derive the expected components of growth and inflation are approximations of the typical process used by voters and "experts" to form economic expectations for the purpose of putting government performance in the proper context when evaluating it. Similarly, while our economic-voting hypotheses are stated as if they apply universally, our theoretical perspective on voter rationality does not preclude the possibility that the hypotheses only apply to a subset of the public. As long as the voting behavior of naive persons does not negate the systematic economic voting of rational persons, the public will appear to vote in a collectively rational manner.

8 The Table 4.2A of Appendix A reports descriptive statistics for the explanatory variables.

9 A number of reviewers and panelists have asked questions about the specification of these models. They are intentionally simplistic and autoregressive in order to best capture what should have been expectations of a rational public. Although the fit of these auxiliary models might have been improved by a more complex lag structure, we felt that this would move us further away from the primary purpose of these estimates. It is worth noting that the fit of these models was quite high. For instance, the R^2-values for models or inflation ranged between 0.709 and 0.865.

10 Although these residuals versus measured values in each figure are drawn from 19 separate regression models, there would appear to be evidence of heteroskedasticity in both sets of models. This is not, however, a problem because the point estimates, which are the only output of interest from these auxiliary models, remain unbiased.

11 We employed overlapping time periods in order to increase the number of observations used to estimate each subsample regression.

12 *Unemployment benefits* were constructed from a five-year moving average of the continuous measure of unemployment benefits summarized in Table 4.1.

Unemployment benefits was coded −1 if the moving average was less than 33.5, 1 if the moving average was greater than 52.0, and 0 otherwise. These thresholds are one-half standard deviation below and above the cross-national mean. We employed a categorical measure because the continuous measure contained considerable year-to-year variation due to changing economic conditions that was largely independent of changes in the government's policy stance on unemployment insurance.

13 Note that the standard deviation of *unemployment* is 4.52 while the standard deviations of *unexpected growth* and *unexpected inflation* are 1.58 and 1.09 (see Table 4.2A of Appendix A).

REFERENCES

Alesina, A. and Rosenthal, H. (1989) Partisan cycles in congressional elections and the macroeconomy. *Am. Political Sci. Rev.*, **83**, 373–398.

Alesina, A., Londregan, J. and Rosenthal H. (1993) A model of the political economy of the United States. *Am. Political Sci. Rev.*, **87**, 12–33.

Anderson, C.J. (1995) *Blaming the Government: Citizens and the Economy in Five European Democracies*. Armonk, NY: Sharpe.

Anderson, C.J. (2000) Economic voting and political context: a comparative perspective. *Electoral Stud.*, **19**, 151–170.

Bartels, L.M. (1993) Messages received: the political impact of media exposure. *Am. Political Sci. Rev.*, **87**, 267–286.

Beck, N. and Katz, J. (1995) What to do (and not to do) with time-series–cross-section data in comparative politics. *Am. Political Sci. Rev.*, **89**, 634–647.

Blanchard, O. and Wolfers, J. (2000) The role of shocks and institutions in the rise of European unemployment: the aggregate evidence. *Economic Journal*, **110**, 1–33.

Chappell, H.W. and Keech W.R. (1985) A new view of political accountability for economic performance. *Am. Political Sci. Rev.*, **79**, 10–27.

Clarke, H.D. and Stewart, M.C. (1994) Prospections, retrospections and rationality: the 'bankers' model of presidential approval reconsidered. *Am. J. Political Sci.*, **38**, 1104–1123.

Dalton, R.J. (1988) *Citizen Politics: Public Opinion and Political Parties in Advanced Industrial Democracies*. Chatham, NJ: Chatham House.

Dalton, R.J., Flanagan, S.C. and Beck, P.A. (eds) (1984) *Electoral Change: Realignment and Dealignment in Advanced Industrial Democracies*. Princeton, NJ: Princeton University Press.

Duch, R.M., Palmer, H.D. and Anderson, C.J. (2000) Heterogeneity in perceptions of national economic conditions. *Am. J. Political Sci.*, **44**, 635–652.

Flanagan, S.C. (1987) Value Change in Industrial Societies. *Am. Political Sci. Rev.*, **81**, 1303–1319.

Greene, W. (1997) *Econometric Analysis*. Upper Saddle River, NJ: Prentice-Hall.

Hetherington, M.J. (1996) The media's role in forming voters' national economic evaluations in 1992. *Am. J. Political Sci.*, **40**, 372–395.

Hibbs, D.A. (1979) The mass public and macroeconomic performance: the dynamics of public opinion toward unemployment and inflation. *Am. J. of Political Sci.*, **23**, 705–731.

Hibbs Jr., D.A., Rivers, R.D. and Vasilatos, N. (1982) On the demand for economic outcomes: macroeconomic performance and mass political support in the United States, Great Britain, and Germany. *J. of Politics*, **44**, 426–462.

Inglehart, R. (1977) *The Silent Revolution: Changing Values and Political Styles among Western Publics*. Princeton, NJ: Princeton University Press.

Katzenstein, P.J. (1985) *Small States in World Markets*. Ithaca, NY: Cornell University Press.

Lipset, S.M. and Rokkan, S. (1967) *Party Systems and Voter Alignments*. New York: Free Press.

Lupia, A. (1994) Shortcuts versus encyclopedias: information and voting behavior in California insurance reform elections. *Am. Political Sci. Rev.*, **88**, 63–76.

MacKuen, M.B., Erikson, R.S. and Stimson, J.A. (1992) Peasants or bankers? The American electorate and the US economy. *Am. Political Sci. Rev.*, **86**, 597–611.

Nadeau, R., Niemi, R.G. and Amato, T. (1999) Elite economic forecasts, economic news, mass economic judgments, and presidential approval. *J. Politics*, **61**, 109–135.

Nadeau, R., Niemi, R.G. and Amato, T. (2000) Elite economic forecasts, economic news, mass economic expectations and voting intentions in Great Britain. *Eur. J. Political Res.*, **38**, 135–170.

Nadeau, R., Niemi, R.G. and Yoshinaka, A. (2002) A cross-national analysis of economic voting: taking account of the political context across time and nations, *Electoral Stud.*, **21**, in press.

Nannestad, P. and Paldam, M. (1994) The VP function: a survey of the literature on vote and popularity functions after 25 years. *Public Choice*, **79**, 213–245.

Norpoth, H. (1996) Presidents and the prospective voter. *J. Politics*, **58**, 776–792.

Paldam, M. (1986) The distribution of election results and the two explanations of the cost of ruling. *Eur. J. Political Economy*, **2**, 5–24.

Paldam, M. and Skott, P. (1995) A rational-voter explanation of the cost of ruling. *Public Choice*, **83**, 159–172.

Palmer, H.D. (1995) Effects of authoritarian and libertarian values on conservative and Labour Party support in Great Britain. *Eur. J. Political Res.*, **27**, 273–292.

Palmer, H.D. and Whitten, G.D. (1999) The electoral impact of unexpected inflation and economic growth. *Brit. J. Political Sci.*, **29**, 623–639.

Peltzman, S. (1990) How Efficient Is the Voting Market? *J. Law Economics*, **33**, 27–63.

Popkin, S.L. (1991) *The Reasoning Voter: Communication and Persuasion in Presidential Campaigns*. Chicago, IL: University of Chicago Press.

Powell, G.B. and Whitten, G.D. (1993) A cross-national analysis of economic voting: taking account of the political context. *Am. J. Political Sci.*, **37**, 391–414.

Stevenson, R. (n.d.) The cost of ruling, cabinet duration, and the 'median-gap' model. *Public Choice*, in press.

Suzuki, M. (1991) The rationality of economic voting and the macroeconomic regime. *Am. J. Political Sci.*, **35**, 624–642.

Suzuki, M. and Chappell Jr., H.W. (1996) The rationality of economic voting revisited. *J. Politics*, **58**, 224–236.

Whitten, G.D. and Palmer, H.D. (1999) Cross-national analyses of economic voting. *Electoral Stud.*, **18**, 49–67.

5 Group economic voting

A comparison of the Netherlands and Germany

Han Dorussen and Michaell Taylor

5.1 INTRODUCTION

It has become widely accepted that economics matters for voting. However, the consensus hides a considerable amount of confusion and disagreement about basic issues in the relationship between economic variables and the calculus of political support. The lines in the debate have been drawn already for a long time and are well known. Are aggregate "objective" economic data preferable to individual perceptions of the state of the economy? Is the vote choice based on experience or on expectations of future economic performance? Do voters carefully evaluate the contribution of government policy to national or personal welfare, or is economic voting a knee-jerk reaction to changing economic times? Clearly, the answers given to these questions are not independent. At the same time, we may need to recognize that economic voting may vary from country to country, from person to person, and even over time (Lin, 1999). In this chapter, we pay special attention to the political and personal contexts of the economic voter. For one, we examine how coalition governments may aid economic voting in multi-party systems. Further, we account for voter heterogeneity based on the salience of economic issues to groups. We argue that economic subgroups present a more appropriate level of analysis than either the personal or collective level. The model of conditional responsibility is evaluated using longitudinal data for Germany and the Netherlands.

The starting point of most economic voting researches is still the reward–punishment hypothesis, originally formulated by V.O. Key.[1] Here, the central expectation is that the electorate rewards an incumbent for economic prosperity and punishes it for economic downturns. Voters base their decision on experience, and disregard party platforms or other macroeconomic policy statements. It is worthwhile to trace the argument in more detail. The reward–punishment hypothesis requires voters to hold an incumbent party *responsible* for the state of the economy. In particular, the economy should reveal information about the *competency* of the government. Moreover, the voter believes that recent experience is a *reliable* indicator for what to expect in the future. Finally, voters have *no loyalty* towards specific parties; in other words, all parties are equivalent alternatives. Are these assumptions generally reasonable? Multi-party systems may provide an important exception. Downs (1957), for example, claims that coalition government renders parties less reliable and less responsible.[2] We make, however, a slightly different argument, namely that coalitions *influence* the perception of reliability and responsibility. In addition, we will argue that subgroups of the electorate differ systematically with respect to their loyalty to incumbent parties and their perception of government competency; in other words, voter heterogeneity matters.

Although the reward–punishment model has been dominant for some time, it is not unchallenged. Alternative models of economic voting represent different views on the ability of the "economic voter" to evaluate the economy retrospectively or prospectively, and to distinguish between various dimensions of economic policy. Basically, three alternatives have received most attention. Briefly, these three variants see voters as either: (1) mainly retrospective, but evaluating competency along different policy dimensions, (2) mainly forward looking, or prospective, but they do not discriminate, or (3) prospective and discriminating between policy dimensions. Even though the models vary in their assumptions about voter sophistication and also yield different predictions in some circumstances, they are close alternatives. There is a real danger that eventually a model is preferred based on the *ad hoc* criterion that it fits the data best in a particular case. A further problem with the various models is that occasionally none appears to fit particularly well. Conditions of coalition complexity and voter heterogeneity are two such settings.

Issue-salience, or issue-priority, models emphasize that parties invest in building a reputation of competency in a given policy domain.[3] Voters are expected to support a party perceived to be best able to handle the most urgent economic problems. Thus, a central assumption is that voters recognize differences in issue priority and competency.[4] Clearly, the additional complexity because of coalition government may influence the applicability of issue-salience models. In multi-party systems the competition for issues is likely to be fierce, and an incumbent party has to share any credit or blame with its coalition partners. However, coalitions can also help voters to evaluate issue priority. Information about the composition of coalition government is readily available and may provide valuable cues about issue priority and competency. Voters also differ in how they process economic and political information. Finally, any investment in a reputation of competency is often directed at specific subgroups in society. For example, a labor party is particularly interested in solidifying its reputation as a competent manager of the labor market with the working classes. Voters are thus likely to differ in their assessment of competency. A specific subgroup of voters may remain loyal to a party as long as it is able to deliver goods to them.

The electorate has been typified as either "peasants," who base their voting decisions retrospectively on the economic record of the parties while they were in office, or "bankers," who vote prospectively based on their expectations how parties would act in office (MacKuen *et al.*, 1992). The rational-expectations approach assumes that voters are exclusively forward looking.[5] The assumption is that the electorate evaluates incumbent parties by contrasting actual with expected economic performance. It is, however, easy to overstate the difference between retrospective and prospective decision making. Clearly, the evaluation of a party's record helps the electorate to formulate expectations for the future (Kuklinski and West, 1981; and Lewis-Beck, 1988; Popkin, 1991). Coalition government may be relevant in this respect as well. Parties will share responsibility for the coalition's record in office. Further, voters elect parties and not coalitions. The extent to which a party's platform and record (as member of an incumbent government) are reliable indicators of future policies depends on the choice of coalition partner(s). More recently, the argument has been restated as the "clarity-of-responsibility" effect (Powell and Whitten, 1993). The prediction is that under "fuzzy" institutions, incumbent support is less sensitive to economic fluctuations.

It remains a reasonable assumption that voters formulate expectations based at least in part on experience. The electorate is concerned about the economic record of an incumbent government exactly because it provides the best, relatively easily available, information about how such a government would handle economics in the future. Also in this respect, coalition government and voter heterogeneity do not just inhibit the strength of economic voting. They also provide additional sources of information that may affect the direction of the economic vote. The circumstances under which a party governs (or is in opposition) determine the economic issue for which it is considered responsible. Of course, the need to mollify coalition partners and to hold a coalition together may limit the freedom of parties in power to pursue particular policy prescriptions. However, the policy preference of the parties and distribution of votes will determine the precise constraints on the coalition parties. Changes in the distribution of votes affect either these constraints and/or open the possibility of an alternative coalition. Whereas some voters may accept coalition constraints as an excuse, others will try to affect these constraints. Although the connection between the electorate and the incumbent may be weakened by "fuzzy" institutions, economic voting still exists under such circumstances and is directionally conditioned by the composition of coalition government.

In Sections 5.2 and 5.3, we present in more detail the argument for economic voting given coalition government and voter heterogeneity. Next, we summarize the hypotheses of – what we have coined – the *conditional-responsibility model of economic voting*, and we briefly introduce the data and research design. We continue with evaluating the conditional-responsibility model for two countries: the Netherlands and Germany. We conclude with a summary and discussion of the main findings.

5.2 COALITION GOVERNMENT AND ECONOMIC VOTING

Coalition government is common in most West European parliamentary democracies. In the Netherlands and Germany, democratic governments have generally been coalitions and are thus a mere fact of political life. Scholars, however, tend to emphasize the added complexity of coalition government. To summarize, coalitions would make it more difficult to assign credit or blame, because several parties share responsibility for the government's record. Moreover, parties vary in the amount of influence they have over the political decisions of a coalition government. Finally, the formation of a coalition government makes compromises inevitable, and the choice of coalition partner(s) affects governmental policies. Consequently, a party's platform and record (as part of an incumbent coalition) are less reliable predictors of future policies.

Coalitions, however, not only increase the amount of required information, but also provide a context helping voters to process information; in other words, knowing whether a party has joined a specific coalition helps a voter to evaluate that party's position. Political news is often presented in terms of coalition and opposition parties. Moreover, a party is expected to join only a coalition that enables it to advance its political agenda. The failure to do so cannot simply be unloaded onto the other members of the coalition. Conflict between coalition members is highly newsworthy, especially if the survival of the government is at stake. In fact, forming and breaking coalition is a commonly used method for parties to define and communicate their issue priority. In their turn, voters use a government's record to evaluate the competency of parties and, if necessary, to signal their desire for change.

Partisan attribution of responsibility is central to issue-priority models of economic voting. These models assume that voters are able to discriminate between parties with respect to issue priority. Voters may use placement on an underlying ideological dimension as a means to determine party priority; for example, a left–right continuum. A common assumption is that along the socioeconomic dimension, center–left parties prioritize full employment policies and anti-cyclic government intervention in the economy. In contrast, center–right parties emphasize price stability and balanced budgets (Hibbs, 1987).[6]

In multi-party systems, this is still insufficient to yield an unambiguous assignment of issue priority. More than one party may try to locate itself on either the left or right side of the ideological spectrum. For example, the main social-democratic party often faces competition from radical or "green" parties. Center parties, moreover, face competition from both their right and left. Thus, if voters wanted to give more weight to unemployment, they could turn to the center party instead of the conservative party. Others – most likely voters who originally voted for the center party – may now prefer the social-democratic party to the center party. The center party would lose on its left but gain from its right. The situation would be reversed in case of inflation. Regardless, the overall effect of economics on the support for center parties is indeterminate.

The circumstance under which a party governs (or is in opposition) may shed some additional light on its issue priority. First, the main social-democratic and liberal-conservative parties often insist that their more extreme alternatives are unfit to govern. Votes for the extreme alternatives are characterized as protest votes or called wasted. The appeal of such arguments, however, depends on being in government or opposition. In opposition, the main party can present itself as a viable option for a change of government. Incumbent parties have to take responsibility for actual economic performance given the existing coalition. In this case, a call for change may either mean being forced into opposition, or the inclusion of the more extreme parties into the government. The prioritized issue is thus particularly valuable whenever a party is in opposition. In government, parties benefit less strongly from their priority issue and, given competition for issue priority, they may even lose.

The political context of coalitions can also clarify the evaluation of issue priority of center parties. In this respect, it is important to be explicit about the link between voting and coalition formation. We propose a simple heuristic: basically, voters evaluate the impact of their vote on the creation and removal of alternatives to the incumbent coalition. Voters for centrist coalition parties face different constraints than voters for more extreme parties. The former cannot create an alternative to the incumbent coalition by switching to an opposition party, because such a move is zero-sum with respect to the distribution of votes between possible coalition. For example, suppose that the center and left parties together have majority support in parliament, while the center and right parties do not hold a majority. By definition, seats gained by the right party but lost by the center party cannot alter this situation. Voters can, however, remove an alternative by switching to more extreme parties. To continue our previous example, if the center party loses enough seats, a center–left coalition may no longer have a majority of seats. Voters for the extreme coalition partner can create an alternative by voting for another party (to a center or opposition party), or remove the alternative of the current coalition by voting for an opposition party.[7]

The asymmetric constraints force coalition parties in the direction of opposite issue priorities. By way of example, suppose that a center–left coalition government is in power. Whenever inflation becomes a problem, the centrist voters should be the first with an interest in forcing their party to form a coalition with the conservative opposition. They can only achieve this objective by removing the incumbent government as a feasible alternative. The center party loses votes because it is incapable of demonstrating competency in the conservative issue. Increasing unemployment does not necessarily suggest a center–right coalition as an attractive alternative. The left party will be held primarily responsible for failing to demonstrate competency in creating jobs, because this is supposedly its salient issue. There will be defection towards radical parties, but also towards the center. The objective of the latter is to create an alternative to the incumbent coalition. Consequently, the coalition parties are being held responsible for failure along different policy dimensions. A similar argument applies in case of a center–right coalition. In this case, the center party will lose votes if unemployment increases, and the conservative party will be held responsible for inflation. Thus, the coalition partner conditions the issue responsibility of a center party.

It goes almost without saying that political circumstances can become so complex that the electorate will be unable to attribute responsibility. Under such conditions, Down's (1957, p. 163) pessimistic conclusion about the possibility of rational voting is certainly warranted: "Eventually each voter either abstains, votes after cutting off his deliberation at some unpredictable point, or decides that it is easier just to vote for his favorite party." However, it should be quite rare that voters find themselves in such dire straits. Excluding these cases – where we should actually expect discontent with the political system that goes beyond ordinary economic voting – information about coalition government should help voters to assign issue responsibility. We have formulated two general expectations: (1) "extreme" parties are held responsible for their issue priority when in government, and (2) "centrist" parties will be held responsible for the mirror issue priority of their coalition partner.

5.3   GROUP ECONOMIC VOTING

A recurring theme in the economic voting literature is whether voters react more to the overall condition of the economy or to their personal financial situation. Beginning with Kinder and Kiewiet (1979), research has shown that general economic conditions tend to be more important than personal economic conditions.[8] Perhaps this finding should not come as a great surprise, since most people find it generally far fetched to blame or credit the government for their personal finances (Weatherford, 1983; Peffley, 1984). There is, however, widespread agreement that a government bears some responsibility for central economic statistics, like growth, unemployment, price stability, and interest rates. If the relative importance of these variables varies across members of society, voter heterogeneity characterizes economic voting. A model that includes the central economic statistics, while ignoring variation in their effects, proceeds at a level of aggregation that is too high (Duch *et al.*, 2000; Gomez and Wilson, 2001; Duch and Palmer, Chapter 7, this volume).

To ignore voter heterogeneity has serious ill effects on inference. First, differences in preferences in society inflate the standard errors of the regression estimates. To the extent that the differences are systematic instead of random, the regression estimates will be biased. Suppose public employees weigh unemployment rates lower in political salience than to public expenditure levels, and that the reverse holds true for unskilled labor. Pooling of these groups assumes a common slope for the unemployment and results in biased (and inefficient) estimates. The magnitude of the bias will be a function for the actual slopes and the comparative size of each group in society.

It would seem appropriate to turn to the group level to assess the magnitude of economic voting. Weatherford (1983) argued that lower occupational skill groups react to economic conditions in a much stronger manner than higher skilled groups, reflecting the much more uncertain economic position of the former. Hibbs (1977, 1987) has argued consistently that economic groups vary in their reaction to economic conditions. Underlying the magnitude of the reaction is a complex calculation comparing economic management competencies of the incumbent government and the main opposition. Hibbs' approach highlights the close affinity between models of group economic voting and issue-priority models. The argument holds that parties represent the interests of their core constituencies. The core constituency of center–left parties, low- and middle-income groups, is more concerned about unemployment. The core constituency of center–right parties, middle- and high-income groups, is more worried about inflation. Assuming, moreover, a trade-off between unemployment and inflation, the distribution of issue priority along the left–right dimension follows almost directly. Parties on the left are more willing to allow for inflation to achieve higher levels of employment, and for parties on the right the reverse holds (Hibbs, 1992; Swank, 1993).

Using groups as the focus of analysis has recently regained some favor in the literature (Mutz and Mondak, 1995). Nagler and Niemann (1997) have returned to Weatherford's analysis to argue that groups not only assign different salience to overall economic conditions but also may actually react to different economic cues. In other words, individuals vote according to how "people like them" are doing in the economy. Teixeira (1998) argues that these differences are only observable recently due to greater separation of group interests in the last ten years or so. Yet, Taylor (1998) demonstrates strong group-level differences in the salience of economic indicators across major European countries over the last two decades.[9]

The most obvious division of economic interests relies on the level of skills one brings to the labor market place. Labor market cycles are part of market economies. However, there is ample evidence that the price associated with labor market fluctuations is not paid equally by all groups in society. Differences in the risk of unemployment vary by industry, region, company, union influence, etc., but worker skill level is without doubt of crucial importance. Lesser-skilled labor runs a much higher risk to become unemployed when aggregate unemployment rates are rising. Hibbs (1987) provides a thorough analysis of the effects of unemployment and inflation on various subelectorate groups in the United States. During the late 1950s, blue-collar unemployment levels during times of recession were roughly three times that of white-collar unemployment. In the late 1970s, the difference was still two and a half times. Feldman (1982) found that during the first two years of the Reagan administration, blue-collar workers faced a shift in risk of unemployment 5 percent higher than white-collar workers did. Compston (1997) and Taylor (1998) show similar effects for western Europe.

Moreover, even though wages tend to be sticky downwards, aggregate unemployment rates show a much stronger negative effect on blue-collar income than white-collar income. Gramlich and Laren (1984) show that, in the United States, a 1 percent increase in aggregate unemployment results in a 5.8 percent decline in pretax and transfer payment income for the least-skilled workers in the workforce. In Europe, strong labor unions and/or social commitment to avoid unemployment result in hour and wage cutbacks affecting a larger pool of workers. Here, the risk of unemployment is borne in particular by young people entering the job market with minimal work experience.

Group economic voting is not entirely immune to the problems of coalition complexity. However, there are several reasons to believe that coalitions are less likely to reduce voter ability to assign unique group representation to political parties. First, the representation of group interests by political parties is founded upon strong and enduring institutional ties between these groups and various parties. In other words, group representation is the institutional equivalent of issue priority. The concerned constituency can be remarkably loyal. In case of disappointing policy results, it will be the first to point towards uncontrollable circumstances or to cast blame on the coalition partner(s). Second, the effects of institutional clarity are reversed under group economic voting. If it is less clear what party is responsible for specific policies, it becomes more important to have access to government. Groups will reward "their" party for providing them with access, i.e. joining a (coalition) government. Group representation may thus compensate for concerns about competency. To the extent that voters are prospective, they assign greater value to the willingness of a party to join a government. Access to government outweighs preferences about the composition of the government.

Those economic groups most vulnerable to unemployment, the low skilled and young, are important constituencies for parties on the left of the political spectrum. We expect these groups to behave with a certain loyalty, because left parties prioritize full employment. If labor market conditions worsen, they will stick (or even return) to their party. Other economic groups are more easily swayed by concerns about competency and thus more inclined to abandon incumbent left parties if unemployment goes up. For example, public service employees are relatively immune from rising unemployment rates. This strengthens the argument presented in the previous section, because the coalition partner then gains from the inability of the main party on the left to demonstrate competence.

5.4   HYPOTHESES

We have argued that most models of economic voting overly simplify voter calculations. For example, the dominant reward–punishment model assumes that voters only use information about parties being in or out of government. Voters, however, also consider information about existing coalitions and expectation about likely future coalitions. Moreover, it is rational for voters to be loyal to a party, at least up to a certain degree. On the other hand, in issue-priority models, voters act with complete loyalty towards parties perceived to prioritize an issue that is most in need of attention. Here, however, voters do not care at all about the constraints of coalition government or information about competency. The record of a party in government becomes wholly irrelevant. Instead we propose a modified version which takes some elements from each of these theories. First, the evaluation of competency is modified by coalition constraints. Second, groups of voters have clear notions of economic issue priority for each party. The attribution of issue priority affects their reaction to macroeconomic fluctuations. The eventual model emphasizes conditional responsibility.

To summarize, the voter reaction to macroeconomic fluctuations is determined by three factors: (i) a party's issue priority, or "portfolio" (Austen-Smith and Banks, 1990), (ii) the position of a party in a coalition government, if any, and (iii) the nature of the coalition partner(s), if any. Specifically, we propose the following set of hypotheses.

Hypothesis 1. Given coalition government, the economic issue responsibility of center parties gets defined in opposition to their (main) coalition partner. Specifically:

> *Hypothesis 1a.* Center parties in coalition with the right are punished for increasing unemployment rates. The coalition parties on the right lose from inflation.

Hypothesis 1b. Center parties in coalition with the left lose from inflation. The coalition parties on the left are punished for increasing unemployment rates.

Hypothesis 2. Extreme coalition partners get rewarded for their issue priority but only when in opposition. Specifically, left parties benefit only from increasing unemployment when they are in opposition, while right parties benefit only from inflation when they are in opposition.

Table 5.1 contrasts the expectations of the conditional-responsibility model with its two main competitors, the reward–punishment model and the issue-priority model. We distinguish two possible coalition structures: a center–left and a center–right coalition government.[10] The conditional-responsibility model formulates predictions for center parties (in contrast to issue-priority models), but the coalition partners affect the specific predictions (in contrast to reward–punishment models). For extreme parties, the predictions of the conditional-responsibility model depend on being in or out of government and the perceived issue priority of the party.

Finally, we formulate the effects of group loyalty on economic voting. We expect that individuals belonging to an economic group tend to have information concerning those macroeconomic indicators that most directly affect, or threaten to affect, their economic interests. Consequently, they will react strongly to swings in these indicators.

Table 5.1 Expectations of conditional-responsibility model compared with reward–punishment and issue-priority models

		Center–right coalition		Center–left coalition	
		Unemployment worsens	*Inflation*	*Unemployment worsens*	*Inflation*
Left party	Cond. responsibility	++	0	–	0
	IP/RP	+/+	–/+	+/–	–/–
Center party	Cond. responsibility	–	+	+	–
	IP/RP	?/–	?/–	?/–	?/–
Right party	Cond. responsibility	0	–	0	++
	IP/RP	–/–	+/–	–/+	+/+

Notes
IP = issue-priority model. RP = reward–punishment model. Cond. responsibility = +conditional-responsibility model. Double signs indicate stronger reactions; zeros indicate nonsignificant relationship; question marks indicate unclear prediction.

Hypothesis 3. Groups react to economic indicators that primarily affect their economic interests.

In the remainder, we will focus primarily on the risks of unemployment. We thus expect individuals vulnerable to unemployment (low-skilled and young people) to react strongly to rising unemployment levels but to remain loyal to parties on the left. If individuals are less vulnerable to unemployment concerns, they respond less strongly to unemployment concerns and are also less loyal to parties on the left.

5.5   DATA AND METHODS

As an initial test of the conditional-responsibility model, we test the hypotheses using two West European countries, Germany and the Netherlands, for a period of approximately 20 years. In both countries, coalition governments are extremely common. Even though the competition for government in these two countries has been open, coalition government was generally either center–left or center–right in the period under study. In the Netherlands, the main parties are the social democratic PvdA, the progressive liberal D'66, the centrist Christian democratic CDA, and the conservative liberal VVD. Coalition government consisted either of PvdA and CDA (with or without D'66), or of CDA and VVD. In Germany, the main parties are the social democratic SDP, the progressive liberal FDP, and the conservative Christian democratic CDU/CSU. Coalition governments were either SDP–FDP or FDP–CDU/CSU.

We have gathered individual-level data for both countries. Data on the Netherlands were originally collected by the Netherlands Institute for Public Opinion and Market Research (NIPO). Since the early 1970s, the NIPO has conducted weekly surveys of about 2000 respondents based on random national samples. The political part of these omnibus surveys asks respondents to recall the party they voted for at the last election and to indicate what party they would vote for if elections were to be held today. Other variables contain socioeconomic and demographic information (Eisinga and Felling, 1992). We have collected these data for the period 1975–1993. In total, the data contain approximately two million observations. The German data are based on monthly Gallup surveys. We have only used data from West Germany. The period covered is 1975–1995. The German data contain originally approximately 120,000 cases.

The original individual-level data are aggregated in two different ways. First, we look at monthly data, because we are unaware of weekly level GDP growth and inflation data – unemployment data are likely available. Second, we look at *group-level support*. We distinguish groups who are weakly, moderately, or highly sensitive to unemployment. High sensitive respondents are low-skilled and young respondents. Low sensitive respondents are civil service employees and retirees. The other respondents are moderately sensitive.[11] For each of these groups, we determine the average group support for a given political party. We chose this technique with the understanding that we destroy information through aggregation. However, we feel that the benefit of lower error of the independent variables is worth the amount of information lost. Given the amount of data we have, we are quite certain to have made the correct decision.[12]

For each country, we examine party support regressed against economic and demographic variables under various government coalitions. The economic variables are monthly aggregate OECD statistics for unemployment, inflation, and GDP growth. Inflation is measured as the consumer price index for all goods. The unemployment definition used is the OECD standardized definition. In case of GDP growth, which is available only in quarterly format over this period, the monthly data are "feathered" from the quarterly indicators (Dorussen and Taylor, 2001). The party support variables and the demographic variables are derived from the individual-level data.

Our approach allows testing for institutional and economic differentiation in an overtime perspective. The models are basic linear regression models with a correction for autocorrelation in the dependent variables. ARIMA analyses suggest generally a first-order nonintegrated autocorrelation in the party support variables. Moreover, the Durbin M-statistic indicates continuing autocorrelation in two of the 36 models if we include only the first lag. Correlograms indicated a fourth-order autoregressive process. As the Durbin M-values shown in the last row indicate, the stochastic process has been eliminated in every model, although the fourth lag is usually not significant. For parsimony and comparability, the first and fourth lags have been included in each model.[13]

Since we are using linear models, the interpretation of the coefficients is straightforward. There is, however, a risk to overestimate the importance of inflation relative to unemployment, since the variation in unemployment figures was considerably larger than in inflation. We assess the relative importance of an independent variable, say X_k, by using the following formula $\beta_k(\mathrm{UL}(X_k)-\mathrm{LL}(X_k))$, where the upper limit (UL) and lower limit (LL) are calculated by using three times the standard deviation from the mean.

5.6   CONDITIONAL RESPONSIBILITY IN THE NETHERLANDS

In several ways, the Netherlands presents an ideal case to test our theory. There is not only an extremely rich set of data available, but coalition governments vary regularly between center–left and center–right. Finally, the left, center, and right comprise each about one-third of the popular vote. In the period covered, the PvdA led a center–left coalition until 1977. The center party CDA was in charge of a center–left coalition for a short period in the early 1980s and from 1989 on. The rest of the period, the CDA headed a center–right coalition with the VVD. As in most other industrialized countries, the government re-evaluated its role in management of the economy during the 1980s, in part in response to frustration with dealing with high unemployment. From the late 1970s, inflation has been a relatively minor problem.[14] The polarization between left and right remained limited in the Netherlands. It is illustrative that the same prime minister, Lubbers (CDA), headed center–right and center–left coalitions. Further, beginning in August 1994, the Netherlands was government by a "purple" coalition of PvdA, D'66, and VVD, excluding the Christian democratic CDA.[15]

We present our analyses of party support for each of the three major parties. Moreover, for each party we distinguish between the two common coalition structures and the three sensitivity levels of groups to unemployment. The three tables thus contain 18 models in total.

Table 5.2 presents the analyses of support for the Christian democrats, CDA, the main center party. In the first three models, estimates are for the periods of a center–right CDA–VVD coalition. The estimates in the other models are based on the periods of center–left CDA–PvdA coalitions. The parameters for the center party, CDA, provide the easiest test of Hypothesis 1, and we observe that the issue responsibility of CDA varies conditional on coalition structure. The unemployment coefficients for CDA given a center–right coalition are negative and significant for respondents who are moderately or highly sensitive to unemployment. Thus, given a CDA–VVD coalition, CDA is held responsible for unemployment. In the same models, the inflation coefficients are positive and generally significant. We observe, however, that the coefficients are quite small and so were the inflation rates during the same period. The substantive significance of inflation is clearly less than that of unemployment.

The results are less clear-cut for the period in which CDA was in coalition with the social democratic PvdA. In accordance with Hypothesis 1b, respondents who are moderately sensitive to unemployment punish the CDA for inflation. However, the least sensitive actually seem to reward the CDA for inflation. As expected, the substantive significance of inflation is larger during the periods of center–left government. Whereas in a CDA–VVD coalition, the CDA is punished for rising unemployment, it tends to benefit from unemployment when in coalition with the PvdA. Given the latter coalition, the substantive importance of unemployment on CDA support is, however, smaller. Focusing on the highly sensitive respondents, the effect of unemployment now equals 2.64 percent, while the CDA loses 16.35 percent when in coalition with the VVD.

Political support for the liberal conservative VVD is analyzed in Table 5.3. In opposition, the VVD gains from inflation, but it is held responsible for

Table 5.2 Group-level political support for the CDA under different coalition conditions (linear regression)

	CDA–VVD coalition						CDA–PvdA coalition					
	Least sensitive		Moderate		Highly sensitive		Least sensitive		Moderate		Highly sensitive	
	β	Δ	β	Δ	β	Δ	β	Δ	β	Δ	β	Δ
Constant	28.36** (4.06)		8.52** (1.28)		18.36** (2.20)		36.24** (8.56)		11.24** (2.70)		8.00* (3.39)	
Unemployment rate	−0.02 (0.01)	−0.27	−0.80* (0.40)	−10.99	−1.19** (0.21)	−16.35	−0.36 (1.20)	−2.38	0.12* (0.06)	0.79	0.40* (0.18)	2.64
Inflation	0.04* (0.02)	0.16	0.12 (0.12)	0.47	−0.002** (0.00)	−0.008	0.36* (0.17)	1.08	−0.26** (0.06)	0.78	0.03 (0.10)	0.09
GDP growth	0.04 (0.03)	0.18	0.24* (0.10)	1.09	0.09** (0.02)	0.41	1.23** (0.42)	5.24	1.24* (0.52)	5.28	0.004 (0.003)	0.17
Dependent ($t-1$)	0.48* (0.20)		0.23** (0.05)		0.29 (0.23)		0.38 (1.63)		0.23** (0.05)		0.65* (0.31)	
Dependent ($t-4$)	0.01 (0.03)		0.09 (0.40)		0.11 (0.17)		0.23* (0.12)		0.09 (0.40)		−0.36 (0.24)	
N	162		162		162		83		83		83	
R^2	0.87		0.95		0.65		0.83		0.86		0.79	
Durbin M	1.12		0.24		0.96		1.63		0.23		0.00	

Notes
* Significant at 0.05.
** Significant at 0.01.

Table 5.3 Group-level political support for the VVD under different coalition conditions (linear regression)

	CDA–VVD coalition						CDA–PvdA coalition					
	Least sensitive		Moderate		Highly sensitive		Least sensitive		Moderate		Highly sensitive	
	β	Δ	β	Δ	β	Δ	β	Δ	β	Δ	β	Δ
Constant	6.52** (1.50)		18.52** (4.37)		12.24** (13.32)		3.23 (2.38)		4.24* (1.79)		−0.12** (0.03)	
Unemployment rate	−0.23* (0.10)	−3.16	0.24** (0.09)	3.30	−1.24** (0.19)	−17.04	−0.13 (0.07)	−0.86	−0.26* (0.13)	−1.72	−1.77* (0.87)	−11.68
Inflation	0.004 (0.005)	0.02	−1.86** (0.57)	−7.25	−0.69** (0.26)	−2.69	0.62* (0.30)	1.86	0.13** (0.03)	0.39	0.03* (0.01)	0.09
GDP growth	0.36 (0.21)	1.64	0.0002* (0.00)	0.0009	−0.36* (0.18)	−1.64	0.03 (0.02)	0.13	0.03 (0.06)	0.13	0.004** (0.001)	0.017
Dependent (t − 1)	0.64** (0.11)		0.02** (0.01)		0.52 (0.36)		0.38 (1.63)		0.47* (0.19)		0.01 (0.02)	
Dependent (t − 4)	−0.26 (0.27)		0.02 (0.11)		0.18 (0.28)		0.05 (0.66)		−0.45 (0.57)		−0.65 (0.81)	
N	162		162		162		83		83		83	
R^2	0.90		0.91		0.90		0.85		0.86		0.92	
Durbin M	0.64		0.12		0.00		1.63		0.24		0.08	

Notes
* Significant at 0.05.
** Significant at 0.01.

this issue when it is in government – only support of the least sensitive respondents is unaffected. These results support Hypotheses 1a and 2. Unemployment generally suppresses VVD support regardless of whether it is in government or in opposition.[16] In most cases, the substantive importance of the independent variables is strongest when the VVD is in government. An interesting comparison is that the moderately and highly sensitive punish the VVD for inflation when in government, but only slightly reward it when in opposition. Inflation is, however, clearly important for the least sensitive when the VVD is in opposition. Finally, inflation matters really only for the VVD. The substantive importance of inflation for VVD support is clearly larger than for CDA and PvdA support.

Table 5.4 shows that the pattern of political support for the PvdA fits Hypothesis 2. In opposition, the PvdA makes strong gains in support when unemployment rates go up. Given a center–left coalition, respondents who are moderately or highly sensitive to unemployment still turn to the PvdA if unemployment rates go up. The substantive significance of unemployment for PvdA support is, however, much smaller: 11.82 versus 0.01 for the moderately sensitive, and 24.73 versus 0.79 for the highly sensitive. Although an incumbent PvdA is not actually punished for unemployment as predicted in Hypothesis 1b, it fails to turn its issue priority into actual support. Inflation has hardly any significant impact on PvdA support. Inflation is generally significant only when the PvdA is in opposition, but even then its substantive importance never exceeds 1 percent.

These findings are not simply what one would expect based on the reward–punishment hypothesis or the issue-priority model. In each case, CDA is part of the coalition government and its relative standing (to other parties) in the political space is constant. Yet CDA's popularity reacts largely in opposite directions in the different coalitions. We find clear evidence that, in the Netherlands, voters respond to shifts in the economy in a manner contingent not only on whether a party is in government or opposition, but also contingent upon their coalition partner. In support of the second hypothesis, the left and right parties gain from their issue priority, but particularly when in opposition. Our findings suggest that evaluations of issue priority and competency are weighed differently depending on the party being in or out of government.

We also find clear support for the third hypothesis, i.e. economic groups respond more strongly to economic issues that are more likely to affect their economic interests. The unemployment rate is always significant for the groups that are moderately or highly sensitive to this issue. Further, the unemployment coefficient for the highly sensitive is always at least twice the comparable coefficient for the moderately sensitive. Finally, only one of the six unemployment coefficients for least sensitive respondents is significant. The effect of GDP growth is quite similar for the main parties. It is generally positive, but small and unaffected by coalition

Table 5.4 Group-level political support for the PvdA under different coalition conditions (linear regression)

| | CDA–VVD coalition | | | | | | CDA–PvdA coalition | | | | | |
	Least sensitive β	Δ	Moderate β	Δ	Highly sensitive β	Δ	Least sensitive β	Δ	Moderate β	Δ	Highly sensitive β	Δ
Constant	12.36* (5.24)		0.06 (2.68)		21.66** (3.80)		11.24 (11.20)		4.24 (2.59)		14.88** (4.07)	
Unemployment rate	−0.52 (0.37)	−7.15	0.86** (0.33)	11.82	1.80** (0.43)	24.73	−0.60 (0.38)	−3.96	0.001* (0.00)	0.01	0.12* (0.06)	0.79
Inflation	−0.20 (1.67)	−0.78	−0.25* (0.11)	−0.98	0.21** (0.08)	0.82	−0.24* (0.10)	−0.72	0.04 (0.03)	0.12	0.001 (0.00)	0.003
GDP growth	0.11 (0.08)	0.50	0.003 (13.81)	0.01	0.09 (0.36)	0.41	0.01 (0.01)	0.04	0.06 (0.10)	0.26	0.29* (0.11)	1.24
Dependent (t − 1)	0.23** (0.07)		0.13* (0.05)		0.02 (0.02)		0.24 (0.45)		0.45* (0.20)		0.24* (0.10)	
Dependent (t − 4)	−0.26 (0.27)		0.02 (0.11)		0.18 (0.28)		0.05 (0.66)		−0.45 (0.57)		−0.65 (0.45)	
N	162		162		162		83		83		83	
R^2	0.75		0.86		0.86		0.80		0.76		0.86	
Durbin M	0.47		1.23		0.10		0.03		0.10		0.75	

Notes
* Significant at 0.05.
** Significant at 0.01.

structure. It is somewhat remarkable that the CDA gets rewarded for GDP growth especially in a center–left coalition.

To summarize, in the case of the Netherlands, our findings generally support the conditional-responsibility model. Coalition structure conditions the issue responsibility of CDA, whose issue responsibility mirrors that of the main coalition partner. The extreme parties cannot turn their issue priority into support when in government. In opposition, they clearly benefit from their issue priority. Moreover, economic groups vary in their sensitivity to unemployment. Interestingly, the conditional-responsibility model outperforms simple reward–punishment or issue–priority models. Whenever its predictions deviate from the other two models, the results generally support the conditional-responsibility model.

5.7 COALITIONS AND ECONOMIC VOTING IN (WEST) GERMANY

Between 1969 and 1982, West Germany was governed by center–left FDP–SDP coalitions of Chancellor Schmidt. Next came several center–right FDP–CDU/CSU coalitions under leadership of Chancellor Kohl. Chancellor Kohl oversaw the reunification of East and West Germany in 1990. Here, we consider data only from the area of former West Germany. Relative to the Netherlands, German politics is more polarized with a small center party, FDP. During the period we analyze the German and Dutch economies were very similar. The German economy had slightly higher growth, but slightly lower unemployment and even lower inflation.[17]

Tables 5.5–5.7 show the analyses of party support in Germany conditioned by coalition structure. The German and Dutch results agree to a large degree. There is a striking similarity between our findings for the Dutch center party CDA and the German center party FDP. Table 5.5 shows that the FDP loses clearly from rising unemployment and gains weakly from inflation when in coalition with CDU/CSU. The pattern of conditional responsibility is less clear for periods where FDP joined center–left FDP–SDP coalitions. Most remarkable is that respondents highly sensitive to unemployment turn to the FDP when unemployment goes up. The importance of unemployment for FDP support is independent from coalition structure. Finally, the substantive effects show that inflation becomes more important for the FDP in coalition with the SDP, but the coefficients are signed inconsistently across electoral groups.

The findings for the conservative parties, CDU/CSU in Germany and VVD in the Netherlands, are also quite similar. The CDU/CSU consistently benefits from concerns about inflation when in opposition. As in the case of the Netherlands, inflation has a substantive effect only for the conservative party. In support of Hypothesis 2, the CDU/CSU is unable

Table 5.5 Group-level political support for the FDP under different coalition conditions (linear regression)

	FDP–CDU/CSU coalition						FDP–SDP coalition					
	Least sensitive β	Δ	Moderate β	Δ	Highly sensitive β	Δ	Least sensitive β	Δ	Moderate β	Δ	Highly sensitive β	Δ
Constant	27.98** (4.30)		20.11** (3.43)		19.55** (2.50)		42.24** (11.51)		16.39** (2.64)		9.18* (3.87)	
Unemployment rate	−0.03 (0.02)	−0.08	−0.99 (0.43)	−2.55	−1.48** (0.32)	−3.82	−0.53 (1.87)	−2.77	0.17 (0.10)	0.89	0.28** (0.11)	1.46
Inflation	0.05* (0.02)	0.14	0.15 (0.13)	0.41	−0.003** (0.001)	−0.008	0.44** (0.15)	1.43	−0.32** (0.06)	1.04	0.03 (0.09)	0.1
GDP growth	0.04 (0.03)	0.18	0.22* (0.10)	1.02	0.08** (0.03)	0.37	0.99** (0.31)	3.86	1.32** (0.55)	5.15	0.003 (0.003)	0.01
Dependent (t − 1)	0.42* (0.20)		0.26** (0.06)		0.31 (0.24)		0.33 (1.36)		0.24** (0.06)		0.57* (0.29)	
Dependent (t − 4)	0.01 (0.03)		0.10 (0.48)		0.12 (0.19)		0.25* (0.11)		0.08 (0.40)		−0.33 (0.21)	
N	138		138		138		56		56		56	
R²	0.86		0.84		0.72		0.81		0.85		0.91	
Durbin M	1.34		0.28		1.16		1.91		0.28		0.003	

Notes
* Significant at 0.05.
** Significant at 0.01.

Table 5.6 Group-level political support for the CDU/CSU under different coalition conditions (linear regression)

	FDP–CDU/CSU coalition						FDP–SDP coalition					
	Least sensitive		Moderate		Highly sensitive		Least sensitive		Moderate		Highly sensitive	
	β	Δ	β	Δ	β	Δ	β	Δ	β	Δ	β	Δ
Constant	7.41** (1.48)		21.86** (5.89)		74.11** (13.60)		3.46 (2.27)		5.03** (1.83)		-0.09** (0.02)	
Unemployment rate	-0.28* (0.13)	-0.77	0.27* (0.12)	0.70	-1.70** (0.25)	-4.39	-0.03* (0.01)	-0.16	-0.06* (0.03)	-0.31	0.35* (0.16)	1.83
Inflation	0.001 (0.001)	0.003	-1.25** (0.37)	-3.38	-0.90** (0.30)	-2.43	0.63** (0.22)	2.04	0.15** (0.03)	0.49	0.04* (0.02)	0.13
GDP growth	0.40 (0.22)	1.85	0.0002* (0.00)	0.0009	-0.29* (0.13)	-1.34	0.03 (0.02)	0.12	0.03 (0.08)	0.12	0.003** (0.001)	0.01
Dependent $(t-1)$	0.58** (0.11)		0.03* (0.01)		0.59 (0.49)		0.36 (1.59)		0.38** (0.17)		0.01 (0.01)	
Dependent $(t-4)$	-0.27 (0.26)		0.02 (0.09)		0.16 (0.31)		0.04 (0.51)		-0.42 (0.47)		-0.75 (0.53)	
N	138		138		138		56		56		56	
R^2	0.85		0.88		0.91		0.79		0.85		0.83	
Durbin M	0.76		0.15		0.004		1.96		0.28		0.10	

Notes
* Significant at 0.05.
** Significant at 0.01.

Table 5.7 Group-level political support for the SDP under different coalition conditions (linear regression)

	FDP–CDU/CSU coalition						FDP–SDP coalition					
	Least sensitive		*Moderate*		*Highly sensitive*		*Least sensitive*		*Moderate*		*Highly sensitive*	
	β	Δ	β	Δ	β	Δ	β	Δ	β	Δ	β	Δ
Constant	11.60** (4.27)	−1.81	0.11 (3.98)	2.97	24.41** (4.55)	5.44	16.20 (11.25)	−4.54	4.94 (3.05)	0.01	14.77** (4.77)	−0.78
Unemployment rate	−0.70 (0.41)	−0.68	1.15* (0.51)	−0.92	2.11** (0.51)	0.70	−0.87 (0.51)	−0.81	0.001 (0.001)	0.16	−0.15* (0.07)	0.003
Inflation	−0.25 (1.81)		−0.34* (0.15)		0.26** (0.08)		−0.25** (0.08)		0.05 (0.03)		0.001 (0.001)	
GDP growth	0.11 (0.10)	0.51	0.003 (13.16)	0.01	0.10 (0.39)	0.46	0.01 (0.01)	0.04	0.06 (0.10)	0.23	0.28* (0.13)	1.09
Dependent (t − 1)	0.61** (0.21)		0.10* (0.05)		0.02 (0.02)		0.28 (0.55)		0.50* (0.19)		0.25* (0.12)	
Dependent (t − 4)	−0.32 (0.28)		0.03 (0.11)		0.22 (0.28)		0.05 (0.67)		−0.54 (0.58)		−0.77 (0.65)	
N	138		138		138		56		56		56	
R²	0.69		0.82		0.84		0.91		0.84		0.82	
Durbin M	0.56		1.48		0.12		0.04		0.13		0.90	

Notes
* Significant at 0.05.
** Significant at 0.01.

to benefit from its issue priority while in government. Rising unemployment decreases support for the CDU/CSU regardless of whether the party is in opposition or in government. An interesting difference with the Netherlands is that when the CDU/CSU is in opposition and unemployment goes up, the highly sensitive respondents are more likely to support the CDU/CSU. This finding is more in accordance with the reward–punishment model, and may be the result of the FDP being a small center party.

In Table 5.7, we present the results for the German social democratic party. In opposition the SDP gains from rising unemployment, while the effect of unemployment is mainly insignificant when the SDP is in government. Respondents who are highly sensitive to unemployment actually punish an incumbent SDP somewhat for poor unemployment figures. Inflation has hardly any significant impact on SDP support. It is generally significant only when the SDP is in opposition, but even then its substantive importance never exceeds 1 percent. When the SDP is in government, the least sensitive to unemployment will punish the party for inflation, but the substantive importance of inflation remains low.

The German case also provides support for the third hypothesis, i.e. economic groups respond more strongly to economic issues that are more likely to affect their economic interests. The results are, however, not as strong as in the case of the Netherlands. The unemployment rate remains always significant for the group that is highly sensitive to this issue. Further, the unemployment coefficient for the highly sensitive is always at least twice the comparable coefficient for the moderately sensitive. However, we observe that the substantive importance of unemployment is much smaller in the German case than the Netherlands. The effect of GDP growth is quite similar for the main parties. It is generally positive, but small and unaffected by coalition structure. The center party FDP gets the most reward for economic growth – not unlike the Dutch case.

The results for Germany are thus generally similar to the Netherlands. The conditional-responsibility model also applies quite well to the German situation during the period in which the FDP acted as a pivotal center party. We observe, however, two important differences. First, in Germany, both the CDU/CSU and FDP benefit from discontent with unemployment given a center–left government. In the Netherlands, only the CDA benefits in this case. Second, in the Netherlands the independent variables generally have a much larger effect than in Germany. A reasonable explanation for both differences is that in the Netherlands the center party, CDA, is a much more viable alternative than the relatively small FDP in Germany. It is perhaps unrealistic to expect that voters would hold a minor coalition member responsible for a particular issue dimension.[18] In a way, this is informative. It may well be that issue responsibility is conditioned by issue position as well as relative strength in the coalition (Anderson, 1995b).

5.8   CONCLUSIONS AND DISCUSSION

In this chapter, we have posited a model of economic voting based on conditional responsibility. The model expands the reward–punishment model of economic voting in several ways. It is important to recognize the considerable staying power of the reward–punishment model. Minimally rational and informed voters can reward and punish incumbent governments without evaluating the specifics of economic news or the exact responsibility of the government. In certain political settings and for certain groups of voters, this may be all that we should expect. However, there is a lingering sense that it fails to adequately describe voters' reactions in all situations, or perhaps completely in any situation. The shortcomings are particularly apparent in the European developed democracies. There is evidence that European voters are more ideologically driven. Issue-priority models encompass this view in economic-voting models by introducing explicit policy dimensionality into the voter decision calculus. However, strict adherence to the issue-priority model can lead to unsatisfactory and counterintuitive hypotheses. For example, it seems unreasonable that voters continue to support a party that has demonstrated to be incompetent in handling its self-proclaimed issue priority.

We suggest that voters actually use a combination of decision rules in economic voting. In agreement with the reward–punishment model, we expect that voters are willing to punish incumbents for poor economic management and are especially likely to punish parties they hold responsible for failures in a specific policy area. The discrimination of issue responsibility becomes particularly important in multi-party systems, where marginal shifts in votes affect expectations about possible coalition governments. This puts center parties in a particularly interesting position. Essentially they are held responsible for whichever issue dimension their coalition partners are not responsible for. In other words, the choice of coalition partners dictates economic-issue priority to the party leaders of center parties. The model assumes that voters are not necessarily baffled by the complexities of multi-party systems with coalition government. Instead, coalition politics becomes a framework in which the "rationality" of the economic vote is evaluated. Empirically, we find the strongest support for this part of our model in the Netherlands. This is not entirely unexpected because here the left, center, and right of the political spectrum are about equally sized, and coalitions vary regularly between center–right and center–left.

Moreover, we expect specific groups of voters to be more loyal towards parties than others. They are willing to ride out hard economic times with "their" party or even return to "their" party when their group faces serious economic problems. In this respect, voter heterogeneity coincides with the expectations of issue-priority models. The underlying assumption is that political parties direct their message of issue priority at specific subgroups of the society. For example, social-democratic parties not just claim to be best able to deal with unemployment, they have targeted this message in particular at groups that are most exposed to the risk of unemployment. In Europe, claims of issue priority and concrete institutional ties often go hand-in-hand. It is clearly important to account for such voter hetero-geneity. First of all, ignoring it leads to underspecified models with biased coefficients. Second, it allows for an alternative explanation of economic voting along the line predicted by issue-priority models.

The empirical evidence is generally encouraging for the conditional-responsibility model of economic voting. However, we also find evidence that other conditioning factors play an important role; in particular, the distinction between two- and multi-party systems is overly broad. For example, in the period covered by our analysis German politics behaved in some respects as a two-party system, because the centrist FDP was relatively small. In other systems, the politics of coalition may be so complex as to render economic voting infeasible – in support of the original clarity-of-responsibility hypo-thesis. We are left, however, with a important middle ground where coalitions have a real effect on the direction of economic voting. The assumption of rational ignorance is probably quite reasonable for a lot (or lack) of political behavior. However, occasionally voters demonstrate considerable amounts of sophistication. We believe that the confirmation of the expectations of the conditional-responsibility model is evidence of such sophistication.

APPENDIX A

Table 5.A Descriptive statistics for variables used in group-level-political-support models

The Netherlands		CDA–VVD coalition		CDA–PvdA coalition	
		Mean	Std. Dev.	Mean	Std. Dev.
Inflation	Monthly change (%)	0.66	0.65	0.87	0.50
Unemployment	Rate	8.90	2.29	7.64	1.10
GDP growth	Monthly growth (%)	0.55	0.76	0.37	0.71
VVD support	Monthly	18.21	4.23	8	2.11
CDA support	Monthly	43.5	3.25	21.2	5.15
PvdA support	Monthly	45.21	5.23	29.63	8.52

Germany		FDP–CDU/CSU coalition		FDP–SDP coalition	
		Mean	Std. Dev.	Mean	Std. Dev.
Inflation	Monthly change (%)	0.19	0.45	0.39	0.54
Unemployment	Rate	7.86	0.43	8.01	0.87
GDP growth	Monthly growth (%)	0.67	0.77	0.38	0.65
CDU support	Monthly	44.32	5.96	43.77	3.66
SDP support	Monthly	42.3	4.3	44	5
FDP support	Monthly	5.6	1.8	8.26	2.1

ACKNOWLEDGMENT

Earlier versions of this chapter were presented at the 1999 Annual Meeting of the Midwest Political Science Association, Chicago, IL, the 1999 Annual Meeting of the American Political Science Association, Atlanta, CA, and at the Special Conference on Institutions and Economic Voting, Trondheim, Norway, 9–12 April 2000. This project was made possible in part by funding from the Norwegian Research Council, NFR-1217149/530 and NFR-134517/530. Data made available by ZA, Germany, and NIWI, the Netherlands. Håvard Strand and Hanne Svendsen provided valuable research assistance. Authors bear responsibility for all use and interpretation of data.

NOTES

1 The literature on economic voting is vast. Important studies are Key (1968), Kramer (1971), Lewis-Beck (1988), Norpoth *et al.* (1991), and Anderson (1995b). We further refer to studies mentioned below. For recent surveys, see Schneider and Frey (1988), Nannestad and Paldam (1994), and Lewis-Beck and Paldam (2000). Powell and Whitten (1993) argue forcefully for the importance of the political context on economic voting. Examples of other studies on how political institutions affect economic voting are Lewis-Beck and Lockerbie (1989), Taylor (1998), Whitten and Palmer (1996, 1999), Dorussen and Taylor (2000, 2001), and Anderson (2000).

2 In a cogent essay, Pappi (1996) analyses the problem of reasoning voters in multi-party systems; see also Dorussen and Taylor (2000, 2001).

3 Budge and Farlie (1983) and Kuechler (1991a,b) use issue salience to study the perception of parties' (economic) competence. Peffley (1984) and Peffley *et al.* (1987) carefully study the attribution of responsibility; see also van der Eijk *et al.* (1999). The related issue-priority model is examined in Clarke *et al.* (1986, 1994), Anderson (1995a,b), and Dorussen and Taylor (2000, 2001). The rational partisan model is also related, but more focused on policy output, see Hibbs (1977, 1987, 1992) and Swank (1993).

4 The economic-voting literature is unclear about the relative importance of issue competency and priority. Issue-priority models generally follow Downs (1957) in treating competence as a secondary consideration to issue priority (e.g. Clarke *et al.*, 1986; Anderson, 1995a,b; Dorussen and Taylor, 2001). Alternatively, research that starts out with the reward–punishment hypothesis, like this paper, tends to emphasize competency over issue priority (e.g. Powell and Whitten, 1993; Norpoth, 1996; Whitten and Palmer, 1999). Finally, Kuechler (1991a,b) and van der Eijk *et al.* (1999) study the perception of parties' (economic) competence directly.

5 Whether voters are predominantly retrospective, as the reward–punishment hypothesis assumes, or prospective is a hotly debated question in the economic-voting literature. Norpoth (1996) and Clarke and Stewart (1994) argue against the view of the electorate as mainly prospective in MacKuen *et al.* (1992, 1996).

6 Dorussen and Taylor (2000, 2001) present evidence that, at least in the Netherlands, information about the party composition of the incumbent government is widespread. Moreover, voters understand party issue priority even within the context of the coalition. They present some indirect evidence that this knowledge matters for the vote decision.

7 The heuristic is based on formalized models of coalition bargaining (Austen-Smith and Banks, 1990; Laver and Shepsle, 1990, 1996, 1998). Dorussen and Taylor (2001) trace the implications of the model of issue-priority voting in case of the Netherlands.

8 The debate is also known as "pocketbook" or "egotropic" versus "sociotropic" voting. For example, Lewis-Beck (1988) shows that also in Europe the electorate is more sociotropic than egotropic. However, Sanders (1995) presents evidence that the British electorate is somewhat exceptional in their concern for their pocketbook.

9 Taylor also demonstrates strong institutional clarity effects in support of Powell and Whitten (1993).

10 These are not the only possible or even actual coalition structures. Germany as well as the Netherlands have also had "grand" coalitions, i.e. coalitions encompassing parties from the right and left. In these cases, the expectations of the conditional-responsibility model are straightforward: the left party is held responsible for unemployment and the right party for inflation. The center party benefits on both accounts. Coalitions of more than two parties may have parties located centrist of the main coalition partners. In this case, the conditional-responsibility model predicts that the issue responsibility of these centrist parties remains unclear.

11 We have excluded respondents who were working for the military.

12 The aggregation affects the autocorrelation structure. It would have been incorrect to estimate the autocorrelation structure at the weekly level and then to aggregate our data. Instead, we estimated the autocorrelation structure directly using the grouped-monthly level data.

13 The Durbin M-statistics in the FDP and CDU models for the least sensitive, given a SDP–FDP coalition, are nearly significant, indicating that some autocorrelation may still be left. We decided, however, against "overfitting" the stochastic process.

14 Descriptive statistics for the Netherlands and Germany are presented in Appendix.

15 For other studies on economic voting in the Netherlands, see Alvarez and Nagler (1998), van der Eijk and Niemöller (1987), Middendorp and Kolkhuis Tanke (1990), and Anderson (1995a). The period of the purple coalition is excluded from this study. Dorussen and Taylor (2000) focus exclusively on economic voting for the purple coalition.

16 We have no explanation for the anomalous finding that the moderately sensitive increase their support for the VVD when the party is in government and unemployment rises. We found a similar result for the German case.

17 Anderson (1993) and Lewis-Beck (1988) are examples of other studies of economic voting specifically in Germany.

18 Dorussen and Taylor (2000) present similar results for D'66 in the Netherlands. D'66 and FDP share a progressive liberal ideology, and both parties are minor partners in coalitions. Our analyses find no evidence that either of these parties is held responsible for a particular economic issue dimension.

REFERENCES

Alvarez, R.M. and Nagler, J. (1998) When politics and models collide: estimating models of multiparty elections. *Am. J. Political Sci.*, **42**(1), 55–96.

Anderson, C.J. (1993) Modeling mass support for German chancellors and their parties: some problems and some results. *Historical Social Res.*, **18**(4), 4–30.

Anderson, C.J. (1995a) The dynamics of public support for coalition governments. *Comp. Political Stud.*, **28**(3), 350–383.

Anderson, C.J. (1995b) *Blaming the Government: Citizens and the Economy in Five
European Democracies*. Armonk: Sharpe.

Anderson, C.J. (2000) Economic voting and political context: a comparative
perspective. *Electoral Stud.*, **19**(2/3), 151–170.

Austen-Smith, D. and Banks, J. (1990) Stable governments and the allocation of
policy portfolios. *Am. Political Sci. Rev.*, **84**(3), 891–906.

Budge, I. and Farlie, D.J. (1983) *Explaining and Predicting Elections: Issue Effects
and Party Strategies in 23 Democracies*. London: George Allen & Unwin.

Clarke, H.D. and Stewart, M.C. (1994) Prospections, retrospections, and rationality: the "bankers" model of presidential approval reconsidered. *Am. J. Political
Sci.*, **38**(4), 1104–1123.

Clarke, H.D., Elliott, E. and Seldon, B.J. (1994) A utility function analysis of
competing models of party support: key assumptions reconsidered. *J. Theoret.
Politics*, **6**(3), 289–305.

Clarke, H.D., Stewart, M.C. and Zuk, G. (1986) Politics, economics and party
popularity in Britain, 1979–1983. *Electoral Stud.*, **5**(2), 123–141.

Compston, H. (1997) *The New Politics of Unemployment*. New York: Routledge.

Dorussen, H. and Taylor, M. (2000) The sophisticated voter: coalition complexity
and group economic voting in the Netherlands. NTNU-Trondheim.

Dorussen, H. and Taylor, M. (2001) The political context of issue-priority voting:
coalitions and economic voting in the Netherlands, 1970–1998. *Electoral Stud.*,
20, 399–426.

Downs, A. (1957) *An Economic Theory of Democracy*. New York: Harper & Row.

Duch, R., Palmer, H.D. and Anderson, C.J. (2000). Heterogeneity in perceptions
of national economic conditions. *Am. J. Political Sci.*, **44**(4), 635–652.

Duch, R.M. and Palmer, H.D. (2002) Heterogenous perceptions of economic
conditions in cross-national perspective. In H. Dorussen and M. Taylor (eds),
Economic Voting, London: Routledge, 139–172.

Eisinga, R. and Felling, A. (1992) *Confessional and Electoral Alignments in the
Netherlands, 1962–1992*. Amsterdam: Steinmetz Archive Codebook P1089.

Feldman, S. (1982) Economic self-interest and political behavior. *Am. J. Political
Sci.*, **26**, 426–443.

Gomez, B.T. and Wilson, J.M. (2001) Political sophistication and economic voting
in the American electorate: a theory of heterogeneous attribution. *Am. J.
Political Sci.*, **45**(4), 899–914.

Gramlich, E.M. and Laren, D.S. (1984) Migration and income redistribution
responsibilities. *J. Human Resourc.*, **19**, 489–511.

Hibbs, D. (1977) Political parties and macro-economic policy. *Am. Political Sci.
Rev.*, **71**, 1467–1487.

Hibbs, D. (1987) *The Political Economy of Industrial Democracies*. Cambridge:
Harvard University Press.

Hibbs, D. (1992) Partisan theory after Fifteen years. *Eur. J. Political Economy*, **8**,
361–373.

Key, V.O. (1968) *The Responsible Electorate*. New York: Vintage.

Kinder, D.R. and Kiewiet, D.R. (1979) Economic discontent and political
behavior: the role of personal grievances and collective economic judgments
in congressional voting. *Am. J. Political Sci.*, **23**, 495–527.

Kramer, G. (1971) Short-term fluctuations in US voting behavior, 1896–1964. *Am. Political Sci. Rev.*, **65**(1), 131–143.

Kuechler, M. (1991a) Issues and voting in the European elections 1989. *Eur. J. Political Res.*, **19**, 81–103.

Kuechler, M. (1991b) Public perception of the Parties' economic competence. In H. Norpoth, M.S. Lewis-Beck and J.-D. Lafay (eds), *Economics And Politics: The Calculus Of Support*. Ann Arbor, MI: University of Michigan Press, pp. 221–238.

Kuklinski, J.H. and West, D.M. (1981) Economic expectations and voting behavior in the United States House and Senate elections. *Am. Political Sci. Rev.*, **30**, pp. 315–346.

Laver, M. and Shepsle, K.A. (1990) Coalitions and cabinet government. *Am. Political Sci. Rev.*, **84**(3), 873–890.

Laver, M. and Shepsle, K.A. (1996) *Making and Breaking Governments*. Cambridge: Cambridge University Press.

Laver, M. and Shepsle, K.A. (1998) Events, equilibria, and government survival. *Am. J. Political Sci.*, **42**(1), 28–54.

Lewis-Beck, M.S. (1988) *Economics and Elections. The Major Western Democracies*. Ann Arbor, MI: University of Michigan Press.

Lewis-Beck, M.S. and Lockerbie, B. (1989) Economics, votes, protests: western European cases. *Comp. Political Stud.*, **22**, 155–177.

Lewis-Beck, M.S. and Paldam, M. (2000) Economic voting: an introduction. *Electoral Stud.*, **19**(2/3), 113–123.

Lin, T.-M. (1999) The Historical significance of economic voting, 1872–1996. *Social Sci. History*, **23**, 561–591.

MacKuen, M.B., Erikson, R.S. and Stimson, J.A. (1992) Peasants or bankers? The American electorate and the US economy. *Am. Political Sci. Rev.*, **86**(3), 597–611.

MacKuen, M.B., Erikson, R.S. and Stimson. J.A. (1996) Comment on Helmut Norpoth, "Presidents and the Prospective Voter". *J. Politics*, **58**(3), 793–801.

Middendorp, C.P. and Kolkhuis Tanke, P.R. (1990) Economic voting in the Netherlands. *Eur. J. Political Res.*, **18**(5), 535–555.

Mutz, D.C. and Mondak, J.J. (1995) Dimensions of sociotropic behavior: group-based judgements of fairness and well-being. In *Annual Meeting of the Midwest Political Science Association, Chicago, IL*.

Nagler, J. and Niemann, J. (1997) Economic voting: enlightened self-interests and economic reference groups. In *Paper Presented at Annual Meeting of the Midwest Political Science Association, Chicago, IL*.

Nannestad, P. and Paldam, M. (1994) The VP function: a survey of the literature on vote and popularity functions after 25 years. *Public Choice*, **79**, 213–245.

Norpoth, H. (1996) Presidents and the prospective voter. *J. Politics*, **58**(3), 776–792.

Norpoth, H., Lewis-Beck, M.S. and Lafay, J.-D. (eds) (1991) *Economics And Politics: The Calculus Of Support*. Ann Arbor, MI: University of Michigan Press.

Pappi, F.U. (1996) Political behavior: reasoning voters and multi-party systems. In R.E. Goodin and H.-D. Klingemann (eds), *A New Handbook of Political Science*. Oxford: Oxford University Press, pp. 255–275.

Peffley, M. (1984) The voter as juror: attributing responsibility for economic conditions. *Political Behav.*, **6**(3), 275–294.

Peffley, M., Feldman, S. and Sigelman, L. (1987) Economic conditions and party competence: processes of belief revision. *J. Politics*, **49**(1), 100–121.

Popkin, S.L. (1991) *The Reasoning Voter*. Chicago, IL: University of Chicago Press.

Powell, G.B. and Whitten, G.W. (1993) A cross-national analysis of economic voting: taking account of the political context. *Am. J. Political Sci.*, **37**(2), 391–414.

Sanders, D. (1995) The economy and support for the Conservative Party in Britain. In *Conference on the Economy and Political Behavior*, Rice University, Houston, 22–23 April.

Schneider, F. and Frey, B.S. (1988) Politico-economic models of macroeconomic policy. In T.D. Willet (ed.), *Political Business Cycle*. Durham: Duke University Press.

Swank, O.H. (1993) Popularity functions based on the partisan theory. *Public Choice*, **75**, 339–356.

Taylor, M. (1998) *Economic interests, institutions, and ego-centric political behavior*. Dissertation. University of Houston.

Taylor, M. (2000) Channeling frustration: institutions and reactions to economic distress. *Eur. J. Political Res.*, **38**, 95–134.

Teixeira, R. (1998) The new economics of voting. *Challenge*, **41**(1), 19–37.

van der Eijk, C. and Niemöller, K. (1987) Electoral alignments in the Netherlands. *Electoral Stud.*, **6**(1), 17–30.

van der Eijk, C., Franklin, M.N. and van der Burg, W. (1999) Policy preferences and party choice. In H. Schmitt and J. Thomassen (eds), *Political Representation and Legitimacy in the European Union*. Oxford: Oxford University Press, pp. 161–185.

Weatherford, M.S. (1983) Parties and classes in the political response to economic conditions. In K.R. Monroe (ed.), *The Political Process and Economic Change*. New York: Agathon Press.

Whitten, G. and Palmer, H. (1996) Heightening comparativists concern for model choice – voting behavior in Great Britain and the Netherlands. *Am. J. Political Sci.*, **40**(1), 231–260.

Whitter, G. and Palmer, H. (1999) Cross-national analyses of economic voting. *Electoral Stud.*, **18**, 49–67.

6   On a short leash

Term limits and the economic voter

Helmut Norpoth

"No person shall be elected to the office of the President more than twice ... "
– 22nd Amendment to the US Constitution, 1951

Few elections seemed as poised to bear out the logic of economic voting as the 2000 American presidential contest. Economic growth was brisk, inflation tame, unemployment invisible, the stock market booming, and the federal budget in the black. How could the party in the White House not retain office under such fabulous circumstances? What is more, how could it fail to win by a landslide? There are at least three broad answers. One, and most disconcerting for proponents of economic voting, is the possibility that the economy may not be a major issue in electoral decisions. With a myriad of non-economic concerns vying for the electorate's attention, some of them trumped the economy. Two, it is not that the economy failed to matter, but that the basic model of economic voting (how voters translate economic considerations into their voting decisions) may be flawed. That still leaves open the possibility that alternative models may capture an economic influence on the vote. And three, while the basic model is a sound one, obstacles of an institutional sort may have prevented it from performing as expected in the 2000 election. While tabling the first possibility but without prejudice to the second, this chapter proposes to probe the third line of inquiry. American presidential elections are subject to an institutional feature that is bound to impinge on the way the economy, among others, may shape the voters' decisions. That condition is term limits.

By tradition or law, US Presidents have refrained from seeking more than two terms. The first holder of the office set a precedent that was broken by only one successor, Franklin Roosevelt, until it was carved in stone by the 22nd Amendment in 1951. Having been elected twice, Bill Clinton was ineligible to be on the ballot in the 2000 election. Many presidential contests are, to use a congressional expression, open-seat races. None of the candidates is an incumbent. In such contests, strictly speaking, a voting model presuming a retrospective, incumbent-oriented calculus should not be applicable. How can voters base their electoral decisions on the president's economic record when the incumbent responsible for that record is not running for re-election? Not very well, it would seem, in general, and in 2000, in particular. It is really quite a stretch to assign such responsibility to the candidate of the incumbent party just because his party was in office before the election. Few electoral students would agree that US presidential elections are simply generic partisan contests, regardless of the personalities on the ballot.

This chapter proposes a model of the presidential vote under conditions of term limits. The results will resolve a major puzzle about the 2000 presidential election: how a good economy failed to keep the incumbent party in office. The fact that the president responsible for the economy was off the ballot in 2000 sharply dampened the influence of the economy on the presidential vote. It did not matter that the Democratic candidate was the vice president. Regardless of the electoral benefit Al Gore may have derived from that status, he was unable to capitalize on the good economy in the way the sitting president would have been able to. That is not Al Gore's fault, but a general feature of non-incumbent candidates; it actually may turn into a blessing under a bad economy. Beyond the 2000 election, the results help illuminate economic voting in presidential elections more generally. The analysis below covers those elections during a time-span of more than 125 years. While the economy is the only determinant of the vote considered here, the findings also speak to any other one fitting the bill of retrospective incumbent-oriented behavior. Put in the most general terms, this chapter aims at sharpening our understanding of how institutional rules impinge on vote decisions. But first, let us introduce the economic variables used for the analysis of the presidential vote from 1872 to 2000. What did those conditions, taken by themselves, predict for the incumbent-party vote in 2000?

6.1   THE ECONOMY AND PRESIDENTIAL ELECTIONS

Few would quibble with the notion that good economic times spell re-election for incumbents, while bad times spell defeat. During the 1980 presidential campaign, Ronald Reagan hit an electoral home run when he posed the question "Ask yourself, are you better off now than you were four years ago?" A vast literature has explored economic voting in its various dimensions (for recent reviews, see the introduction by Dorussen and Palmer; Lewis-Beck and Stegmaier, 2000; Norpoth, 1996a). Survey research has documented the imprint of the economy on the choices of American voters in presidential elections (e.g. Kiewiet, 1983). And so have aggregate studies of election outcomes over time (Fair, 1978; Tufte, 1978; Norpoth *et al.*, 1991). It also helps that few variables are measured as regularly and provided as easily as are economic-performance indicators. Indeed it appears as if the economy is not simply the major key to elections, but the only key. The economy, by far, is the leading indicator of choice among forecasters of presidential elections (Lewis-Beck and Rice, 1992; Campbell and Garand, 2000).

Yet most of those efforts have tracked the economy no further back than 40 years ago, leaving barely a dozen elections for the estimation of the vote function. With several economic variables and additional ones for political events included in vote models, that does not leave many degrees of freedom. What is more, all these models have a very short track record of forecasting – in a true *ex-ante* sense – future elections. While they performed very well in 1996 (Campbell and Garand, 2000), their record in the 2000 election was a disappointment (Clymer, 2000; Kaiser, 2000). Until recently, only one economic-voting model reached significantly further back into the history of presidential elections (Fair, 1978). Kramer (1971) did cover elections as far back as 1896, as did Bloom and Price (1975), but both studies dealt with the congressional vote, not the presidential one.

This study has tracked data on the US economy as far back as 1872, the measures being GNP growth and inflation.[1] Figure 6.1 plots the vote share of the incumbent party in presidential elections (based on the major-party vote total) against the growth rate of real GNP during the election year.[2] When examined over such a long time-span, the relationship between one of the key indicators of economic performance

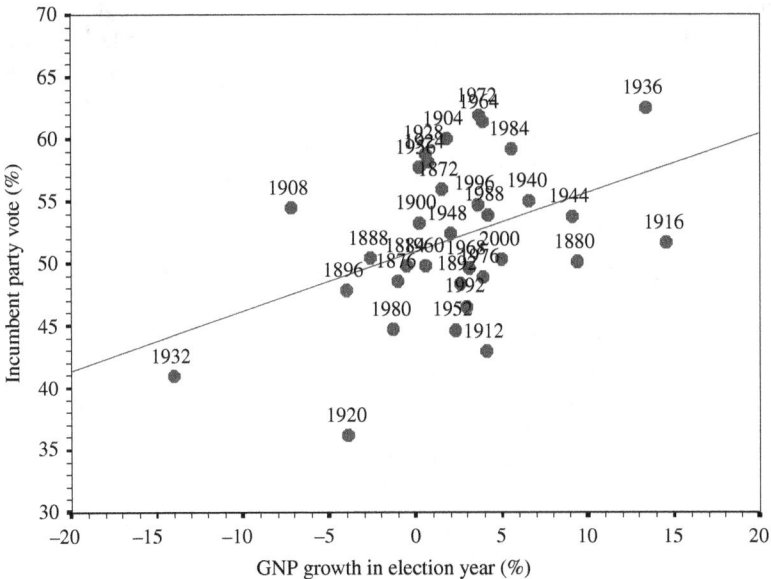

Figure 6.1 US presidential vote by GNP growth.

and support for the party in the White House appears rather modest (adjusted R^2 of 0.14). Much of it, moreover, may owe to two extreme instances: 1932 and 1936. The economic collapse during the Great Depression, as captured by the nearly 15 percent decline in 1932, and the New Deal recovery, as witnessed by a growth of similar magnitude in 1936, anchor the GNP/vote relationship. Adding the inflation rate to the vote equation enhances the fit somewhat while leaving both measures with highly significant effects (standard error in parentheses):

$$\text{INC.VOTE}_t = 53.1 + 0.55\,\text{GNP}_t - 0.83\,\text{INF}_t$$
$$\phantom{\text{INC.VOTE}_t = 5}(1.2)\quad(0.17)\qquad(0.27)$$
$$\text{Adj.}\,R^2 = 0.33,\quad \text{SER} = 5.1,\quad N = 33(1872-2000)$$

The combination of economic growth and inflation in 2000 predicts a vote share of 54.1 percent for the White House party. That, of course, is not an *ex-ante* forecast, since the outcome of the 2000 election is included in the estimation, but it goes to show that a comfortable victory for the Democrats that year was consistent with the historic performance of this economic-voting model. Indeed, the election year numbers for real economic growth (5.0 percent) and the price deflator (2.1 percent) are among the best in the past 50 years. The last time those two measures predicted a higher vote share for the incumbent party was back in 1944. It seems hard to fathom that these economic indicators could predict less of an electoral edge for Bill Clinton in 1996, Ronald Reagan in 1984, Richard Nixon in 1972, and Lyndon Johnson in 1964, all of whom were victorious. What did these four have in common that eluded Al Gore in 2000? The answer is quite simple. All were sitting presidents running for re-election. Term limits prevented the sitting president in 2000 to carry the banner of the White House party that year. Why should that have made the difference between winning and losing?

6.2   TERM LIMITS AND ELECTORAL DECISIONS

For good reasons, the institutional context of electoral choice is attracting growing attention among students of economic voting (Paldam, 1991; Powell and Whitten, 1993; Anderson, 2000). As Dorussen and Palmer, in the introduction to this volume make clear, "political reality does not necessarily match the ideal of democratic accountability," which may sap the incentives of elected officials to pay attention to the electorate's economic concerns. A two-party system, for example, affords the electorate a much better opportunity to hold elected officials responsible for economic deeds than is true for a multi-party system. But even a two-party system may muddle the clarity of responsibility if the constitutional system of separation of powers spawns divided government (Norpoth, 2001), or if term limits remove incumbents from electoral contests. Term limits for elective officials, as advocates of this blunt weapon of reform clearly wish, are meant to break the stranglehold of incumbency. Even though not all incumbents keep running until they drop dead and a fair proportion of them gets unseated by the voters, it is indisputable that setting a limit on the number of terms forces out a good number of incumbents who otherwise might run for and win re-election. Without an incumbent in the race, how are voters supposed to make up their minds about which of the candidates to support at the polls? To be sure, there are voting theories where that would make no difference whatsoever, but for one theory of voting the presence or absence of an incumbent in the race is crucial. That is the retrospective theory. It is a dominant one in the study of economic voting, especially at the aggregate level.

Elections offer the public an opportunity to act, in the immortal words of the late V.O. Key, as a "rational god of vengeance and reward." The voters' calculus is rational, but simple: "If the performance of the incumbent [. . .] is 'satisfactory' [. . .] retain the incumbent [. . .] in office, while if the government's performance is not 'satisfactory' [. . .] vote against the incumbent" (Kramer, 1971: 34). Besides focusing on the incumbent, this calculus stipulates that voters make retrospective judgments, rather than prospective ones, and key on performance rather than policies. The economy would seem to be a classic case for such a calculus to apply. So, as long as the recent performance of the economy is satisfactory, the voter would push the re-election button, while hitting the ejection button and "throwing the rascals out" at times of unsatisfactory performance of the economy.

A vast literature has shown this to be true, in one form or another, be it with cross-sectional studies of individual voting, or with time-series analyses of the public in aggregate form (Norpoth, 1996a). To be sure, the retrospective, incumbent-centered, reward–punishment theory has its detractors. It pays no attention to the economic policies that produced the economic performance (Chappell and Keech, 1991; Norpoth, 1992). Nor does it make an allowance for partisan distinctions on economic issues (Hibbs, 1992). It also fails to consider the possibility that voters may be far more inclined to punish incumbents for bad economic performance than to reward them for good times (Bloom and Price, 1975). And it also has a blind spot for economic performance in the future (Lewis-Beck, 1988; MacKuen *et al.*, 1992). This is not the place to delve into those controversies. Suffice to say that in the battle with more sophisticated competitors, the retrospective theory has held up remarkably well whenever the object of the public's judgment is an incumbent (Clarke and Stewart, 1994; Norpoth, 1996b).

Remove, however, the incumbent from the decision situation and you are bound to strip the retrospective theory of its appeal. Of what use to a voter is the "performance of the incumbent" if that incumbent is not running for re-election? Strictly speaking, incumbent performance, including economic performance, should not be expected to affect the voting decision in such elections. Most studies employing the retrospective theory skirt this problem by taking for granted that voters key on the party in office, not the individual incumbent. Kramer (1971) says so explicitly in the decision rule quoted above in abbreviated form. It is the performance of the *incumbent party* that determines the voter's decision. From that perspective, it makes no difference whether the incumbent party is running with the same or a new candidate. The party overshadows the individual candidate.

That may very well be true for elections where candidates are little known to most voters, but it is hard to accept for electoral contests featuring highly visible contenders. The vote for president in American politics bears a heavy imprint of candidate evaluations, as demonstrated by one of the voting classics, *The American Voter* (Campbell *et al.*, 1960, Chapters 3 and 4), as well as many studies since (e.g. Tufte, 1978, pp. 120–123; Erikson, 1989). While past performance in office leaves a mark on those evaluations, the effect varies sharply according to whether an incumbent president is in the race or not. True, incumbent presidents seeking re-election are overwhelmingly evaluated by retrospective performance, but fresh candidates of the incumbent party much less so (Miller and Wattenberg, 1985). While an incumbent vice president running for the presidency may be subject to a "succession" effect (Mattei and Weisberg, 1994), there are too few instances of that sort in the time frame of this analysis (only 1960, 1968, and 1988, besides 2000) to parcel out a vice presidential effect. Note, however, that three of those four vice presidents lost. Sitting presidents, in contrast, rarely suffer defeat at the polls.

This view of incumbency stands in marked contrast to the celebrated "cost-of-ruling" hypothesis. Nannestad and Paldam (Chapter 2, this volume) claim, with considerable evidence from western democracies, that "the average government in an established democracy loses about 2.5 per cent of the vote." Governing is a costly exercise, as far as popular support is concerned. A governing party alone or a coalition of parties must reckon with a loss of voter support at the next election. The United States, with presidential elections, is part of the set of countries examined, and appears to fit the general pattern quite well. That appearance, however, is misleading. As can be seen in Table 6.1, the incumbent party in presidential contests suffers no loss, on an average, after its first term in office. Indeed, in nearly 120 years there is but one instance where the party controlling the White House lost it after just one term (1980). The electoral price is extracted, and with a vengeance it seems, after the second term. But that may have more to do with the absence than the presence of incumbency. Whoever was elected two terms earlier, as a rule, is not leading his party into battle for a third term.

Table 6.1 Vote change of presidential party by terms of office, 1828–2000 (in per cent)

Terms in office	Vote change of presidential party	Elections
1	+0.2	19
2	−6.4	12
More than 2	−5.6	12

In deciding against seeking a third term, the first president, George Washington, set a precedent not violated for nearly a century and a half. Franklin Roosevelt's departure from that tradition in 1940 sparked an effort to make a two-term limit a constitutional requirement. The 22nd Amendment adopted in 1951 set term limits in stone for American presidents. But whether by law or tradition, the two-term limit has been the rule (with one exception) in presidential elections. The rule guarantees that incumbent presidents are missing from those contests with some predictable regularity. Hence the hypothesis: the two-term limit on presidential tenure produces a corresponding cycle in the presidential vote. The following section presents a test tracking presidential elections back to the beginning of popular voting.

6.3 THE DYNAMICS OF THE PRESIDENTIAL VOTE

For a country with an uninterrupted history of elections spanning more than two centuries, the flow of the vote should be expected to yield some reliable clues. Popular voting for President on a broad scale can be traced as far back as 1824. What is more, for most of that time, just two parties, and the same two parties, have claimed the lion's share of the vote. Every president since 1860 has either been a Democrat or a Republican, and before that, one of those parties was a constant competitor for the control of the White House. Between 1828 and 1860, the (Jacksonian) Democrats dueled with a succession of major-party adversaries (National Republicans and Whigs) for control of the federal government. It makes sense to focus on the Democratic share of the vote, given that this party boasts the longest continuity (America's true Grand Old Party). To be precise, the vote share of interest is the Democratic share of the major-party vote for President. Note that this is not the incumbent-party vote share examined above in the section on economic effects on the presidential vote. The shift to the vote share of one and the same party is unavoidable at this point. Because the incumbent-party vote switches back and forth from Democrat to Republican (or predecessors), that series is not suitable for the analysis of the dynamics of the presidential vote. In a later stage, we will incorporate

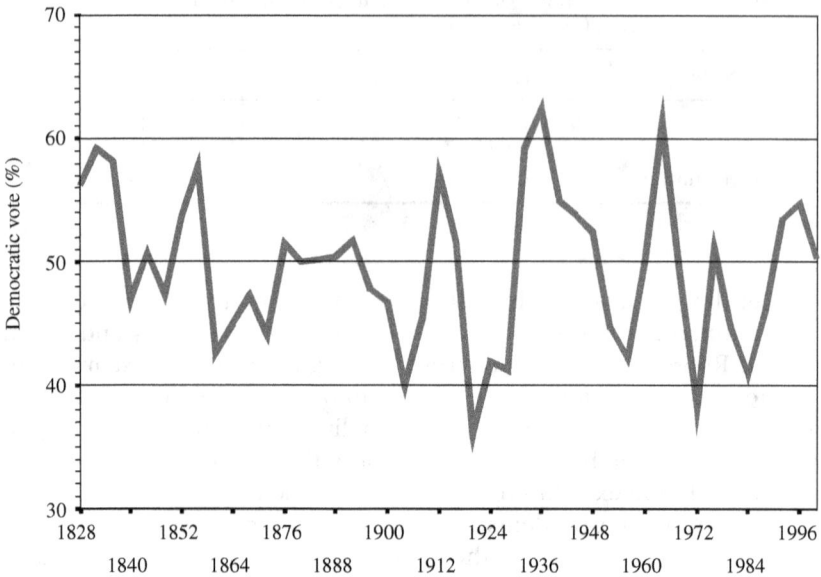

Figure 6.2 The US Democratic vote 1828–2000.

the economic variables, through proper transformation, into a vote model using the Democratic vote share instead of the incumbent-party vote.

Figure 6.2 charts the Democratic percentage of the major-party vote for President from 1828 to 2000, a period covering 44 elections altogether. Like the Republican vote series examined for the 1860–1992 period before (Norpoth, 1995), the longer Democratic series exhibits all the features of a phenomenon in equilibrium. On the one hand, there is remarkable stability: the movement of the two-party division of the vote is constrained within boundaries of roughly 35 and 65 percent. On the other hand, within that range the vote moves about with wild abandon, crossing the 50 percent line a total of 17 times in 44 trials, as it were. No sooner does the vote stray beyond 60 percent, or drop below 40 percent, than it bounces back with a sharp jolt toward the point of equal division. That is the familiar dynamic of a stationary process for which Figure 6.2 furnishes a textbook case. The standard test for a random-walk allows us to reject that hypothesis beyond a shred of doubt (Dickey–Fuller $t = -4.7$, $p < 0.01$). Equilibrium is the trademark of presidential elections in the United States.

Even more important that equilibrium is anchored in an equally sized partisan division. The Democratic share of the two-party vote throughout nearly 175 years averages 49.6 percent, which is not significantly different from 50 percent. In the long run, the balance of party support in presidential elections is dead even suggesting that the major parties are operating under conditions of perfect competition. The winning party of a presidential contest cannot expect to hold on to the White House for very long. How long, on the average? The existence of an effective two-term limit would predict that the vote division exhibits a two-term cycle. That is exactly what a second-order autoregressive model of the presidential vote proves (see Box and Jenkins, 1976; Clarke *et al.*, 1998). For the Democratic vote series (VOTE), centered around its overall mean, the estimates are as follows, with standard errors in parentheses:

$$VOTE_t = 0.41 VOTE_{t-1} - 0.35 VOTE_{t-2}$$
$$(0.14) \qquad\qquad (0.14)$$
$$\text{Adj.} R^2 = 0.21, \quad SER = 5.6, \quad N = 44$$

Most telling, the parameter for $VOTE_{t-2}$ is negative, whereas the parameter for $VOTE_{t-1}$ is positive, and both are roughly equal in absolute size.[3] These results confirm estimates derived for the Republican vote series, 1860–1992 (Midlarsky, 1984; Norpoth, 1995). The positive sign for the $VOTE_{t-1}$ parameter indicates that a party winning a presidential election can expect to hold on to much of its above-equilibrium vote portion in the immediately following election, just as the losing party will hold on to much of its below-equilibrium vote portion. In other words, after one term in office re-election is a safe bet. At the same time, the winning party must reckon with a reversal at elections after that, given the negative sign for $VOTE_{t-2}$. So after two terms defeat looms large. The average length of the presidential vote staying above (or below) the 50 percent mark is exactly 2.5 terms. When a president leaves the White House after two terms, the party's hold on that office is in peril. That was Al Gore's predicament in the 2000 election.

Indeed long before Election Day 2000, the second-order cyclical model of the presidential vote produced a forecast that said just that. It predicted vote shares of 50.2 percent for the Republican candidate, and 49.8 for the Democrat in the 2000 presidential election.[4] It came closer to the final tally than any other forecast known to the author, and it did so without any reference to economic conditions or any other predictor, let alone the identity of the two major-party candidates. The forecast promised an extremely close election, the closest since 1960, when a bare two-tenths of a percentage point separated Kennedy from Nixon, and only the second closest since 1884. To dispel any suspicion that this model invariably forecasts close outcomes, note that the forecast for 1996 was a Democratic victory by 52.3 percent of the major-party vote, just 2.4 points short of the actual result (Norpoth, 1995). Neither the difference between 1996 and 2000 nor the similarity between 1960 and 2000 is simply a matter of coincidence. In the 2000 election, the incumbent who won easy re-election four years earlier was not a candidate anymore, casualty of the two-term limit. The same was true in 1960. On both occasions, the absence of a sitting president from the ballot was a key to the election outcome.

6.4   ECONOMIC VOTING UNDER TERM LIMITS

To probe the impact of the economy on the presidential vote under the two-term limit, we have to return to the time horizon for which the economic variables are available (1872–2000). But we retain the definition of the electoral variable as the Democratic share of the major-party vote. The focus on the vote for one and the same party, regardless of whether it holds office or not, requires a transformation of the way economic conditions enter the vote model. Obviously, whenever the White House is not in Democratic hands, the retrospective theory does not predict that good times will help that party's electoral fortune, or that bad times will hurt it. It is just the other way around. So for elections where Republicans held the presidency the economic variables must be inverted.[5] For the sake of parsimony, the two economic variables, real GNP growth and inflation, have been converted into an index of economic performance (ECON):

Index of economic performance = {real GNP growth − 1.5 inflation}

The weight for inflation (1.5) takes into account the different variation of the two indicators. The standard deviation of the GNP measures is 50 percent larger than the one for the inflation measure. The impact of the presidential term limit will be estimated through the second-order autoregressive dynamic as identified for the vote series all the way back to 1828 in the previous section. The vote equation for the Democratic percentage of the major-party vote in presidential elections (VOTE) yields the following estimates for the economic performance index (ECON) and the term-limit induced dynamic (standard errors in parentheses):[6]

$$VOTE_t = 48.9 + 0.51\ ECON_t + 0.41\ VOTE_{t-1} - 0.40\ VOTE_{t-2}$$
$$(7.6)\quad (0.12)\qquad\quad (0.13)\qquad\qquad (0.13)$$
$$Adj.\ R^2 = 0.60,\quad SER = 4.5,\quad \chi^2_{(8)} = 6.5,\quad N = 33(1872-2000)$$

Certainly the model combining those two components fits much better than either one separately. While the economy retains an effect on the presidential vote, that influence must now contend with the fall-out from the two-term limit, as registered by the autoregressive dynamic, especially the negative weight attached to the vote two elections before. What

Table 6.2 Model predictions and actual Democratic vote for president, 1872–2000 (percentages)

Year	Predicted	Actual	Deviation
1872	47.2	44.1	−3.1
1876	48.4	51.5	3.1
1880	50.0	50.0	0.0
1884	47.6	50.2	2.6
1888	47.7	50.4	2.7
1892	46.7	51.7	5.0
1896	48.4	47.8	−0.6
1900	47.8	46.8	−1.0
1904	47.2	40.0	−7.2
1908	48.8	45.5	−3.3
1912	50.0	57.1	7.1
1916	55.4	51.6	−3.8
1920	34.2	36.1	1.9
1924	41.3	41.9	0.6
1928	49.9	41.2	−8.7
1932	54.7	59.2	4.5
1936	64.2	62.5	−1.7
1940	53.3	55.0	1.7
1944	50.6	53.8	3.2
1948	45.3	52.4	7.1
1952	49.6	44.6	−5.0
1956	47.2	42.3	−4.9
1960	48.0	50.1	2.1
1964	54.0	61.3	7.3
1968	52.4	49.6	−2.8
1972	45.0	38.2	−6.8
1976	46.1	51.1	5.0
1980	47.7	44.7	−3.0
1984	45.6	40.8	−4.8
1988	46.8	46.1	−0.7
1992	50.4	53.5	3.1
1996	53.5	54.7	1.2
2000	51.5	50.3	−1.2

Notes
Model used for predictions: $\text{VOTE}_t = 48.9 + 0.51\ \text{ECON}_t + 0.41\ \text{VOTE}_{t-1} - 0.40\ \text{VOTE}_{t-2}$.

does the combined model predict for the Democratic vote in the 2000 election? As can be seen in Table 6.2, the predicted vote is 51.5 percent. That still means the model picks Al Gore as the winner, but now by only a razor-thin margin. The margin is much closer than it is with the economic variables alone (54.1 percent). A superior economy delivers only a portion of its electoral benefit to the incumbent party when the two-term limit keeps the incumbent himself from taking full advantage of that economic record.

The 2000 election turned out very much as the economic-voting model under term limits would have predicted. Indeed, seen in historical perspective since 1872, the 2000 performance is one of the model's better years. With just 1.2 points off the mark, the 2000 prediction is way below the standard error (4.5). There are only five other elections, out of a total of 33, where the model exceeds the 2000 performance. Seen in that light, there is nothing puzzling about the 2000 election. What happened to the influence of the economy in the contest between Al Gore and Bush? Though undeniably fabulous, it was of little electoral value to a candidate who was not the sitting president. Yes, Al Gore carried the banner of the same party as that president, served as his vice president, and arguably had a hand in economic policy making. However much that may have counted in the election, it fell way short of what a good economy would have done for the incumbent himself.

To take another stab at this point, one could introduce more explicitly the distinction between elections featuring sitting presidents and those that do not. The simplest way of doing so is to return to the incumbent-party vote and estimate separate vote functions for those two types of contests.[7] The results, with standard errors in parentheses, are as follows:

Elections *with* presidential incumbents:

$$\text{INC.VOTE}_t = 53.8 + 0.49 \ \text{ECON}_t$$
$$(0.93) \ (0.17)$$
$$\text{Adj.} R^2 = 0.19, \quad \text{SER} = 5.1, \quad N = 22$$

Elections *without* presidential incumbents:

$$\text{INC.VOTE}_t = 50.8 - 0.14 \ \text{ECON}_t$$
$$(1.5) \ (0.45)$$
$$\text{Adj.} R^2 = -0.11, \quad \text{SER} = 4.1, \quad N = 10$$

The contrast could not be sharper. When a sitting president is running for re-election, the economy influences the vote in American presidential elections; and when the contest is between two non-incumbent candidates, the economy does not matter for the vote to a significant extent. In the context of the 2000 election, Al Gore had nothing to gain from a good economy since he was not the incumbent president; there is little consolation from the corollary that he would not have been hurt by a bad economy. In American presidential elections, proponents of economic voting would do well to confine their models and forecasts to the type of contest that includes a sitting president. The successor candidate within the incumbent party cannot count on the electoral effects of economic performance under the sitting president. While incumbent vice presidents might claim an exemption, the sparse incidence of such elections does not allow a conclusive test as to whether or not that claim is warranted. The outcome of the 2000 election certainly is not encouraging.

6.5   CONCLUSION

This chapter has told a story and offered a lesson. The lesson is that institutional rules such as the two-term limit in US presidential elections require our attention if we want to grasp the influence of the economy on voters' decisions. These rules, whether just by tradition or by force of constitutional law, bear on the operation of decision models applying to the voting public; those rules rarely are neutral bystanders. For the retrospective theory of voting – so pervasive in the study of economic voting – any rule that affects incumbency must raise a red flag immediately. Halt, and consider how such a rule changes the game of playing "rational god of vengeance and reward" on Election Day.

The story of this chapter deals with the 2000 presidential contest and resolves a maddening puzzle: where was the electoral benefit of economic prosperity? If ever economic conditions had to deliver electoral victory to the incumbent party, the most recent American presidential election should have been that case. What went wrong? As the analysis above has shown, the missing link in the economic–electoral connection was the absence of the sitting president from the race – a casualty of the two-term limit. Removing the incumbent responsible for economic conditions from the ballot sharply dampens the electoral influence of the economy. Al Gore was unable to capitalize on good times in 2000 the way Bill Clinton would have been able to.

In American presidential elections incumbent performance does not automatically transfer to successor candidates, not even those who served as vice presidents. These electoral contests are too personalized to come down to generic partisan decisions. Even though party identification leaves a strong stamp on voter perceptions of economic and political matters, American voters make a sufficient distinction between incumbent and non-incumbent candidates when assigning responsibility for the state of the economy. Whether or not that is true for voters in other countries, where the choice of the chief executive is often out of the hands of the electorate, remains to be seen.

ACKNOWLEDGMENT

I am grateful to Lynch (1999) for making available these data. For data since 1988, see the Bureau of Economic Analysis (BEA) website, Table 6, 31 January 2001.

134 *Helmut Norpoth*

NOTES

1 In the presidential elections of 1912 and 1924, third-party intrusions severely distort the vote shares of the major parties. To avoid problems with such outliers, I have replaced the presidential vote with the vote for House candidates in 1912 and 1924.
2 It should be noted that such a process is by no means common among stationary phenomena. The presidential vote series, however, is a textbook case for an AR(2) process with opposite signs. The main diagnostic tool for identifying this process, the partial autocorrelation function, yields the following values: +0.32 for lag one, and −0.36 for lag two, each significant at the 0.05 level, given a standard error of 0.15. Also note that the parameter estimates of the AR(2) model are such that the stationarity conditions are met: (1) $\phi_2 + \phi_1 < 1$; (2) $\phi_2 - \phi_1 < 1$; (3) $-1 < \phi_2 < 1$.
3 I first presented that forecast for the 2000 election at the Foreign Policy Association meeting, New York, 19 October 1999; later at Trondheim University, 12 April 2000.
4 To be precise, the overall mean was removed from each economic series (2.15 for GNP growth, and 2.86 for inflation), and the deviations from the mean were inverted (multiplied by −1) for the elections with Republican control of the White House.
5 The estimates for the model with the two economic variables entered separately are as follows:

$$\text{VOTE}_t = 48.9 + 0.50 \text{ GNP}_t - 0.77 \text{ INF}_t + 0.41 \text{ VOTE}_{t-1} - 0.40 \text{ VOTE}_{t-2}$$
$$(7.7) \quad (0.16) \qquad (0.25) \qquad (0.13) \qquad\qquad (0.13)$$
$$\text{Adj.} R^2 = 0.59, \quad \text{SER} = 4.6, \quad \chi^2_{(8)} = 6.5, \quad N = 33(1872 - 2000)$$

6 The 1920 election had to be excluded from the set of elections lacking a presidential incumbent. With a score of −27 on the economic index, the 1920 case is an extreme outliner nearly eight standard deviations (3.0) from the mean for this group (−1.6). In the total set of elections, given a much larger variation of the economic index, the 1920 case has a less pronounced effect. Still, its inclusion accounts for the curious fact that the overall analysis shows a stronger effect for the economy than is true for the subset of elections featuring presidential incumbents.

REFERENCES

Anderson, C.J. (2000) Economic voting and political context: a comparative perspective. *Electoral Stud.*, **19**, 151–170.
Bloom, H.S. and Price, H.D. (1975) Voter response to short-run economic conditions: the asymmetric effect of prosperity and recession. *Am. Political Sci. Rev.*, **69**(4), 1240–1254.
Box, G.E.P. and Jenkins, G.W. (1976) *Time Series Analysis: Forecasting and Control.* San Francisco, CA: Holden-Day.
Campbell, J.E. and Garand, J.C. (eds) (2000) *Before the Vote.* Thousands Oaks: Sage.
Campbell, A., Converse, P.E., Miller, W.E. and Stokes, D.E. (1960) *The American Voter.* New York: Wiley.

Chappell Jr., H.W. and Keech, W.R. (1991) Explaining aggregate evaluations of economic performance. In H. Norpoth, M. Lewis-Beck and J.-D. Lafay (eds), *Economics and Politics: The Calculus of Support*. Ann Arbor, MI: University of Michigan Press.

Clarke, H.D. and Stewart, M.C. (1994) Prospections, retrospections and rationality: the bankers model of presidential approval reconsidered. *Am. J. Political Sci.*, **38**(4), 1104–1123.

Clarke, H.D., Norpoth, H. and Whiteley, P. (1998) It's about time: modelling political and social dynamics. In E. Scarbrough and E. Tanenbaum (eds), *Research Strategies in the Social Sciences*. Oxford: Oxford University Press.

Clymer, A. (2000) And the winner is Gore, if they got the math right. *The New York Times*, September 4.

Erikson, R.S. (1989) Economic conditions and the presidential vote. *Am. Political Sci. Rev.*, **83**, 567–573.

Fair, R.C. (1978) The effect of economic events on votes for president. *Rev. Economics Statist.*, **60**, 159–173.

Hibbs Jr., D.A. (1992) Partisan theory after 15 years. *Eur. J. Political Economy*, **8**, 361–373.

Kaiser, R. (2000) And the winner will be...: Al Gore, according to the election soothsayers' nearly foolproof formulas. *Washington Post Weekly*, June 5.

Kiewiet, D.R. (1983) *Macroeconomics and Micropolitics*. Chicago, IL: Chicago University Press.

Kramer, G.H. (1971) Short-term fluctuations in US voting behavior. *Am. Political Sci. Rev.*, **65**(1), 131–143.

Lewis-Beck, M.S. (1988) *Economics and Elections: The Major Western Democracies*. Ann Arbor, MI: University of Michigan Press.

Lewis-Beck, M.S. and Rice, T.W. (1992) *Forecasting Elections*. Washington, DC: CQ Press.

Lewis-Beck, M.S. and Stegmaier, M. (2000) Economic determinants of electoral outcomes. *Annu. Rev. Political Sci.*, **3**, 183–219.

Lynch, G.P. (1999) Presidential elections and the economy 1872 to 1996: the times they are a 'chaning or the song remains the same? *Political Res. Quart.*, **52**(4), 825–844.

MacKuen, M.B., Erikson, R.S. and Stimson, J.A. (1992) Peasants or bankers? The American electorate and the US economy. *Am. Political Sci. Rev.*, **86**(3), 597–611.

Mattei, F. and Weisberg, H.F. (1994) Presidential succession effects in voting. *Brit. J. Political Sci.*, **24**, 495–516.

Midlarsky, M.I. (1984) Political stability of two-party and multiparty systems: probabilistic bases for the comparison of party systems. *Am. Political Sci. Rev.*, **78**, 929–951.

Miller, A.H. and Wattenberg, M.P. (1985) Throwing the rascals out: policy and performance evaluations of presidential elections. *Am. Political Sci. Rev.*, **79**, 359–372.

Norpoth, H. (1992) *Confidence Regained: Economics, Mrs. Thatcher, and the British Voter*. Ann Arbor, MI: University of Michigan Press.

Norpoth, H. (1995) Is Clinton doomed? An early forecast for 1996. *PS* **28**, 201–207.

Norpoth, H. (1996a) The economy. In L. LeDuc, R. Niemi and P. Norris (eds), *Comparative Democratic Elections*. Newbury Park: Sage.

Norpoth, H. (1996b) Presidents and the prospective voter. *J. Politics*, **58**(3), 776–792.

Norpoth, H. (2001) Divided Government and Economic Voting. *J. Politics*, **63**(2), 414–435.

Norpoth, H., Lewis-Beck, M.S. and Lafay, J.-D. (eds) (1991) *Economics and Politics: The Calculus of Support*. Ann Arbor, MI: University of Michigan Press.

Paldam, M. (1991) How robust is the vote function? A study of 17 nations over four decades. In H. Norpoth, M.S. Lewis-Beck and J.-D. Lafay (eds), *Economics and Politics: The Calculus of Support*. Ann Arbor, MI: University of Michigan Press.

Powell, B.G. and Whitten, G.D. (1993) A cross-national analysis of economic voting: taking account of the political context. *Am. J. Political Sci.*, **37**, 391–414.

Tufte, E.R. (1978) *Political Control of the Economy*. Princeton, NJ: Princeton University Press.

Part II
Voter heterogeneity and economic voting

7 Heterogeneous perceptions of economic conditions in cross-national perspective

Raymond M. Duch and
Harvey D. Palmer

7.1 INTRODUCTION

There have been two particularly important recent contributions to our understanding of economic voting. One of these contributions, primarily based on American data, is that economic voting exhibits considerable heterogeneity and thus different segments of the population respond differently to objective fluctuations in the economy. A second recent contribution to this literature concerns the importance of institutions in shaping the manner in which vote choice or incumbent evaluation responds to the economy. This chapter builds on both these recent contributions in an effort to better understand the cross-national economic voting. We demonstrate that systematic differences between subjective and objective characterizations of the economy at the aggregate level are, to some extent, the result of subjective heterogeneity in economic evaluations at the individual level. We speculate that different institutional contexts may affect the extent, or direction, of this subjective heterogeneity that in turn may contribute to cross-national variations in economic voting.

Aggregation of individual evaluation series is a common practice in much of the cross-national work on economic voting (e.g. Clarke *et al.*, 1998). A widely accepted advantage of aggregation is that it avoids the high degree of "noise" or random variation associated with survey data (e.g. Converse, 1990; Page and Shapiro, 1992). Aggregation of individual responses presumably "cancels out" the random variation, thereby leaving only the underlying meaningful component of public opinion. A growing literature exploits this characteristic of aggregated opinion data to demonstrate the extent to which political outcomes respond to shifts in public opinion (e.g. Stimson *et al.*, 1995).

This argument presumes, however, that individual errors in measures of public opinion are random rather than systematic. As Bartels (1996) points out, if these individual errors are actually systematic, aggregation will not produce unbiased aggregate measures of public sentiment. Rather, these aggregate measures will include systematic variation with factors unrelated to objective economic performance such as partisanship and demographic characteristics.

In a similar fashion, we argue here that individual errors in national economic evaluations are not random. As a result, aggregate deviations of individual-level economic evaluations from objective economic conditions are not idiosyncratic but rather constitute the systematic effects of respondent characteristics (i.e. subjective variation). The politically engaged segments of the population, for example, might rationalize their perceptions of the macroeconomy consistent with their partisan predispositions (Zaller, 1992). Thus, aggregated evaluations of economic performance might reflect the systematic impacts of partisanship as well as the latent objective evaluation.

We hypothesize that subjective variation in economic evaluations poses a serious problem on the grounds that it accounts for a substantial portion of total variation. As a result, systematic "noise" at the individual level causes measures of economic evaluations derived by aggregating survey responses to deviate widely from objective economic performance. We also hypothesize that the magnitude and direction of the systematic bias is not constant across time and elections. Because the systematic bias is not constant, we cannot generalize the nature of the distortion in aggregate measures of economic perceptions. Thus, systematic biases aggregated to the national level cannot be easily accounted (corrected) for in aggregate-level models. The implication here is that ignoring the individual-level "noise" when conducting aggregate-level analyses of economic voting could produce misleading conclusions.

In an earlier work, based on American National Election Study data, we demonstrated that subjective heterogeneity in evaluations of economic performance at the individual level introduces systematic biases into the aggregated evaluation series and thus distorts aggregate-level economic voting results (Duch *et al.*, 2000). The research presented here extends this earlier work in two important ways. First, it explores the extent to which subjective heterogeneity in economic evaluations poses a problem for political behavior research in non-US political contexts. In turn, it highlights a potential methodological problem for comparative economic-voting studies that employ evaluation series aggregated from individual-level survey responses. Second, it investigates whether the evidence of subjective heterogeneity in economic evaluations is sensitive to model specification. It is possible that part of the subjective heterogeneity represents a meaningful individual-level variation in economic policy preferences. Individuals might respond differently to different indicators of economic performance – inflation, unemployment, and GDP growth – and thus objectively evaluate economic performance differently. In the analyses presented here, we consider this possibility (i.e. counter-argument) and thereby provide a stronger test of our principal hypothesis about the presence of subjective heterogeneity in evaluations of economic performance.

In addition, by extending our earlier work to a cross-national perspective, this chapter highlights the importance of institutional differences and political context. Institutional differences account for cross-national variation in the extent and nature of heterogeneity in economic voting (e.g. Palmer and Whitten, 1999; Powell and Whitten, 1993; Whitten and Palmer, 1999; Nadeau *et al.*, 2002). Similarly, the problems associated with heterogeneous economic voting in the American context might not generalize to all other democratic contexts. We speculate that institutional features could have two effects. First, institutional features might significantly attenuate heterogeneity in certain contexts by making accountability for economic outcomes very transparent. Second, institutional features might affect the nature of heterogeneity – inducing policy-related heterogeneity that poses no systematic bias in aggregation as opposed to subjective heterogeneity that has been shown to induce systematic bias in aggregation.

To better understand heterogeneity from a cross-national perspective, we conduct an extensive analysis of economic perceptions in Canada, Hungary, the Netherlands, the United States, and West Germany. This analysis seeks to determine to what extent individual-level "noise" distorts economic evaluations and whether the magnitude of the "noise" (particularly the systematic component or measurement bias) differs across institutional contexts. Specifically, we investigate the sources of heterogeneity in economic evaluations and attempt to identify to what extent they are driven endogenously by individual-level characteristics as opposed to being driven exogenously by policy-related concerns. This investigation employs survey data from a national election study (NES) in each country to estimate ordered probit models of retrospective and prospective national economic evaluations.

7.2 THEORETICAL ARGUMENT

The literature on economic voting generally recognizes that voters are not fully informed about the economy. But how do less than fully informed voters form opinions? This section explores the process of mass opinion formation under limited information and speculates about what strategies voters adopt under these circumstances. We also present a theoretical explanation for why deviations from full information have serious implications for models of economic voting.

Suppose that an individual's evaluation is a stochastic variable

$$Y = Y_O + Y_S + \varepsilon$$

where Y_O is the latent objective evaluation (i.e. variation due to economic policy preferences), Y_S captures systematic differences due to information and subjective factors (e.g. partisan rationalization), and ε the stochastic term. This formal definition highlights the two forms of "noise" that plague individual-level evaluations: subjective considerations and random fluctuations. Both forms of "noise" constitute sources of non-attitudes or perhaps more appropriately labeled here as non-evaluations.

Some recent research debates the relevance of non-attitudes and low levels of information by arguing that citizens can employ heuristics to behave as if fully informed (e.g. Sniderman *et al.*, 1991; Lupia, 1992, 1994). Such research implies that heuristics can reduce the influence of subjective considerations and random fluctuations on public attitudes about government policy and performance. If this implication is true, information-gathering shortcuts must eliminate or dramatically reduce the magnitude of Y_S.

Aggregation also plays a central role in overcoming the problem of individual errors in survey responses. Aggregate-level analyses of public opinion presume that aggregation eliminates the "noise" contained in mass opinion (e.g. Page and Shapiro, 1992; Stimson *et al.*, 1995). More formally, aggregate-level analyses implicitly assume that, in the equation above, Y_S and the stochastic term have zero means. Given these assumptions, the mean of Y across individuals represents a "clean" aggregate-level measure of public opinion that is not plagued by individual-level "noise" due to subjective non-policy considerations. Thus, aggregate-level studies "solve" the statistical problems posed by survey data by using mean evaluations.

In this chapter, we debate this conclusion by positing that individual economic evaluations contain subjective sources of systematic variation and thus aggregation does not eliminate these distortions (i.e. $Y_S \neq 0$). This hypothesis is consistent with the central theme of Kramer's (1983) theory about why individual-level evidence of egocentric ("pocketbook") economic voting contrasts with the strong aggregate-level evidence of a causal connection between objective economic conditions and election results. This micro–macro-dichotomy poses a paradox since early studies attributed the aggregate-level relationship to egocentric economic voting by individuals (e.g. Kramer, 1971).[1] Kramer argues that individual-level measurement error accounts for this dichotomy in empirical evidence. According to Kramer, only government-induced changes in personal financial situation matter to the economic-voting relationship while other sources of systematic variation, such as life-cycle effects and partisan rationalization, are meaningless noise. Consequently, survey evidence of economic voting is "drowned out" by the noise.

The crux of our theoretical contribution is extending Kramer's theory about evaluations of personal financial situation to evaluations of national economic performance. This extension follows the logic of Kramer's

(1983: 95) contention that "we are ultimately interested only in how real economic outcomes affect voting decisions and not in economic rhetoric or perceptual imagery." The crucial question for this chapter is whether or not evaluations of the national economy are plagued by subjective considerations. If subjective factors do not explain a significant portion of the total variation in economic evaluations, it is reasonable to assume that those evaluations are largely objective in nature.

Past research tends to support the position that evaluations of the national economy are largely objective. Survey research has found that evaluations of the national economy perform better than evaluations of personal finances in economic-voting models (e.g. see Lewis-Beck, 1988; compare Kinder and Kiewiet, 1979 with Fiorina, 1978, 1981). Aggregate-level analyses of economic voting have produced a similar pattern of results (e.g. MacKuen *et al.*, 1992; Clarke and Stewart, 1994; Norpoth, 1996). Additionally, research has shown that people do not generally attribute responsibility for their personal circumstances to political causes (e.g. Brody and Sniderman, 1977; Sniderman and Brody, 1977; Sears *et al.*, 1980). In other words, people do not use their personal experiences as a heuristic for making political judgments. This generalization holds most strongly for economic issues (e.g. Weatherford, 1983; Conover *et al.*, 1986; but see Hetherington, 1996). Yet, people politicize their personal experiences more in some situations than others (Feldman, 1985) and debate exists over whether media exposure facilitates or hinders self-interested political attitudes (Sears *et al.*, 1980; Weatherford, 1983; Conover *et al.*, 1986; Mutz, 1992, 1994). Mutz (1994) finds, for instance, that news media exposure politicized personal-level judgments regarding unemployment, causing them to influence presidential performance evaluations in the United States.

Finally, some of the work on aggregate-level measures of economic expectations suggests the existence of systematic "error" in individual assessments of future economic performance. For example, while Haller and Norpoth (1994) find that certain economic assessments result from a form of adaptive expectations, their results also indicate asymmetry in how economic expectations respond to positive versus negative economic times. These authors point to different "psychological" processing of economic information as an explanation for systematic differences in the objective and subjective economic evaluations. In this chapter, we hypothesize that systematic differences between subjective and objective characterizations of the economy at the aggregate level might actually be the result of subjective heterogeneity in economic evaluations at the individual level.

To investigate this hypothesis, first we must specify the sources of subjective variation. In this effort, we build upon recent research efforts that identify how subjective considerations matter in the formation of public opinion (i.e. the factors shaping Y_S). More specifically, our analysis focuses on four distinct sources of subjective heterogeneity in national economic evaluations: information, political attitudes, personal experiences, and socioeconomic characteristics.

7.2.1   Information

Bartels (1996) debates the assumption that $Y_S = 0$ by demonstrating that the decision calculus of voters differs with their level of political knowledge. In the American context, Bartels finds that poorly informed voters do not behave as if they were fully informed. Rather, actual and "fully informed" vote probabilities for American presidential elections from 1972 to 1992 differ by 10 percent points on average. This large difference is particularly surprising given that presidential elections produce an abundant supply of low-cost cues and voting heuristics. Moreover, Bartels finds that this informational difference is systematic – favoring incumbent presidents and Democratic candidates – rather than random. This finding implies that aggregate outcomes are unlikely to conform to the "complete information majority preferred alternative," as suggested by Lupia (1992).

A number of recent findings suggest that Bartels' "information" findings for voting behavior – an expression of preference on government policy – extend to evaluations of policy outcomes. Building on Bartels' analysis, Althaus (1998) used survey data to simulate "fully informed" collective preferences and found that aggregated measures of public opinion on a range of policy issues were significantly distorted by group differences in information (at the individual level). Similarly, Hetherington (1996) demonstrates that American voters in 1992 evaluated the national economy differently depending on their level of media usage, though this result does not extend to the 1984 and 1988 presidential elections. In sum, citizens in aggregate do not behave as if they are fully informed and, more generally, aggregation does not eliminate the distortion of systematic subjective differences in public opinion.

The research of Bartels, Althaus, and Hetherington demonstrates that public opinion differs systematically with the level of information. Similarly, we expect national economic evaluations to vary with factors that influence how individuals collect and interpret information about the political economy. To the extent that poorly informed opinions differ from well-informed ones, evaluations of the national economy – past, present, and future – should vary systematically with the extent to which individuals are "informed" about the political economy. Certainly, persons with broader and "cheaper" access to and greater incentive to obtain information about the economy should have more accurate or, at least, more consistent economic evaluations. Thus, we expect citizens to perceive economic performance differently depending on their levels of political sophistication and education. We hold a similar expectation for mass media exposure based on the assumption that media usage distinguishes among citizens in terms of their access to and interpretation of information about the economy.[2] We label this set of theoretical expectations the *information* hypothesis.[3]

7.2.2 Political attitudes

Previous research has recognized that partisan predispositions influence economic perceptions (e.g. Macdonald and Heath, 1997; Wlezien *et al.*, 1997; Markus, 1988). Some voters positively or negatively evaluate economic performance based on their partisan and ideological biases, regardless of whether those biased perceptions are contradicted by actual changes in national economic conditions. These biases may stem from short-run reactions to government policies or more persistent partisan attachments. Thus, we posit that individuals with stronger attachments to the parties in government (president's party) perceive the national economy more positively.

Zaller (1992) theorizes that information has a polarizing effect on the opinions of individuals with strong political predispositions. Paraphrasing his explanation, individuals with strong political predispositions interpret new information so that it reinforces previously held attitudes, thereby augmenting rather than tempering the differences between their beliefs and those of individuals with opposing political pre-dispositions. In the present context, Zaller's argument implies that partisan biases produce greater heterogeneity in economic perceptions among better-informed persons than among poorly informed ones. Thus, we hypothesize that political sophistication strengthens the effect of government party attachment, thereby magnifying the subjective heterogeneity in economic evaluations attributable to partisan preferences. We label the set of theoretical expectations associated with partisan preferences the *political-attitudes* hypothesis.

7.2.3 Personal financial experience

Even if individuals are exposed to the same amount of information about objective economic conditions, their subjective interpretations of those conditions may differ. We expect that personal financial circumstances will shape individuals' perceptions of actual economic outcomes. There is considerable empirical evidence suggesting that personal financial circumstances weigh more heavily on the political decisions of the less informed as opposed to the informed (Weatherford, 1983; Conover *et al.*, 1987; Delli Carpini and Keeter, 1996; Krause, 1997; but see Hetherington, 1996). Hence we expect that reliance on personal experience as a heuristic for overall economic outcomes should vary with political sophistication. For example, those experiencing personal financial troubles (e.g. unemployed, recently laid off) should perceive national economic conditions more negatively (Funk and Garcia-Monet, 1997). As Conover *et al.* (1986: 583) argue, the "... well-informed tend to ignore their own personal economic experiences, while the uninformed draw heavily upon them." Thus, we expect political sophistication to weaken the effect of personal financial situation on national economic evaluations. We label these theoretical expectations the *personal financial-experience* hypothesis.

7.2.4   Group self-interest

Collecting and processing information takes time and effort – incurs costs on the information user. As suggested above in our discussion of the information hypothesis, some individuals face lower costs due to their higher levels of political sophistication and mass media attention. Although we expect such individuals, on average, to be more knowledgeable about the national economy, we do not believe that people gather information and read/watch the national news simply to have better-informed opinions. For most individuals, what they know about national economic conditions is a byproduct of activities engaged in for other purposes (e.g. entertainment, business). In other words, most individuals do not acquire information about the national economy simply to make better voting decisions or to form more consistent political attitudes about government policy outcomes. In turn, individuals who derive greater benefits from having economic information (e.g. those with greater investments in stocks) tend to have a better understanding of national economic conditions.

Similarly, MacKuen and Mouw (1995) find, based on their analysis of consumer attitudes from 1978 to 1990, that high-status individuals are more likely to hold accurate economic perceptions and that systematic variation across socioeconomic groups exists in the content of information utilized to make sense of the economy. Consistent with the notion that self-interested citizens seek out information that reflects their particular economic circumstances (e.g. employment status, occupation, amount of debt), MacKuen and Mouw (1995) reveal that people react differently to different economic indicators depending on their social status and situation in the economic structure.[4] Homeowners, for example, can be expected to pay closer attention to interest rates, and people out of work or in marginal occupations can be expected to pay greater attention to the unemployment rate. Thus, economic self-interest, as reflected in demographic characteristics, constitutes a source of heterogeneity in perceptions of the economic performance. We label this the *group self-interest* hypothesis.

Overall, our theoretical expectations specify that perceptions of economic performance vary for a variety of reasons relating to information and self-interest. Public assessment of the national economy might vary independently of objective economic conditions due to differences in political sophistication, media exposure, partisan attachments, personal financial experiences, and demographic characteristics. We can summarize the hypotheses that compose our individual-level model of subjective heterogeneity in economic evaluations as follows:

1   Citizens who are more sophisticated and better informed evaluate the national economy differently than those who are less sophisticated and poorly informed.
2   Economic self-interest and partisan preferences bias economic evaluations. Citizens with stronger attachments to incumbent parties and more favorable personal financial experiences evaluate the national economy more positively. Similarly, citizens' perceptions of economic performance vary with their socioeconomic situation.
3   Partisan biases in national economic evaluations are greater for citizens who are better informed about politics. On the other hand, political sophistication weakens the effect of personal financial situation on economic perceptions.

7.3   DATA AND METHODOLOGY

Our statistical investigation estimates individual-level, ordered probit models of national economic evaluations using survey data from West Germany (1990), Canada (1993), the United States (1996), Hungary (1997), and the Netherlands (1998). This investigation proceeds in two stages. The first stage adopts the same approach as our earlier research (Duch *et al.*, 2000), but applies it with a cross-national perspective. The second stage applies a more conservative approach that provides a stronger test of our null hypothesis.

The primary purpose of the analysis is to evaluate the null hypothesis that national economic evaluations do not vary systematically with information, political attitudes, personal financial situation, and group self-interest, and thus are purely objective. Evidence to the contrary would demonstrate that individual-level "noise" in economic evaluations is systematic rather than random. Such a finding would refute the presumption that aggregation solves the statistical problems posed by non-attitudes and thereby produces a "clean" measure of the public's objective evaluation of the economy.

The first stage of our analysis applies a simple test of this null hypothesis that only includes measures of subjective heterogeneity in the model specification. Our earlier research also adopted this approach (Duch *et al.*, 2000). One criticism of this simple approach is that the model should control for objective sources of variation in economic evaluations. Even if individuals are exposed to the same information about objective economic conditions, their subjective interpretations of those conditions might differ

in meaningful ways. There are multiple indicators of economic performance (e.g. unemployment, inflation, GDP growth, international trade
balance) and even experts disagree about which of these indicators is most
important. Individuals who focus on different performance indicators thus
can often reach different conclusions about the state of the national economy. We speculate that individuals' economic policy preferences influence how much attention they give to the various indicators of economic
performance. If this speculation is valid, economic policy preferences
represent an objective source of variation in national economic evaluations.

This criticism provides a counter-interpretation of first-stage results
that reject the null hypothesis: the sources of subjective heterogeneity
are correlated with economic policy preferences that account for meaningful individual-level variation in economic evaluations. The second
stage of our analysis addresses this counter-argument by adding measures of economic policy preferences to the model specification. More
specifically, we employ factor analyses of economic policy questions to
construct factor scales that capture respondents' preferences on the issues
of government regulation of the economy and the (Phillips Curve) trade-
off between inflation and unemployment.[5] For Hungary, the model also
includes a third factor scale that reflects policy preferences on the issue of
market reform. By controlling for these objective, policy-related sources
of heterogeneity, the second-stage models provide stronger, more conservative tests of the null hypothesis that subjective considerations are not
significant sources of variation in national economic evaluations.

A secondary goal of the analysis is to consider the extent to which
institutional context influences the magnitude and sources of systematic
"noise" in national economic evaluations. The cross-national perspective
adopted in this chapter allows us to consider two general questions. First,
is subjective heterogeneity greater in some countries than in others? One
could posit that Hungarian citizens evaluate the national economy more
objectively than their counterparts in other countries due to the high
salience of economic issues during the initial stages of market reform in
Hungary. In contrast, one could speculate that subjective considerations
exert greater influence on economic evaluations in the highly partisan
atmosphere of American politics.

Second, do particular sources of subjective heterogeneity have greater
relevance in some countries than in others? Institutional differences might
produce cross-national differences in the relative importance of different
sources of subjective heterogeneity. In the United States, where politics is
highly partisan and receives extensive media attention, we expect partisanship, media usage, and political sophistication to exert the greatest influence
on economic evaluations. In the Netherlands and West Germany, where
group-party ties are stronger, we expect demographic characteristics to have
greater relevance as sources of subjective heterogeneity (particularly in the
Netherlands, which has a pure system of proportional representation).

Finally, in Hungary, the economic dislocation caused by market reform might increase the importance of personal financial experiences as a determinant of assessments of the national economy.

The dependent variables in the ordered probit models are standard measures of national economic evaluations with three or five response categories. The corresponding survey questions ask respondents to compare current economic conditions to those in the past year (retrospective) and those expected during the next year (prospective). Responses to these questions have been coded so that they range from (much) "worse" to (much) "better." Given that the economic evaluations are ordered categorical variables, ordered probit is a more appropriate econometric method than linear regression. Ordered probit, like linear regression, assumes a particular ordering of the responses along a single dimension but, unlike linear regression, does not impose the assumption that all adjacent responses are equidistant apart.

The ordered probit model is a generalization of the binomial probit model that allows for more than two observed outcomes. In the specific context of our analyses, survey responses on the national economy are derived from latent economic evaluations expressed as continuous random variables. The stochastic components of latent evaluations are assumed to be normally distributed with a mean of zero and variance of one (if homoskedastic). The probability of obtaining a particular survey response corresponds to the probability that the latent evaluation is within a particular range and hence is a function of the standard normal cumulative distribution. See Greene (2000) for a more detailed exposition of the ordered probit model.

As in the binomial probit model, the marginal effects of regressors on response probabilities are not equal to the coefficients. Moreover, the marginal effects on the probabilities for mid-range responses (e.g. "same") do not necessarily have the same signs as the coefficients. If a regressor's coefficient is positive, an increase in that regressor always produces a decrease in the probability of the lowest response (e.g. "much worse") and an increase in the probability of the highest response (e.g. "much better"). The directions of probability changes for mid-range responses, however, are ambiguous since they depend on the probability densities prior to the increase in the regressor.

7.4 ARE EVALUATIONS OF THE NATIONAL ECONOMY PURELY OBJECTIVE?

If national economic evaluations are purely objective, they are not a function of information, media exposure, partisanship, personal financial experiences, and demographic characteristics. Thus, our statistical analyses focus on whether such variables prove significant in ordered probit models of national economic evaluations. Tables 7.1(a,b) present ordered

Table 7.1(a) Retrospective national economic evaluations in West Germany (1990), Canada (1993), and USA (1996) (ordered probit regression)

Explanatory variables	West Germany, 1990		Canada, 1993		USA, 1996	
	Coeff.	T-stat.	Coeff.	T-stat.	Coeff.	T-stat.
Partisanship	0.070*	2.25	0.007	0.19	−0.095**	−2.95
Partisanship × political sophistication	−0.015	−1.02	0.027	1.86	−0.022	−1.83
Retrospective personal financial situation	0.659**	5.57	0.184**	3.97	0.293**	5.85
Retrospective PFS × political sophistication	−0.094	−1.52	−0.006	−0.28	0.004	0.18
Media usage	–		−0.074*	−2.30	0.101**	2.73
Political sophistication	–		0.021	0.50	0.127*	2.06
Education	0.290**	2.79	0.027*	2.03	0.057*	2.37
Family income	–		0.020*	2.04	0.044	1.51
Professional/self-employed	0.05	0.33	−0.08	−1.32	0.02	0.27
Manual worker	−0.03	−0.32	−0.07	−0.99	−0.12	−0.50
Union membership	0.14	1.59	−0.12*	−2.34	−0.04	−0.54
Age	0.023	1.51	−0.0029	−1.81	0.0073**	4.21
Ethnicity (French/Black)	–		−0.34**	−6.18	−0.10	−1.23
Female	−0.08	−1.07	−0.29**	−5.93	−0.18**	−3.31
Constant	−0.22**	−0.90	0.65**	4.74	0.77**	4.08
μ_1	1.61**	27.19	0.99**	32.97	0.86**	15.47
μ_2	–		2.12**	45.43	2.26**	34.81
μ_3	–		3.45**	27.40	3.64**	47.53
χ^2-Statistic of overall model	124.4**		236.9**		353.1**	
% Predicted correctly	53.0		40.3		49.6	
% Error reduction	2.1		7.5		10.1	
N	998		2295		1697	

Notes
For West Germany, the dependent variable is a 3-point scale ranging from "worse" to "better" in response to the standard question on national economic situation over the past year. For Canada and USA, the dependent variable is a 5-category scale ranging from "much worse" to "much better". The naive model that everyone gives the modal response correctly predicts 52.0% of the West German cases, 35.5% of the Canadian cases, and 43.9% of USA cases. ** $p < 0.01$; * $p < 0.05$.

Table 7.1(b) Retrospective national economic evaluations in Hungary (1997), and the Netherlands (1998) (ordered probit regression)

Explanatory variables	Hungary, 1997		The Netherlands, 1998	
	Coeff.	T-stat.	Coeff.	T-stat.
Partisanship	0.062*	2.17	0.063*	2.19
Partisanship × political sophistication	0.028*	1.97	−0.004	−0.43
Retrospective personal financial situation	0.580**	9.59	–	
Retrospective PFS × political sophistication	−0.068*	−2.04	–	
Media usage	0.095*	2.47	0.008	0.58
Political sophistication	0.317**	5.36	0.007	0.36
Education	0.046	1.54	0.011	0.90

Family income	0.001	0.06	0.022	1.19
Professional/self-employed	0.03	0.22	–	
Manual worker	−0.02	−0.22	–	
Social class	–		0.13**	4.25
Union membership	–		0.29	1.78
Age	−0.0026	−1.37	−0.0054**	−2.90
Female	−0.18**	−2.94	−0.08	−1.35
Constant	0.18	1.01	2.04**	8.11
μ_1	0.99**	21.61	0.74**	6.89
μ_2	1.89**	33.98	2.55**	21.58
μ_3	4.39**	28.67	3.99**	32.58
χ^2-Statistic of overall model	487.9**		61.9**	
% Predicted correctly	45.7		51.5	
% Error reduction	20.1		8.5	
N	1482		1754	

Notes
For both countries, the dependent variable contains five categories ranging from "much worse" to "much better" in response to the standard question on national economic situation over the past year. The naive model that everyone gives the modal response correctly predicts 32.1% of the Hungarian cases and 47.0% of the Dutch cases. ** $p < 0.01$; * $p < 0.05$.

probit models of retrospective evaluations in West Germany, Canada, the United States, Hungary, and the Netherlands, each estimated with survey data from a national election survey in the country. Similarly, Table 7.2 presents ordered probit models of prospective evaluations in West Germany, Canada, the United States, and Hungary.[6] The Statistical Appendix discusses the measurement of the explanatory variables (regressors) in these ordered probit models.

The χ^2-statistics of overall model significance reported in Tables 7.1(a,b) and 7.2 decisively reject the null hypothesis that national economic evaluations are purely objective. Clearly, information and subjective factors produce systematic variation across individuals in their assessments of the economy, particularly in their retrospective assessments. Furthermore, the evidence of subjective heterogeneity in national economic evaluations generalizes across countries – it is clearly not unique to the American case.

On the basis of their statistical significance, personal financial experiences and partisanship have the strongest and most consistent influence on economic evaluations. The effect of *personal financial situation* is significant at the 1 percent level for both retrospective and prospective evaluations and for all of the countries. Similarly, the effect of *partisanship* achieves statistical significance at the 5 percent level in all the retrospective models, except the one for Canada, and at the 1 percent level in the prospective models for the United States and Hungary.

Information and group self-interest also have relevance as determinants of economic evaluations. *Political sophistication* proves significant in the retrospective model for the United States and in the retrospective and

Table 7.2 Prospective national economic evaluations in West Germany (1990), Canada (1993) USA (1996), and Hungary (1997) (ordered probit regression)

Explanatory variables	West Germany, 1990		Canada, 1993		USA, 1996		Hungary, 1997	
	Coeff.	T-stat.	Coeff.	T-stat.	Coeff.	T-stat.	Coeff.	T-stat.
Partisanship	0.034	1.15	−0.040	−1.08	−0.105**	−3.20	0.071**	2.66
Partisanship × sophistication	−0.003	−0.17	0.030*	2.02	−0.001	−0.06	0.012	0.88
Prospective PFS	0.911**	6.37	0.281**	5.27	0.444**	7.72	0.733**	11.83
Prospective PFS × sophistication	−0.204**	−2.69	0.027	1.19	−0.042	−1.70	−0.081*	−2.47
Media usage	–		0.074*	2.29	0.036	0.92	0.063	1.59
Political sophistication	–		−0.057	−1.01	0.146	1.94	0.313**	4.33
Education	0.326**	3.53	0.007	0.53	−0.033	−1.29	0.021	0.66
Family income	–		−0.002	−0.21	−0.051	−1.63	0.057*	2.38
Professional/ self-employed	−0.14	−1.00	−0.03	−0.46	0.11	1.50	0.24	1.87
Manual worker	0.02	0.16	−0.09	−1.31	−0.02	−0.06	−0.05	−0.60
Union membership	0.01	0.04	−0.11*	−2.07	−0.08	−1.00	–	
Age	0.082**	5.23	0.0036*	2.09	0.0038*	1.98	0.0047*	2.42
Ethnicity (French/Black)	–		0.02	0.35	0.12	1.52	–	
Female	−0.13	−1.66	−0.13*	−2.51	−0.06	−1.07	−0.03	−0.42
Constant	−1.54**	−6.46	0.01	0.05	1.20**	5.62	0.05	0.28
μ_1	1.26**	22.35	1.52**	41.95	0.91**	13.49	1.13**	15.84
μ_2	–		–		2.83**	36.88	2.38**	30.30
μ_3	–		–		4.03**	43.17	5.02**	34.32
χ^2-Statistic of overall model	107.6**		180.5**		205.3**		469.5**	
% Predicted Correctly	54.4		54.1		61.9		55.5	
% Error Reduction	6.0		2.0		0.2		23.5	
N	990		2211		1683		1417	

Notes
For West Germany and Canada, the dependent variable is a 3-category scale ranging from "worse" to "better" in response to the standard question on national economic situation during the next year. For USA and Hungary, the dependent variable is a 5-category scale ranging from "much worse" to "much better." The naive model that everyone gives the modal response correctly predicts 51.5% of the West German cases, 53.1% of the Canadian cases, 61.8% of USA cases, and 41.7% of the Hungarian cases. ** $p < 0.01$; * $p < 0.05$.

prospective models for Hungary. Similarly, *media usage* achieves the 5 percent significance level in the retrospective and prospective models for Canada and in the retrospective models for the United States and Hungary. Several demographic characteristics, as proxies for group self-interest, have significant effects in more than one model. *Education* is significant in both models for West Germany and in the retrospective models for Canada and the United States. *Female* proves significant in both models for Canada and in the retrospective models for the United States and Hungary. *Age* is significant in the retrospective models for the United States and the Netherlands and in all of the prospective models. Finally, union membership, ethnicity, family income, and social class image achieve statistical significance in various models. In sum, all four sources of subjective heterogeneity contribute to individual-level variation in evaluations of the national economy.

As stated above, the marginal effects of regressors in ordered probit models are not equal to their coefficients. Thus, to better understand the estimated substantive impacts, we illustrate how "typical" respondents' economic evaluations vary with information and subjective factors. We define a "typical" respondent as someone whose initial probability of giving a "better" (somewhat or much) evaluation is equal to the sample frequency. For example, a typical West German respondent has an initial 0.332 probability of stating that national economic conditions are "better" today than a year ago.[7] Using the ordered probit coefficients, we can characterize the magnitudes of the explanatory variables' estimated effects for typical respondents.

Personal financial experiences have the strongest estimated effects on evaluations of the national economy. For typical respondents, one-category improvements in their personal financial evaluations (e.g. from "same" to "somewhat better") increase their predicted probability of a positive retrospective evaluation by 25.7 percentage points in West Germany, by 3.0 points in Canada, by 11.6 points in the United States, and by 22.5 points in Hungary.[8] Over the entire range of personal financial evaluations, a typical respondent's predicted probability of positively evaluating the economy's past performance increases by 45.2 percentage points in West Germany, by 10.8 points in Canada, by 42.8 points in the United States, and by 70.8 points in Hungary. Similar effects occur for prospective evaluations with a one-category improvement producing increases of 26.8 percentage points in West Germany, 9.5 points in Canada, 15.9 points in the United States, and 28.2 points in Hungary. Not surprisingly, personal financial experiences exert greater influence on assessments of future economic performance than on assessments of past economic conditions.

The strong impact of personal financial experiences on national economic evaluations might not surprise some readers, especially since such a relationship is consistent with a "pocketbook" explanation of economic voting. However, this finding contradicts research demonstrating that people do not generally attribute personal experiences to government policy and political events (e.g. Brody and Sniderman, 1977; Sniderman and Brody, 1977; Sears *et al.*, 1980). Furthermore, most of the models reject the hypothesis that reliance on personal financial experiences as a heuristic for judging national economic conditions decreases with the person's level of political sophistication. The principal exception here is Hungary.[9] The estimated marginal impact of personal financial experiences on retrospective evaluations is 5.4 percentage points lower for typical respondents who have "very high" rather than "average" levels of political knowledge. A similar interactive effect occurs for prospective evaluations, resulting in a 5.8 point decrease. These findings are consistent with the view that the economic turbulence generally associated with market reform increases the information requirements of evaluating the economy and thereby increases the use of personal financial experiences as a heuristic (note that the total effect is greatest for Hungary).

Partisanship also exerts substantial influence on national economic evaluations. A one-unit increase in partisan attachment to the government increases typical respondents' predicted probabilities of a "better" retrospective evaluation by 2.6 percentage points in West Germany, by 3.6 points in the United States, by 2.3 points in Hungary, and by 2.5 points in the Netherlands.[10] Over the entire range of partisan attitudes, a typical respondent's predicted probability of positively evaluating the past economy increases by 25.0 percentage points in West Germany, by 21.7 points in the United States, by 22.1 points in Hungary, and by 19.9 points in the Netherlands. Similar but more limited effects occur for prospective evaluations as well. Over the entire range of partisan attitudes, a typical respondent's predicted probability of positively evaluating the future economy increases by 19.8 percentage points in the United States and by 27.3 points in Hungary. Thus, as expected, one's optimism about the national economy increases with the strength of one's attachment to the government parties.[11]

Tables 7.1(a, b) and 7.2 also reveal evidence of systematic variation in national economic evaluations due to information and demographic characteristics, though these factors have more modest influence than do political attitudes and personal financial experiences. Among typical respondents, a one-unit increase in *political sophistication* increases the likelihood of responding "better" to a retrospective question about the national economy by 5.0 percentage points in the United States and by 12.1 points in Hungary. *Political sophistication* also significantly influences prospective evaluations in Hungary with an estimated marginal impact of 12.4 percentage points for typical respondents.

Mass media exposure also contributes to information differences but to a lesser extent than political sophistication. Among typical respondents, a one-unit increase in *media usage* increases the predicted probability of a positive retrospective evaluation by 3.9 percentage points in the United States and by 3.5 points in Hungary. In Canada, media exposure has opposite effects on past and future assessments of the economy. Among typical Canadian respondents, a one-unit increase in *media usage* decreases the likelihood of a positive evaluation of the past economy by 1 percent point but increases the likelihood of a positive evaluation of the future economy by 2.4 percentage points. The fact that the sign of the *media usage* coefficient differs across the two equations for Canada suggests that this variable actually captures a media effect rather than some general attribute associated with political interest and sophistication. Note that in West Germany and Hungary, the more educated or more politically sophisticated tended to hold more optimistic views of economic performance.

Overall, demographic characteristics contribute the least to systematic variation in national economic evaluations, though they prove to be statistically and substantively significant in some models. The more notable demographic effects are those for education in both West German models, social class image in the retrospective model for the Netherlands, and ethnicity in the retrospective model for Canada. Education contributes greatly to variation in the economic evaluations of West Germans. Among typical West German respondents, a one-category increase in *education* increases the likelihood of a positive retrospective evaluation by 11.1 percentage points and the likelihood of a positive prospective evaluation by 7.5 percentage points. Similarly, a one-category increase in *social class* produces a 5.2 percentage point increase in the typical Dutch respondent's predicted probability of positively evaluating the past economy. Finally, ethnicity has both substantive and statistical significance in Canada where typical French respondents are 3.8 percentage points less likely than their English counterparts to positively evaluate the economy's performance over the past year.

Our discussion of the ordered probit results highlights several interesting cross-national differences in the sources of subjective heterogeneity in economic evaluations. As theorized earlier, the effect of *partisanship* is particularly strong in the United States, especially in terms of its statistical significance. In contrast, partisan attitudes have little to no effect in Canada and only influence retrospective evaluation in West Germany. This pattern is consistent with the fact that party identification plays a much less significant role in shaping policy preferences and vote choice in national contexts other than the United States (Budge *et al.*, 1976; Dalton, 1988). Yet, this inference is far from universal. In terms of substantive import, the effect of *partisanship* in the United States was similar in magnitude to its effects in Hungary and, to a lesser extent, in West Germany and the Netherlands.

The ordered probit results also reveal interesting cross-national differences in the effects of personal financial experiences, media exposure, political sophistication, and demographic characteristics. Personal financial experiences clearly have the greatest influence in Hungary with total effects of 70.8 percentage points for retrospective evaluations and 85.0 percentage points for prospective evaluations. This finding is consistent with our expectations about how citizens form economic evaluations in a nascent democracy in the midst of market transition. Also, as expected, *media usage* and *political sophistication* strongly influence economic evaluations in the United States where the scope of the mass media is arguably greater than in Canada and Europe. Yet, the information effects are even stronger in Hungary. Again, this finding is consistent with the market reform setting of Hungary, which increases the information requirements of following changes in the national economy (Duch, 2001). Finally, there is some evidence consistent with the expectation that group self-interest is a more important source of subjective heterogeneity in countries with stronger group-party ties such as the Netherlands and West Germany.

For instance, social class image and age are by far the most important determinants of economic evaluations in the Netherlands. This evidence is only suggestive, however, since no definitive cross-national pattern emerges in the effects of the demographic characteristics.

So far, we have considered the statistical significance of the explanatory variables individually and in total (i.e. the statistical significance of the entire model). Our discussion has highlighted the existence of systematic variation in national economic evaluations due to information and subjective factors, and attempted to distinguish among the different sources of systematic variation in terms of the strength of their influence. In the latter context, we can more concisely distinguish among the different sources of systematic variation by comparing the joint significance of different subsets of variables (i.e. how much different subsets of explanatory variables contribute to overall model significance). Table 7.3 presents likelihood ratio (LR) statistics that measure the joint significance of variables in four different subsets: political attitudes, personal financial experiences, information, and demographic characteristics. These groupings of variables should be self-evident. In Table 7.1(a), for instance, the first two variables are included in the political attitudes subset, the next two variables are

Table 7.3 Likelihood ratio statistics for different sources of subjective variation in national economic evaluations (USA, Canada, Hungary, West Germany, and the Netherlands)

Excluded variables	USA	Canada	Hungary	West Germany	The Netherlands
Retrospective evaluations					
Political attitudes	121.5	24.8	93.7	12.1	11.7
	(<0.0001)	(<0.0001)	(<0.0001)	(0.0024)	(0.0029)
Personal financial experiences	132.9	67.4	193.6	74.8	–
	(<0.0001)	(<0.0001)	(<0.0001)	(<0.0001)	
Information	11.7	5.9	36.4	–	0.5
	(0.0028)	(0.0523)	(<0.0001)		(0.7634)
Demographic characteristics	40.1	94.6	17.0	12.8	43.2
	(<0.0001)	(<0.0001)	(0.0092)	(0.0456)	(<0.0001)
Prospective evaluations					
Political attitudes	57.0	6.8	56.6	5.1	–
	(<0.0001)	(0.0340)	(<0.0001)	(0.0797)	
Personal financial experiences	102.5	140.3	275.4	77.8	–
	(<0.0001)	(<0.0001)	(<0.0001)	(<0.0001)	
Information	4.0	5.9	21.0	–	–
	(0.1367)	(0.0523)	(<0.0001)		
Demographic characteristics	19.0	17.3	17.2	35.9	–
	(0.0151)	(0.0273)	(0.0087)	(<0.0001)	

Notes
Likelihood ratio statistics evaluate whether the excluded variables significantly improve the overall performance of the model and hence test whether national economic evaluations vary significantly with each source of subjective variation. p-values for the statistics are reported in parentheses.

included in the personal financial experiences subset, *media usage* and *political sophistication* are included in the information subset, and the remaining variables are included in the demographic subset.

The LR statistics in Table 7.3 indicate whether a particular source of subjective considerations produces systematic variation in national economic evaluations. Additionally, comparisons of LR statistics' significance across variable subsets characterize the relative strength of different sources of subjective considerations. Political attitudes and personal financial experiences have uniformly high LR statistics and are statistically significant in all countries and in both retrospective and prospective equations.[12] In contrast, the statistical significance of information and demographic characteristics varies considerably across countries. This variation reflects some interesting cross-national differences in the relative importance of different sources of subjective heterogeneity. In the United States and Hungary, personal financial experiences are most important followed by political attitudes. In contrast, demographic characteristics are most important in the Netherlands and in the retrospective model for Canada. They are also the second most important source of subjective heterogeneity in West Germany and in the prospective model for Canada. These cross-national differences in the relative importance of the different sources of subjective heterogeneity is, at least broadly, consistent with theorized differences in the institutions and political context of these five countries.

For readers sympathetic to our argument, the first stage of our analysis (Tables 7.1(a,b)–7.3) provides strong evidence against the null hypothesis that national economic evaluations are purely objective and thus independent of information differences and subjective considerations. Skeptical readers, however, could question this conclusion on the grounds that the ordered probit models do not include measures of economic policy preferences, which might account for objective, policy-related variation in economic evaluations. Omitting these measures potentially produces misleading evidence against the null hypothesis to the extent that the sources of subjective heterogeneity are correlated with economic policy preferences.

The second stage of our analysis addresses this counter-argument by adding economic policy preferences to the model. Tables 7.4 and 7.5 present ordered probit models that add measures of economic policy preferences to the model specifications applied in Tables 7.1(a,b) and 7.2.[13] As discussed earlier, we constructed three measures of policy preferences. *Government regulation of economy* captures attitudes toward the extent of government intervention in the economic markets for labor and goods and services. *Phillips curve trade-off* measures the importance of reducing unemployment relative to controlling inflation and government spending. *Market reform*, which is unique to the Hungary models, captures the strength of support for implementing market reform of the

Table 7.4 Retrospective national economic evaluations in Canada (1993), USA (1996), Hungary (1997), and the Netherlands (1998) with economic policy controls (ordered probit regression)

Explanatory variables	Canada, 1993		USA, 1996		Hungary, 1997		The Netherlands, 1998	
	Coeff.	T-stat.	Coeff.	T-stat.	Coeff.	T-stat.	Coeff.	T-stat.
Government regulation of economy	–		-0.017	-1.59	-0.027	-1.61	-0.001	-0.11
Phillips curve trade-off	-0.070**	-3.12	-0.100**	-4.99	0.030	0.71	-0.043	-1.67
Market reform	–		–		-0.011	-0.51	–	
Partisanship	0.020	0.63	-0.101**	-3.08	0.062*	2.15	0.064*	2.22
Partisanship × sophistication	0.017	1.70	-0.014	-1.07	0.029*	1.99	-0.004	-0.43
Retrospective PFS	0.144**	3.77	0.290**	5.75	0.581**	9.57	–	
Retrospect. PFS × sophistication	0.012	0.63	0.003	0.14	-0.071*	-2.11	–	
Media usage	-0.078**	-3.02	0.099**	2.67	0.095*	2.48	0.007	0.53
Political sophistication	-0.054*	-2.28	0.087	1.38	0.317**	5.34	0.003	0.14
Education	0.025	1.94	0.037	1.51	0.038	1.28	0.008	0.65
Family income	0.018	1.69	0.039	1.31	0.0004	0.02	0.019	1.12
Professional/self-employed	-0.12	-1.88	0.004	0.05	0.01	0.08	–	
Manual worker	-0.07	-1.14	-0.11	-0.46	-0.01	-0.08	–	
Social class	–		–		–		0.13**	4.22
Union membership	-0.10*	-2.04	-0.05	-0.63	–		0.30	1.87
Age	-0.0053**	-2.28	0.0082**	4.61	-0.0025	-1.31	-0.0051**	-2.74
Ethnicity (French/Black)	-0.32**	-5.54	-0.04	-0.54	–		–	
Female	-0.25**	-5.13	-0.16**	-2.93	-0.17**	-2.85	-0.08	-1.46
Constant	1.00**	6.62	1.23**	5.58	0.22	1.11	2.26**	8.34
μ_1	0.98**	32.78	0.87**	15.49	0.99**	21.56	0.74**	6.88
μ_2	2.10**	45.01	2.29**	34.81	1.89**	33.94	2.56**	21.57
μ_3	3.41**	27.06	3.68**	47.50	4.40**	28.52	3.99**	32.56
χ^2-Statistic of overall model	228.7**		383.6**		490.8**		65.2**	
χ^2-Statistic of base model	197.0**		287.1**		455.1**		55.8**	
N	2295		1697		1482		1754	

Notes

See notes to Tables 7.1(a,b). ** $p < 0.01$; * $p < 0.05$.

Table 7.5 Prospective national economic evaluations in Canada (1993), USA (1996), and Hungary (1997) with economic policy controls (ordered probit regression)

Explanatory variables	Canada, 1993		USA, 1996		Hungary, 1997	
	Coeff.	T-stat.	Coeff.	T-stat.	Coeff.	T-stat.
Government regulation of economy	–		−0.014	−1.38	0.029	1.60
Phillips curve trade-off	−0.037	−1.47	−0.003	−0.13	−0.010	−0.23
Market reform	–		–		−0.016	−0.66
Partisanship	−0.045	−1.58	−0.104**	−3.16	0.070**	2.59
Partisanship × political sophistication	0.032**	2.93	0.004	0.28	0.013	0.95
Prospective personal financial situation	0.356**	6.75	0.446**	7.62	0.733**	11.75
Prospective PFS×political sophistication	−0.014	−0.42	−0.042	−1.68	−0.077*	−2.35
Media usage	0.053	1.86	0.037	0.95	0.063	1.58
Political sophistication	0.050	1.02	0.136	1.79	0.310**	4.30
Education	0.002	0.22	−0.035	−1.33	0.025	0.80
Family income	−0.003	−0.34	−0.050	−1.58	0.058*	2.43
Professional/self-employed	−0.06	−0.89	0.11	1.45	0.25	1.95
Manual worker	−0.08	−1.19	−0.03	−0.13	−0.06	−0.71
Union membership	−0.11*	−2.05	−0.08	−1.10	–	
Age	0.0034*	2.04	0.0041*	2.10	0.0043*	2.20
Ethnicity (French/Black)	0.03	0.51	0.12	1.51	–	
Female	−0.10*	−2.11	−0.07	−1.19	−0.03	−0.51
Constant	−0.08	0.45	1.34**	5.70	0.11	0.51
μ_1	1.51**	41.60	0.91**	13.38	1.13**	15.85
μ_2	–		2.83**	36.56	2.38**	30.30
μ_3	–		4.03**	42.91	5.03**	34.26
χ^2-Statistic of overall model	183.2**		207.1**		472.9**	
χ^2-Statistic of base model	152.6**		176.5**		463.8**	
N	2211		1683		1417	

Notes
See notes to Table 7.2. ** $p < 0.01$; * $p < 0.05$.

economy. See the Statistical Appendix for details on the coding and construction of the economy policy measures.

It is clear from Tables 7.4 and 7.5 that including economic policy measures does not alter our conclusions about the extent of subjective heterogeneity in economic evaluations. Comparisons across the two sets of models reveal few changes – almost all the significant factors in Tables 7.1(a, b) and 7.2 still prove significant in Tables 7.4 and 7.5. The constancy across models is most concisely demonstrated by the χ^2 (LR)-statistics of base model reported in Tables 7.4 and 7.5. The base model is defined as the set of explanatory variables used in the corresponding model from Tables 7.1(a,b) and 7.2. These statistics test the null hypothesis that the (base model) sources of subjective heterogeneity, when considered together, are not jointly significant. We would expect this null hypothesis to hold if our conclusion from the first stage of our analysis was incorrect, i.e. if the evidence of subjective heterogeneity was spurious due to the omission of economic policy preferences from the model. Comparison of these statistics with the χ^2-statistics of overall model in Tables 7.1(a,b) and 7.2 indicates the extent to which the importance of subjective heterogeneity has changed as a result of controlling for policy preferences. This comparison reveals that the statistical significance of the sources of subjective heterogeneity changes little across model specifications. In sum, this more conservative test of the null hypothesis increases our confidence in the conclusion that evaluations of the national economy are not purely objective and instead are plagued by measurement bias attributable to personal experiences, partisan attitudes, information, and group self-interest.

7.5   CONCLUSION

It is widely accepted that aggregation of individual-level economic evaluations produces a good measure of citizens' average perception of economic performance because individual-level "noise" – or measurement error – in public opinion is largely, if not entirely, random and thus "cancels out" when aggregated. For this reason, some argue that macrolevel models of economic voting tend to perform better than their microlevel counterparts. In this chapter, we explore the validity of this argument by investigating the importance of information differences and subjective considerations as a source of individual-level variation in economic evaluations.

We estimate individual-level models of both prospective and retrospective economic evaluations in five countries – the United States, West Germany, Canada, Hungary, and the Netherlands. Our individual-level results confirm what most believe: voters' assessments of economic performance only approximate objective economic conditions. But contrary to what some might believe, distorted individual-level perceptions of economic performance are not plagued by random noise alone. Rather, our individual-level statistical analysis provides fairly conclusive evidence that how people view economic performance is shaped by their political predispositions, personal financial experiences, socioeconomic situation, and level of understanding about the political economy. Moreover, this result holds even when the model controls for objective, policy-related sources of variation in economic evaluations.

To the extent that assessments of economic performance reflect information differences and subjective considerations (e.g. the better informed tend to be more optimistic about the economy), national economic evaluations are not entirely exogenous in equations explaining vote choice and government support. Furthermore, if the net effects of information differences and subjective considerations do not "cancel out" across individuals, as previous research has shown (Duch *et al.*, 2000), this heterogeneity produces systematic measurement (error) biases in aggregated evaluation series. The presence of these systematic biases implies that aggregation is not a panacea for the statistical problems associated with individual-level "noise" in survey data. Thus, aggregate-level models of the economic-voting relationship cannot rely on aggregation as a means of escaping misleading statistical inferences due to measurement error.

Our results clearly indicate that the subjective factors shaping economic perceptions at the individual level vary considerably from one country to the next. For example, partisanship and media influences seem to matter much more in some countries than in others. This of course suggests that the extent of systematic biases in aggregated evaluation series will vary cross-nationally. For example, it might be the case that in some countries media exposure significantly exaggerates negative economic outcomes, while in other countries it has little impact. This suggests us a potential new direction for understanding cross-national variations in aggregate economic voting results. Traditionally, the literature has explored institutional explanations for cross-national variations in economic voting ("clarity-of-responsibility" explanations, for example). The results reported here suggest that it might be useful to explore factors that directly shape the manner in which individuals get information about the economy. It would appear, for example, that in some contexts such as the United States and Hungary partisan cues about the economy are more prevalent than in other national contexts. Similarly, the media seems to play a particularly important role in shaping information about the economy in the United States and Hungary, but to a lesser extent in Canada and apparently not at all in Germany. A better understanding of how these different agents shape subjective perceptions of the economy may significantly contribute to our understanding of cross-national differences in economic voting.

STATISTICAL APPENDIX

This section reports the coding of the explanatory variables in the ordered probit models presented in Tables 7.1(a,b)–7.5 and in the factor analyses presented in Tables 7.7–7.9. These variables were constructed with survey data from the 1990 German Election Study (Forschungsgruppe 1994),[14] The 1993 Canadian Election Study,[15] the 1996 ANES,[16] The 1997 Hungarian Markets and Democracy Study,[17] and the 1998 Dutch Election Study.[18] See the study codebooks for further details on question format. Whenever possible, we adopted the same coding across countries. Missing values were set to the sample means to avoid losing observations. Table 7.6 reports descriptive statistics.

Partisanship measures the strength of the respondent's attachment to the incumbent party. For the United States, *partisanship* ranges from 0 for strong Democrats to 6 for strong Republicans. For Canada, West Germany, Hungary, and the Netherlands, *partisanship* is the product of *party attachment* and *strength of party attachment*. For Canada and West Germany, *party attachment* is coded 1 for respondents stating that they feel close to a government party, −1 for those stating that they feel close to an opposition party, and 0 otherwise (e.g. do not feel close to any party). For Hungary and the Netherlands, *party attachment* is coded similarly on the basis of the respondent's vote intention. *Strength of party attachment* measures how closely respondents feel to the party for which they stated an attachment (vote intention) and ranges from 1 to 5 for West Germany and Hungary, from 1 to 3 for Canada, and from 1 to 4 for the Netherlands.

Retrospective personal financial situation (PFS) measures respondents' evaluations of their personal financial situations compared to a year ago. While the question wording varies somewhat across countries, the coding ranges from 0 for "much worse" to 4 for "much better" for the United States, Canada, and Hungary, and from 0 for "worse" to 2 for "better" for West Germany. PFS measures respondents' expectations about their future personal finances 1 year ahead. While the question wording varies somewhat across countries, the coding ranges from 0 to 4 for the United States, Canada, and Hungary, and from 0 to 2 for West Germany (with category labels analogous to those above). The Dutch survey does not include retrospective and prospective questions on personal financial situation.

Media usage measures the respondent's level of exposure to political information in the mass media. For the United States, *media usage* is the sum of *television news* and *newspaper usage*, both divided by 7, and *campaign media*, divided by 4. For Canada, *media usage* is the sum of *television news*, *newspaper usage*, and *radio news*, divided by 7. *Television news, newspaper usage* and *radio news* are the numbers of days per week (0–7) that the respondent watches the national news on television, reads a newspaper, and listens to news on the radio, respectively. *Campaign media* is the number of media sources – radio, newspapers, magazines, and television – from which the respondent learnt about the election campaign, divided by 4. For Hungary, *media usage* is the sum of coded responses to three questions on media consumption, divided by 4. The three questions ask respondents how often they watch television news, listen to radio news, and read newspapers/magazines. Responses to these questions were coded from 0 for "hardly ever" to 4 for "every day." For the Netherlands, *media usage* was constructed from three questions on how frequently the

Table 7.6 Descriptive statistics for the explanatory variables used in the ordered probit models and factor analyses

Explanatory variables	West Germany		Canada		USA		Hungary		The Netherlands	
	Mean	Std. Dev.	Mean	Std. Dev.	Mean	Std. Dev.	Mean	Std. Dev.	Mean	Std. Dev.
Partisanship	-0.29	2.95	-0.52	1.52	2.68	2.09	-0.06	2.49	0.19	1.69
Partisanship × political sophistication	-0.53	5.85	-1.16	3.85	6.32	6.44	0.09	5.11	0.32	4.92
Retrospective personal financial situation	1.50	0.65	1.64	1.11	2.22	1.06	1.50	0.90	–	
Retrospective PFS × political sophistication	2.76	1.88	3.41	3.13	5.00	3.47	2.45	2.31	–	
Prospective personal financial situation	0.93	0.61	2.13	0.88	2.38	0.84	1.95	0.87	–	
Prospective PFS × political sophistication	1.72	1.49	4.43	3.04	5.32	3.24	3.14	2.59	–	
Media usage	–		1.65	0.83	1.43	0.83	1.18	0.82	4.66	2.10
Political sophistication	–		2.09	1.08	2.24	1.05	1.56	0.97	1.85	1.61
Education	1.78	0.83	5.08	2.09	3.02	1.50	2.07	1.31	4.21	2.69
Family income	–		3.19	2.55	1.87	1.07	1.97	1.46	7.01	3.27
Social class	–		–		–		–		1.79	0.96
Age	6.06	2.59	42.3	15.4	47.4	17.3	47.8	17.7	44.7	16.2
Government regulation of economy	–		–		10.28	3.14	0.35	1.82	4.81	2.63
Phillips curve trade-off	–		1.30	1.05	1.77	1.49	3.40	1.32	4.33	1.12
Market reform	–		–		–		0.62	0.68	–	
% of cases for										
Professional/self-employed	15.8		22.8		33.5		7.5		–	
Manual worker	69.0		16.6	1.5	67.9		–			
Union membership	29.4		31.9		17.3		–		96.6	
Ethnicity (French/Black)	–		21.6		11.8		–		–	
Female	50.9		48.9		55.0		54.3		50.1	

respondent watches three television news broadcasts (NOS TV, RTL4 TV, and NOVA). Coded responses to these questions, ranging from 0 for less than once a week to 3 for daily, were summed. Hence, *media usage* ranges from 0 to 9 for the Netherlands and from 0 to 3 for the United States, Canada, and Hungary. The West German survey does not includes a measure of mass media exposure.

For the United States, Canada, and Hungary, *political sophistication* is the interviewer's evaluation of the respondent's general level of inform-ation about politics, ranging from 0 for "very low" to 4 for "very high." For the Netherlands, *political sophistication* ranges from 0 to 5 and is the average of two political knowledge variables included in the Dutch survey. The first variable measures the respondent's ability to identify pictures of leading Dutch politicians. The second measures the respondent's ability to correctly answer a series of questions about Dutch politics (e.g. which parties are in the governing coalition). The West German survey does not includes a question on the respondent's level of political information and so we replaced *political sophistication* with *education* for the purpose of creating interaction terms.

Education is a categorical measure of the respondent's education level. For the United States, *education* is coded from 0 for 8 grades or less to 5 for BA-level degree or better. For the Netherlands, *education* ranges from 0 for elementary or less to 9 for university. Similarly, for the other countries, *education* measures the respondent's highest level of education, ranging from 0 to 10 for Canada, 0 to 3 for West Germany, and 0 to 5 for Hungary.

Family income is a categorical measure of household income. For the United States, *family income* is coded from 0 for incomes in the 0–16 per-centile to 4 for incomes in the 96–100 percentile. For Canada, the coding ranges from 0 for less than $20,000 to 9 for greater than $100,000. For Hungary, the coding ranges from 0 for 30,000 Ft/month or less to 5 for 101,000 Ft/month or more. For the Netherlands, the coding ranges from 0 for less than 17,000 to 11 for 73,000 or more. The West German survey does not includes a measure of personal or household income.

Professional and *manual worker* are binary variables denoting whether the respondent is employed in a professional or manual labor occupation, respectively. For Hungary, *professional* denotes identification with the "intelligentsia" since the survey did not distinguish among non-manual occupations in terms of whether they were professional or white-collar. The Dutch survey did not include occupation categories equivalent to pro-fessional and manual labor, and so *social class* was used instead. *Social class* measures respondents' self-image of their social class, ranging from 0 for "working class" to 4 for "upper class." *Union membership* is a binary variable coded 1 if the respondent or a family member belongs to a labor union. The Hungarian survey does not includes a question on union membership.

The analysis also includes several demographic variables. *Age* is the respondent's age in years for the United States, Canada, Hungary, and the Netherlands. For West Germany, *age* is a categorical variable ranging from 1 for 18–20 years to 10 for 70 years and older. *Ethnicity* (Black/French) is a binary variable coded 1 for African-American respondents in the United States and French respondents in Canada. *Female* is a binary variable coded 1 for women.

Government regulation of economy, *Phillips curve trade-off*, and *market reform* are measures of the respondent's economic policy preferences. For Canada, *Phillips curve trade-off* is the coded response to a question on whether or not the government should increase spending to reduce unemployment, ranging from 0 for strongest unemployment concern to 4 for strongest spending/inflation concern. For the United States, Hungary, and the Netherlands, these measures are factor scales constructed with the factor analysis results presented in Tables 7.7–7.9.[19]

The United States factor analysis (Table 7.7) includes several variables designed to capture economic policy preferences: *environmental regulation, guaranteed job, ideology, isolationism, jobs/environment, government regulation, reduce federal budget deficit*, and *reduce federal taxation*. *Environmental regulation* ranges from 1 for "tougher regulations needed to protect the environment" to 7 for "regulations to protect environment already too much of a burden on business." *Guaranteed job* ranges from 1 for "government should see to a job and good standard of living" to 7 for "government should let each person get ahead on own." *Ideology* ranges from 1 for "extremely liberal" to 7 for "extremely conservative." *Isolationism* ranges from −2 for "opposing new limits on foreign imports and tolerating greater immigration" to 2 for "favoring new limits on imports and a large decrease in immigration". *Jobs/environment* ranges from 1 for "protect environment, even if it costs jobs, standard of living" to 7 for "jobs, standard of living more important than environment." *Government*

Table 7.7 Factor analysis for economic policy measures, United States, 1996

Factors	Loadings	
	Government regulation of economy	Phillips curve trade-off
Environmental regulation	0.730	0.136
Guaranteed job	0.643	−0.240
Ideology	0.733	0.118
Isolationism	−0.019	0.521
Jobs/environment	0.543	0.409
Reduce federal budget deficit	0.385	−0.743
Reduce federal taxation	0.451	0.515
Reduce government regulation	0.698	−0.272
Eigenvalue	2.62	1.42
Percent of variance explained	32.7	17.7

Table 7.8 Factor analysis for economic policy measures, Hungary, 1997

Factors	Loadings		
	Government regulation of economy	Market reform	Phillips curve trade-off
Market economy	−0.543	−0.014	−0.025
Guaranteed jobs	0.781	0.187	0.037
Price controls	0.796	0.187	0.046
Inflation concern	0.190	−0.073	0.790
Unemployment concern	0.344	0.026	−0.741
Reduce spending on health care	−0.227	0.771	0.016
Reduce spending on pensions	−0.216	0.793	−0.016
Reduce spending on unemployment insurance	0.142	0.342	0.181
Eigenvalue	1.81	1.42	1.21
Percent of variance explained	22.6	17.7	15.1

Table 7.9 Factor analysis results for economic policy measures, the Netherlands, 1998

Factors	Loadings	
	Government regulation of economy	Phillips curve trade-off
Importance of unemployment	−0.444	0.387
Inflation priority	−0.166	0.872
Left–Right ideology	0.702	0.323
Level of social benefits	0.657	0.037
Income differences	0.694	0.093
Eigenvalue	1.63	1.02
Percent of variance explained	32.7	20.5

regulation was constructed from two questions about the scope of government and ranges from −1 for "need a stronger government that is doing more things" to 1 for "less government is better and free market can handle today's economic problems".

Reduce federal budget deficit and *reduce federal taxation* were constructed from a series of questions about trade offs among federal budget deficit, taxes, and spending on domestic programs. *Reduce federal budget deficit* ranges from −2 for "increase budget deficit to cut taxes and increase spending" to 2 for "increase taxes and cut spending to decrease budget deficit". *Reduce federal taxation* ranges from −2 for "increase taxes to increase spending and reduce budget deficit" to 2 for "cut spending and increase budget deficit to cut taxes".

The Hungary factor analysis (Table 7.8) includes: *market economy, guaranteed jobs, price controls, inflation concern, unemployment concern, reduce spending on health care, reduce spending on pensions,* and *reduce spending on unemployment insurance. Market economy* ranges from 1 for "the state should play an important role in controlling the market economy" to 10 for "the state should not control the market economy." *Guaranteed jobs* was constructed from two questions about the state's intervention in the labor market. This measure ranges from 0 for "respondents who fully disagree" to 2 for "those who fully agree" with the following two statements: (1) the state should secure work for everybody needing it, and (2) the number of jobs available will increase if the state restricts the number of employees that firms can layoff.

Price controls was constructed from two questions about the state's intervention in the market for goods and services to control prices and ranges from 0 to 2. At the low end are respondents who fully disagree with the statement that "If the government did not regulate the prices enterprises may set for their products, prices will go loose," and choose the opinion that "It is better if we can choose from many goods and services, even if their prices are high and uncontrolled." At the high end are respondents who fully agree with the statement above about government-regulated prices and choose the opinion that "It is better if there are less goods and smaller variety but the prices are low and controlled by the state."

Inflation concern and *unemployment concern* were constructed from two questions asking respondents to rank different economic problems and policy outcomes and ranges from 0 to 2. At the high end of *inflation concern* are respondents who: (1) ranked the headline that "The inflation rate has been decreasing in Hungary for two years," as the most favorable for the country among four economic news headlines, and (2) choose "rising prices" as the most important concern from among four national economic problems. At the low end are respondents who: (1) ranked the inflation headline as the least favorable for the country, and (2) did not choose "rising prices" as an important concern (i.e. not selected as first or second choice). At the high end of *unemployment concern* are respondents who: (1) ranked the headline that "Today the Hungarian Prime Minister announced in Parliament that in this year the level of unemployment is the lowest in the last 5 years," as the most favorable for the country, and (2) choose "increase of unemployment rate" as the most important national economic concern. At the low end are respondents who: (1) ranked the unemployment headline as the least favorable for the country, and (2) did not choose "increase of unemployment rate" as an important concern.

Reduce spending on health care ranges from 1 for "respondents who fully disagree" to 5 for "those who fully agree" with the statement that "To complete the economic reforms, the government should reduce its expenses on health care." Similarly, *reduce spending on pensions* and *reduce spending on unemployment insurance* were constructed from analogous questions posing a trade-off between economic reform and government spending on pensions and unemployment benefits. These measures also range from 1 to 5, with 5 representing full agreement with reducing government spending to ensure the success of economic reform.

The Netherlands factor analysis (Table 7.9) includes: *importance of unemployment, inflation priority, Left–Right ideology, level of social benefits,* and *income differences. Importance of unemployment* was coded according to how respondents evaluated unemployment as a national concern, ranging from 1 for "very unimportant" to 10 for "very important". *Inflation priority* was constructed from the standard question on postmaterialist priorities and ranges from 0 for respondents who did not select "fight rising prices" as a first or second priority to 2 for those who selected this political goal as the first priority. *Left–Right ideology* was coded according to the respondent's self-placement on an 11-point scale ranging from 0 for "left" to 10 for "right." *Level of social benefits* captures the respondent's position on the level of social benefits and ranges from 1 for "much too low" to 7 for "much too high." *Income differences* represents the respondent's position on the issue of income differences and ranges from 1 for "larger differences" to 7 for "smaller differences."

ACKNOWLEDGMENT

We thank Harold Clarke and Guy Whitten for helpful comments and Leesa Boeger and Vanessa Baird for research assistance. This research was generously supported by Duch's NSF Grant No. SBR 9600306.

NOTES

1 For further discussion of this dichotomy, see Lewis-Beck (1988) and Nannestad and Paldam (1994).
2 This expectation is consistent with the findings of Hetherington (1996) and Nadeau *et al.* (1999), though their research focuses exclusively on the American case.
3 The focus here is on the existence of a systematic effect rather than its direction.
4 It also seems plausible that individuals who are more insulated from changes in national economic conditions (e.g. union members, welfare recipients, and more affluent respondents) are generally more positive about them.
5 Unfortunately, the 1993 Canadian NES only included one economic policy question, which dealt with the relative importance of unemployment and inflation. See Statistical Appendix for further details on the construction of the economic policy measures.
6 The 1998 Dutch NES did not include a measure of prospective evaluations of the national economy.

7 When calculating the marginal probability effect of a non-binary variable, we assume that typical respondents initially have the variable's mean value. For binary variables, we assume that typical respondents have the modal characteristic denoted by the variable (e.g. no family member belongs to a union).

8 *Retrospective personal financial situation* ranges from "much worse" to "much better" in Canada, the United States, and Hungary, but only from "worse" to "better" in West Germany.

9 The prospective model for West Germany represents the other exception.

10 For the United States, a one-unit increase in partisan attachment to the government constitutes a one-unit decrease in partisanship since Democrat Bill Clinton was President in 1996 and partisanship ranges from 0 for "strong Democrats" to 6 for "strong Republicans". Also, the estimated effect for Canada is trivial in magnitude (0.1 points) as well as statistically insignificant.

11 The evidence of an interactive effect with *political sophistication* is generally weak. The exceptions are the retrospective model for Hungary and the prospective model for Canada. In both these models, as expected, the estimated effect of partisanship on economic evaluations increases with the respondent's level of political knowledge. This finding is broadly consistent with Zaller's (1992) hypothesis that information has a polarizing effect on the attitudes of individuals with strong political predispositions.

12 The only notable exception here is the effect of political attitudes on prospective evaluations in West Germany, which only prove significant at the 10 per cent level.

13 Tables 7.4 and 7.5 do not report models for West Germany since the 1990 West German election study did not include questions that could serve as reliable proxies for economic policy preferences.

14 Forschungsgruppe Wahlen (Mannheim). GERMAN ELECTION STUDY, 1990 [Computer file]. Köln, West Germany: Zentralarchiv für empirische Sozialforschung [producer], 1993. Köln, West Germany: Zentralarchiv fuer empirische Sozialforschung and Ann Arbor, MI: Interuniversity Consortium for Political and Social Research [distributors], 1994.

15 Data from the 1993 Canadian Election Study were provided by the Institute for Social Research, York University. The survey was funded by the Social Sciences and Humanities Research Council of Canada (SSHRC), Grant Nos. 411-92-0019 and 421-92-0026, and was completed for the 1992/1993 Canadian Election Team of Richard Johnston (University of British Columbia), Andre Blais (Universite de Montreal), Henry Brady (University of California at Berkeley), Elisabeth Gidengil (McGill University), and Neil Nevitte (University of Calgary). Neither the Institute for Social Research, the SSHRC, nor the Canadian Election Team is responsible for the analyses and interpretations presented here.

16 Warren E. Miller, Donald R. Kinder, Steven J. Rosenstone, and the National Election Studies, 1993, *American National Election Study, 1992: Pre- and Post-Election Survey* [Enhanced with 1990 and 1991 data; computer file]. Conducted by the University of Michigan, Center for Political Studies. ICPSR ed. Ann Arbor: University of Michigan, Center for Political Studies, and Interuniversity Consortium for Political and Social Research [producers]. Ann Arbor: Interuniversity Consortium for Political and Social Research [distributor].

17 The 1997 Hungarian Markets and Democracy Study was funded by Raymond Duch's NSF Grant No. SBR-4600-306. The survey questionnaire was designed by Raymond Duch, and translated and administered by TARKI. The survey sample includes 1544 respondents, interviewed from 26 November to

8 December. It is a probability sample, selected in multiple stages without proportional stratification. In the first stage, localities were divided into eight strata and then 71 localities were selected from these strata with simple probability sampling. In the second stage, the number of the individuals to be sampled from each strata was set according to the proportion of the adult population in that strata. These proportions were modified according to the presumed dropout rate, which was derived with 1996 Census characteristics. For further details, see the markets and democracy website: http://crystal. cpp.uh.edu/uhdps/markets.

18 Aarts, Kees, Henk van der Kolk, and Marlies Kamp. DUTCH PARLIAMEN-TARY ELECTION STUDY, 1998 [Computer file]. ICPSR version. Amsterdam, the Netherlands: NIWI-Steinmetz Archive/Dutch Electoral Research Foundation (SKON) [producers], 1999. Amsterdam, the Netherlands: NIWI-Steinmetz Archive/Köln, Germany: Zentralarchiv fuer Empirische Sozialforschung/Ann Arbor, MI: Interuniversity Consortium for Political and Social Research [distributors], 1999.

19 Extraction method was principal components with no rotation.

REFERENCES

Althaus, S. (1998) Information effects in collective preferences. *Am. Political Sci. Rev.*, **92**, 545–558.

Bartels, L.M. (1996) Uninformed votes: information effects in presidential elections. *Am. J. Political Sci.*, **40**, 194–230.

Brody, R.A. and Sniderman, P.M. (1977) From life space to polling place: the relevance of personal concerns for voting behavior. *Brit. J. Political Sci.*, **7**, 337–360.

Budge, I., Crewe, I. and Farlie, D. (eds) (1976) *Party Identification and Beyond.* New York: Wiley.

Clarke, H.D. and Stewart, M.C. (1994) Prospections, retrospections and rationality: the 'bankers' model of presidential approval reconsidered. *Am. J. Political Sci.*, **38**, 1104–1123.

Clarke, H.D., Stewart, M.C. and Whiteley, P.F. (1998) New models for new labour: the political economy of Labour Party support, January 1992–April 1997. *Am. Political Sci. Rev.*, **92**, 559–575.

Conover, P.J., Feldman, S. and Knight, K. (1986) Judging inflation and unemployment: the origins of retrospective evaluations. *J. Politics*, **48**, 565–588.

Conover, P.J., Feldman, S. and Knight, K. (1987) The personal and political underpinnings of economic forecasts. *Am. J. of Political Sci.*, **31**, 559–583.

Converse, P.E. (1990) Popular representation and the distribution of information. In J.A. Ferejohn and J.H. Kuklinski (eds), *Information and Democratic Processes.* Urbana, IL: University of Illinois Press.

Dalton, R.J. (1988) *Citizen Politics: Public Opinion and Political Parties in Advanced Industrial Democracies*, 2nd ed. Chatham, NJ: Chatham House Publishers.

Delli Carpini, M.X. and Keeter, S. (1996) *What Americans Know about Politics and Why It Matters.* New Haven, CT: Yale University Press.

Duch, R. (2001) A developmental model of heterogeneous economic voting in new democracies. *Am. Political Sci. Rev.*, **95**, 895–910.

Duch, R., Palmer, H. and Anderson, C. (2000) Heterogeneity in perceptions of national economic conditions. *Am. J. Political Sci.*, **44**(4), 635–652.

Feldman, S. (1985) Economic self-interest and political behavior. *Am. J. Political Sci.*, **26**, 446–466.

Fiorina, M. (1978) Economic retrospective voting in American national elections: a micro-analysis. *Am. J. Political Sci.*, **22**, 426–443.

Fiorina, M. (1981) *Retrospective Voting in American National Elections*. New Haven, CT: Yale University Press.

Funk, C.L. and Garcia-Monet, P. (1997) The relationship between personal and national concerns in public perceptions about the economy. *Political Res. Quart.*, **50**, 317–342.

Greene, W.H. (2000) *Econometric Analysis*, 4th edn. Upper Saddle River, NJ: Prentice-Hall.

Haller, B.H. and Norpoth, H. (1994) Let the good times roll: the economic expectations of US voters. *Am. J. Political Sci.*, **38**, 625–650.

Hetherington, M.J. (1996) The media's role in forming voters' retrospective economic evaluations in 1992. *Am. J. Political Sci.*, **40**, 372–395.

Kinder, D.R. and Kiewiet, D.R. (1979) Economic grievances and political behavior: the role of personal discontents and collective judgments in congressional voting. *Am. J. Political Sci.*, **23**, 495–527.

Kramer, G.H. (1971) Short-term fluctuations in US voting behavior, 1896–1964. *Am. Political Sci. Rev.*, **65**, 131–143.

Kramer, G.H. (1983) The ecological fallacy revisited: aggregate vs. individual-level findings on economics and elections, and sociotropic voting. *Am. Political Sci. Rev.*, **65**, 131–143.

Krause, G.A. (1997) Voters, information heterogeneity, and the dynamics of aggregate economic expectations. *Am. J. Political Sci.*, **41**, 170–200.

Lewis-Beck, M.S. (1988) *Economics and Elections: The Major Western Democracies*. Ann Arbor, MI: University of Michigan Press.

Lupia, A. (1992) Busy voters, agenda control, and the power of information. *Am. Political Sci. Rev.*, **86**, 390–403.

Lupia, A. (1994) Shortcuts versus encyclopedias: information and voting behavior in california insurance reform elections. *Am. Political Sci. Rev.*, **88**, 63–76.

Macdonald, K. and Heath, A. (1997) Pooling cross-sections: a comment on Price and Sanders. *Political Stud.*, **45**, 928–941.

MacKuen, M.B. and Mouw, C. (1995) Class and competence in the political economy. University of Missouri, St. Louis.

MacKuen, M.B., Erikson, R.S. and Stimson, J.A. (1992) Peasants or bankers? The American electorate and the US economy. *Am. Political Sci. Rev.*, **86**, 597–611.

Markus, G.B. (1988) The impact of personal and national economic conditions on the presidential vote: a pooled cross-sectional analysis. *Am. J. Political Sci.*, **32**, 137–154.

Mutz, D.C. (1992) Mass media and the depoliticization of personal experience. *Am. J. Political Sci.*, **36**, 483–508.

Mutz, D.C. (1994) Contextualizing personal experience: the role of mass media. *J. Politics*, **56**, 689–714.

Nadeau, R., Niemi, R.G., Fan, D.P. and Amato, T. (1999) Elite economic forecasts, economic news, mass economic judgments, and presidential approval. *J. Politics*, **61**, 109–135.

Nadeau, R., Niemi, R.G. and Yoshinaka, A. (2002) A cross-national analysis of economic voting: taking account of the political context across time and nations. *Electoral Stud.*, **21**, forthcoming.

Nannestad, P. and Paldam, M. (1994) The VP function: a survey of the literature on vote and popularity functions after 25 years. *Public Choice*, **79**, 213–245.

Norpoth, H. (1996) Presidents and the prospective voter. *J. Politics*, **58**, 776–792.

Page, B.I. and Shapiro, R.Y. (1992) *The Rational Public*. Chicago, IL: University of Chicago Press.

Palmer, H.D. and Whitten, G.D. (1999) The electoral impacts of unexpected inflation and economic growth. *Brit. J. Political Sci.*, **29**, 623–639.

Powell Jr., B., Allen Jr., H.M. and Whitten, G.D. (1993) A cross-national analysis of economic voting: taking account of the political context. *Am. J. Political Sci.*, **37**, 391–414.

Sears, D.O., Lau, R.R., Tyler, T.R. and Allen Jr., H.M. (1980) Self-interest versus symbolic politics in policy attitudes and presidential voting. *Am. Political Sci. Rev.*, **74**, 670–684.

Sniderman, P.M. and Brody, R.A. (1977) Coping: the ethic of self-reliance. *Am. J. Political Sci.*, **21**, 501–521.

Sniderman, P.M., Brody, R.A. and Tetlock, P.E. (1991) *Reasoning and Choice: Explorations in Political Psychology*. New York: Cambridge University Press.

Stimson, J.A., MacKuen, M.B. and Erikson, R.S. (1995) Dynamic representation. *Am. Political Sci. Rev.*, **89**, 543–565.

Weatherford, M.S. (1983) Economic voting and the 'symbolic politics' argument: a reinterpretation and synthesis. *Am. Political Sci. Rev.*, **77**, 158–174.

Whitten, G.D. and Palmer, H.D. (1999) Cross-national analyses of economic voting. *Electoral Stud.*, **18**, 49–67.

Wlezien, C., Franklin, M.N. and Twiggs, D. (1997) Economic perceptions and vote choice: disentangling the endogeneity. *Political Behav.*, **19**, 7–17.

Zaller, J.R. (1992) *The Nature and Origins of Mass Opinion*. New York: Cambridge University Press.

8 Economic voting in subnational government

Catalonian evidence

Clara Riba and Aida Díaz

8.1 ECONOMICS, POLITICS, AND THE ATTRIBUTION OF RESPONSIBILITIES TO SUBNATIONAL GOVERNMENTS

In the late 1960s, it became a common journalistic assumption that economic factors play an important role in determining government popularity. In March 1968, Harold Wilson asserted that "all political history shows that the standing of the government depends on the success of its economic policy" (Heath *et al.*, 1991, p. 159). The notion of some kind of link between economic conditions and government support is firmly established within the scientific community, and the literature dealing with it has grown considerably.[1] Most popularity functions assume the classical "reward–punishment" model of the type suggested by Key (1968). It is simple: if economic conditions are good, so the most common argument goes, the electorate will reward incumbents, while it will punish them if economic conditions are less than satisfactory. The implicit assumption behind this statement is that the government is directly responsible for economic conditions. Butler and Stokes argued that government responsibility for the economy is a fundamental assumption in the dialogue between parties and the electorate.

> Modern electorates tend to solve [the] problem of causal reasoning by assuming that certain causal relationships must exist rather than by discerning what they are. Electors focus their attention primarily on certain conditions, which they value positively or negatively and simply assume that past or future governments affect them. The public can call for a government's dismissal in economic hard times just as it calls for a team manager's dismissal in a losing season, in each case concluding that causal relationships must exist without knowing in detail what they are (Butler and Stokes, 1976: 25).

This hypothesis contrasts with the strict notion of rationality that would consider that voters differentiate between changes attributable to the government and those caused by other factors. For instance, Spanish citizens attribute the current rise in oil prices to the oil companies. Considering that the crisis is affecting the majority of Western economies, they regard it as a factor over which the government has no influence.[2] In this case, voters do find it unreasonable to blame the government for such a situation.

One of the assumptions that lies behind the reward–punishment hypothesis is that there is a "clarity of responsibilities" in terms of which party (or parties) is (are) responsible for macroeconomic policy and performance (Powell and Whitten, 1993). Without clarity of responsibility, there is no reason that there should be any correlation between party support patterns and the economy. A second assumption behind the hypothesis is the existence of a viable and credible opposition of which citizens may approve or vote for if they do not like the incumbent party's performance (Sanders and Carey, this volume; Fraile, this volume). If, for whatever reasons, voters believe that the opposition fails to offer a credible alternative to the incumbent party, then, regardless of the political image of the incumbent, macroeconomic performance need not necessarily damage the government (Sanders, 2000: 277–278). It turns out that the question of why and how people should attribute economic changes to the incumbent's actions remains unclear. It is questionable whether the responsibility model, which is in part based on the British parliamentary system, works in a similar way in other political contexts where political control is not in the hands of a single party.[3] Responsibility is frequently shared by competing political actors through, e.g. coalition government, or simply obscured because of multiple levels of decision making and political control (Anderson, 2000: 153). In parliamentary democracies, cases of single-party majority government are rare. Strøm (1990) demonstrates that governments shared by different parties are surprisingly common in many parliamentary democracies. In such cases of power sharing, exactly which part is responsible for the many and varied aspects of policies and legislature?

The question of assignment of responsibility has been addressed in several ways in the literature on vote and popularity functions. One of them is concerned with the effects of the political context and the consequences of dual responsibilities. Powell and Whitten (1993) and Anderson (1995) consider that the structure of credit and blame is filtered by political context. Specifically, they use some measures of institutional complexity to clarify the attribution of responsibilities. In this volume, this topic is discussed by Palmer and Whitten (Chapter 4), and Stevenson (Chapter 3) examines the electoral context from the economic perspective.

Another line of research has addressed the issue of clarity of responsibility in contexts where political power is shared or divided into several institutions. For instance, some authors have modeled popularity functions on the French case during the cohabitation period, with the President and the Prime Minister belonging to different political parties (Lewis-Beck, 1988; Lafay, 1991). Others have concentrated on the attribution of responsibilities in cases of divided government in the United States (Alesina and Rosenthal, 1995; Leyden and Borrelli, 1995).

Coalition governments or divided governments are not the only possible forms of power sharing: an additional possibility is the existence of different levels of government. In many situations, the lives of citizens are influenced not only by national governments but also by regional or state executives, whose ideology or political composition may differ from the national one. The sharing of power between national and subnational government varies greatly from country to country. Germany, with its Federal System, is characterized by the existence of Land (state) governments with substantial power and autonomy. Spain, with its 17 Autonomous Communities, provides another example of strong subnational powers, although their level of autonomy is still less than the German Länder. Italy has regional powers that were extended in the 1970s. France still has a low degree of decentralization compared with its Western partners, in spite of the decentralization laws implemented during the 1980s. Finally, the British situation seems to be changing due to the "New Labour" devolution project in which Scotland is benefiting from the decentralization of competencies. In this chapter, we address the problem of attributing responsibilities in a context of multi-level governance in Spain.

Do voters judge subnational governments on their local or regional management? It varies according to countries and types of elections. According to Jêrome and Jêrome-Speziari (2000), in Britain the national and local offices are so separated that there is no national message in local elections. Moreover, they conclude that elections of the German Länder take into account the regional, political, and economic situation, although the results imply responsibility for the Federal government; in contrast, Spanish electors seem to consider mainly local issues in subnational elections, as they are held so much in a regionalist spirit. On the French case voters seem to be less sensitive to regional economic issues than to national ones (Jêrome and Lewis-Beck, 1999; Jêrome and Jêrome-Speziari, 2000).

The classic form of government based on the asymmetrical distribution of political responsibilities, with absolute predominance of the nation-state, is being subjected to a process of redefinition. The near-monopoly rule of the nation-state is transforming into a complex institutional framework on multiple levels, with new territorial balances, often in favor of supranational or subnational levels. European politics is an interplay about a limited number of projects by coalitions of actors at three levels: the regional, national, and supranational level (Hooghe and Marks, 1997).

The political process of the European Union is a good example of this increasing complexity, as it is both a supranational institution and wants to embody the idea of the "Europe of the Regions." The transfer of power to new and powerful regional authorities has started to build new forms of European integration, where the principle of subsidiariness can be interpreted as a devolution of powers from the European institutions not to a national but to a subnational or regional level. In analyzing the territorial complexity of many European countries, we must consider two simultaneous dynamics: "Europeanization," understood as displacements of government towards the European Union and "territorialization," as movements towards regional and local governments. Both processes are happening in different dimensions of the political system: the dimension of policy making and the symbolic institutional dimensions (Brugué *et al.*, 2000). The process of regionalization can be seen, at least partly and with varying intensity, in many European countries such as the United Kingdom, Germany, Spain, Italy or even in a centralized system of government as France with its regional councils.[4]

This dynamics of transformation from single to multilevel governance will affect models of party support. It may be that the most predictable scenario for the European Union in some years to come, is that part of the power of the state-based governments will be transferred to a European supranational institution, which will then give rise to strong subnational institutions. We will have to investigate how the new configuration of institutions affects voters' electoral behavior. How do citizens cope with different decision levels? In this respect, the attribution of responsibilities is a crucial step in the decision-making process of economic voting. People must believe that economic conditions are a consequence of government policies. "The attribution of blame thus comes close to constituting a necessary condition for the subsequent politicization of economic events, in that the impact of economic perceptions on political behavior is mediated by judgments of accountability" (Peffley, 1985: 192).

This chapter aims not only to explore whether or not people attribute responsibility for economic issues to subnational governments but also to reveal the machinery of the system and show the "nuts and bolts" of it. Catalonia is a pertinent case to study for several reasons. First of all, Catalonia represents a multilevel, territorially organized system of governance. Second, it has a level of considerable autonomy from the national government. Third, previous research (Diaz, 1999; Diaz and Riba, 1999) on popularity functions demonstrates that economic variables statistically correlated with the state government's popularity exhibit the same effect on regional governments without important explicit competencies in this area.

This pattern will allow us to clarify the underlying factors that shape government support at the individual level, bringing new insights into the attribution-of-responsibilities debate. In this chapter, we first give an overview of Catalan politics, then we discuss the hypothesis underlying the process of attribution of responsibilities, and finally we present the main findings of the study performed.

8.2 AN OVERVIEW OF CATALAN POLITICS

Democracy brought a new form of territorial organization of political power in Spain, known as "Autonomous State" or "State of the Autonomies." This is undoubtedly one of the main innovations of the 1978 Spanish Constitution, which aims to solve the historical problem of articulating Spain's national and cultural plurality within a new political unit. This new form of territorial organization implies a vertical distribution of state power between the central institutions and the territorial ones, granting to each of them some competencies and resources (Fossas and Colomé, 1993). Thus, the autonomous communities are territorial entities with a legal constitutional power.[5]

The approval of the Catalan Statute of Autonomy in the 1979 referendum made it possible to hold the first autonomous elections a few months later, on 20 March 1980, turning the Catalan autonomous government into the fundamental basis and most symbolic expression of Catalan self-government.[6] Since then, six elections have been held, with five full-term governments. The autonomous elections have been the basis for the legitimization of the Catalan autonomy and for Spanish democracy itself.

The democratic and autonomous stability over a relatively long period allows us to study the regional government support in Catalonia and to depict with assurance some features of the autonomous electoral processes. The nationalist coalition Convergencia i Unió (CiU) has been in power since the first democratic elections and had an absolute majority of parliamentary seats from 1984 to 1995.[7] The hegemony of CiU in Catalan politics at the electoral level, as well as at the institutional level, can be explained by a set of factors. Among them are the following: the strength and stability of the governing coalition, the lack of an effective opposition, campaigning on strong personalities, and a "presidentialization" of Catalan politics (Vallès and Molins, 1990; Pallarès and Font, 1995).

Besides the above phenomena and connected to them, the electoral alignments and the interplay of competition have been structured in the space defined by the inter-relation of two main attitudinal axes. The left/right continuum is the main dimension of political conflict as it occurs in most of the European party systems, while the vertical axis of nationalism (or subjective national identification) expresses the conflict derived from problems related to the national integration between Catalonia and Spain. The Catalan government's political discourse adopts moderate tones in relation to nationalism, with irregular emphasis depending on the circumstances. At a socioeconomic level, the Catalan government finds itself at the center of the left/right axis, displaying a liberal point of view. Its general discourse is essentially economic, emphasizing the role of businessmen and small to medium size companies in the development of the country.[8]

The support that underlies the CiU's absolute majority at an auto-nomous level is unique compared to other types of elections in Catalonia. In fact, since the first democratic elections, the Socialist Party has won all the general elections, while the nationalist coalition party has won all the autonomous ones. The literature suggests that this discrepancy is pro-duced by the phenomena of "differential abstention" and "dual vote," which have acquired great significance in Catalan politics (Montero and Font, 1991; Riba, 2000). By differential abstention, we understand an electoral behavior consisting of voting in the general elections and abstaining in the autonomous ones; by dual vote we understand voting for different parties in different types of elections. Catalonia is the only autonomous community in Spain where such behavior takes place. The theory of the dual vote in the Spanish literature is similar to the ticket-splitting phenomenon in the United States (Beck *et al.*, 1992). This type of voting is based on the perceived differential competence of the political actors with regard to issues belonging to a specific territorial context. To consider or characterize such voting as "territorial-oriented voting" is not to imply that voters need a sophisticated understanding of policy instru-ments. Rather, it requires only that they perceive differences between parties in the amount of skill they apply in comparing Spanish and Catalan interests. In some ways territorial-oriented voting can be consid-ered as a mechanism of "checks and balances" between the central and the autonomous government. However, the vote in the Spanish autonomous elections does not resemble the so-called "barometer elections" – which may be the case for British by-elections or German Landër elections – as they are not used by the electorate to send a message of approval or disapproal to the national government.

Reconsidering the above information, the progressive recovery of self-governance over the last two decades has meant the eruption of a Catalan national perspective in policy making. Although the government of Catalonia has become an actor in policy formulation, with the Spanish state and the European Union playing highly restricted, merely selective roles, the state does maintain an important degree of centrality in the perception of its citizens (Brugué *et al.*, 2000: 3).

8.3   THE ATTRIBUTION-OF-RESPONSIBILITIES MODEL

Diaz's (1999) study on Catalan popularity functions uses aggregate monthly data from 1991 to 1995 and includes Catalan as well as Spanish data indicators. Its conclusions are that aggregate Catalan economic

Table 8.1 Aggregate effects of economic conditions on Catalan government support, 1991–1995 (regression estimators)

	Coefficient	t-Ratio (sig)
Catalan government evaluation ($t-1$)	0.21	3.58 (0.001)
Δ Catalan unemployment ($t-2$)	−0.63	−4.14 (0.010)
Δ Catalan economic retrospective evaluations	0.67	1.79 (0.080)
Corruption	−0.46	−4.47 (0.000)
Δ Leadership	0.38	4.26 (0.000)
Constant	3.79	5.47 (0.000)
Model diagnosis		
Adjusted R^2		0.73
Serial correlation: Durbin Watson		2.22
Serial correlation: Lagrange multiplier test of residual serial correlation		12.93 (0.374)
Functional form: Ramsey's RESET test using the square of fitted values		4.46 (0.065)
Normality: based on a test of skewness and kurtosis residuals		0.77 (0.678)
Heteroscedasticity: based on the regression of squared residuals on squared fitted values		1.05 (0.305)

Source: Díaz (1999).

conditions influence support for its regional politicians. The model seems to perform according to the simple reward–punishment hypothesis, as people attribute the regional economic situation to their regional government regardless of the competencies it holds (see Table 8.1).

Are these aggregate findings compatible with the individual voter calculus of the naive reward–punishment theory? Maybe citizens do not perceive where the real economic power is. Perhaps they do not distinguish between Spanish and Catalan economic government management. Possibly they see the regional government as a central political economic authority. Many studies compare the variation of governmental approval over time with the rise and fall of a set of possible explanatory variables, assuming that people evaluate the government in terms of its performance regarding economic issues. But is it not just coincidence? Why do people really evaluate the government the way they do?

To respond to these questions, microlevel analysis is especially important because it allows us to test the causal relations associated with aggregate popularity models and, consequently, to validate their results. We must remind that popularity functions are basically descriptive. The models serve to discover the factors that affect government popularity, but they do not really serve us in knowing what the inherent process is that generates individual perceptions leading to this support. For this reason, the two bodies of research (with aggregate and individual level data) are intimately related to one another, and they need each other to validate our hypothesis in a more conclusive way. Individual data can help us to strengthen the macro-results.

To gain insight in the attribution of responsibilities, we need to investigate the causal link between government performance, government approval, and vote intention for the government party. The responsibility hypothesis is accepted as the theoretical base for the relations found in aggregate popularity models. Individual data provide us with the opportunity to empirically test if this hypothesis really works in the way it is supposed to. The responsibility hypothesis can be divided into two parts. First, it is assumed that citizens make the government responsible for the state of the economy. As a result, they approve or disapprove the government according to the evaluation of how well it is managing the economy. Second, if citizens approve the government record, they reward the party that is supporting it, voting for the incumbent, and giving the government the possibility to rule the country for another term. On the contrary, if people do not approve the government, they use to vote for a different party with expecting of a better government.

In consequence, to test the responsibility hypothesis empirically requires collecting data about government evaluation and vote intention, and estimating the effect of the first over the latter. It might be argued that it is difficult to distinguish between government approval and vote intention. This assertion is corroborated by the fact that in studies with aggregate data, both measures have been used alternatively as indicators of government popularity. Our opinion is that vote intention is influenced by government approval, yet conceptually and empirically it is a different thing. There are structural, political, and contextual factors that induce vote intention independent of the perceptions of government record. In some cases, the lack of precise indicators has forced the use of vote intention as a proxy of government approval. But, when there are other available alternatives, we can model vote intention as a function of government evaluation, controlling the rest of the explanatory variables.

However, the strategy just described forms only one part of the test. There is a previous stage in the causal chain of responsibility attribution. It refers to the way in which people form their own perceptions about government performance and use them to evaluate the government. In this respect, it seems quite reasonable to assume that to evaluate the government, people take into account the policies designed and applied by its departments. The results of governmental actions can be seen through several specific policies dealing with economic (and non-economic) issues that are implemented during its period in office. And it is easier for people to express an opinion about more tangible things, such as policies relating to specific issues, than about "general government perform-ance." In consequence, policy evaluations are the first link in the causality chain of attribution of responsibilities, and can be used as predictors of government approval.

In addition to the fact that they shape government approval, evalu-ations of specific policies provide us with more detailed information about the judgments citizens make of the different aspects of the governmental tasks, and show the degree of salience people give to these issues. In an earlier work, Kernell and Hibbs (1981) argue that respondents would voice approval of the government's record only if they evaluate that performance above some critical point. Extending this argument, Hud-son (1982) maintains that respondents would indicate vote intention for the government in an election if they also evaluate their performance above some critical approval point. This critical approval point will vary from person to person, being smaller for those who identify themselves closely with the governing party. As a result, Hudson concludes that, in some cases, people feeling close to the government party may vote for it even when they do not approve its performance. This is another argu-ment for considering government approval as something different from vote intention.

Finally, when dealing with economic expectations we should take into account the assumptions of psychological models of electoral behavior (Conover and Feldman, 1986; Conover *et al.*, 1987). In contrast with rational-voting behavior, the majority of people react emotionally when they evaluate the economic situation. According to this view, there is not only a cognitive content but also an affective one these models should incorporate. For example, when things go well, people can develop a sense of euphoria that is unrelated to rational evaluations of the govern-ment record, but that does affect their vote. This can be the expression of an overall feelgood factor that can influence vote intention directly, apart from the indirect effect by way of government approval.

As a result of the previous discussion, we assume that there is a causal chain that links the evaluation of policies to vote intention in two ways: directly, and indirectly through government approval (see Figure 8.1).

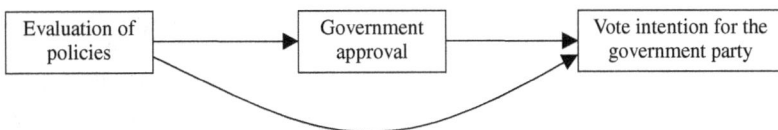

Figure 8.1 Chain of attribution of causal responsibility.

8.4   METHOD AND DATA

The data used in the analysis are from a Catalan survey conducted in November 1998. It contains 12 questions about policy evaluations that reflect citizens' perceptions of how well the different departments of the government are performing. The data show that these policy evaluations are fairly high correlated. This is the case, for instance, with evaluations of policies concerning occupation and housing, culture and education, or health and welfare. As a result, we hypothesize that there are some common latent factors underlying policy evaluations that cause the observed correlation. Even though people are asked about several specific policies, their answers are the upshot of their perceptions of more general policy successes or failures. In this sense, policy evaluations can be considered as specific indicators of a small number of factors that citizens take into account when evaluating government performance. These latent factors are responsible for the correlation of policy variables and we are interested in highlighting them. As soon as we are capable of finding these factors underlying government evaluation, they can be used as predictors of government approval and vote intention in a more parsimonious and accurate way than when using the values of single policy variables only.

These considerations suggest that one possible strategy for testing the responsibility hypothesis at the microlevel is to create a three-stage model with individual survey data. The first step consists of determining the factors underlying evaluations of government policies. The second step consists of estimating government approval as a function of these policy factors. The final step consists of estimating vote intention for the governmental party as a function of policy factors and government approval.

For the third step, we introduce two interaction terms between government approval on the one hand and party identification and leadership on the other. We assume that these latter variables affect the causal link between government approval and vote intention for the party in office. In addition, we introduce other individual and contextual variables to estimate the separate effects of the variables we are interested in (see Figure 8.2).

With this approach, if the findings of the models turn out to be significant, we will be more confident in accepting the connection between the initial and final links in the causality chain of attributing responsibilities to government for the state of the economy.

In the first step, we apply the factor analysis technique to the policy evaluations. This allows us to extract three uncorrelated factors that contain most of the variance of the original variables and eliminate data noise. In the second step, we estimate government approval from the factors imbedding policy evaluations determined in step one. Because the dependent variable is binary, we apply logistic regression, which estimates

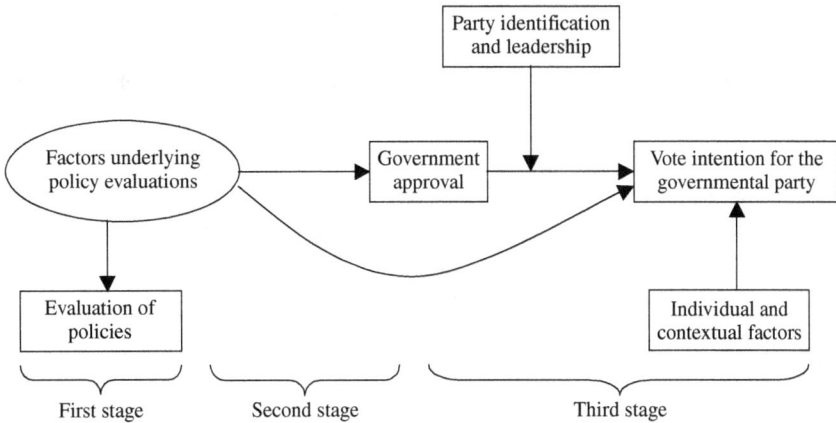

Figure 8.2 Three stage model of attributing responsibilities to government.

the probability of the respondent approving the government. In the third step, vote intention for the governmental party is estimated using as predictors the government approval, its interactions with party identification and leadership, and other control variables. Given that vote intention is a dichotomous variable, we apply logistic regression here as well. Finally, we integrate the second and third stages in a combined model that estimates vote intention using as predictor the probability of approving the government, derived from policy evaluations (and from the interaction terms, and individual and contextual variables included in the third step).

8.5 RESULTS

8.5.1 Factors underlying the evaluation of government policies

An initial exploratory factor analysis of the 12 variables recording policy evaluations has led to the extraction of three factors. One of them strongly emphasizes the culture, Catalan language, and education policy variables. We label this the *cultural factor*, given the contents of the policy variables it correlates with. The important variables in the second factor are financial aid to business, occupation, housing, and public works. The economy-related characteristics of these policies suggest that it can be interpreted as an *economic factor*. Finally, the third factor is strongly correlated with the health and welfare policy variables, which are clearly related to social policies. Hence, we identify this as a *social factor*. The rest of the variables, youth, law and order, and environmental policies, are somewhat correlated with the three factors mentioned above, but they are less well explained by them. In consequence, we did not include these three rest variables in a second confirmatory factor analysis. We also excluded the variable financial aid to business, because of the few responses to this question.[9]

The three factors we found together explain more than 68 percent of the total variance in policy evaluations, the percentage of variance explained being quite similar for each factor: 24, 23, and 22 percent for economic, cultural, and social factors, respectively. Therefore, we can conclude that the evaluations citizens give to specific policies carried out by the departments of the regional government are mainly realizations of their perceptions of cultural, economic, and social governmental performance (see Figure 8.3).

Let us discuss the coherence of these factors with those one can expect to find from the theoretical perspective. From an external point of view, it might appear somewhat strange that citizens give importance to economic policies in the evaluation of a subnational government, which has little control of economic issues and no power in macroeconomic policies. However, this fact is consistent with other results found at the aggregate level (Díaz, 1999) and it is also reflected in the responses to other questions in the same survey. When asked in an open question about what the most important problem in the country is, 76 percent of the respondents consider problems of economic nature. When asked about the problems that worried them at a personal or family level, 51 percent reported economic issues. Moreover, when asked about important achievements of the autonomous government, half of those who give an answer describe economy-related policies. In summary, Catalan citizens express great

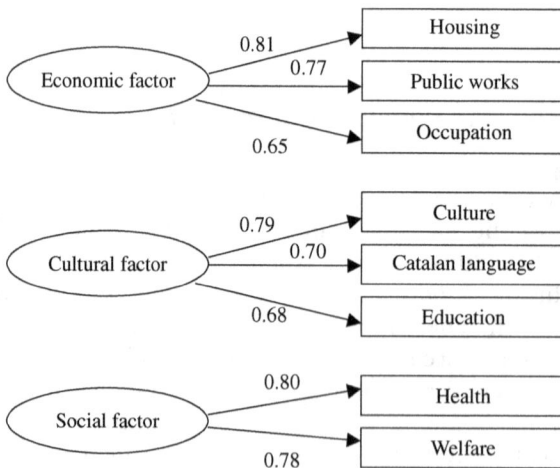

Figure 8.3 Factors underlying policy evaluations in Catalonia.

concern about economic issues and it seems logical that, when evaluating the results of specific policies, they take into account the underlying economic factor.

The existence of a cultural factor in policy evaluations is coherent with the reality of politics in Catalonia. In fact, the nationalist parties, in particular CiU, claim a greater level of autonomy, due to the so-called "differential fact" of the region based on the Catalan historical and linguistic characteristics. It is quite natural that a subnational government emphasizes all the cultural policies oriented towards increasing citizens' "national" identity. By strengthening Catalan identification, it gains more support for negotiating the transference of power with the Spanish government. In such circumstances, cultural policies acquire great importance and people recognize this when considering them as one of the main aspects of government evaluation.[10]

Finally, the social factor is also quite coherent because Catalonia is one of the autonomous communities in Spain with a higher level of competencies. Among these competencies there are health and some welfare policies that have high salience in the public opinion. Health policy is very important not only because of its impact on the daily life of people and the great amount of resources devoted to it, but also because of the innovation, introduced by the Catalan government, in the way the services are provided.[11] Welfare policies are important mainly for their symbolic and propagandistic use. The Catalan Government has a Department of Social Welfare that carries out certain social policies, especially distributing financial aid among institutions, associations, and non-governmental organizations that work in favor of the needy. The charitable nature of most of these policies and the lack of transparency in the distribution of the subsidies have generated some criticism. As a result, there are different opinions about the quality of the social policies carried out by the regional executive and this aspect of the government record is taken into account by citizens when evaluating its policies. The work of Fraile in this volume (Chapter 12) corroborates the importance of social policies in the Spanish framework.

8.5.2   Influence of policy evaluations on government approval

We will use the three main factors underlying policy evaluations as predictors of government approval. Table 8.2 shows the results of the estimation of a logistic regression predicting governmental approval from the values of the cited variables.

The model is highly significant and correctly predicts 88 percent of the cases. The three factors are significant at the 0.001 level and its coefficients are positive, indicating that the higher the evaluation in economic, cultural, and social policies, the higher is the probability of approving the government.

Table 8.2 Govermental approval, Catalonia (1998) (logistic regression)

	Coefficient	Wald (sig)
Evaluation of government performance		
Economic factor	0.90	94.92 (0.000)
Cultural factor	0.80	81.72 (0.000)
Social factor	0.76	66.99 (0.000)
Constant	2.20	404.71 (0.000)
Model diagnosis		
N	1269	
$-2\log$ likelihood initial	1099.12	
Model χ^2	268.27	(DF = 3)
Correct prediction government approval (%)	97.67	
Overall correct prediction (%)	87.55	
$R^2_{LA} \times 100$ (%)	23.86	

Notes
$R^2_{LA} = $ (Model $\chi^2 - 2$DF)/($-2\log$ likelihood initial); DF = degrees of freedom.

8.5.3   Influence of government approval on vote intention

The third step in our analysis consists of estimating vote intention for the party in office as a function of government approval. Because our hypothesis is that this relation can be affected by the identification with that party and by the evaluation of its leader, we test for the existence of interaction effects between government approval and two variables: party identification and leadership. We also include in the model the three factors of policy evaluation to test whether the evaluation of government policies can affect vote intention directly, as it is assumed in Figures 8.1 and 8.2. In this model, we have introduced as controls a large set of variables capturing individual characteristics and contextual economic and non-economic evaluations, although only a small number of them show themselves as having significant independent effects on vote intention.

As individual sociological variables, we have considered age, gender, subjective social class, urbanization, education, and Catalan origin. The latter is an ordinal variable that aims to reflect the degree of identification that the respondent has with Catalonia. The inclusion of such an indicator as a background variable is quite common in all Catalan electoral studies. The reason for this practice can be found in the internal migratory processes that occurred in Spain during the 1960s and 1970s. Because of the more advanced industrialization process in some of the Spanish regions, mainly Catalonia and the

Basque Country, many people from other regions migrated to these areas in search of better opportunities. Most of them established themselves and their families in the adopted region. However, some of them have not developed Catalan nationalist feelings despite living in Catalonia for several decades, and still consider themselves Andalusian or Galician, for example. Almost all studies on electoral behavior coincide in finding high levels of differential abstention and low level of vote for nationalists parties among these groups of citizens (Montero and Font, 1991; Pallarés and Font, 1995; Riba, 1995, 2000; Font *et al.*, 1998). For this reason, it seems necessary to control on the basis of Catalan origin when estimating vote intention for the governmental (nationalist) party. This specification assumes the existence of voter heterogeneity in the same way as Duch and Palmer do in another part of this volume (Chapter 7).

Because of the relation between Spanish and Catalan politics in a context of multilevel governance, it is necessary to control for those contextual variables that reproduce the political and economic situation at the national level. For this purpose, we have introduced some variables concerning the Spanish situation. Specifically, we have introduced an overall evaluation of the Spanish government performance, the leadership of the Spanish president, and the perception about the Spanish political situation into the model. In addition, we have used another group of economy-related variables based on the responses given to four open questions in the survey. The first two items ask what people perceive as the most important recent events in Spain and Catalonia, while the other two items ask about what they find to be the most important problems at a general and individual level.

Out of the set of individual and contextual variables, only Catalan origin and negative perceptions of the Spanish economy have shown to have an independent significant effect on vote intention for the governmental party, and have been included in the final model estimation.

Table 8.3 presents, in the column labeled Model 2, the estimated coefficients for the variables just described as predictors of vote intention.[12] The model is highly significant with an overall correct prediction of 88 per cent of cases.

The interaction terms have significant positive coefficients (at the 0.001 level). This means that identification with the governing party and evaluating its leader positively increases the effect of government approval on vote intention. There are two other significant coefficients in the model. The first one, negative perceptions of the Spanish economy, tells us that perceptions of the national economy influence the regional vote in the following sense: when they are negative the probability to vote for the regional governing party increases. This result is consistent with our expectations that negative perceptions of the Spanish economy explain the differential performance of the Catalan government. The second one, Catalan origin, tells us that Catalan origins have a remarkable impact

Table 8.3 Vote intention for the incumbent party using actual government approval, Catalonia (1998) (logistic regression estimators)

	Model 2	*Model 3*
Economic factor	−0.22	
Cultural factor	−0.05	
Social factor	−0.02	
Government approval × leadership	0.55***	0.52***
Government approval × party identification	4.01***	3.99***
Government approval	−4.33***	−4.29***
Negative perceptions of Spanish economy	1.54*	1.52*
Catalan origin	−0.39***	−0.40***
Constant	−1.67***	−1.47***
Model diagnosis		
N	753	753
−2 log likelihood initial	1014.2	1014.2
Model χ^2	543.3 (DF = 8)	540.2 (DF = 5)
Correct prediction for governmental vote (%)	88.7	88.7
Overall correct prediction (%)	88.3	87.9
$R^2_{LA} \times 100$ (%)	52.2	52.3

Notes
$R^2_{LA} = $ (Model $\chi^2 − 2DF$)/($−2$ loglikelihood initial); DF = degrees of freedom.
*** Significant at 0.001 level; ** Significant at 0.01 level; * Significant at 0.05 level.

on the nationalist vote: deep Catalan roots increase the probability of voting for the governing party in Catalonia. The significance of this variable is also theoretically consistent and confirms previous results. None of these three factors of policy evaluation have significant independent direct effects on vote intention.

Given that the factors driving the evaluation of government policies are nonsignificant, we have re-estimated the model while excluding them. The results are also shown in Table 8.3, in the column labeled Model 3. The coefficients are basically the same, with the same sign, the same significance, and almost the same value. The diagnostic statistics are very similar and a χ^2-test comparing the two models indicates that there is no significant improvement in the model when these three factors of policy evaluation are added (at the 0.01 level). In consequence, we will retain Model 3 since it is more parsimonious than Model 2.

8.5.4   Influence of predicted government approval on vote intention

In the last part of our analysis, we combined the two models that integrate the results of Tables 8.2 and 8.3. That is, we have re-estimated vote intention employing the same predictors as in Models 2 and 3, but using predicted government approval (following the results of Model 1) instead

Table 8.4 Vote intention for the incumbent party using predicted government approval, Catalonia (1998) (logistic regression estimators)

	Model 4	Model 5
Economic factor	−0.64**	
Cultural factor	−0.41*	
Social factor	−0.39*	
Predicted government approval × leadership	0.72***	0.61***
Predicted government approval × party identification	4.73***	4.64***
Predicted government approval	−3.60*	−6.76***
Negative perception of Spanish economy	1.76*	1.78**
Catalan origin	−0.34***	−0.36***
Constant	−3.63**	−0.26
Model diagnosis		
N	725	725
−2 log likelihood initial	986.74	986.74
Model χ^2	562.3 (DF = 8)	552.6 (DF = 5)
Correct prediction for governmental vote (%)	90.2	90.8
Overall correct prediction (%)	87.7	88.0
$R^2_{LA} \times 100$ (%)	55.4	55.0

Notes
R^2_{LA} = (Model χ^2 − 2DF)/(−2 log likelihood initial); DF = degrees of freedom. *** Significant at 0.001 level; ** Significant at 0.01 level; * Significant at 0.05 level.

of actual government approval. The results are displayed in Table 8.4. Model 4 shows the results of the estimation parallel to Model 2; Model 5 shows those parallel to Model 3.

Coefficients in Model 4 are basically the same as those in Model 2 except for the increase in significance of the policy evaluation factors. Although all of them remain nonsignificant at the 0.001 level, the first factor is significant at the 0.01 level and the others at the level of 0.05. In the same way, coefficients in Model 5 are very similar to those in Model 3 except for the bigger absolute value of the coefficient of predicted government approval. This is because the coefficient captures the direct effects of the excluded factors of policy evaluation.

The diagnostic statistics for Models 4 and 5 are very similar. In both cases, there is an overall correct prediction of 88 percent of the cases and of 90 percent for government vote. The χ^2-test for comparison between these two models leads to the acceptance of the null hypothesis of no improvement when these three factors of policy evaluation are added (at the 0.01 level).[13] In consequence, as in the preceding case, we will retain Model 5 since it is more parsimonious than Model 4.

Bearing in mind the three steps used in this analysis for modeling vote intention, the following overall picture emerges. First, people take into account three main aspects when evaluating government policies: economic, cultural, and social factors. Second, perceptions about government performance influence government approval. The better the evaluations of economic, cultural, and social policies, the higher is the probability that the citizen/respondent approves the government. Third, government approval positively affects vote intention for the incumbent party. In addition, party identification and leadership affect this relationship. The effect is bigger for people identifying themselves with the governing party and for people who evaluate its leader positively.

The final model combines these three steps linking the evaluation of policies implemented by the Catalan government with vote intention for the party in office. To resume, all other things being equal, the better the evaluations of government policies, the higher is the probability of voting for the governmental party in the next election.

8.5.5   Visualization of the effects

Due to the fact that the logistic model is not linear, it is difficult to see which variables have a major impact on the dependent variable. In Models 1 to 5, the effects vary depending on the values of the explanatory variable under consideration, and on the values of the remaining independent variables.

For example, from the results displayed in Table 8.2, one can deduce the following. A typical citizen, with average perceptions about government record in cultural and social policies, has a probability of approving the government that ranges from 0.20 to 0.99, depending on his/her perceptions of the economy. However, this difference is not always the same. For a more optimistic individual, with a slightly positive evaluation of cultural and social policies, the probability of approving the government ranges from 0.55 to 0.99, depending on his/her perceptions of the economy. That is, the effect of the economy perception is smaller for an optimistic citizen than for a typical one.[14] Similarly, the effect of a unit increase in the value of the economic evaluation for a typical citizen with cultural and social evaluations equal to the mean is greater when the economy perception is negative than when it is positive.

Given the difficulties for interpretation, the best way to decode the information provided by the models is displaying graphically the effects of each variable depending on the specific values of the remaining variables. Figure 8.4 represents the conditional effects of economic policy evaluations on government approval, conditioned by cultural evaluation for those electors with social policy evaluations equal to the mean (following Model 1). It shows a clear asymmetry with respect to the mean. Specifically, the effects of a unit increase in the value of the economic evaluations are bigger when a citizen has a negative perception than when he/she has a positive perception. It also shows that the effect of an increase on the cultural evaluation depends on the economic evaluation.

Figure 8.5 shows the impact of leadership on vote intention conditioned by Catalan origin (following Model 3). The probability of voting

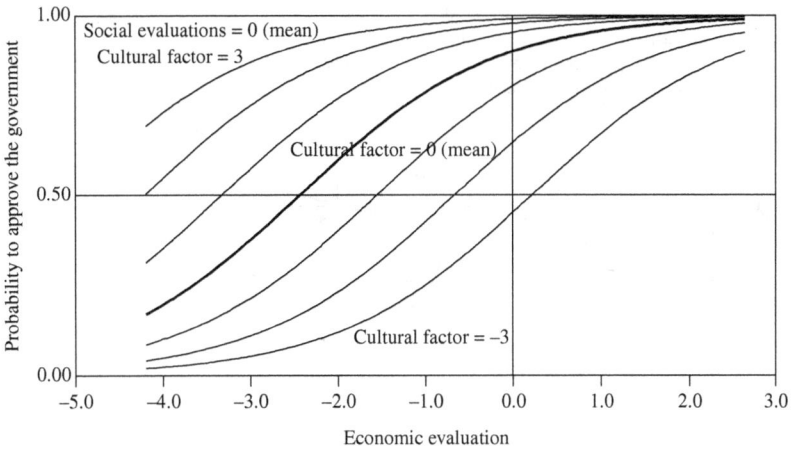

Figure 8.4 Effects of economic evaluation on government approval conditioned by cultural evaluation.

for the governmental party increases along with the positive evaluation of its leader. Moreover, this probability is always higher for people with Catalan parents than for those with parents from other Spanish regions. And it is higher for the latter, who are natives of Catalonia, than for those not born in this region.

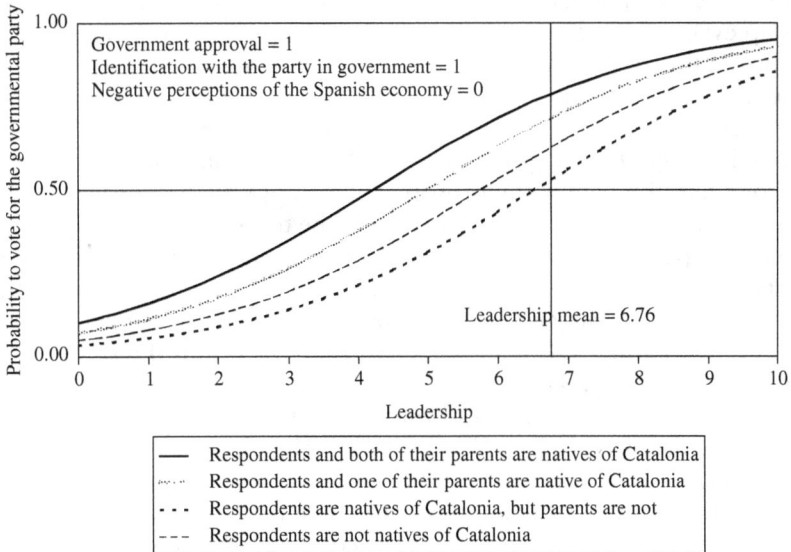

Figure 8.5 Vote intention: effects of leadership conditioned by Catalan origin (with the rest of variables fixed to the median).

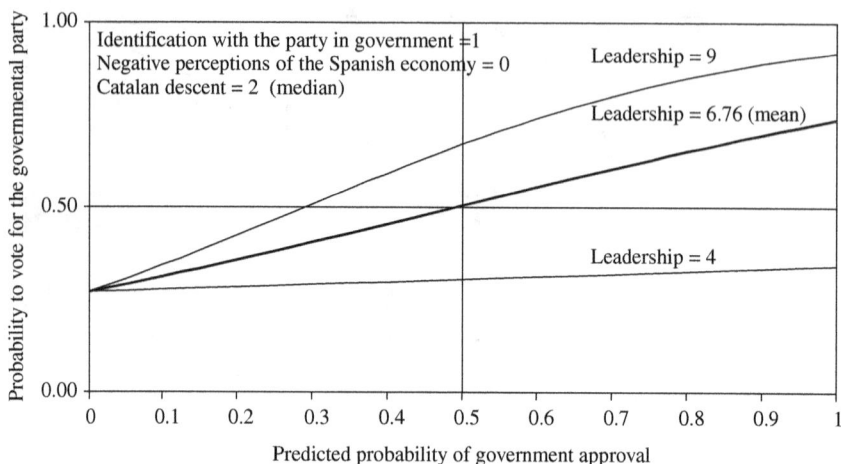

Figure 8.6 Catalan vote intention: effects of predicted government approval conditioned by leadership.

It can be observed that citizens with deep Catalan roots have a probability to vote for the nationalist party ruling the government greater than 50 percent even when evaluating its leader negatively. On the contrary, the probability that people who are not native of Catalonia vote for the governmental party is above 50 percent only when their leadership evaluation is equal to or above the mean. This confirms the importance of the variable reflecting regional identification in the vote for the subnational government.

Figure 8.6 displays the effects of predicted government approval on vote intention for the government, according to the results of Model 5. It shows that the higher the probability is to approve the government, the higher it is to vote for it. In this respect, the three curves of the graph put into perspective three different situations. First, people who evaluate the Catalan president very negatively will never vote for the governing party, even when approving its record. Second, people with an average evaluation of the president will vote for the incumbent party only if they evaluate its policies positively. Third, people with a very positive evaluation of the Catalan President will claim to vote for his party, even when they do not approve the government. Because of the significant interaction between leadership and government approval, its effect on vote intention increases along with the positive evaluation of the Catalan President. The differences in the slopes of the curves show the differential effect of government approval on vote intention due to leadership.

Figure 8.7 visualizes the link between the first and the third link in the causality chain for the attribution of responsibilities. It combines

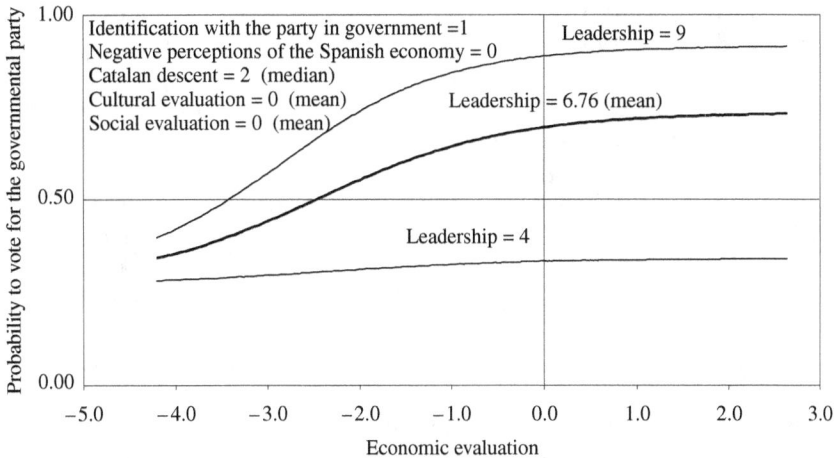

Figure 8.7 Catalan vote intention: effects of economic evaluation (through government approval) conditioned by leadership.

the results of the estimations of the two logistic equations displayed in Tables 8.2 and 8.4. Because we are interested in showing how economic evaluations affect vote intention, we have kept constant all the other variables included in both models. From the estimated probabilities of approving the government as a function of economic evaluations (derived from Model 1), we have calculated the probability of voting for the incumbent (derived from Model 5).

As a result, Figure 8.7 shows the effects of economic evaluations on vote intention through governmental approval. These results are somewhat surprising. We see that when economic perceptions are negative, a more positive economic evaluation increases the probability to vote for the governmental party. However, when economic perceptions are positive, the effect on vote intention is almost nonexistent, since the probability curves are almost horizontal. Hence, we observe here for a second time a considerable asymmetry. It seems that economic perceptions matter when they are negative, while they have no effect when they are positive. The slopes of the curves on the left side of Figure 8.7 also show the accelerating effect of leadership on the relation between economic perceptions and vote intention.

From the last figure we can deduce that the effects on vote intention of citizens' evaluations of economy-related policies implemented by the Catalan government differ depending on the values they take. If the economic evaluation is positive, the effect is hardly noticeable, whereas the effect is very strong when it is negative.[15]

To test the existence of grievance asymmetry, we split our data file into two groups, with negative and positive economic evaluations, respectively, and re-estimated Model 5 for each group. The results indicate that the model for the people with negative economic perceptions: (a) fits the data better, and (b) shows stronger effects of predicted government approval on vote intention. Therefore, voters give more weight to negative information, tending to punish the incumbent party when they have negative evaluations of its policies, rather than rewarding it when their evaluations are positive.

These results conform to the findings of Bloom and Price (1975) in the sense that economic downturns hurt congressional candidates of the in-party but upturns do not help them.[16] There is also a theoretical support for this bias. Lau (1982, 1985) draws upon the literature in cognitive psychology to provide both empirical evidence and theoretical justification for negativity bias operating at the level of attitudes. Nannestad and Paldam (1997) discuss some assumptions regarding the theoretical support for grievance asymmetry and the way in which it can be modeled. In our case, the patterns of the graphs confirm the grievance asymmetry.

8.6   CONCLUSIONS

This chapter contributes to the debate about the attribution of responsibilities to the government for the economic situation. We have examined with individual data the causal link that relates government performance with government approval and vote intention. We have taken the case of the Catalan government, as it serves well as an example of subnational government in a context of multilevel governance. The empirical results clearly show the following points.

The responsibility hypothesis is valid for political institutions without explicit macroeconomic competencies. With individual data, we disentangled the causal process of attributing responsibilities to the government and brought empirical evidence for the importance of policy evaluations in government approval. It turns out that the relation between responsibility and economic power is not so straightforward as it seems. An alternative way to see if people attribute economic changes to the incumbent is to use evaluations of policies, where the attribution of responsibilities looks clear. Our analysis has shown that, in the Catalan case, there are three factors underlying policy evaluations, namely the economic, the cultural, and the social factors, that affect Catalan government approval.

Government approval is not synonymous with vote intention for the incumbent and this can be empirically distinguished. Citizens express approval of the government's record if they evaluate its performance above some critical value. Taking this one step further, we can see that citizens will also indicate their intention to vote for the government if they evaluate its performance above some critical value, which varies from person to person. In the Catalan case, this critical value is strongly related with *leadership* and *Catalan origin*. People who evaluate the president very positively will declare their intention to vote for the government, even when evaluating its economic policies negatively; people with a very negative evaluation of the president will declare not to vote for the government, even when approving its economic record. In a similar way, this vote intention threshold depends in part on Catalan origins, being lower for those with deep Catalan roots than for the rest.

The grievance-asymmetry hypothesis is empirically grounded. Our results provide empirical support for a negativity disposition with regard to government popularity. In the case of Catalonia, the effect of economy evaluations on vote intention is strong when these evaluations are negative, while it is hardly noticeable when they are positive. It supports the hypothesis that an economy in decline harms the incumbent's support but an economy that is improving does not benefit the government accordingly. The graphical displays presented in this chapter clearly visualize these findings.

Although the attribution of responsibility is diffused in contexts of multilevel governance, citizens are able to credit and blame the government for the economic situation. Government has ceased to be a unidirectional, hierarchical, and monopolistic entity and is developing into a network of relationships by means of which power is more or less distributed among multiple actors. Taking into account the breakdown in traditional conceptions of government, the tensions due to nation-state resistance, and the increase of public decisions on a territorial level, people are able to attribute economic responsibilities to a subnational government such as the Catalan one. The European Union is undergoing a period of fundamental change and the patterns and factors underlying Catalan government support could be extrapolated to the future situation in Europe. Although most of the macroeconomic competencies would be centralized in a supranational institution, with the existence of a single Currency Unit and a European Central Bank, our study suggests that citizens in each European country will most likely continue to attribute responsibilities to their state government.

NOTES

1 For overviews, see Lewis-Beck (1988), Norpoth *et al.* (1991), and Nannestad and Paldam (1994).
2 The data proceed from the results of a CIS survey published in *El País* on 3 November 2000.
3 Sørensen (1987) finds weak and contradictory effects in the Norwegian case and Lewis-Beck (1988) points out that the economic vote diminishes when the complexity of the coalition government increases. For the Italian case, Bellucci (1991) shows that the traditional reward–punishment pattern has not been

working during the *pentapartito* government period; however, it does seem to work in the newly institutional context set in the 1990s (Bellucci, 1999; this volume).

4 Related to the issue of decentralization, see De Vries (2000).

5 The Catalan government has assumed competencies in issues such as culture, research, tourism, mountains, fishing, publicity, sport, public works, guardianships of minors, and foundations and associations. For other issues, it only assumes the execution of the state legislation: penitentiary issues, labor, international exhibitions (Fossas and Colomé, 1993 p. 21). In relevant issues such as industry, agriculture and trade, education, media, health, or police force, the Catalan government has ruling powers but within the state laws. Issues directly related to sovereignty (nationality, international affairs, armed forces, and monetary system), certain branches of law (commercial, penal, and labor), or issues related to macroeconomic policies or to the general planning of economic activity correspond to the State.

6 The Spanish Constitution states that the Statute of Autonomy, approved by law in the Spanish Parliament, is "the essential institutional rule of each Autonomous Community" (Article 147.1).

7 The CiU is a pre-electoral coalition, composed of two parties: Convergencia Democràtica de Catalunya (CDC), with a close-to-liberal ideology, and Unió Democràtica de Catalunya (UDC), which is a Christian-democratic party.

8 This economic discourse has been used, e.g. when the nationalist coalition justified its support for the state government. The pacts reached in 1993 with the Socialist Party, and from 1996 with the Popular Party, have been explained by the necessity for economic stability to achieve the convergence criteria for entrance into the European Currency Unit (EURO).

9 The fact that there were three other good indicators for the economic factor was another reason for not including this variable.

10 For example, there has recently been a great debate in Catalonia concerning the politics of language due to the discussion of a new Language Law in the Catalan Parliament. In contrast to the 1983 Linguistic Normalization Law that was reached by consensus, there were opposing views between parties regarding the necessity for and content of the 1998 Linguistic Policy Law. As the former law has succeeded in the sense that almost all people understand Catalan, the new one intends to increase its use among people and institutions. This goal was seen as a threat for an important sector of Spanish speakers living and working in Catalonia. The supporters and opponents have different views about the Catalan government's record on cultural aspects and, consequently, will report different positions regarding the evaluation of language policies.

11 In fact, Catalonia was the pioneer in Spain in introducing some aspects of private management in the service of public health. This initiative has been somewhat controversial, as it means an improvement of the service for some people, whereas for others it represents the privatization of one of the pillars of the welfare state.

12 Along with the interaction terms, we have not included the leadership and party identification variables because they introduce multicollinearity problems in the model.

13 However, the test is not so conclusive than when comparing Models 2 and 3. In fact, we should reject the null hypothesis if we were using a significance level of 0.05.

14 The economic, cultural, and social variables are standardized. As a result, the mean is zero and the standard deviation 1. Negative values correspond to evaluations below the mean and positive values to those above the mean.

15 We have drawn the figures corresponding to other simulations and in all cases we found similar patterns.
16 Previous to Bloom and Price, Mueller (1970) looked at a different type of asymmetry. Mueller's grievance asymmetry implies that voters react to an economic variable when the variable rates above or below a certain level.

REFERENCES

Alesina, A. and Rosenthal, H. (1995) *Partisan Politics, Divided Government, and the Economy*. Cambridge: Cambridge University Press.

Anderson, C. (1995) *Blaming the Government. Citizens and the Economy in Five European Democracies*. London: Sharpe.

Anderson, C. (2000) Economic voting and political context: a comparative perspective. *Electoral Stud.*, **19**, 151–170.

Beck, P.A., Baum, L., Clausen, A.R. and Smith Jr., C.E. (1992) Patterns and sources of ticket splitting in subpresidential voting. *Am. Political Sci. Rev.*, **86**(4), 916–928.

Bellucci, P. (1991) Italian economic voting: a deviant case or making a case for a better theory? In H. Norpoth, M.S. Lewis-Beck and J.D. Lafay (eds), *Economics and Politics: The Calculus of Support*. Ann Arbor, MI: University of Michigan Press.

Bellucci, P. (1999) *Economic issues and economic voting in a democratic transition: the 1994 and 1996 Italian national elections*. Paper Presented at the ECPR Joint Sessions of Workshops, Mannheim, Germany.

Bloom, H. and Price, H. (1975) Voter response to short-run economic conditions. *Am. Political Sci. Rev.*, **69**, 124–154.

Brugué, Q., Gomà, R. and Subirats, J. (2000) *Multilevel Governance: The Case of Catalonia*. Departament de Ciència Política i de Dret Públic de la Universitat Autònoma de Barcelona (unpublished).

Butler, D. and Stokes, D. (1976) *Political Change in Britain*. New York: St Martin's Press.

Conover, P.J. and Feldman, S. (1986) Emotional reactions to the economy: I am mad as hell and I am not going to take it anymore. *Am. J. Political Sci.*, **30**, 50–78.

Conover, P.J., Feldman, S. and Knight, K. (1987) The personal and political underpinnings of economic forecasts. *Am. J. Political Sci.*, **31**, 559–583.

De Vries, M.S. (2000) The rise and fall of decentralisation: a comparative analysis of arguments and practices in European countries. *Eur. J. Political Res.*, **38**, 193–224.

Díaz, A. (1999) *Evolució de la Popularitat del Govern de Catalunya: La Influència de la Conjuntura Econòmica i dels Esdeveniments Polítics*. Departament de Ciència Política i de Dret Públic, Universitat Autònoma de Barcelona (unpublished).

Díaz, A. and Riba, C. (1999) *The Effects of Economic Conditions in Sub-national Government Approval: The Catalan Case*. Paper Presented at the 1999 ECPR Joint Sessions of Workshops in Mannheim, Germany.

Font, J., Contreras, J. and Rico, G. (1998) *L'Abstenció en les Eleccions al Parlament de Catalunya*. Barcelona: Editorial Mediterrània, Collecció Polítiques 23.

Fossas, E. and Colomé, G. (1993) *Political Parties and Institutions in Catalonia*. Barcelona: Institut de Ciències Polítiques i Socials.

Heath, A., Jowell, R., Evans, G., Fields, J. and Witherspoon, S. (1991) *Understanding Political Change: The British Voter 1964–1983*. Oxford: Pergamon Press.

Hooghe, L. and Marks, G. (1997) *The Making of a Polity: The Struggle over European Integration*. Working Paper RSC No. 97/31. Florence: European University Institute.

Hudson, J. (1982) The relationship between government popularity and approval for the government's record in the United Kingdom. *Brit. J. Political Sci.*, **12**(2), 165–186.

Jêrome, B. and Jêrome-Speziari, V. (2000) The 1998 French regional elections: why so much political instability? *Electoral Stud.*, **19**, 219–236.

Jêrome, B. and Lewis-Beck, M.S. (1999) Is local politics local? French evidence. *Eur. J. Political Res.*, **35**, 181–197.

Kernell, S. and Hibbs, D.A. (1981) A critical threshold model of presidential popularity. In D.A. Hibbs and H. Fassbender (eds), *Contemporary Political Economy*. Amsterdam: North-Holland, pp. 49–71.

Key Jr., V.O. (1968) *The Responsible Electorate: Rationality in Presidential Voting, 1936–1960*. New York: Vintage Books.

Lafay, J.-D. (1991) Political dyarchy and popularity functions: lessons from the 1986 French experience. In H. Norpoth, M.S. Lewis-Beck, and J.-D. Lafay, (eds), *Economics and Politics: The Calculus of Support*. Ann Arbor, MI: University of Michigan Press, pp. 123–140.

Lau, R. (1982) Negativity in political perceptions. *Political Behav.*, **4**, 353–378.

Lau, R. (1985) Two explanations for negativity effects in political behavior. *Am. J. Political Sci.*, **29**, 119–138.

Lewis-Beck, M.S. (1988) *Economics and Elections: the Major Western Democracies*. Ann Arbor, MI: Michigan University Press.

Leyden, K.M. and Borrelli, S.A. (1995) The effect of state economic conditions on gubernatorial elections: does unified government make a difference? *Political Res. Quart.*, **48**(2), 253–274.

Montero, J.R. and Font, J. (1991) El voto dual: lealtad y transferencias de votos. In Equip de Sociologia Electoral (ed), *Estudis Electorals 10: L'electorat Català a Les Eleccions Autonòmiques de 1988: Opinions, Actituds i Comportaments*. Barcelona: Publicacions de la Fundació Jaume Bofill.

Mueller, J.E. (1970) The presidential popularity from Truman to Johnson. *Am. Political Sci. Rev.*, **64**, 18–39.

Nannestad, P. and Paldam, M. (1994) The VP function: a survey of the literature on vote and popularity functions after 25 years. *Public Choice*, **79**, 213–245.

Nannestad, P. and Paldam, M. (1997) The grievance asymmetry revisited: a microstudy of economic voting in Denmark, 1986–1992. *Eur. J. Political Economy*, **13**, 81–99.

Norpoth, H., Lewis-Beck, M.S. and Lafay, J.-D. (eds) (1991) *Economics and Politics: The Calculus of Support*. Ann Arbor, MI: University of Michigan Press.

Pallarès, F. and Font, J. (1995) *The Autonomous Elections in Catalonia (1980–1990)*. Barcelona: Institut de Ciències Polítiques i Socials.

Peffley, M. (1985) The voter as juror: attributing responsibility for economic conditions. In M.S. Lewis-Beck and H. Eulau (eds), *Economic Conditions and Electoral Outcomes in the United States and Western Europe*. New York: Agathon, pp. 187–206.

Powell, G.B. and Whitten, G.D (1993) A cross-national analysis of economic voting: taking account of the political context. *Am. J. Political Sci.*, **37**, 314–334.

Riba, C. (1995) *Vot Dual i Abstenció Diferencial*. Doctoral Thesis Presented at the Departament de Ciència Política i de Dret Públic de la Universitat Autònoma de

Barcelona, Bellaterra: Publicacions de la Universitat Autònoma de Barcelona (microfiche).

Riba, C. (2000) Voto dual y abstención diferencial. Un estudio sobre el comportamiento electoral en cataluña. *Revista Española de Investigaciones Sociológicas*, **91**, 59–87.

Sanders, D. (2000) The real economy and the perceived economy in popularity functions: how much do voters need to know? A study of British Data, 1974–1997. *Political Stud.*, **19**, 275–294.

Sørensen, R.J. (1987) Macroeconomic policy and government popularity in Norway, 1963–1986. *Scand. Political Stud.*, **10**, 301–321.

Strøm, K. (1990) *Minority Government and Majority Rule*. New York: Cambridge University Press.

Vallès, J.M. and Molins, J.M. (1990) La vida electoral a Catalunya: eleccions i referèndum entre 1982 i 1988. In Equip de Sociologia Electoral (ed.), *Estudis Electorals 9: Atlas Electoral de Catalunya 1982–1988*. Barcelona: Publicacions de la Fundació Jaume Bofill.

9 Temporal variations in economic voting

A comparative cross-national analysis

David Sanders and Sean Carey

Research over the past three decades has demonstrated that there is considerable cross-national variation in the relationship between the economy and the democratic political support. In some countries, such as Britain and Denmark, economic voting appears to play a significant role in the calculus of party support (Clarke and Stewart, 1995; Nannestad and Paldam, 1996, 1997). In others, such as Norway and Italy, the effects appear far weaker (Lewis-Beck, 1988; Paldam, 1991). In the early 1990s, Powell and Whitten made an important contribution to our understanding of the sources of this general pattern of cross-national variation (Powell and Whitten, 1993). They argued that the clarity of responsibility tended to be highest in situations where a single party (as opposed to a coalition) was in government, where there were majority as opposed to minority governments, and in systems where the separation of executive and legislative powers was not associated with "divided government". In those contexts, where it was clear that the governing party was responsible for macroeconomic policy and performance, it was to be expected that voters would be more inclined to reward governments for economic success and to punish them for economic failure. By the same token, where the clarity of responsibility was low, voters would be less able and less likely to base their electoral judgments on economic factors because it was less clear which party should be blamed or credited for economic failure or success. Powell and Whitten (1993) found significant empirical support for their propositions. There has subsequently been a continuing debate both about how clarity of responsibility should be measured and about the extent to which it explains cross-national variations in the strength of economic voting (Whitten and Palmer, 1999; Royed *et al.*, 2000).

In this analysis, we develop what we regard as the logical corollary to Powell and Whitten's analysis. We argue that, in addition to the systematic *spatial* variation in economic voting that occurs across countries, there is also systematic *temporal* variation in economic voting, within countries,

over time. Our analysis concentrates on the relationship between subjective economic perceptions and patterns of party support. We show that
there are quite marked fluctuations in the strength of this relationship
over time. Crucially, we also show that these variations are related –
though not in all countries – both to the underlying "objective" strength
of the macroeconomy and to the electoral credibility of the main opposition party or parties. We offer an explanation of these cross-national
variations based on the idea that voters' "political risk orientations" under
conditions of uncertainty vary according to cultural context.

The first part of this chapter outlines our core theoretical arguments
about the sources of temporal variation in the effects that economic
perceptions exert on party support. It also outlines the basic research
design that we employ to analyze these variations. The second part
applies this research design to aggregate monthly time-series data from
UK for the period 1974–1999. The final part extends this analysis to a
limited number of other countries for which comparable data are available: the United States, Germany, Denmark, Australia, and Spain.

9.1   THEORY AND RESEARCH DESIGN

A common folk wisdom in many countries is that governments which take
good care of the economy – as measured by unemployment, inflation,
GDP growth, or whatever – are likely to be re-elected, while those that
preside over economic failure are likely to be ousted. Academic research
into the relationship between the economy and voting has shown that the
reality is rather more ambiguous and that the impact of economic factors
on party support varies significantly from country to country (Lewis-
Beck, 1988; Norpoth *et al.*, 1991; Chappell and Veiga, 2000). One source
of variation, of course, is that "taking good care of the economy" means
different things in different contexts. Another is that there may be a
mismatch between a government's "objective" economic performance
and voters' "subjective" assessments of it. Yet another is that voters in
some political contexts may not hold the government responsible for
certain economic outcomes. These ambiguities about the potential relevance of "the economy" have led analysts to focus on the "subjective
economy," on economic perceptions.

In principle, there are four general types of economic perception
that are potentially of relevance to economic voting. The first is a
cluster of perceptions that is sometimes labeled as the "feelgood factor."
This refers to voters' general sense of economic well-being and is
usually assumed to have four components: national retrospections (how
well has the general economy been performing), personal retrospections (how well has the individual's household been doing), national
expectations (how well will the general economy perform), and personal

expectations (will the individual's position improve or deteriorate). Nannestad and Paldam (2000) have shown that it is almost impossible to disentangle the connections among these four elements. Indeed, it seems likely that to a considerable degree they all measure the same underlying "feelgood" phenomenon. A second type of economic perception involves the question of culpability. This aspect of perceptions concerns the extent to which voters hold governments responsible for overall economic performance and/or for their personal economic circumstances. The third dimension relates to voters' perceptions of the relative economic management competencies of the rival political party leaderships: poor economic performance will not necessarily damage an incumbent government if the alternative governments appear substantially less competent to manage the economy than those currently in control. The final dimension concerns voters' perceptions about specific indicators of macroeconomic performance. Inflation, for example, may objectively be low. But if voters do not perceive it to be low or if they do not, for whatever reason, consider inflation to be an important electoral issue, then a good record on inflation is unlikely to assist an incumbent party's campaign for re-election.

A full empirical analysis of the role of subjective economic perceptions in determining political preferences would require a consideration of the interplay of all these dimensions of perceptions. Suitable time-series data, however, are simply not available for sufficiently long periods of time to make such an analysis possible. This said, relatively long-running time-series data on various aspects of the "feel-good" subset of perceptions *are* available – and for a number of different countries. For this reason, we focus our theoretical discussion on this latter set of perceptions. We do not enter the debate as to whether it is the prospective or retrospective, or the egocentric or sociotropic, components of these perceptions that are the most important in determining political preferences. The core theoretical idea that we deploy, however, is simple. If voters feel that economic conditions have improved or that they are likely to improve in the future, then they are more likely, other things being equal, to wish to preserve the political status quo that has created their current or projected sense of economic well-being. In short, to the extent voters feel good or optimistic, they are more likely to support the incumbent party or parties; to the extent they feel bad or pessimistic, they are more likely to support the opposition.

There is abundant evidence, from a wide range of national contexts and for both individual and aggregate-level data, that feelgood perceptions correlate with patterns of party support (Fiorina, 1981; Anderson, 1995, 2000; Nadeau *et al.*, 1996; Alvarez *et al.*, 2000; Clarke *et al.*, 2000; Sanders, 2000). Figure 9.1 displays a typical relationship using UK data. This figure shows variations in aggregate personal expectations and support for the governing party between January 1974 and July 1999. (We use aggregate personal expectations here because, of the four

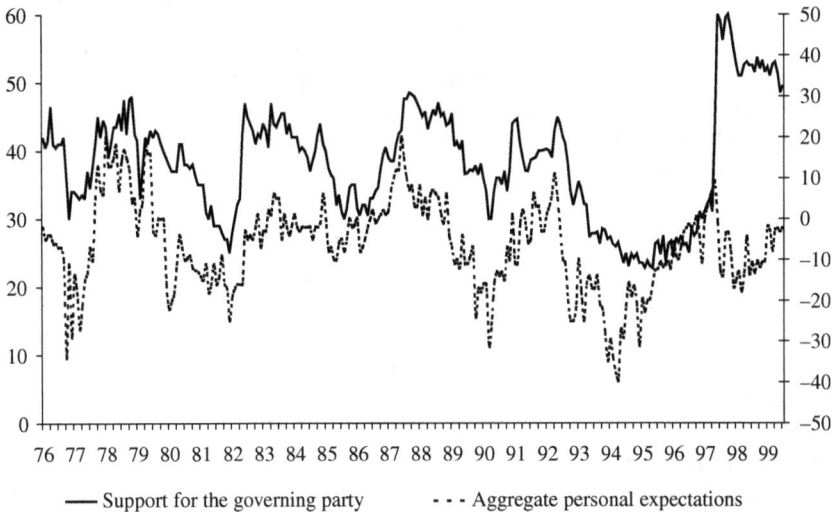

Figure 9.1 Aggregate personal economic expectations and support for the governing party in the UK, January 1976–December 1999.

feelgood components, it offers the best-fit with party popularity in UK: similar results, though not quite so strong, are obtained using the other three feelgood measures.) The two graphs move together remarkably closely though, inevitably, there are occasions when they diverge. As we show below, formal tests strongly support the notion that expectations and incumbent support are closely connected. From Powell and Whitten's perspective, of course, this strong relationship between expectations and support in UK makes extremely good sense. UK is a high "clarity-of-responsibility" system. Since 1945, UK has been ruled almost continuously by single-party majority governments that have dominated both the executive and legislative branches. Even during the brief exception of the Lib–Lab pact of 1977–1978, Labour ministers held all the economic portfolios, suggesting that "clarity of responsibility" was still high.

As intimated above, however, there is reason to suppose that aggregate expectations (or indeed other aggregate measures of voters' economic perceptions) do not always exert the same effect on party support. We can easily test to see if any "clarity-of-responsibility" effects were evident during the Lib–Lab pact period referred to above. (Indeed, we conduct precisely such tests in our second section.) In our view, there are two other major sources of variation in the relationship between economic expectations and incumbent party support.

The first of these, unsurprisingly, is the objective macroeconomy itself. Economic perceptions are only partly determined by economic realities. Governments regularly attempt to "talk up" the economy as part of their efforts to secure their own re-election (Butler and Kavanagh, 1997). Media outlets, especially newspapers, frequently engage in similar partisan efforts to raise economic confidence in advance of elections – and with some success (Sanders *et al.*, 1993). It is entirely possible for there to be a significant increase in feelgood perceptions even though the underlying "objective" macroeconomic position – as measured by, say, unemployment – remains unchanged. In these circumstances, rational voters will not equate their economic optimism with government management of the economy, and therefore not be so strongly motivated to translate their economic optimism into incumbent support – the preservation of the political *status quo* – as when there is an accompanying improvement in "objective" economic conditions. Accordingly, we hypothesize that, when macroeconomic conditions are objectively weak, then the effects of economic perceptions – in this case measured as aggregate personal expectations – on party support will be smaller. When unemployment is low, we would expect the effect of expectations on support to be relatively large; when unemployment is high, we would expect the effect to be relatively small. In short, we expect a negative relationship between the level of unemployment and the magnitude of the effect of expectations on incumbent party support (H1).

The second potential influence on the magnitude of the expectations-support effect is the political credibility of the major opposition party or parties. Economic factors do not impinge on voters' electoral preferences in a political vacuum. Rational voters may well wish to vote against an incumbent government because it has failed – or looks as though it will fail – to satisfy their economic aspirations. But if those voters also believe that the main alternative government is likely to fail them even more – if the opposition lacks credibility as a government – then they are less likely to translate their low expectations into support for the opposition. Anderson (2000) finds that too many available alternatives for dissent tends to reduce the defection away from the governing party. Fraile (this volume) finds that, after a return to democracy, it took almost two decades for the main opposition party in Spain to gain credibility and thus for the economic voter to emerge. By the same token, in the face of a non-credible opposition, voters with high expectations are even more likely to support the incumbent party than they would be if the opposition offered a credible political alternative. The immediate difficulty with the notion of "non-credible opposition," of course, is that it is by no means self-evident how we would know if an opposition were "non-credible." A plausible surrogate measure is the size of the opinion poll gap between the two leading parties or coalitions of parties. There is considerable evidence, at least in UK, to suggest that voters are very well informed about opinion poll party support levels. There is a very high correlation, e.g. between voters' expectations about which party will win the next general election, and the size and direction of the opinion poll gap between the two major UK parties. We would argue that the larger (smaller) the gap between the government and its main opposition rival, the less (more) electorally credible the opposition party will be. We accordingly hypothesize that there should be a positive relationship between the size of the government–opposition polling gap (which measures the non-credibility of the opposition) and the magnitude of the effect that voters' economic expectations exert on incumbent support. The expectations–support relationship should be strongest when the gap is larger and weakest when the gap is smaller (H2).

9.1.1 Research design

Our research design for investigating these hypotheses, initially as applied to UK data, is composed of three distinct steps. The first step consists in showing that aggregate economic expectations are indeed linked to governing party support levels in a theoretically predictable way. This step simply involves specifying and estimating a model, covering the period 1974–1999, in which governing party support is analyzed as a function of expectations and a series of "event dummies" which represent unusual political "shocks" to party support. These include terms for the 1982 Falklands War and for Tony Blair's New Labour government in 1997. It has been shown elsewhere that the standard measures of the objective condition of the economy (and in particular unemployment and inflation) do not exert direct effects on UK party support, over and above the effects of expectations (Sanders, 1999). Hence our first step model specification is:

$$\text{Government popularity}_t = a + b_1 \text{ government popularity}_{t-1}$$
$$+ b_2 \text{ aggregate personal expectations}_t$$
$$+ \sum b_k \text{event dummy}_k + u_t \qquad (9.1)$$

The second step involves using a statistical test – rolling recursive OLS – that is conventionally deployed to test for the stability of the coefficients in a model (originally developed by Brown *et al.*, 1975; but see Charemza and Deadman, 1997, pp. 47–57). Rolling recursive techniques involve estimating the magnitude of the effect of X on Y in a rolling "estimation window." For example, if a given time-series consists of 90 observations, a rolling window of $N = 30$ could be employed to test for parameter stability. The first window would involve observations 1–30, the second would involve 2–31, the third 3–32, and so on, through to 61–90. Note that this is different from simply segmenting the series into different parts (e.g. observations 1–30, 31–60, and 61–90). For any given time point at the end of a 30-month "window," rolling recursive estimates indicate the magnitude of the effect of X on Y over the previous 30 months. Rolling recursive coefficients offer a remarkably sensitive instrument for assessing the way in which the effect of X and Y varies over time. Note, however, that rolling recursive models can be estimated only if there is variation in all the variables in the model in each estimation "window." To maximize the number of cases over which we estimate the rolling recursive coefficients, therefore, we drop the dummy variables from the specification as follows:

$$\text{Government popularity}_t = a + b_1 \text{ government popularity}_{t-1} \\ + b_2 \text{ aggregate personal} \\ \text{expectations}_t + u_t \qquad (9.2)$$

There are a total of 307 monthly observations (January 1974–July 1999) in our data. We report the results of using rolling window sizes of $N = 30$, 40, and 50, though similar results were obtained using windows of intermediate and greater sizes. With $N = 30$, we first estimate Eq (9.2) for January 1974–June 1976. This yields an estimate of the effect of expectations on support that we assign to June 1976. Next, we estimate (2) for February 1974–July 1976, which yields an effect magnitude for July 1976. We replicate this process iteratively through to February 1997–July 1999, which yields an effect magnitude for July 1999. This yields a total of 277 observations for the next stage of our analysis (or 267 if we use a window size of $N = 40$).

The third step of our modeling procedure involves using our rolling estimates of the effects of expectations on support as a dependent variable that we seek to model. In essence, we seek to estimate hyperparameters that model the changes in the value of the expectations coefficient. Our specification contains terms for the following:

1   The lagged values of the dependent variable.
2   The objective condition of the economy, measured as the level of unemployment. In line with H1, we expect this term to exert a *negative* effect on the size of the expectations effect.
3   The opinion poll gap between the government and the main opposition party (NONCRED). In line with (H2), we expect this term to exert a *positive* effect on the magnitude of the expectations effect.
4   A dummy variable term which corresponds to the period of the 1977–1978 Lib–Lab pact. We include this term to determine whether or not, in line with Powell and Whitten (1993), there is a reduced "clarity-of-responsibility" effect during this period.
5   An additional set of dummy variable terms for the unusual events that are known to have affected party support during the test period. These terms are included for control purposes to ensure that the model is correctly specified rather than for the express purpose of estimating their respective effect magnitudes.

Formally, our specification is:

$$\text{Magnitude of effect coefficient}_t = a + b_1 \text{ magnitude of effect}$$
$$\text{coefficient}_{t-1} + b_2 \text{ unemployment}_t$$
$$b_3 \text{ NONCRED}_t + b_4 \text{ Lib--Lab pact}$$
$$+ \sum b_k \text{ event dummies}_k + u_t \quad (9.3)$$

Having applied these models to UK data, we proceed in the third part of this chapter to apply analogous models to data from the United States, Germany, Denmark, Australia, and Spain.

9.2 EMPIRICAL RESULTS FOR BRITAIN

Table 9.1 describes the results of a simple OLS model of governing party support in UK for the period 1974–1999. The main independent variable is aggregate personal economic expectations, the difference between the percentage of respondents who expect their personal finances to get better over the next 12 months minus the percentage who think they will get worse.[1] As intimated above, this prospective, egocentric dimension of "feel-good" economic perceptions is chosen partly because it is continuously available for the longest time period in UK and partly because it is more closely related to UK party support patterns than other feel-good variables. The expectations variable is measured in levels, though a change specification (using the change in expectations at $t - 1$) produces virtually identical results. A range of different dummy variables were included in the initial specification, including terms for the switch to a Conservative government in June 1979 and for the introduction of the poll tax in March 1990. The reported equation includes only those terms that proved to exert statistically significant effects on government popularity: for the October 1976 IMF loan crisis; the 1982 Falklands war; Thatcher's removal from office in November 1990; and the switch to New Labour in May/June 1997. The results in Table 9.1 suggest a straightforward conclusion. Personal expectations exert a significant, if modest, effect on government popularity in UK. Over the 1974–1999 period, the magnitude of the effect is $b = 0.06$: governing party support increases (falls) by 0.06 of a percentage point for each percentage point increase (fall) in aggregate expectations.

But how stable is the magnitude of this effect? Based on the specification in Eq (9.2), Figure 9.2 plots the rolling recursive estimates of the variations in the magnitude of the personal expectations coefficient for a window size of $N = 30$. There are clear variations in the size of the coefficient over time – even though these are estimates derived from a 30-month rolling window, in which each window represents two-and-a-half years of monthly

Table 9.1 Aggregate personal economic expectations and governing party support in the UK, 1974–1999 (OLS estimators)

Constant	3.20***
	(0.72)
Government support $(t-1)$	0.78***
	(0.05)
Government support $(t-2)$	0.14**
	(0.05)
Personal expectations	0.06***
	(0.01)
IMF loan crisis – November 1976	−7.07**
	(2.20)
Falklands – May 1982	9.39***
	(2.20)
Falklands – June 1982	6.46**
	(2.23)
Thatcher removal – December 1990	6.98**
	(2.20)
Blair government – May/June 1997	14.76***
	(1.58)
N	307
R^2	0.93
Durbin Watson	2.10
Sample	1974 m1–1999 m7

Notes
* Coefficient significant at 0.05; ** at 0.01; *** at 0.001. Standard errors in parentheses. Estimation by OLS. Dependent variable is government support at time t. A dependent variable lagged twice (government support at $t-2$) was included to reduce first-order autocorrelation. Dummy variables that were insignificant in the model were omitted. These include: Thatcher's election victory (May/June 1979), Poll Tax (March 1990), and ERM crisis (September–November 1992).

data. Some, though by no means all, of the variation is due to the distorting effects of "events" such as the Falklands war. However, these effects cannot be controlled for in the rolling specification because for the majority of the windows (e.g. January 1984–March 1988 with regard to the Falklands effect), the appropriate dummy terms have no variance and therefore cannot be included in the estimation. We consider below how far this variation in effect magnitude over time *within* a single country compares with variations *across* countries. We simply note here that the variation is quite marked, ranging from a maximum of $b = 0.34$ to a minimum of $b = -0.08$. We also repeated this exercise for rolling windows of $N = 40$ and 50. The overall pattern of variation in all three figures is similar, though not surprisingly the variation is slightly larger when shorter windows are used. The rolling estimates for a window of $N = 40$ vary from $b = 0.27$ to -0.05; and for a window of $N = 50$ from $b = 0.19$ to $b = -0.05$.

Figure 9.2 Rolling recursive estimates of the variations in the magnitude of the personal expecations coefficients in the UK, July 1976–December 1999, window size = 30.

Is there any systematic pattern to the coefficient variation observed in Figure 9.2? In line with the hypotheses advanced above, Table 9.2 correlates the variations in effect magnitudes for $N = 50$, 40, and 30 with the level of unemployment, with the degree of non-credibility of the main opposition party (NONCRED), and with the existence (or not) of the Lib–Lab pact. The correlations provide support for both (H1) and (H2). Regardless of window size, the magnitude of the expectations effect varies negatively with unemployment (when the objective economy is not performing well, voters are more reluctant to translate their optimism into incumbent support and vice versa). And it varies positively with NONCRED (when the main opposition party lacks political credibility, voters are even more likely to translate their optimism into support for the government and vice versa). It is also clear that the period of the

Table 9.2 Rolling recursive estimates of the size of the expectations effect correlated with unemployment, non-credibility of opposition and the Lib–Lab pact in the UK, 1976–1999 (bivariate correlations)

Window size (N)	Sample	Unemployment	Non-credibility of opposition	Lib–Lab pact
50	1978m2–1999m7	−0.37	+0.23	+0.02
40	1977m4–1999m7	−0.45	+0.41	+0.08
30	1976m6–1999m7	−0.50	+0.43	+0.07

Lib–Lab pact made no difference to the effect of expectations on government support. If the "clarity of responsibility" was reduced in Britain during this period, it clearly did not affect the economic perceptions – government support relationship in the way implied by the Powell–Whitten model.

These relationships are modeled formally, for a window size of $N = 30$, in Table 9.3, though virtually identical results are obtained using larger windows. This window size is used to facilitate the cross-national comparisons that are developed in the next section. For most other countries, comparable data are available over much shorter time periods. This in turn means that for these countries, it is necessary to use a relatively short window to maximize the number of time periods for which the magnitude of the effect coefficients can be estimated. The results in Table 9.3 confirm the conclusions derived from the correlations shown in Table 9.2. Even when the effects of the relevant "event shocks" are controlled

Table 9.3 Predicting variations in the effects of aggregate personal economic expectations on governing party support in UK, 1976–1999

	Window size	
	$N = 40$	$N = 30$
Constant	0.03***	0.03***
	(0.01)	(0.01)
Effect magnitude (−1)	0.88***	0.89***
	(0.03)	(0.03)
Unemployment	−0.001**	−0.002**
	(0.00)	(0.00)
Non-credibility	0.0003**	0.0002*
	(0.00)	(0.00)
Lib–Lab pact	−0.003	−0.01
	(0.01)	(0.01)
Falklands – May 1982	−0.02	−0.02
	(0.02)	(0.03)
Falklands – June 1982	0.01	0.06*
	(0.02)	(0.03)
Thatcher removal	0.05*	0.05
	(0.02)	(0.03)
Blair government	−0.03*	−0.06***
	(0.01)	(0.02)
N	267	277
R^2	0.88	0.86
Durbin Watson	2.01	1.96
Sample	1977m5–1999m7	1976m7–1999m7

Notes
* Coefficient significant at 0.05; ** at 0.01; *** at 0.001. Standard errors in parentheses. Estimates are maximum likelihood estimations with an autoregressive error specification AR(1). Dependent variable is the magnitude of the effect of expectations of support at time t.

for, the expectations coefficient is significantly affected negatively by unemployment ($b = -0.002$, which supports (H1)) and positively by the non-credibility of the opposition ($b = +0.0002$, which supports (H2)). Substantively this means that the lower the unemployment rate and the perceived credibility of the opposition, the greater is the positive effect of economic expectations on governing party support. The coefficient magnitude is clearly unaffected by the Lib–Lab pact, suggesting that, within UK at least, the impact of economic perceptions on party support is unrelated to variations in clarity of responsibility.

The preliminary conclusion suggested by these empirical results is clear. There is considerable within-country variation in the effects that economic perceptions exert on government support. Different window sizes imply different levels of coefficient variation, but even the largest windows produce high levels of variation. As far as Britain is concerned, in contrast to Powell and Whitten (1993), this coefficient variation is not linked systematically to variations in clarity of responsibility, though it should be emphasized that during the 1974–1999 period there was not much clarity variation. Rather, in Britain, the impact of economic perceptions on government popularity is smaller when the economy is in trouble and larger when the opposition lacks electoral credibility.

9.3 EMPIRICAL RESULTS FOR SIX COUNTRIES

The intriguing question that follows from these UK results, of course, is whether or not they extend to other countries. In this section, as far as data permit, we attempt to develop comparable models for UK, the United States, Germany, Denmark, Australia, and Spain. This selection is not intended to constitute a representative sample of the countries in which economic voting is alleged to occur. Rather, these were simply the only countries for which we could obtain suitable time-series data on party support patterns and economic perceptions.

Several preliminary observations need to be made about the cross-national data that we employ. First, while our data for UK, the United States, Germany, Denmark, and Australia are monthly, the Spanish data are quarterly. Notwithstanding this difference, the strong similarities between the Spanish and other models that are developed suggest that this does not invalidate the use of the Spanish data as part of our sample. Second, the political data that we use for the United States refer to "presidential approval" rather than to the popularity of the governing political party or parties. Again, we would argue that this distinctiveness does not invalidate our cross-national comparisons: presidential approval ratings represent the standard means of assessing support for the US government; and our comparisons in any case focus primarily on the within-country variations in effect-magnitudes over time.[2] Third, the time periods for which data are available vary considerably from country to country. As we saw in the previous section, monthly UK data are available for the period January 1974–July 1999. The time series that we were able to obtain for other countries were rather more restricted: January 1978–December 1997 for the United States; January 1992–December 1998 for Germany, April 1986–December 1997 for Denmark, January 1976–December 1990 for Australia, and 1983Q1–1995Q3 for Spain. Given this temporal asymmetry, we are clearly unable to develop a single integrated model for all six of our sample countries. However, it does not prevent us from exploring the magnitudes of economic-voting coefficients in a wide range of spatial and temporal contexts.

A fourth observation that needs to be made relates to the character of the aggregate economic perceptions data that we employ. These data are not available uniformly across all of our sampled countries either in terms of the dimensions of economic perceptions that are measured (personal versus national and retrospective versus prospective) or in terms of the different time periods for which the various measures are available. For example, although both personal and national expectations are measured in the Spanish data, the personal expectations series is so short as to be unusable for the sort of rolling recursive analysis that we seek to develop here. In UK, in contrast, the national expectations series is considerably shorter than the personal expectations series. The Australian data are even more intractable. They merely provide a summary measure of "consumer satisfaction" which combines forward- and backward-looking assessments of both personal and national perceptions. To maximize the cross-national comparability of our investigation and the number of time points for which data are available, we focus on measures of personal and national expectations. Our data for Australia necessarily combine both of these, along with measures of retrospections. However, the consumer satisfaction index does correlate highly with both measures, and particularly with national expectations.[3]

Our fifth observation concerns our measures of unemployment. Unemployment is a notoriously difficult variable to calibrate cross-nationally. However, because we are interested only in the extent to which unemployment varies with effect-magnitudes *within* countries, we are able to side-step these potential calibration difficulties and use the unemployment rate as published in official government statistics.

Finally, note that our measure of "opposition non-credibility" – defined as the gap between the support ratings of the governing and major opposition parties – is broadly similar in meaning for most of our countries. In UK, it is the gap between Labour and the Conservatives; in Germany, the gap between the Christian Democrats and the Social Democrats; in Denmark the gap between the Social Democrats and the Conservatives (including Liberals when in government); in Spain, the gap between the Socialists and the Peoples' Party; and in Australia, the gap between Labor and the National Liberal Party. In the United States, no such gap measure is available because party support as such is not measured on a continuing monthly basis. In these circumstances, we defined the United States "opposition non-credibility" as one-hundred minus the presidential approval rating. This means that our opposition non-credibility index for the United States is by definition exactly collinear with presidential approval. However, the similarity between the US results and those of other countries (where opposition non-credibility is *not* collinear with government support) suggests that this collinearity does not seriously distort our empirical findings.

9.3.1 Comparative results

Table 9.4 reports the simple bivariate correlations between governing party support (presidential approval for the United States) and (1) aggregate personal expectations and (2) aggregate national expectations for six countries. The correlation levels are quite similar for UK, the United States, and Spain – where support correlates more strongly with personal rather than with national expectations. For Germany and Denmark, however, support correlates more strongly with national expectations than personal expectations. And for Australia, it is impossible to distinguish between the two because the consumer satisfaction measure incorporates both sets of expectations – as well as personal and national retrospections. We could easily speculate as to why these differential patterns are observed in the different countries. However, we prefer to suspend this exercise until we have explored the within-country similarities and between-country differences more fully.

Tables 9.5 (a–f) report the results of a series of models that were estimated on the basis of the specification outlined in Eq (9.1). For each country, and for each expectations dimension, Eq (9.1) was estimated

Table 9.4 Governing party support correlated with aggregate personal and national economic expectations in the UK, USA, Germany, Denmark, Australia, and Spain, varying time periods (bivariate correlations)

	Personal expectations	*National expectations*
UK	0.47 (1974–1999)	0.33 (1976–1997)
USA*	0.42 (1978–1997)	0.35 (1978–1997)
Germany	0.17 (1994–1997)	0.53 (1992–1998)
Denmark	0.10 (1986–1997)	0.32 (1986–1997)
Australia	[0.66 (1976–1990)]**	
Spain	0.42 (1986–1995)	0.30 (1983–1995)

Notes
* Presidential approval.
** Consumer satisfaction includes both personal and national expectations, as well as personal and national retrospections.

Table 9.5(a) The effects of aggregate personal and national economic expectations on governing party support in the UK, 1974–1999 (OLS estimators)

	Aggregate personal-expectations model	Aggregate national-expectations model
Constant	3.46***	3.14***
	(0.72)	(0.76)
Government support $(t-1)$	0.92***	0.92***
	(0.02)	(0.02)
Personal expectations	0.06***	
	(0.01)	
National expectations		0.04***
		(0.01)
IMF loan crisis	−6.31*	−5.79**
	(2.22)	(2.08)
Falklands – May 1982	9.18***	8.57***
	(2.22)	(2.08)
Falklands – June 1982	5.20***	4.75*
	(2.22)	(2.08)
Thatcher removal	6.56***	7.07***
	(2.22)	(2.07)
Blair government	13.95***	
	(1.58)	
N	307	254
R^2	0.92	0.91
Durbin Watson	2.35	2.74
Sample	1974m1–1999m7	1975m12–1997m1

Notes
* Coefficient significant at 0.05; ** at 0.01; *** at 0.001. Standard errors in parentheses. Estimation by OLS.

Table 9.5(b) The effects of aggregate personal and national economic expectations on presidential approval in USA, 1978–1997 (OLS estimators)

	Aggregate personal-expectations model	Aggregate national-expectations model
Constant	−5.05	1.79
	(2.89)	(1.31)
Presidential approval $(t-1)$	0.89***	0.90***
	(0.02)	(0.02)
Personal expectations	0.09***	
	(0.03)	
National expectations		0.03***
		(0.01)
Reagan's inauguration	16.3***	16.11***
	(3.79)	(3.76)
Bush's inauguration	−11.56**	−11.56**
	(3.78)	(3.75)
Bush's inauguration $(t-1)$	11.26**	11.20**
	(3.77)	(3.75)

Gulf war	24.51***	25.99***
	(3.77)	(3.77)
Clinton's inauguration	6.30	6.56
	(3.77)	(3.74)
N	239	239
R^2	0.88	0.88
Durbin Watson	1.85	1.89
Sample	1978m2–1997m12	1978m2–1997m12

Notes
* Coefficient significant at 0.05; ** at 0.01; *** at 0.001. Standard errors in parentheses.
Estimation by OLS. Dependent variable is presidential approval at time t.

Table 9.5(c) The effects of aggregate personal and national economic expectations on governing party support in Germany, 1993–1998 (OLS estimators)

	Aggregate personal-expectations model	*Aggregate national-expectations model*
Constant	−3.30	9.29**
	(4.27)	(2.72)
Government support $(t-1)$	0.86***	0.78***
	(0.06)	(0.07)
Personal expectations	0.20*	
	(0.09)	
National expectations		0.08**
		(0.02)
Schröder's election victory	9.79**	8.37**
	(3.03)	(2.94)
N	72	72
R^2	0.73	0.74
Durbin Watson	2.57	2.56
Sample	1993m1–1998m12	1993m1–1998m12

Notes
* Coefficient significant at 0.05; ** at 0.01; *** at 0.001. Standard errors in parentheses.
Estimation by OLS. Dependent variable is government support at time t.

Table 9.5(d) The effects of aggregate personal and national economic expectations on governing party support in Denmark, 1986–1997 (OLS estimators)

	Aggregate personal-expectations model	*Aggregate national-expectations model*
Constant	3.82**	3.78**
	(1.21)	(1.21)
Government support $(t-1)$	0.88***	0.88***
	(0.08)	(0.04)
Personal expectations[a]	0.17**	
	(0.06)	
National expectations[a]		0.11***
		(0.02)

Table 9.5(d) (Continued)

	Aggregate personal-expectations model	Aggregate national-expectations model
1987 election	−4.29**	−5.05***
	(1.30)	(1.29)
1994 election	3.66**	4.17**
	(1.29)	(1.26)
N	139	139
R^2	0.81	0.81
Durbin Watson	2.07	2.05
Sample	1986m6–1997m12	1986m6–1997m12

Notes
* Coefficient significant at 0.05; ** at 0.01; *** at 0.001. Standard errors in parentheses. Estimation by OLS. Dependent variable is government support at time t. [a] Augmented Dickey–Fuller tests suggest that the expectations terms needed differencing for the Danish data. Empirically, the effects of expectations in the Danish context are much stronger. For these reasons, we use change in expectations terms from $t−(t − 1)$ as independent variables in the Danish equations.

Table 9.5(e) The effects of aggregate economic expectations/retrospections on governing party support in Australia, 1976–1990 (OLS estimators)

	Consumer-satisfaction model
Constant	2.85***
	(0.01)
Government support $(t − 1)$	0.79***
	(0.04)
Consumer satisfaction	0.06***
	(0.01)
Hawke's election victory	10.36***
	(1.75)
N	180
R^2	0.82
Durbin Watson	2.06
Sample	1976m1–1990m12

Notes
* Coefficient significant at 0.05; ** at 0.01; *** at 0.001. Standard errors in parentheses. Estimation by OLS. Dependent variable is government support at time t.

Table 9.5(f) The effects of aggregate personal and national economic expectations on governing party support in Spain, 1983–1995 (OLS estimators)

	Aggregate personal-expectations model	Aggregate national-expectations model
Constant	4.57	3.99
	(3.32)	(2.92)
Government support $(t − 1)$	0.86***	0.92***
	(0.07)	(0.06)

Personal expectations	0.20*	
	(0.09)	
National expectations		0.11*
		(0.05)
N	38	51
R^2	0.85	0.85
Durbin Watson	2.32	2.34
Sample	1986q2–1995q3	1983q1–1995q3

Notes
* Coefficient significant at 0.05; ** at 0.01; *** at 0.001. Standard errors in parentheses. Estimation by OLS. Dependent variable is government support at time *t*.

incorporating a series of "event" dummy variables. These dummies corresponded to either (a) switches from one governing (presidential) party to another or (b) events that had been shown by previous studies to exert a major influence on government (presidential) popularity. Measures of unemployment and inflation were also added to each estimated equation to confirm that the expectations coefficient estimates were unaffected by the inclusion of terms for the objective economy: the empirical results (not reported) indicated that they were not.[4]

The results shown in Tables 9.5(a–f) suggest a complex but consistent pattern. Although the time periods and countries analyzed vary, the terms for personal and for national expectations are all correctly signed and statistically significant. Thus, for all the models in all the countries in this study, increases in economic optimism lead to increases in support for the governing party. This said, it is clear that the magnitudes of the coefficients vary from country to country. The personal expectations coefficient ranges from $b = 0.06$ in the UK to $b = 0.20$ in Germany and Spain; its national counterpart from $b = 0.03$ in USA to $b = 0.11$ in Spain and Denmark.

Table 9.6 relates these coefficient magnitudes to Powell and Whitten's clarity-of-responsibility index. On the face of it, there appears to be little support for a Powell–Whitten explanation of this cross-national pattern of variation. Germany and Denmark exhibit the lowest level of clarity (2.6 and 2.8, respectively); yet they exhibit the largest expectations effects. Similarly, UK exhibits the smallest coefficients and the highest level of clarity. If Powell and Whitten's clarity mechanism were operating here, we would have expected the highest clarity countries to have the largest coefficients and vice versa. However, given that all the countries sampled here exhibit relatively high levels of responsibility, the results presented in Table 9.6 cannot be regarded as an adequate *test* of the Powell–Whitten thesis.

But as we noted earlier, we are less interested here in cross-national variations in the magnitudes of the expectations coefficients and rather more interested in variations over time *within* countries. We showed

Table 9.6 "Full-series" OLS estimates of aggregate personal and national economic expectations coefficients by country, compared with Powell and Whitten's clarity-of-responsibility index

	Personal expectations	National expectations	Powell and Whitten's clarity-of-responsibility score*
UK	0.06	0.04	0.2
USA	0.09	0.03	1.0
Germany	0.20	0.08	2.6
Denmark	0.17	0.11	2.8
Australia***	[0.06]	0.4	
Spain	0.20	0.11	**

Notes
* The smaller the numerical score on this index, the greater is the clarity of responsibility; ** Not in Powell and Whitten's sample; no score available; *** This is a measure of consumer satisfaction, which includes both personal and national expectations, as well as personal and national retrospections.

earlier how the personal expectations coefficient varies over time in UK. Figure 9.2, for example, showed how the magnitude of the coefficient varied using a rolling window of $N = 30$. To maximize cross-national comparability (and because far fewer data points are available, particularly for Spain and Germany), the remainder of our analysis uses an $N = 30$ window. Figures 9.3(a–d) are the direct counterparts of Figure 9.2.

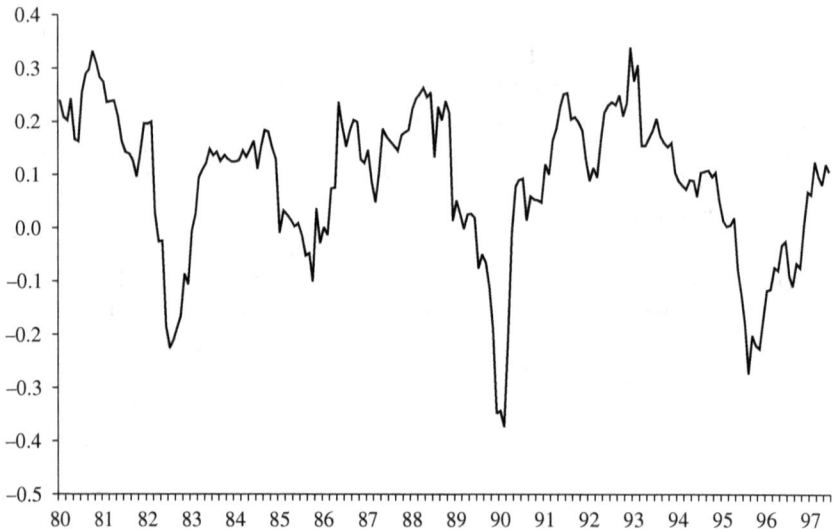

Figure 9.3(a) Rolling recursive estimates of the variations in the magnitude of the personal expectations coefficients in USA, July 1980–December 1997, window size = 30.

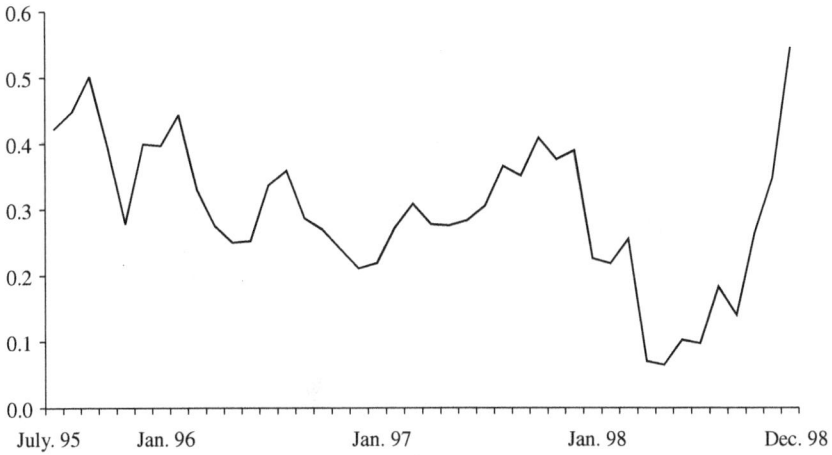

Figure 9.3(b) Rolling recursive extimates of the variations in the magnitude of the personal expectations coefficients in Germany, July 1995–December 1998, window size = 30.

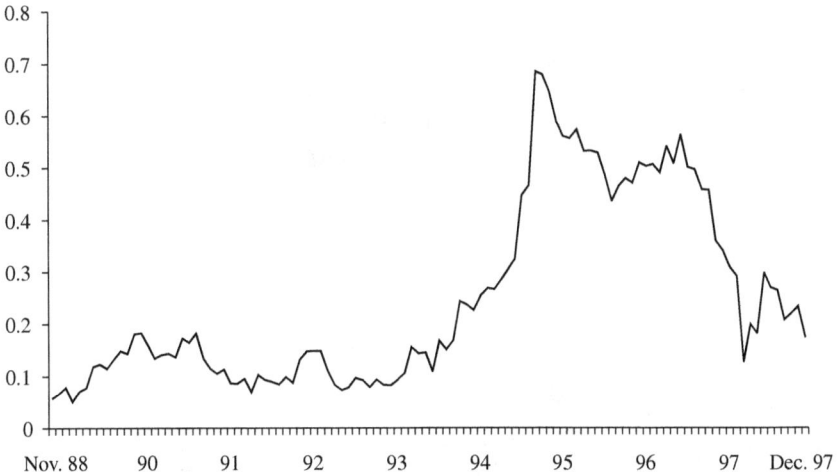

Figure 9.3(c) Rolling recursive estimates of the variations in the magnitude of the personal expectations coefficients in Denmark, November 1988–December 1997, window size = 30.

Based on the model outlined in Eq (9.2), they provide rolling recursive estimates of the *personal* expectations coefficient, using $N = 30$, for the United States, Germany, Denmark, and Australia, respectively.[5] Visual inspection of the figures clearly indicates that there is considerable over-time variation in the sizes of the coefficients. Figures 9.4(a–e) provide the

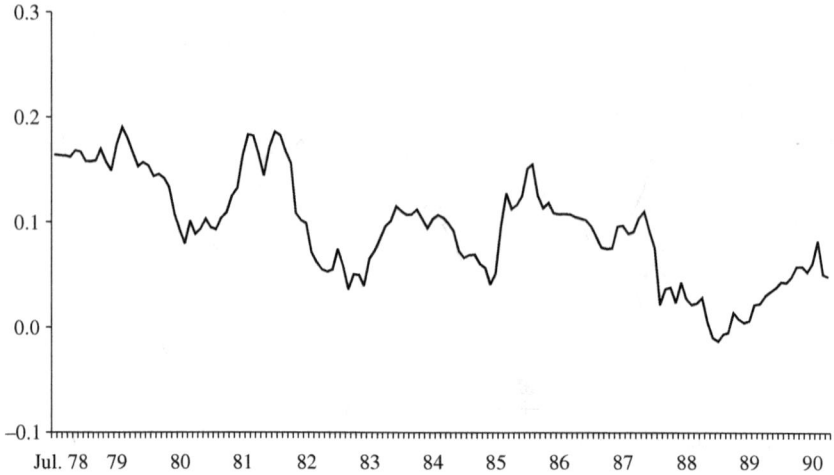

Figure 9.3(d) Rolling recursive estimates of the variations in the magnitude of the consumer satisfaction coefficients in Australia, July 1978–December 1990, window size = 30.
Note: Consumer satisfaction includes both personal and national expectations, as well as personal and national retrospections.

corresponding rolling recursive estimates of the *national* expectations coefficient for UK, the United States, Germany, Denmark and Spain. Again, visual inspection of the figures shows that the coefficient magnitudes vary quite considerably in each of the countries analyzed.

Figure 9.4(a) Rolling recursive estimates of the variations in the magnitude of the national expectations coefficients in the UK, July 1978–January 1997, window size = 30.

Figure 9.4(b) Rolling recursive estimates of the variations in the magnitude of the national expectations coefficients in USA, July 1982–December 1997, window size = 30.

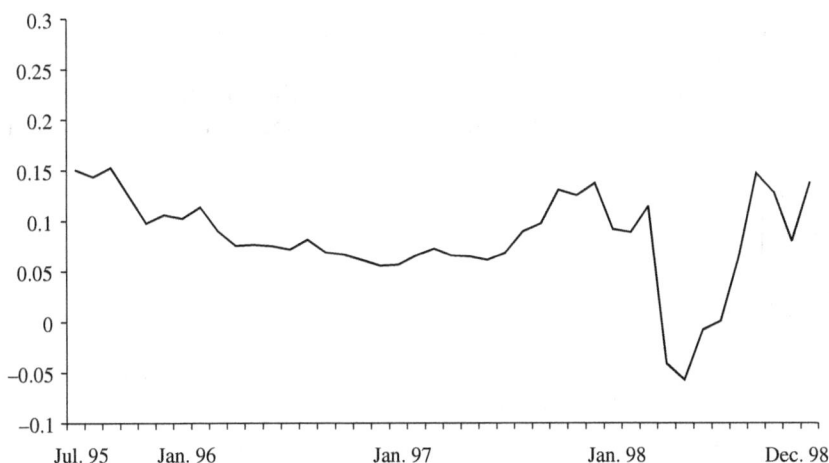

Figure 9.4(c) Rolling recursive estimates of the variations in the magnitude of the national expectation coefficients in the Germany, July 1993–December 1998, window size = 20.

Table 9.7 provides a summary of the information contained in Figures 9.2–9.4(e). The ranges of all the coefficients are quite considerable. The UK coefficient for personal expectations, for example, varies from +0.34 to −0.04 over different 30-month periods – averaging $b = 0.12$. (The best estimate of the coefficient magnitude over the entire period, of course, is

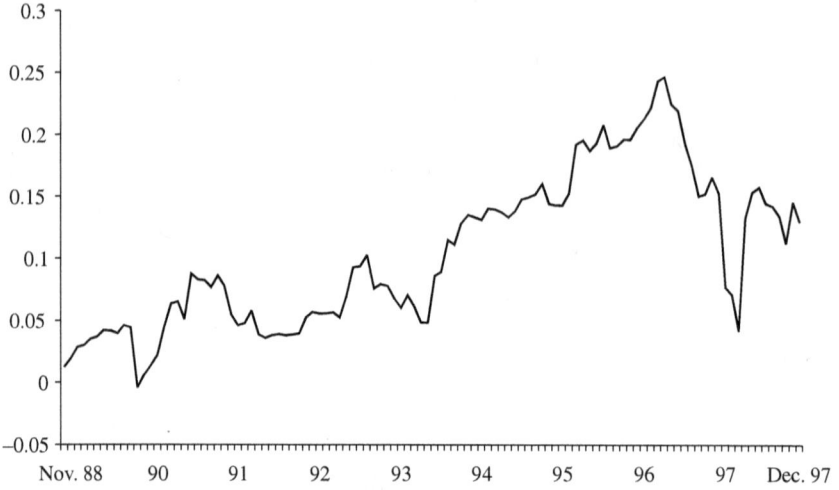

Figure 9.4(d) Rolling recursive estimates of the variations in the magnitude of
the national expectations coefficients in Denmark, November
1988–December 1997, window size = 30.

the "full-series" OLS estimate of $b = 0.06$.) The key inference that needs
to be drawn from Table 9.7, however, is that the variations in coefficient
magnitudes *within* countries are greater than the variations *across* countries. The "full-series" estimates of the personal general expectations

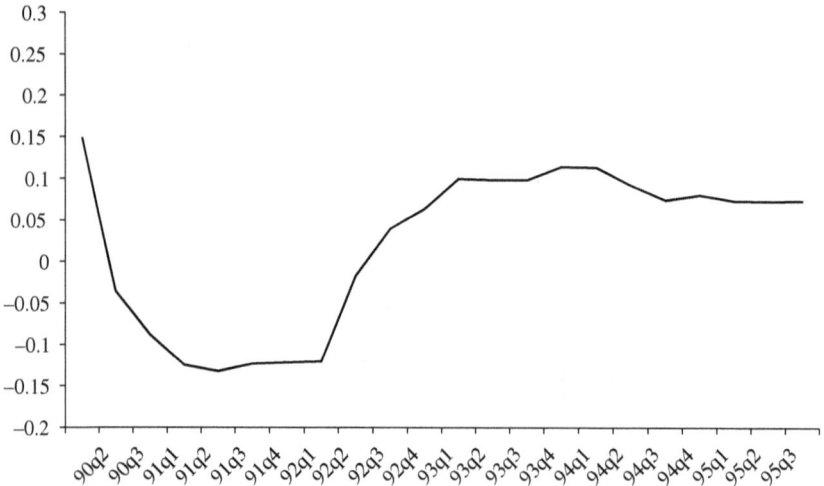

Figure 9.4(e) Rolling recursive estimates of the variations in the magnitude of the
national expectations coefficients in Spain, 1990 (second quarter)–
1995 (third quarter), window size = 30.

Table 9.7 Variations in the personal and national economic expectations coefficients in the UK, USA, Germany, Denmark, Australia and Spain, varying time periods

		Personal expectations coefficient (window N = 30)	National expectations coefficient (window N = 30)
UK	Maximum value	0.34	0.19
	Minimum value	−0.04	−0.07
	Average value	0.12	0.06
	Coefficient estimate over full time-series	0.06	0.04
USA	Maximum value	0.34	0.22
	Minimum value	−0.37	−0.16
	Average value	0.09	0.04
	Coefficient estimate over full time-series	0.09	0.03
Germany	Maximum value	0.55	0.15
	Minimum value	0.06	−0.06
	Average value	0.30	0.08
	Coefficient estimate over full time-series	0.20	0.08
Denmark	Maximum value	0.69	0.25
	Minimum value	0.05	0.00
	Average value	0.25	0.10
	Coefficient estimate over full time-series	0.17	0.11
Australia*	Maximum value	0.19	
	Minimum value	−0.01	
	Average value	0.09	
	Coefficient estimate over full time-series	0.06	
Spain	Maximum value	0.27	0.14
	Minimum value	0.18	−0.13
	Average value	0.22	0.02
	Coefficient estimate over full time-series	0.20	0.11

Note
* This is a measure of consumer satisfaction, which includes both personal and national expectations, as well as personal and national retrospections.

coefficient range from 0.06 to 0.20. For the national expectations coefficient, the equivalent range is from 0.04 to 0.11. Yet in all six countries (with the exception of the personal expectations coefficient in Spain), and across both measures, the range of the rolling window coefficients is considerably greater. This pattern strongly supports the idea that the within-country over-time variations in coefficients demand just as much analysis and explanation as the cross-country variations in those coefficients.

From a purely econometric viewpoint, of course, it could be argued that, whenever the effect of one variable on another is estimated, the longest possible time period should be used for the estimation: anything less fails to use all the available information. This perspective, however, is not necessarily appropriate when political data are being analyzed. There is, as noted above, a considerable volume of theorizing and evidence to suggest that voters respond to economic stimuli when they are deciding which political party they should support. But it is far less evident that voters respond mechanically to economic stimuli – particularly when they arise in different political and cultural contexts. Political symbols, agendas, discourses, and personalities are continuously in flux. In these circumstances, it would be astonishing if identical economic stimuli produced identical reactions among voters.

The results in Table 9.7 show that voters do not react in the same ways in all circumstances. On the contrary, sometimes their optimism is strongly translated into incumbent support; at other times, it can even serve to weaken that support. It would be a brave politician indeed who relied on the long-term "full-series" value of the expectations coefficient in circumstances when, in the recent past, rising expectations had clearly not translated into support for his/her party. From a strict econometric perspective, we should undoubtedly be cautious in seeking to draw inferences from short-term estimates of coefficient magnitudes. Yet the reality may be – and this is certainly the implication of Figures 9.2–9.4(e) – that the coefficient magnitudes really do vary over time. In these circumstances, it is important to seek to understand *why* they vary.

9.3.2   Modeling the sources of temporal variation in effect magnitudes

The analysis conducted in Section 9.2 showed that, for UK, over-time variations in the personal expectations coefficient could be explained, in part, by the level of unemployment (H1) and by the degree of non-credibility of the main opposition party (H2). In this section, we seek to establish whether this finding can be generalized to national expectations and to the other countries in our sample.

For each of our six countries, Table 9.8 correlates the variations in the personal and national expectations coefficients with the level of unemployment and opposition non-credibility (NONCRED). The results shown in the table are mixed. In UK, Germany, and Denmark, the coefficient pattern clearly supports (H1) and (H2): all sets of expectations correlate negatively with unemployment and positively with opposition non-credibility. The results for the United States also show that the coefficients support (H2), that expectations correlate positively with non-credibility of the opposition, but the signs of the coefficients are mixed for (H1). For Spain, however, the signs on the coefficients are the *reverse* of what is predicted by (H1), the expectations terms tend to

Table 9.8 Aggregated personal and national economic expectations correlated with unemployment and non-credibility of opposition in the UK, USA, Germany, Denmark, Australia and Spain (bivariate correlations, rolling recursive windows = 30)

	Unemployment	Non-credibility of the opposition	Time period
UK			
Personal expectations	−0.50	+0.43	1976m6–1997m7
National expectations	−0.03	+0.67	1978m5–1997m1
USA			
Personal expectations	+0.09	+0.25	1980m7–1997m12
National expectations	−0.004	+0.47	1980m7–1997m12
Germany			
Personal expectations	−0.32	+0.58	1995m7–1998m12
National expectations	−0.27	+0.61	1995m7–1998m12
Denmark			
Personal expectations	−0.05	+0.62	1988m12–1997m12
National expectations	−0.07	+0.69	1988m12–1997m12
Australia			
Consumer satisfaction*	−0.22	−0.17	1978m6–1990m12
Spain			
Personal expectations	+0.60	+0.37	1993q3–1995q2
National expectations	+0.77	−0.72	1990q2–1995q2

Notes
* This is a measure of consumer satisfaction, which includes both personal and national expectations, as well as personal and national retrospections.

correlate positively with unemployment, and are mixed for (H2). In Australia, the consumer satisfaction variable is correctly signed in terms of (H1), but NONCRED is not.

This ambiguous pattern of correlation is confirmed by more formal attempts to model these relationships, using the general specification described in Eq (9.3). The results of these modeling efforts, which included controls for the various event dummies indicated in Table 9.5, are summarized in Table 9.9. The full equations are not reported – only the coefficients for the unemployment and NONCRED terms. The overall pattern of coefficients suggests that (H1) and (H2) are fully supported *only* in UK. Elsewhere, the coefficients are either generally nonsignificant (as they are in the United States, Denmark, Australia, and Spain) or inappropriately signed (as they are in Germany for the unemployment term). Indeed, the main conclusion suggested by Table 9.9 is that there is no general relationship between variations in coefficient magnitudes and either unemployment or opposition non-credibility. Rather, the sources of coefficient variability themselves appear to vary from one country to another.

Table 9.9 Effects of unemployment and non-credibility of the opposition on predicting variations in the effects of aggregate personal and national economic expectations on governing party support in the UK, USA, Germany, Denmark, Australia and Spain summarized, varying time periods (rolling recursive windows = 30)

		Unemployment	Non-credibility of opposition	Time period	Event dummies included in the specification
UK	Personal expectations coefficient	−0.002**	+0.0002**	1976m6–1997m7	IMF loan crisis, Falklands war, Thatcher removal
	National expectations coefficient	−0.0008	+0.0003*	1978m5–1997m1	Blair election (not for national expectations)
USA	Personal expectations coefficient	−0.002	−0.00004	1980m8–1997m12	Inaugurations of Reagan, Bush and Clinton; Gulf war
	National expectations coefficient	−0.001	+0.0003	1980m8–1997m12	
Germany	Personal expectations coefficient	+0.07*	+0.005*	1995m7–1998m12	Schröder's election victory
	National expectations coefficient	+0.04**	+0.002**	1995m7–1998m12	
Denmark	Personal expectations coefficient	+0.004	+0.001	1988m12–1997m12	September 1994 election (not for national expectations)
	National expectations coefficient	+0.001	+0.0003	1988m12–1997m12	
Australia	Consumer satisfaction	−0.0001	+0.0001	1978m6–1990m12	Hawke's election victory
Spain	Personal expectations coefficient	Too few observations			
	National expectations coefficient	+0.01	−0.0004	1990q2–995q2	

Notes
Specification as in Eq. (9.3). Estimation by maximum likelihood AR(1) for UK, USA, Denmark, Australia, and Spain. Estimation by OLS for Germany. Alternative specifications, using change in unemployment and non-credibility (both lagged and unlagged) produced similar results.

9.3.3 The potential relevance of the culture of risk

Is there a simplifying logic that might explain the within-country variations in coefficient magnitudes? In our view, one fruitful avenue may lie in the way voters, in different cultural contexts, orient themselves towards risk taking under conditions of uncertainty. This perspective cannot help to explain the variable effects of opposition non-credibility shown in Table 9.9. However, it can help to explain why unemployment appears to reduce the effects of expectations in Britain, to increase them in Germany and to leave them unaffected in the United States, Denmark, Australia, and Spain.

In principle, voters' attitudes to risk can lie anywhere on a continuum that runs from highly risk averse, through risk neutral, to highly risk acceptant.[6] Voters' risk orientations under conditions of uncertainty could have an important effect on the way in which they translate their economic perceptions into party support under different economic circumstances.

Consider, first, voters who become more risk averse – i.e. they become less prepared to take risks – as uncertainty increases, and more risk acceptant when uncertainty declines. Assume that in economic "bad times" – at high levels of unemployment – economic uncertainty rises. In such circumstances, these voters are less likely to take political risks. Their political opinions become "stickier." They are less likely to translate any changes in their economic expectations into changes in support for the incumbent party. Assume, now, that the converse is also true – that in economic "good times" uncertainty declines. This in turn implies that these voters will become more risk acceptant. They are more prepared to take risks because the costs of failure do not appear to be so great. In these circumstances, their political preferences will be more fluid and, as a result, they will be more likely to adjust their party preferences in response to changes in their economic expectations.

Second, consider voters who become more risk acceptant as uncertainty increases. This is by no means a counter-intuitive possibility. Again, assume that uncertainty increases in economic "bad times." These voters' response to the greater uncertainty of high unemployment will be to take more political risks in order to put things right. In other words, under uncertainty, their political preferences become more fluid. They become more likely to translate changes in expectations into incumbent support. In economic "good times," where there is less uncertainty, these voters are prepared to take *fewer* risks because they want to avoid losing what they already have. As a result, their political preferences become "stickier" and they become less likely to change their party preferences in response to changing economic perceptions.

Finally, consider voters whose risk orientations do not change as the level of uncertainty changes. For these voters, the advent of either

economic "good times" or "bad times" is irrelevant. Their risk orientations remain stable in either case. As a result, the extent to which their
political preferences are affected by their economic perceptions is unaffected by the overall level of uncertainty.

We consider it likely that the electorate in any country will be composed of a mix of these three types of voter. However, it is clearly possible
that different cultural configurations could result in different countries
exhibiting different mixes of the three voter types. Depending on which
group of voters predominates in a particular country, we can generate
three different sets of expectations about the relationship between
(i) macroeconomic uncertainty, as measured by unemployment, and
(ii) the magnitude of the connection between voters' economic perceptions and incumbent party support.[7] Specifically:

a   If voters become more risk averse as uncertainty increases, then we
    would expect to find a *negative* correlation between unemployment
    and the magnitude of the relationship between economic expecta-
    tions and incumbent support.
b   If voters become more risk acceptant as uncertainty increases, then
    we would expect to find a *positive* correlation between unemployment
    and the magnitude of the relationship between economic expecta-
    tions and incumbent support.
c   If voters become neither more risk acceptant nor more risk avoidant
    as uncertainty increases, then we would expect to find *no* correlation
    between unemployment and the magnitude of the relationship
    between economic expectations and incumbent support.

It is clear from Table 9.9 that in UK, voters appear to become more
politically risk averse under uncertainty, whereas in Germany they
appear to become more politically risk acceptant. In USA, Denmark,
Australia, and Spain, uncertainty seems to make no difference to
the distribution of risk.

It could be argued, of course, that the whole notion of "risk orientations under uncertainty" is irrelevant to any understanding of economic
voting. The fact that the pattern of coefficients in Table 9.9 is so vari-
egated could be interpreted as evidence that there is no systematic
connection between unemployment and the expectations–incumbent support relationship precisely because risk orientations have no systematic
effect on anything.

Such an interpretation would do a disservice to the risk orientation
approach described here. The real pay-off of the risk approach is that it
explains more than just the null findings represented by the nonsignificant
coefficients that are reported in Table 9.9. It explains why unemployment
correlates negatively with variations in the expectations coefficients in UK
(UK voters on balance have a tendency to become more risk averse as

uncertainty increases). It explains why unemployment correlates positively with coefficient variations in Germany (German voters on balance become more risk acceptant as uncertainty increases). And it also explains why unemployment fails to correlate with coefficient variation in the United States, Denmark, Australia, and Spain (American, Danish, Australian, and Spanish voters on balance do not change their risk orientations as uncertainty increases). As with any "explanation" in the social sciences, the analysis here inevitably begs the question as to what it is that produces these hypothesized variations in risk orientations. We can offer no answer here beyond the suggestion that it may have something to do with "political culture." But that raises questions far beyond the scope of the present analysis. It also suggests a need to develop independent measures of voters' risk orientations in order that the claims we make for their explanatory role might be more fully developed and tested.

In conclusion, it is important to emphasize that we do not doubt Powell and Whitten's claim that economic effects on voting are strongest in high-clarity systems. What we have shown here supplements rather than contradicts their findings. We have shown that, even in what are consistently high-clarity countries, economic-voting effects vary hugely – not so much across systems as within them. We have provided a tentative explanation for that variation, but it is no more than that. Further research is clearly necessary to develop and test the claims that we have made. On a more pessimistic note, we recognize that we may be searching for a Holy Grail of economic voting that does not exist. There may in fact be no underlying model that will explain all the complex features of economic voting that have variously been observed. Rather, there may be, in the final analysis, merely a multiplicity of cultural differences and historical contingencies.

NOTES

1 Question texts in the UK are as follows: Personal expectations – "How do you think the financial situation of your household will change over the next 12 months?"; National expectations – "How do you think the general economic situation in this country will develop over the next 12 months?"; The response categories for both questions are: get a lot better, get a little better, stay the same, get a little worse, get a lot worse, do not know/refused. There are minor variations in question wording for other countries.

2 Previous economic-voting literature has also attempted to use party identification data in the United States as a proxy for vote intention. However, these data are not comparable with the popularity functions that we employ in the other countries in this study.

3 Data measuring consumer satisfaction (consat), personal expectations (pexp), and national expectations (nexp) are available for the period January 1996–July 1997. The correlation between consat and pexp is $r = 0.72$; between consat and nexp is $r = 0.91$.

230 Sanders Carey OCR

4 The estimates reported in Tables 9.5a–f are all OLS. For some of the models, a first-order autoregressive process was evident in the residuals. The equations were accordingly re-estimated using an AR(1) maximum likelihood specification. These specifications produced minor changes in the magnitude of the expectations coefficients: For UK, the personal expectations coefficient falls from 0.06 to 0.05 and the national expectations coefficient falls from 0.04 to 0.03. For Germany, the personal expectations coefficient falls from 0.20 to 0.17 and the national expectations coefficient falls from 0.08 to 0.06. For Spain, the personal expectations coefficient falls from 0.20 to 0.18 and the national expectations coefficient falls from 0.11 to 0.09.

5 As noted earlier, the Australian series strictly measures consumer satisfaction (a combination of national and personal prospections and retrospections) rather than personal expectations.

6 There is a strong emphasis on political risk in studies that use, in general, game theory approaches to political situations and, in particular, decision theory. For a discussion of risk acceptance, risk averseness, and risk neutrality, see Ordeshook (1986), but also Rohde (1979).

7 We use a single measure of macroeconomic conditions here – unemployment – to ensure that our results are clearly interpretable. Statistical tests for inflation were applied to all the models that we develop here, with no significant differences to the results that we report.

REFERENCES

Alvarez, R.M., Nagler, J. and Willete, J.R. (2000) Measuring the relative impact of issues and the economy in democratic elections. *Electoral Stud.*, **19**, 237–253.

Anderson, C. (1995) *Blaming the Government*. Armonk, NY: Sharpe.

Anderson, C. (2000) Economic voting and political context: a comparative perspective. *Electoral Stud.*, **19**, 151–170.

Brown, R.L., Durbin, J. and Evans, J.M. (1975) Techniques for testing the constancy of regression relationships over time. *J. Roy. Statist. Soc. Ser. B*, **37**, 153–157.

Butler, D. and Kavanagh, D. (1997) *The British General Election of 1997*. Oxford: MacMillan.

Chappell, H.W. and Veiga, L.G. (2000) economics and elections in western Europe: 1960–1997. *Electoral Stud.*, **19**, 183–197.

Charemza, W.W. and Deadman, D.F. (1997) *New Directions in Econometric Practice*, 2nd ed. Cheltenham: Edward Elgar.

Clarke, H.D. and Stewart, M. (1995) Economic evaluations, prime ministerial approval and governing party support: rival models considered. *Brit. J. Political Sci.*, **25**, 15–70.

Clarke, H.D., Ho, K. and Stewart, M. (2000) Major's lesser (not minor) effects: prime ministerial approval and governing party support in Britain since 1979. *Electoral Stud.*, **19**, 255–273.

Fiorina, M.P. (1981) *Retrospective Voting in American National Elections*. New Haven, CT: Yale University Press.

Lewis-Beck, M. (1988) *Economics and Elections: The Major Western Democracies*. Ann Arbor, MI: University of Michigan Press.

Nadeau, R., Niemi, R.G. and Amato, T. (1996) Prospective and comparative or retrospective and individual? party leaders and party support in Great Britain. *Brit. J. Political Sci.*, **26**, 245–258.

Nannestad, P. and Paldam, M. (1996) It's the government's fault! A cross-section study of economic voting in Denmark, 1990–1993. *Eur. J. Political Res.*, **28**, 33–65.

Nannestad, P. and Paldam, M. (1997) The grievance asymmetry revisited: a microstudy of economic voting in Denmark, 1986–1992. *Eur. J. Political Economy*, **13**, 81–99.

Nannestad, P. and Paldam, M. (2000) What do voters know about the economy? A study of Danish data, 1990–1993. *Electoral Stud.*, **19**, 363–391.

Norpoth, H., Lewis-Beck, M. and Lafay, J.-D. (eds) (1991) *Economics and Politics: The Calculus of Support*. Ann Arbor, MI: University of Michigan Press.

Ordeshook, P. (1986) *Game Theory and Political Theory*. Cambridge: Cambridge University Press.

Paldam, M. (1991) How robust is the vote function? A study of 17 nations over four decades. In H. Norpoth, M. Lewis-Beck and J.-D. Lafay (eds), *Economics and Politics: The Calculus of Support*. Ann Arbor, MI: University of Michigan Press.

Powell, G.B. and Whitten, G.D. (1993) A cross-national analysis of economic voting: taking account of the political context. *Am. J. Political Sci.*, **37**, 391–414.

Rohde, D.W. (1979) Risk-bearing and progressive ambition: the case of the members of the United States House of Representatives. *Am. J. Political Sci.*, **23**, 1–26.

Royed, T.J., Leyden, K.M. and Borrelli, S.A. (2000) Is clarity of responsibility important for economic voting? Revisiting Powell and Whitten's hypothesis. *Brit. J. Political Sci.*, **30**, 669–685.

Sanders, D. (1999) Conservative incompetence, labour responsibility and the feelgood factor: why the economy failed to save the conservatives in 1997. *Electoral Stud.*, **18**, 251–270.

Sanders, D. (2000) The real economy and the perceived economy in popularity functions: how much do voters need to know? A study of British data, 1974–1997. *Electoral Stud.*, **19**, 275–294.

Sanders, D., Ward, H. and Marsh, D. (1993) The electoral impact of press coverage of the British economy, 1979–1987. *Brit. J. Political Sci.*, **23**, 175–210.

Whitten, G.D. and Palmer, H. (1999) Cross-national analyses of economic voting. *Electoral Stud.*, **18**, 49–67.

Part III
The changing economic voter

10 Emotions, expectations and the dynamics of party support in Britain

Harold D. Clarke, Marianne C. Stewart and Paul F. Whiteley

10.1 INTRODUCTION

How do people evaluate economic conditions, and how do they use this information to make voting choices? As observed in Chapter 1, these questions have captured the attention of researchers for more than three decades, and they have generated continuing, oftentimes heated, controversies. One such controversy concerns the time horizon of economic evaluations. Challenging numerous analyses that had used Key's (1968) classic reward–punishment model of the impact of *retrospective* evaluations of economic performance (e.g. Goodhart and Bhansali, 1970; Alt, 1979; Fiorina, 1981; Kiewiet, 1983; Moseley, 1984; Hudson, 1985), researchers began to specify more sophisticated models based on the idea that voters employ *prospective* evaluations when making political support decisions (e.g. Chappell and Keech, 1985; Lewis-Beck, 1988; Sanders, 1991, 1993; MacKuen *et al.*, 1992; Clarke and Stewart, 1994). This long-standing debate about whether voters are backward- or forward-looking continues.

Another protracted controversy pits cognition against emotion. Traditionally, most researchers have assumed that perceived costs and benefits of alternative economic outcomes are what matters (Borooah and van Der Ploeg, 1983; Alesina, 1987, 1988; Alesina and Rosenthal, 1995). As noted in Chapter 1, the theory of economic voting has been seen as a special case of the rational choice perspective on electoral behavior: Voting is an instrumental act to maximize individual utility or welfare. However, some analysts have focused on the impact of emotional reactions to economic performance (Conover and Feldman, 1986; Conover *et al.*, 1986, 1987; Marcus and MacKuen, 1993; Clarke *et al.*, 1998a). The presumed significance of cost–benefit calculations derives from neoclassical economics and rational choice theory more generally, whereas the emphasis on the role of the emotions is rooted in social–psychological accounts of how individuals respond to important information about their collective and individual well-being.

A third debate concerns the referent of politically relevant economic judgments. When making such judgments, the familiar "pocketbook-voting" hypothesis maintains that voters focus on their personal well-being rather than that of the country as a whole or some particular group to which they belong (Kinder and Kiewiet, 1979, 1981; Kinder and Mebane, 1983; MacKuen *et al.*, 1992; Clarke and Stewart, 1994; Haller and Norpoth, 1994). An individual-centered (egocentric) focus is broadly consistent with traditional rational choice theories of party support that assume people seek to maximize their *own* utilities (Whiteley, 1995). In contrast, absent an identity between group- and self-interest, group-based (sociotropic) economic evaluations are inconsistent with such theories.

In the present chapter, we consider these controversies in three sets of analyses. First, we investigate factors that explain the formation of expectations regarding the evolution of personal economic conditions over the coming year – the widely touted "feel-good" factor (e.g. Sanders, 1991, 1993) – and examine the effects of these expectations on party support in contemporary Britain. To this end, we develop hypotheses based on recent theories of politico-economic information processing and test them in the context of a major British economic crisis, the exchange rate (ERM) or "currency" crisis that precipitated the ejection of Britain from the European Monetary System in September 1992. By integrating affective and cognitive accounts of the formation of economic expectations, we bring together hitherto distinct lines of research.

In a second set of analyses, we use individual-level survey data to assess relationships between objective economic conditions and subjective economic evaluations. This is a task that traditionally has been inhibited by the limitations imposed by cross-sectional survey designs. Particularly important in this regard is the absence of temporal variation in macro-economic indicators, a lack of variance that vitiates analysis of their effects (Kramer, 1983; see also Markus, 1988).[1] We avoid this problem by taking advantage of a natural experiment (Cook and Campbell, 1979) – the aforementioned ERM crisis. By utilizing data from four successive monthly surveys, two occurring before the event and two afterwards, we have sufficient variation in objective economic conditions to assess links between the objective economy and subjective economic evaluations at the individual level.

In a third set of analyses, we analyze subjective economic evaluations among subgroups in the electorate. To date, most aggregate models of the dynamics of party support have assumed a homogenous electorate. However, there is mounting evidence that the homogeneity assumption may be unrealistic and misleading (e.g. Rivers, 1988; Zaller, 1992; Krause, 1997). With few exceptions (e.g. Hibbs, 1982a,b; Box-Steffens-meier *et al.*, 1997) analysts who have relaxed the assumption have focused on educational achievement, viewing variation in level of formal education as a proxy for differences in voters' information availability and cognitive capacity. We pursue this promising line of inquiry, but also examine the extent to which age and gender condition the dynamics of subjective economic perceptions and political support. The conjecture motivating attention to these latter variables is that groups defined in terms of these variables will react differently to the dynamics of the macroeconomy. These reactions will influence how various groups of voters perceive their economic futures.

The chapter has five sections. After reviewing recent research on political information processing, we offer several hypotheses about the mechanisms that explain the formation of economic expectations. We then examine the dynamics of some of the variables that play an important role in explaining the formation of expectations, and proceed to test various hypotheses. Next, we estimate the influence of these economic expectations on voting intentions. In the conclusion, we briefly consider the implications of our findings for future research.

10.2   POLITICAL INFORMATION PROCESSING AND THE ECONOMY

For nearly half a century, students of voting and elections have struggled to reconcile classical notions in democratic theory of an informed, vigilant citizenry with evidence that the public is largely ignorant of politics and political issues. Data showing that levels of public knowledge about politics is very limited was one of the most widely noted findings in the early election studies in the United States (Berelson *et al.*, 1954; Campbell *et al.*, 1960). These findings soon were replicated in Britain by Butler and Stokes (1974, p. 277) who pointed out that "[u]nderstanding of policy issues falls away very sharply indeed as we move outwards from those at the heart of political decision-making to the public at large". Voters' lack of political knowledge fits well with rational choice theory. In what has become a canonical statement of the argument, Downs (1957, pp. 215–216) contended that voter ignorance is actually rational, since in most cases the acquisition of political knowledge entails costs and does not significantly enhance an individual's ability to influence policy outcomes. The implications are stark – if ignorance is rational, then politicians will not and cannot be held accountable for their actions. Voters cannot accurately assess a government's success in managing the economy and, in any event, it would be a waste of their time and energy to do so.

However, these pessimistic conclusions have been challenged, and there has been a number of attempts to explain how the public might acquire and use information in order to make politicians accountable. All of these efforts share the idea that voters can use informational shortcuts or "heuristics" which allow them to make reasoned judgments without having detailed knowledge. One of the earliest and best known analyses of this type was by Popkin (1991, p. 7) who argued that *low information rationality* is a type of reasoning that "draws on various information short-cuts and rules of thumb that voters use to obtain and evaluate information and to simplify the process of choosing between candidates". Such short-cuts can involve using cues from a variety of sources, including trusted opinion leaders (Berelson *et al.*, 1954), party loyalties (Campbell *et al.*, 1960), political campaigns (Lodge *et al.*, 1995), opinion polls (McKelvey and Ordeshook, 1986), interest group endorsements (Lupia, 1994) and the media (Iyengar and Kinder, 1987; Page and Shapiro, 1992).

The low information approach was developed more fully in the work of Sniderman *et al.* (1991) who introduced a distinction between cognitive and affective heuristics for processing of political information. Sniderman *et al.*'s (1991: 22) "likability heuristic" is a simple rule of thumb that can be used to evaluate political issues. They illustrate the heuristic with the following example: "[s]uppose that a person wants to figure out what she thinks about increasing federal government spending for blacks, it is not necessary that she has elaborated a theory of government, specifying services that alternative levels of government, federal, state and local, are competent and obliged to supply. It suffices that she knows she dislikes blacks: Dislike blacks and it follows immediately that she should oppose an increase in government spending to benefit them". This implies that affective or emotional reactions to a social group can substitute for cognitive judgments about a political issue involving that group when information is lacking about that issue or when voters wish to avoid the costs of acquiring and processing that information.

The general hypothesis that emotions drive calculations when forming expectations has a lengthy and distinguished pedigree (e.g. Keynes, 1936). Frank (1988) has elaborated the hypothesis by suggesting that emotional predisposition can explain apparently irrational behavior within a rational choice theoretical framework. This is because such pre-disposition can help to solve commitment problems, which in turn bring long-run benefits to the actors involved. A familiar example of this is the prisoners' dilemma game. It is well known that the optimal strategy in the one-shot game is defection rather than cooperation, even though this produces a Pareto-inferior outcome for all players (Mueller, 1989: 9–15). However, if players commit to cooperation, as in the repeat prisoners' dilemma game, then their long-term payoffs are higher (see Axelrod, 1984, 1997). In Frank's approach, emotions play the key role in support-ing moral codes which predispose individuals to cooperate, even in situations where their immediate incentive is to defect, or in which their defection cannot be detected easily and thereby sanctioned. Such emotional predisposition helps them to build a reputation for reliability and honesty, which in turn brings them long-term benefits. In this view, emotions undergird cognitive judgments.

Another approach to information processing comes from the literature on signaling games and from cognitive psychology, which specifies circumstances under which voters are likely to use certain kinds of heuristics. For example, Lupia and McCubbins (1998) employ a rational choice framework to investigate the conditions under which voters can be persuaded to accept political messages as truthful and reliable (see also Ferejohn and Kuklinski, 1990; Austin-Smith, 1990, 1993). They contend that "[t]he following conditions are individually necessary and collectively sufficient for persuasion: The principal must perceive the speaker to be trustworthy and the principal must perceive the speaker to have the knowledge she desires. Absent external forces, persuasion requires perceived common interests and perceived speaker knowledge" (Lupia and McCubbins, 1998: 54–55).

This argument builds on the work on "cheap talk" equilibria in signaling games (Crawford and Sobel, 1982), in which players can make costless commitments on which they have an incentive to renege. The trustworthiness of the speaker and the perceived community of interests between the speaker and the audience avoid perverse noncooperative equilibria in such games. This work suggests that the credibility and trustworthiness of the current leader of a governing political party and the identification of interests between voters and that leader should have a significant influence on voters' subjective expectations about the state of the economy.

A third approach to the use of heuristics is exemplified by the work of Zaller (1992) (see also Feldman and Zaller, 1992). The basic conjecture is that different segments of the electorate will react differently to political messages. In Zaller's (1992: 42) work, individuals with greater "cognitive engagement" (i.e. political knowledge) are more likely to receive and understand political messages. This is true regardless of whether they agree or disagree with those messages. In addition, Zaller (1994: 44) argues that individuals with greater knowledge of the context in which political messages occur are more likely to resist them if such messages are inconsistent with their political predisposition. Political knowledge thus acts as a filtering mechanism in situations where individuals have partisan predisposition, which are inconsistent with that knowledge. Zaller's work, therefore, represents an important extension of traditional "Michigan"-school arguments regarding the information-processing effects of partisan attachments (see, e.g. Campbell *et al.*, 1960, Chapter 6).

Economic information processing is a special case of political information processing and so the insights of this literature should apply to the task of explaining how the public processes economic information. We build on these insights in order to derive testable hypotheses about the influence of perceptions of economic management by political leaders on the economic expectations of various segments of the electorate.

A common theme in the literature on political information processing is that voters' knowledge conditions the way in which messages are perceived. A relatively neglected point is that voters also have different interests and, in the case of the economy, are affected differently by economic shocks depending on their socioeconomic status and position in the labor force. In this regard, similar to other advanced industrial democracies, there have been substantial changes in the Britain's economy in recent years. The British Household Panel Survey shows that older male unskilled workers have been particularly vulnerable to economic change, with working class occupations declining from 41 percent of the workforce in 1984 to 34 percent in 1992 (see Buck *et al.*, 1994: 154). Occupational "flexibility" has become a watchword of the "new economy," a development that favors younger, highly skilled workers at the expense of older, unskilled ones. Many of the latter have been forced into early retirement. Additionally, participation in the labor force by women has grown significantly over time, although many of the jobs involved are insecure, low paid and part-time (Buck *et al.*, 1994: 175). These developments imply that levels of economic optimism and pessimism should vary systematically across the electorate by age, skills and gender as a function of (changing) patterns of economic interests.

10.3   HYPOTHESES

The preceding discussion suggests several hypotheses that may be tested in the British case. We focus first on factors that influence voters' prospective evaluations of their personal economic conditions, i.e. their expectations about the evolution of their personal economic circumstances over the next year. The hypothesis that personal economic expectations strongly affect party support in Britain has been argued forcefully by Sanders (1991, 1993), and the impact of such expectations on voting behavior and election outcomes has become part of the shared conventional wisdom of academic observers and media pundits. Although recent time series analyses (Clarke *et al.*, 1997, 1998a, b) indicate that the effects of personal economic expectations in party support models may be more complex and less compelling than earlier studies had concluded, available evidence continues to indicate that such expectations deserve careful attention.

The first three hypotheses concern the impact of interest rates and the September 1992 ERM crisis.

(H1) Personal economic expectations will vary inversely with interest rates.

In addition to Sanders' (1991, 1993) general argument that interest rates will have significant effects on people's forecasts of their personal financial circumstances, there are good reasons to conjecture that interest rates were particularly important in the period in which our survey data were gathered. During the ERM crisis (September 1992), the salience of interest rates was magnified by the fact that these rates exhibited a frightening combination of high levels and extreme volatility. Indeed, on September 16, 1992 ("Black Wednesday"), rates rose by fully 5 percent (from 10 to 15 percent in the space of a few hours, as Chancellor of the Exchequer, Norman Lamont struggled vainly to defend the pound (Denver, 1998: 9). In addition to focusing public attention on a sensitive economic issue, the currency crisis and Britain's subsequent ejection from the European monetary system (only days after the Prime Minister assured the country that exit was not a viable option) severely tarnished the reputation of the governing Conservatives and their leader, prime minister John Major. The crisis starkly demonstrated the futility of government economic policy, and undermined public confidence that the prime minister and his associates could manage the country's business effectively. Pooled survey data covering the August–November 1992 period enable us to study this shock effect at the level of the individual voter. Specifically, we hypothesize:

(H2) The ERM crisis caused a sharp erosion in personal economic expectations.

Our third hypothesis follows from Zaller's (1992) conjecture that news has a greater impact on the perceptions of individuals who are politically knowledgeable than of those who are less well informed.

(H3) Objective economic measures, that is interest rates, and the shock variable measuring Britain's ejection from membership of the European monetary system, will have a greater impact on the expectations of cognitively engaged individuals than on the cognitively disengaged.

As mentioned earlier, Zaller's work also suggests that partisanship can act as a filter for political information, which gives rise to the hypothesis that:

(H4) Voters will use a partisanship heuristic to form personal economic expectations. However, cognitively engaged individuals will tend to rely on this less than cognitively disengaged individuals.

The partisanship heuristic implies that voters with strong partisan attachments will tend to filter out messages that are inconsistent with their beliefs, discounting bad economic news if their preferred party is in power, and emphasizing it if their party is in opposition. In this regard, recall one of the conditions for believing messages in signaling games is that a community of interest exists between the sender and receiver of messages; partisanship provides an indicator of the existence of this community of interests. The partisanship heuristic is very easy to use since it requires very little knowledge of politics and policies, beyond the fact that one's preferred party is in power or opposition. This is why the cognitively disengaged are likely to rely on it more than the cognitively engaged.

A fifth hypothesis involves governing party performance heuristics:

(H5) Voters will use governing party performance heuristics to form personal economic expectations. But cognitively engaged individuals will tend to rely on this heuristic more than cognitively disengaged individuals.

At any point in time, this heuristic means that voters will be more optimistic about their own future economic prospects if they believe in the probity and wisdom of the leadership of the governing party. This particular heuristic satisfies the second condition for believing messages in signaling games discussed earlier, namely, that the receiver believes in the trustworthiness and competence of the sender.

There is a difference between the cognitive requirements for the operation of governing party performance and partisanship heuristics. Evaluating governing party performance implies the ability to monitor that party's policies and to some extent the outcomes which result from those policies. Evaluations of governing party performance are subject to substantial dynamism. This is especially the case if voters evaluate governing party performance exclusively with reference to the actions of the party's current top leaders, i.e. the cabinet and prime minister, because such figures have very short "half-lives" compared to the parties they lead. In contrast, the partisanship heuristic places less stringent demands on voters' cognitive capacities because of the durability of parties and the reference frames (party systems and ideological spaces) within which they operate. Although the strength and direction of voters' partisan attachments can change in response to economic outcomes, policy performance in non-economic policy areas and salient events and conditions, British time series data indicate that partisanship is more stable than governing party performance evaluations or prime ministerial approval (Clarke *et al.*, 1997, 1998a). These varying dynamics suggest that judging governing party performance typically will be a more cognitively demanding exercise than evaluating parties. Use of a governing party performance heuristic, thus, will require a greater knowledge of politics than will the partisanship heuristic. Consequently, cognitively engaged individuals are more likely to use it than are the cognitively disengaged.

The sixth hypothesis concerns *emotional reactions* to economic conditions. Voters will use an affective heuristic to help them form personal economic expectations and this generally will be more important than mediated personal retrospective evaluations, particularly for cognitively disengaged individuals. The notion of an affective heuristic challenges economists' cherished assumption that voters are coldly calculating utility maximizers. But, as discussed above, hypotheses specifying emotional effects on economic behavior are not novel, and during the past decade, the importance of emotions in party-support functions and political psychology more generally has been emphasized in the work of Conover *et al.* (e.g. Conover and Feldman, 1986; Conover *et al.*, 1986, 1987; Frank, 1988; Sniderman *et al.*, 1991). Our specific hypothesis about the role of the emotions is straightforward:

(H6) If voters feel happy, hopeful, confident or proud about the state of the economy and their personal financial circumstances, these emotions will stimulate optimistic personal economic expectations. In contrast, if voters feel uneasy, afraid, angry or disgusted about national or personal economic conditions, these feelings will generate pessimistic expectations.

Retrospective evaluations of the economy are linked to adaptive expectation models of the macro-economy (see Attfield *et al.*, 1985, pp. 1–10; Whiteley, 1986; Clarke and Stewart, 1994; Haller and Norpoth, 1994). In situations where such evaluations are mediated, i.e. voters attribute responsibility to government for economic conditions, retrospective evaluation models imply that voters calculate their future economic prospects on the basis of judgments concerning the incumbent party's influence on their own past economic welfare. Such calculations are linked to governing party performance and partisanship heuristics, but they focus specifically on voters' perceptions of the government's role in influencing the economic welfare of themselves and their families, and not on wider issues of trust and competence. In the famous model of expectation formation advanced by Keynes (1936) nearly 70 years ago, emotions underpin and drive cognitive judgments. If this model is correct, affective evaluations are likely to join with mediated retrospective evaluations as factors influencing the formation of economic expectations.

Similar to the partisanship heuristic, the affective heuristic is very easy to use since individuals can respond to crisis headlines about the economy with feelings of uneasiness, pessimism or even fear, without having detailed knowledge of the crisis. On the other hand, if they are informed about politics and the economy, they will be able to put the facts of the crisis in context and make reasoned judgments about how it may affect themselves and their families. A related point is that informed individuals will tend to track the wider influences on their own personal expectations more closely than uninformed individuals. This implies that:

(H7) Mediated retrospective judgments should be more important for the cognitively engaged voters than for the disengaged, since such judgments require greater knowledge to be formed.

The eighth hypothesis concerns the role of economic interests:

(H8) Economic interests and resources will influence economic expectations independently of cognitive engagement.

Specifically, aforementioned evidence from the British Household Panel Survey on changes in the occupational structure and employment patterns in the workforce suggests that age, gender and employment status will play a role in influencing subjective economic evaluations. However, in the new and relatively insecure economic environment, skills acquired by extensive formal education appear to be an especially important factor governing employment prospects and financial rewards (see Madison, 1991).

10.3.1   Data

Since January 1992 we have included questions on monthly public opinion surveys conducted by the Gallup Organization as part of our ongoing project on the dynamics of political support in contemporary Britain. These questions tap respondents' evaluations of and emotional reactions to national and personal economic conditions. The personal prospective evaluation question asks whether people expect that their personal and household finances will get a lot better or a little better, stay the same, or get a little worse or a lot worse over the coming year (see Appendix A for question wording). Other questions focus on expectations about national economic performance in the coming year, and evaluations of personal and national economic circumstances during the past year. Emotional reactions to economic conditions are measured by showing a card to respondents and asking them which words printed on it – afraid, uneasy, disgusted, angry, proud, confident, hopeful, happy – describe their feelings about the national economy, and which ones express their feelings about their own personal economic circumstances. The monthly surveys also include the standard British Election Study (BES) party identification question battery, as well as questions on prime ministerial approval, vote intentions, and demographic characteristics. These data enable us to test the several hypotheses articulated above.

10.4   EXPECTATIONS AND EMOTIONS IN A CRISIS CONTEXT

We begin by describing the balance of positive and negative personal economic expectations in the run-up to and aftermath of the 1992 ERM Crisis. As Figure 10.1 shows, more people expected that their circumstances would improve, rather than worsen, at the time of the April 1992 General Election. However, in August, the month *before* the

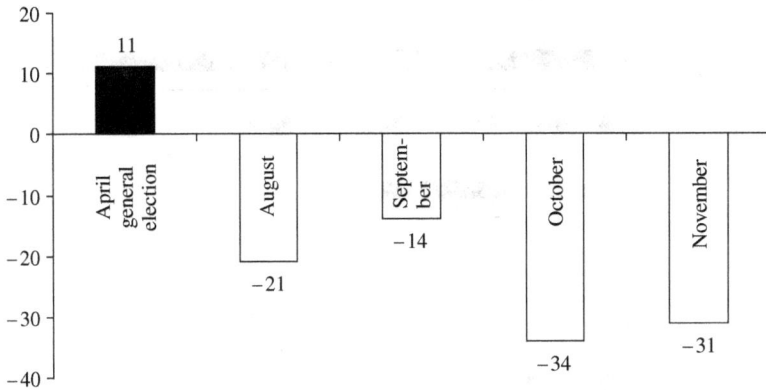

Figure 10.1 Balance of positive and negative personal economic expectations, April 1992 general election and British national surveys
August–November 1992.

government's decision to pull Britain out of the ERM, expectations fell,
with 21 points separating the percentage forecasting "worse" from that
forecasting "better." In the month after the crisis, expectations became
much gloomier – 46 percent stated that their circumstances would get
worse and only 12 percent thought that they would get better. The
situation remained basically unchanged in November when the negative
group exceeded the positive one by 31 percent.

   The same dynamic characterizes emotional reactions to national and
personal economic conditions. Although both before and after the ERM
crisis more of our survey respondents reported that they were afraid,
uneasy, disgusted, or angry, rather than proud, confident, hopeful, or
happy, about national economic conditions, negativity increased afterwards (Figure 10.2). Thus, the crisis is associated with increases in the
percentages of respondents stating that they were disgusted, angry, or
afraid, and with a diminishing sense of hope, about the state of the national
economy. It also is noteworthy that negativity about national economic
conditions was more pronounced than negativity about personal economic
circumstances. For example, before the crisis 53.7 percent as opposed to
31.5 percent said they were uneasy about the national economy, and their
personal economic circumstances, respectively (see Figures 10.2 and 10.3).
In the wake of the crisis, the comparable numbers were 55.6 percent and
38.4 percent. More generally, there was a tendency for people to feel
confident, hopeful, or happy, rather than afraid, disgusted, or angry,
about their personal circumstances than about the national economy.
However, as the "uneasiness" percentages just cited illustrate, emotional
reactions about personal circumstances changed as the crisis unfolded –
negative feelings increased, and positive ones decreased.

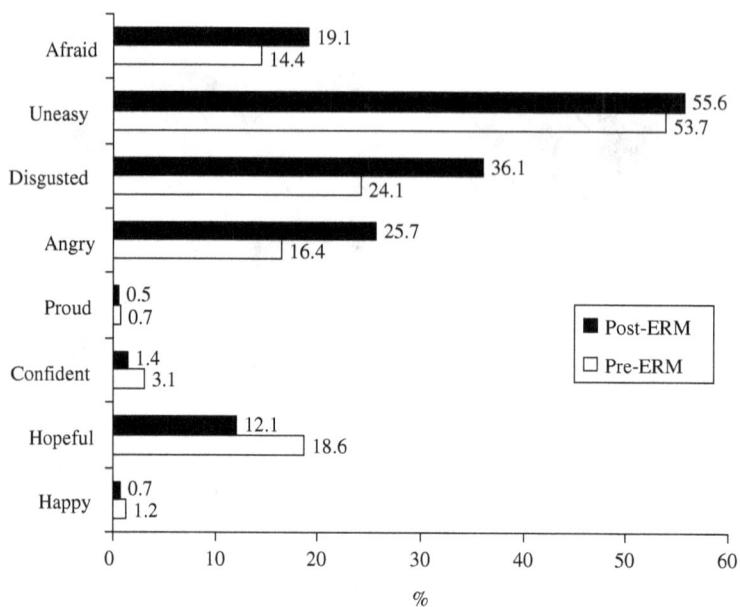

Figure 10.2 Emotional reactions to national economic conditions in pre- and post-ERM surveys.

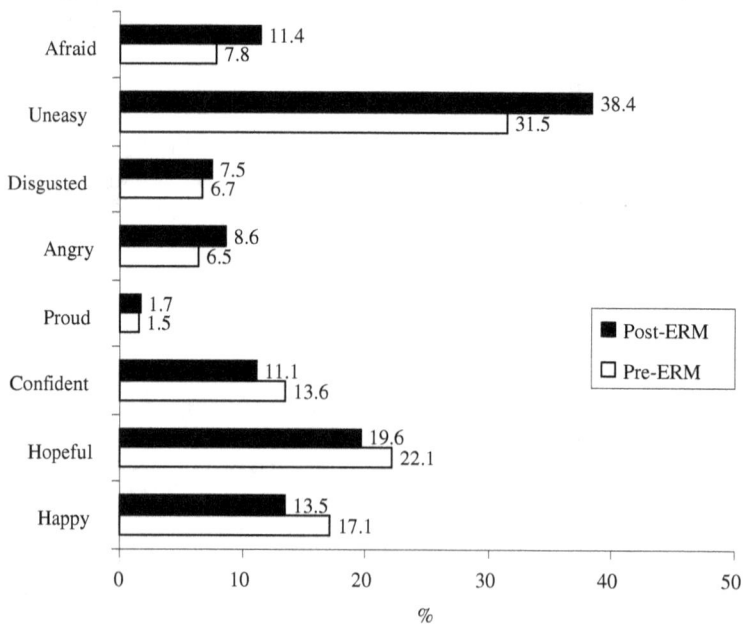

Figure 10.3 Emotional reactions to personal economic conditions in pre- and post-ERM surveys.

10.5 TESTING THE PERSONAL ECONOMIC EXPECTATIONS HYPOTHESES

To test the eight hypotheses advanced previously, we specify a multivariate model with personal expectations as the dependent variable. The independent variables include: (a) additive indices of emotional reactions to national and personal economic conditions;[2] (b) mediated retrospective evaluations of personal economic conditions; (c) partisanship, measured as the strength and direction of identification with the governing Conservatives or one of the opposition parties; (d) evaluations of governing party performance; (e) monthly interest rates; (f) a dummy variable indexing the occurrence the ERM crisis; (g) dummy variables for full- and part-time employment status; (h) other demographics, i.e. age, education, gender. To facilitate comparison and interpretation of the effects of various independent variables, model parameters are estimated using OLS regression.

Table 10.1 contains estimates for the pooled August–November 1992 sample. The table also contains separate estimates for cognitively disengaged and cognitively engaged individuals. Cognitive engagement is measured using a proxy variable, educational level, which has been used by several researchers for this purpose (see, e.g. Converse, 1964; MacKuen, 1984; Granato and Krause, 1995; Krause, 1997). Cognitively disengaged individuals are defined as those who left full-time education at age 16 or less; cognitively engaged individuals are those continuing their education beyond that age.

Considering each of the hypotheses articulated above in turn, we see that both interest rates and the ERM shock variable are statistically significant predictors of personal economic expectations with the correct (negative) signs (Table 10.1). However, there is no evidence that their effects are stronger for the cognitively engaged individuals compared with the cognitively disengaged. The (unstandardized) regression coefficients for the two variables are of virtually identical magnitude for both groups. Model estimates for the entire sample also indicate that a partisanship heuristic is operating. However, partisanship is not a statistically significant predictor of expectations for cognitively engaged individuals, although it is highly significant for the cognitively disengaged. This result is consistent with the hypothesis that partisanship is a relatively easy heuristic to use and, hence is attractive for persons with relatively little political knowledge.

The governing party performance heuristic also operates and, unlike partisanship, its effects are significant for both cognitively engaged and cognitively disengaged groups. The regression coefficient for the governing party performance heuristic is larger for the former group than for the latter one (0.16 versus 0.10, $p = 0.015$). Thus, the evidence is consistent with the hypothesis that well-educated individuals place more emphasis on the governing party performance heuristic than do

Table 10.1 Determinants of personal economic expectations, August–November 1992 (OLS estimates)

Predictor variables	Whole sample	Education	
		16 years or less	*More than 16 years*
Emotional reactions to:			
Personal economic conditions	0.24***	0.24***	0.25***
National economic conditions	0.03*	0.03*	0.02
Mediated personal retrospective			
Economic evaluations	0.08***	0.08***	0.08***
Governing party heuristic	0.12***	0.10***	0.16***
Partisanship heuristic	0.03*	0.07***	−0.04
Interest rates	−0.07**	−0.06*	−0.08*
ERM intervention	−0.24***	−0.24***	−0.25**
Age	−0.04***	−0.04***	−0.03***
Education	0.06*	X	X
Gender	0.01	−0.00	−0.00
Employment status			
Full-time	0.01	−0.04*	0.07
Part-time or unemployed	−0.07*	−0.04*	−0.07
Constant	2.51***	2.54***	0.64***
Adjusted R^2	0.19	0.19	0.17
F-statistic	75.79***	53.32***	25.77***
N	4004	2580	1424

Notes
*$p \leq 0.05$; **$p \leq 0.01$; ***$p \leq 0.001$; one-tailed test; X – variable not included in model.

less educated ones. Taking the partisanship and governing party performance results together, it appears that cognitively engaged individuals are more performance oriented than are their disengaged counterparts, and they are less inclined to let partisanship influence their judgments about their expectations of future economic welfare.

Table 10.1 also provides strong support for the hypothesis that expectations are related to emotional reactions to national and personal economic conditions. Both types of emotional reactions have significant effects ($p \leq 0.05$) in the models for the whole sample and for persons with lower levels of formal education. Personal, but not national, emotional reactions are significant in the model for persons with higher levels of formal education. Comparisons of standardized regression coefficients reveal that the effects of personal emotional reactions are much larger than those associated with national emotional reactions. In the three models, the size of the coefficients for the former variables varies from 0.30 to 0.31, whereas the latter vary from 0.03 to 0.04 (coefficients not shown in tabular form).

Although emotions, especially those involving one's personal circumstances matter, they do not negate the influence of mediated retrospective evaluations. Specifically, the three analyses show that mediated retrospective judgments about one's personal economic conditions exert statistically significant effects. However, the conjecture that cognitively engaged persons rely more on such judgments than do cognitively disengaged ones is not supported. As Table 10.1 shows, the size of the coefficient for this variable is identical ($\beta = 0.08$) in all three analyses. It also is noteworthy that affective reactions to personal economic circumstances have a larger influence than do retrospections. Unlike the standardized regression coefficients for personal emotional reactions ranging from 0.30 to 0.31, the comparable coefficients for mediated personal retrospection are only 0.07 in all three analyses.

Finally, there is some support for the hypothesis that economic interests and resources play a role in shaping expectations. The effects of age are the strongest and most consistent; older voters in the cognitively engaged and cognitively disengaged groups are significantly more pessimistic about their economic prospects than are younger persons. Other effects are less impressive, but there is evidence that skills and employment status matter. In the full sample analysis, persons with higher levels of formal education are more sanguine about their economic futures, and persons with part-time jobs and the unemployed are less optimistic.

10.6 EMOTIONAL REACTIONS TO ECONOMIC CONDITIONS AND POLITICAL SUPPORT

The results of the preceding analyses are consistent with the hypothesis that emotional reactions to personal and national economic conditions affect personal economic expectations. Given the results of time series analyses by Sanders (1991, 1993) and Clarke *et al.* (1997, 1998a), these findings indicate that economic emotions have indirect effects on party support. But, do emotions have other effects, such as direct effects on party support, or indirect ones via influences on prime ministerial approval? Here, we test for such effects by specifying multivariate models of the determinants of: (i) Conservative (governing party) vote intentions, and (ii) prime ministerial approval. Since voting intentions are measured as a dichotomy (vote Conservative $= 1$, vote for another party $= 0$) and prime ministerial approval is measured as a trichotomy (approve job PM is doing $= 2$, undecided or do not know $= 1$, disapprove job PM is doing $= 0$), we use binary and ordered probit, respectively, to estimate parameters in vote intention and prime ministerial approval models.

In addition to the emotional reactions measures, the models include the following independent variables: (a) party identification; (b) personal economic expectations; (c) mediated retrospective evaluations of national and personal economic conditions; (d) a dummy variable for the ERM crisis; (e) general life satisfaction, and (f) demographics (age, education, gender, region, social class). Prime ministerial approval also is included in the vote-intentions model. To determine if the effects of emotional reactions differ for cognitively engaged and cognitively disengaged persons, we include interaction effect variables measured as (national or personal) emotional reaction index times education (age 16 or less = 0, older than age 16 = 1) in the models.

A preliminary analysis of the vote-intention model revealed that neither of the interaction effects is statistically significant (results not shown in tabular form). Mediated personal retrospective economic evaluations also were insignificant. Omitting these variables and re-estimating the model yields the results in Table 10.2. A number of the independent variables exert significant effects and, in every case, the signs on the coefficients are as anticipated. Conservative party identifiers, persons who approve of the job the prime minister is doing, those who judge that government economic policy has had beneficial effects, those who were interviewed before the ERM crisis, those in the upper and middle classes, women, and persons living in the greater London area

Table 10.2 Effects of the determinants of Conservative vote intentions, pooled August–November 1992, British national surveys (binary probit regression)

Predictor variables	β	S.E.	t
Constant	−1.34	0.26	−5.10***
Party identification	0.90	0.03	28.75***
Prime ministerial approval	0.44	0.05	9.31***
Personal economic expectations	0.13	0.05	2.65**
Government impact on national economic conditions	0.23	0.08	2.81**
Emotional reactions to:			
National economic conditions	0.13	0.05	3.05***
Personal economic conditions	−0.02	0.04	−0.39
Exchange rate mechanism crisis	−0.09	0.08	−1.07
General life satisfaction	0.10	0.06	1.58
Age	−0.02	0.01	−1.40
Education	−0.04	0.10	−0.44
Gender	0.15	0.08	1.84*
Social class	0.09	0.04	2.48**
Region			
Wales	−0.34	0.22	−1.51
North	−0.16	0.12	−1.38
Midlands	−0.17	0.14	−1.26
South East	−0.09	0.13	−0.67
South West	−0.04	0.15	−0.29
Scotland	−0.60	0.18	−3.25***

Notes
*$p \leq 0.05$; **$p \leq 0.01$; ***$p \leq 0.001$; one-tailed test; $N = 3520$; likelihood ratio $\chi^2 = 3333.53$; df = 18; $p < 0.001$. Estimated (McKelvey) $R^2 = 0.82$; % of cases correctly classified = 94.1; PRE (Lambda) = 0.91.

(the reference category) rather than Scotland (a traditional Labour bastion) all are more likely to state that they intend to vote Conservative. Net of all these effects, emotional reactions to national economic conditions have the hypothesized positive effect ($p \leq 0.001$). Emotional reactions to personal economic circumstances are not significant ($p > 0.05$).

How strong are the effects of emotional reactions to national economic conditions? Since probit coefficients do not have straightforward interpretations, we answer this question by constructing scenarios in which we manipulate the values of the national emotional reactions index while holding the values of several other variables at their mean values (see, e.g. Long, 1997, Chapter 3). Our hypothetical voter is a man who was interviewed after the ERM crisis. We consider the effects of national emotional reactions on such a voter, making various assumptions about the direction and strength of his party identification. The results clearly indicate that the impact of emotional reactions varies strongly across party identification groups (see Figure 10.4). The impact is very sizable for non-identifiers, weak for weak identifiers, and essentially nonexistent for strong identifiers. Note also that non-identifiers are the only group for which movement across the emotional reactions index from highly negative (−4) to highly positive (+4) propels the probability of voting Conservative across the 0.5 boundary. Given that non-identifiers constitute a very small group in the British electorate (3–5 percent at any particular point in time), this result suggests that, *ceteris paribus*, the direct impact of emotional reactions to national economic conditions is quite

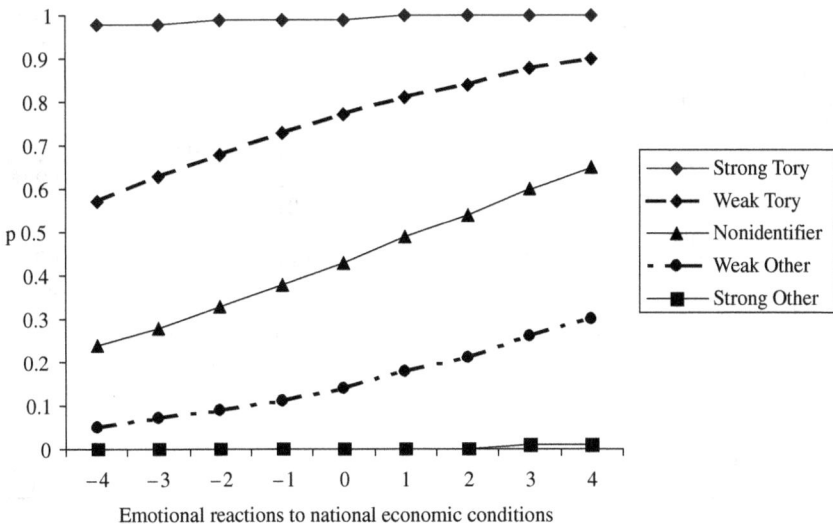

Figure 10.4 Probability of Conservative vote intention by emotional reactions to national economic conditions.

limited. Most voters have weak or moderate partisan attachments and, for such persons, emotional reactions exert only small direct effects on party support.

The effects of the emotional variables on prime ministerial approval are both more complex and more impressive. As Table 10.3 shows, several variables – party identification, personal economic expectations, mediated national economic retrospection, general life satisfaction, and the ERM crisis – significantly influence prime ministerial approval judgments. In all cases, the coefficients for these variables are correctly signed. Controlling for all these variables, emotional reactions to national and personal economic conditions exert significant main effects. Emotional reactions to the national economy also have a significant interaction effect

Table 10.3 Effects of the determinants of prime ministerial approval, pooled August–November 1992, British national surveys (ordered probit regression)

Predictor variables	β	S.E.	t
Party identification	0.27	0.01	19.76***
Personal economic expectations	0.14	0.03	5.55***
Government impact on national economic conditions	0.54	0.04	12.80***
Emotional reactions to			
National economic conditions:			
Main effect	0.15	0.03	5.04***
Education interaction effect	0.09	0.05	1.91*
Personal economic conditions:			
Main effect	0.07	0.03	2.59**
Education interaction effect	−0.03	0.04	−0.70
Exchange rate mechanism crisis	−0.53	0.05	−11.81***
General life satisfaction	0.12	0.03	3.68***
Age	0.01	0.01	1.34
Education	0.11	0.07	1.52
Gender	0.12	0.04	2.62**
Social class	−0.01	0.02	−0.50
Region			
Wales	−0.21	0.11	−1.92*
North	−0.04	0.07	−0.61
Midlands	0.08	0.07	1.15
South East	−0.00	0.08	−0.04
South West	0.05	0.09	−0.53
Scotland	−0.09	0.09	−1.00
Category thresholds			
τ_1	0.65	0.14	4.65***
τ_2	1.02	0.14	7.22***

Notes
* $p \leq 0.05$; ** $p \leq 0.01$; *** $p \leq 0.001$; one-tailed test; $N = 3982$; likelihood ratio $\chi^2 = 1809.93$; df = 19; p < 0.001. Estimated (McKelvey) $R^2 = 0.50$; % of cases correctly classified = 74.2; PRE (Lambda) = 0.61.

($\beta = 0.09$, $p \leq 0.05$) with cognitive engagement (as measured by education). The nature of this interaction effect is such that the impact of emotional reactions to national economic conditions is larger for cognitively engaged (better educated) persons than for cognitively disengaged (less well educated) ones.

To determine the strength of the national emotional reactions variable, we construct scenarios in which we manipulate the values of this variable while setting most other variables at their means. Our interest is in the probability that a voter will express satisfaction with the job being done by the prime minister. We again consider a male voter, and examine the impact of emotional reactions in the pre- and post-ERM periods. In keeping with the presence of a significant interaction effect with the extent of cognitive engagement (education), we calculate the probability of prime ministerial approval for more and less well-educated groups. The results (Figure 10.5) clearly show that this probability increases sharply from a very low value (0.25 or less) as emotional reactions to national economic conditions move from negative to positive. Although all probabilities shift downwards in the post-ERM period, in every case, except that of a less well-educated voter in the post-ERM period, the probabilities exceed 0.5 among persons expressing very positive emotions. One also can see the interaction effect at work. In both the pre- and post-ERM periods, the probabilities of being satisfied with the job that the prime minister is doing are lower among cognitively engaged persons than cognitively disengaged persons when emotional reactions are negative, and higher when emotional reactions are positive (Figure 10.5).

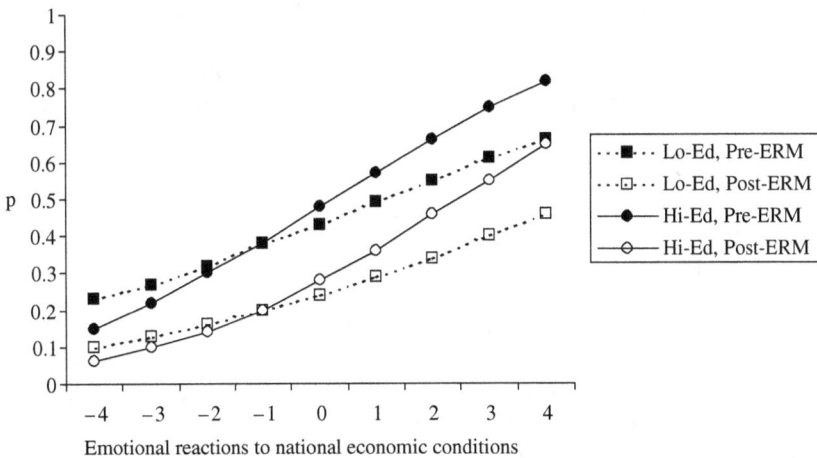

Figure 10.5 Probability of positive prime ministerial approval rating by emotional reactions to national ecomomic conditions for low and high educational groups in the pre- and post-ERM crisis periods.

10.7   CONCLUSION: EMOTIONS, HETEROGENEITY AND PARTY SUPPORT

Although there is an extensive literature on the political economy of party support in mature democracies, very little work has been done on the effects of emotional reactions to economic or other conditions. The conjecture that emotions matter challenges economists' core anthropological assumption that people as cold-blooded, egocentric "agents" who rationally and ruthlessly go about the business of maximizing their personal utilities. The present chapter has subjected this conjecture to empirical testing using data on British voters' emotional reactions to national and personal economic conditions. Analyses of multivariate models of personal economic expectations, prime ministerial approval, and governing party vote intentions using individual-level survey data gathered before and after the ERM crisis in the autumn of 1992 strongly suggest that emotional reactions are indeed influential. Controlling for several variables that have been accorded prominent roles in previous studies of the determinants of party support, emotional reactions to national economic conditions have direct and indirect effects on governing party vote intentions and prime ministerial approval. For their part, emotional reactions to personal economic circumstances influence personal economic expectations, a variable that is commonly viewed as the lynchpin in political economy models of support for governing and opposition parties in contemporary Britain.

The analyses of the impact of emotions is embedded in a larger analytic framework that focuses on the explanatory leverage provided by conceptualizing electorates as heterogeneous entities. Specifically, we consider the performance of multivariate models of personal economic expectations, prime ministerial approval, and governing party vote intentions for persons with varying levels of cognitive engagement. Although the results of our empirical analyses are mixed, there are indications that future studies can profit by recognizing this type of heterogeneity. Specifically, and as hypothesized, partisanship is a significant heuristic in our model of economic expectations only for cognitively disengaged persons. The relative strength of partisanship in the model of personal expectations for this group is consistent with low-information rationality theories. Given their relative paucity of information about current economic and political conditions, persons in the less well-educated group avoid the costs of acquiring such information by relying on partisanship as a convenient surrogate.

Also, while levels of cognitive engagement do not directly condition the effects of emotional reactions to economic conditions on governing party support, there is substantial evidence of indirect conditioning via effects on prime ministerial approval, a key determinant of party support.

Emotional reactions to national economic conditions have significantly stronger effects on prime ministerial approval among cognitively engaged voters than among cognitively disengaged ones. This finding suggests an alternative to Frank's "cognition within emotion" conjecture. Although a variety of strategic interactions may be conditioned as Frank suggests, the process by which the public evaluates the behavior of leading politicians appears to be one where the impact of politically consequential emotions interacts with available information. To the extent that such information is reliable, emotions are tied to "real-world" events and conditions that can have profound effects on the quality of voters' lives. Viewed this way, the political role of emotions appears to have rational component – albeit perhaps "rough-and-ready" – that substantially qualifies the typical juxtaposition of cognition and emotion in accounts of party support provided by rational choice and social psychological theories of party support.

At a less abstract level, the findings presented above buttress the results of recent aggregate-level time series analyses showing that emotional reactions matter for party support (Clarke *et al.*, 1998a). Perhaps particularly intriguing, both the previous aggregate-level and the present individual-level analyses indicate that a major avenue for the effects of emotional reactions concerns voters' judgments of party leader performance. This finding has intuitive appeal; in a media age that metaphorically brings party leaders into everyone's living room, leader images have an immediacy that forges a person-to-person nexus that is missing in voters' more global images of political parties. This interpersonal nexus, in turn, generates emotional reactions to economic conditions consequential for evaluations of party leader performance and, indirectly, for party support. However, emotional reactions are not confined to the economy. Parties and party leaders do and say many things that generate a variety of positive and negative feelings in electorates. Studying the effects of these emotions in models of party support that accommodate voter heterogeneity is a promising avenue for future research.

APPENDIX – QUESTION WORDING

A.1 Economic evaluations

National economic expectations: "How do you think the general economic situation in this country will develop over the next 12 months?" "Will it: 'get a lot better,' 'get a little better,' 'stay the same,' 'get a little worse,' 'get a lot worse'?"

National economic retrospections: "How do you think the general economic situation in this country has changed over the last 12 months?" "Has it: 'got a lot better,' 'got a little better,' 'stayed the same,' 'got a little worse,' 'got a lot worse'?"

Personal economic expectations: "How do you think the financial situation of your household will change over the next 12 months?" "Will it: 'get a lot better,' 'get a little better,' 'stay the same,' 'get a little worse,' 'get a lot worse'?"

Personal economic retrospection: "How does the financial situation of your household now compare with what it was 12 months ago?" "Has it: 'got a lot better,' 'got a little better,' 'stayed the same,' 'got a little worse,' 'got a lot worse'?"

A.2   Emotional reactions to national and personal economic conditions

"Which, if any, of the words on this card describe *your feelings* about *the country's general economic situation* [emphasis added]?"

"Which, if any, of the words on this card describe *your feelings* about the financial condition of *your household* [emphasis added]?"

The words are: "angry," "happy," "disgusted," "hopeful," "uneasy," "confident," "afraid," "proud."

A.3   Governing party performance

"Do you approve or disapprove of the Government's record to date?"

A.4   Party identification

"Generally speaking, do you think of yourself as Conservative, Labour, Liberal Democrat, Plaid Cymru [in Wales], Scottish Nationalist [in Scotland], or what?" Those naming a party are then asked: "Would you call yourself very strong, fairly strong, or not very strong [party named]." Those not naming a party are asked: "Do you feel a little closer to one of the parties?" [If "yes"] "Which one"?

A.5   Prime ministerial approval

"How good a job do you think John Major is doing as prime minister?"

A.6   Vote intentions

"If there were a general election tomorrow, which party would you vote for?" Persons not citing a party are asked: "Which party would you be most inclined to vote for?" Here, those mentioning a party in response to either question are considered as intending to vote for that party.

NOTES

1 There is now a sizable literature employing individual- or aggregate-level time series analyses that pool data across time and space. See, e.g. Anderson (1995, 2000), Hibbs (1982a, b), Krause (1997), Pacek and Radcliff (1995); Weatherford (1978) and Whitten and Palmer (1999).
2 It might be conjectured that there is a risk of simultaneity bias in that expectations might affect emotional reactions to economic conditions. We believe that a more plausible causal sequence is that perceived current national and personal economic conditions/trends influence emotional reactions which, in turn, affect economic expectations. To minimize the possibility of bias, the emotional reaction questions solicit respondents' reactions to prevailing economic conditions, with no reference being made to anticipated future conditions.

REFERENCES

Alesina, A. (1987) Macroeconomic policy in a two-party system as a repeated game. *Quar. J. Economics*, **102**, 651–678.
Alesina, A. (1988) Macroeconomics and politics. In *NBER Macroeconomic Annual*. Cambridge, MA: MIT Press.
Alesina, A. and Rosenthal, H. (1995) *Partisan Politics: Divided Government and the Economy*. Cambridge: Cambridge University Press.
Alt, J. (1979) *The Politics of Economic Decline*. Cambridge: Cambridge University Press.
Anderson, C.J. (1995). *Blaming the Government: Citizens and the Economy in Five European Democracies*. Armonk, NY: Sharpe.
Anderson, C.J. (2000) Economic voting and political context: a comparative context. *Electoral Stud.*, **19**, 151–170.
Attfield, C.L.E, Demery, D. and Duck, N.W. (1985) *Rational Expectations in Macroeconomics*. Oxford: Basil Blackwell.
Austin-Smith, D. (1990) Information transmission debate. *Am. J. Political Sci.*, **34**, 124–152.
Austin-Smith, D. (1993) Information and influence: lobbying for agendas and votes. *Am. J. Political Sci.*, **37**, 799–833.
Axelrod, R. (1984) *The Evolution of Cooperation*. New York: Basic Books.
Axelrod, R. (1997) *The Complexity of Cooperation*. Princeton, NJ: Princeton University Press.
Berelson, B.R., Lazarsfeld, P.F. and McPhee, W.N. (1954) *Voting*. Chicago, IL: University of Chicago Press.
Borooah, V.K. and Van Der Ploeg, F. (1983) *Political Aspects of the Economy*. Cambridge: Cambridge University Press.
Box-Steffensmeier, J.M., DeBoef, S. and Lin, T.-M. (1997) *Macroideology, macropartisanship, and the gender gap*. Paper Presented at the Annual Meeting of the American Political Science Association, Washington, DC.
Buck, N., Gershuny, J., Rose, D. and Scott, J. (1994) *Changing Households – The British Household Panel Survey 1990–1992*. Colchester: University of Essex Research Centre on Micro-Social Change.
Butler, D. and Stokes, D. (1974) *Political Change in Britain*, 2nd edn. London: Macmillan.

Campbell, A., Converse, P.E., Miller, W.E. and Stokes, D. (1960) *The American Voter*. New York: Wiley.

Chappell Jr., H.W. and Keech, W.R. (1985) A new view of political accountability for economic performance. *Am. Political Sci. Rev.*, **79**, 10–27.

Clarke, H.D. and Stewart, M.C. (1994) Prospections, retrospections, and rationality: the 'bankers' model of presidential approval reconsidered. *Am. J. Political Sci.*, **38**, 1104–1124.

Clarke, H.D., Stewart, M.C. and Whiteley, P.F. (1997) Tory trends: party identification and the dynamics of conservative support since 1992. *Br. J. Political Sci.*, **27**, 299–319.

Clarke, H.D., Stewart, M.C. and Whiteley, P.F. (1998a) New models for New Labour: the political economy of Labour Party support, January 1992–April 1997, *Am. Political Sci. Rev.*, **92**, 559–615.

Clarke, H.D., Stewart, M.C. and Whiteley, P.F. (1998b) Political change and party choice: voting in the 1997 general election. In D. Denver *et al.* (eds), *British Elections & Parties Review*, vol i. London: Frank Cass Publishers.

Conover, P.J. and Feldman, S. (1986) Emotional reactions to the economy: I'm mad as hell and I'm not going to take it anymore. *Am. J. Political Sci.*, **30**, 50–78.

Conover, P.J., Feldman, S. and Knight, K. (1986) Judging inflation and unemployment: the origin of retrospective evaluations. *J. Politics*, **48**, 565–588.

Conover, P.J., Feldman, S. and Knight, K. (1987) The personal and political underpinnings of economic forecasts. *Am. J. Political Sci.*, **31**, 559–583.

Converse, P.E. (1964) The Nature of Belief Systems in Mass Publics. In D. Apter (ed.) *Ideology and Discontent*. New York: Free Press.

Cook, T.D. and Campbell, D.T. (1979) *Quasi-experimentation: Design and Analysis for Field Settings*. Boston: Houghton Mifflin.

Crawford, V. and Sobel, J. (1982) Strategic Information Transmission. *Econometrica*, **50**, 1431–1451.

Denver, D. (1998) The Government That Could Do No Right. In A. King (ed.) *New Labour Triumphs: Britain at the Polls*. Chatham: Chatham House Publishers.

Downs, A. (1957) *An Economic Theory of Democracy*. New York: Harper and Row.

Feldman, S. and Zaller, J. (1992) Political culture of ambivalence: ideological responses to the welfare state. *Am. J. Political Sci.*, **36**, 268–307.

Ferejohn, J.A. and Kuklinski, J.H. (eds) (1990) *Information and Democratic Processes*. Urbana, IL: University of Illinois Press.

Fiorina, M.P. (1981) *Retrospective Voting in American National Elections*. New Haven, CT: Yale University Press.

Frank, R.H. (1988) *Passions Within Reason – The Strategic Role of the Emotions*. New York: Norton and Company.

Goodhart, C.A. and Bhansali, R.J. (1970) Political Economy. *Political Stud.*, **18**, 43–106.

Granato, J. and Krause, G.A. (1995) *Asymmetric diffusion of information within the electorate: transmission of inflation expectations*. Paper Presented at the Annual Meeting of the Midwest Political Science Association, Chicago.

Haller, H.B. and Norpoth, H. (1994) Let the good times roll: economic expectations of voters. *Am. J. Political Sci.*, **38**, 625–650.

Hibbs, D.A. (1982a) The dynamics of political support for American presidents among occupational and partisan groups. *Am. J. Political Sci.*, **26**, 312–332.

Hibbs, D.A. (1982b) Economic outcomes and political support for British governments among occupational classes: a dynamic analysis. *Am. Political Sci. Rev.*, **76**,
259–279.

Hudson, J. (1985) The relationship between government popularity and
approval for the government's record in the United Kingdom. *Br. J. Political
Sci.*, **15**, 165–186.

Iyengar, S. and Kinder, D.R. (1987) *News That Matters: Television and American
Opinion*. Chicago, IL: University of Chicago Press.

Key Jr., V.O. (1968) *The Responsible Electorate: Rationality in Presidential Voting,
1936–1960*. New York: Vintage Books.

Keynes, J.M. (1936) *The General Theory of Employment, Interest and Money*. London:
Macmillan.

Kiewiet, D.R. (1983) *Macroeconomics and Micropolitics*. Chicago: University of
Chicago Press.

Kinder, D.R. and Kiewiet, R.D. (1979) Economic discontent and political
behavior: the role of personal grievances and collective economic judgments
in congressional voting. *Am. J. Political Sci.*, **23**, 495–517.

Kinder, D.R. and Kiewiet, R.D. (1981) Sociotropic politics: the American case.
Br. J. Political Sci., **11**, 129–161.

Kinder, D.R. and Mebane, W. (1983) Politics and economics in everyday life. In
K. Monroe (ed.), *The Political Process and Economic Change*. New York: Agathon Press.

Kramer, G.H. (1983) The ecological fallacy revisited: aggregate versus individual-
level findings on economics and elections, and sociotropic voting. *Am. Political
Sci. Rev.*, **77**, 92–111.

Krause, G.A. (1997) The dynamics of aggregate economic expectations.
Am. J. Political Sci., **41**, 1170–1200.

Lewis-Beck, M.S. (1988) *Economics and Elections*. Ann Arbor, MI: University of
Michigan Press.

Lodge, M., Steenbergen, M. and Brau, S. (1995) The responsive voter: campaign
information and the dynamics of candidate evaluation. *Am. Political Sci. Rev.*,
89, 309–326.

Long, J.S. (1997) *Regression Models for Categorical and Limited Dependent Variables*.
Thousand Oaks: Sage Publications.

Lupia, A. (1994) Shortcuts versus encyclopedias: information and voting behavior
in California insurance reform elections. *Am. Political Sci. Rev.*, **88**, 63–76.

Lupia, A. and McCubbins, M.D. (1998) *The Democratic Dilemma*. Cambridge: Cambridge University Press.

MacKuen, M.B. (1984) Exposure to information, belief integration and individual
responsiveness to agenda change. *Am. Political Sci. Rev.*, **78**, 372–391.

MacKuen, M.B., Erikson, R.S. and Stimson, J.A. (1992) Peasants or bankers? The
American electorate and the US economy. *Am. Political Sci. Rev.*, **86**, 597–611.

Madison, A. (1991) *Dynamic Forces in Capitalist Development*. Oxford: Oxford
University Press.

Marcus, G.E. and MacKuen, M.B. (1993) Anxiety, enthusiasm and the vote: the
emotional underpinnings of learning and involvement during presidential
campaigns. *Am. Political Sci. Rev.*, **87**, 672–685.

Markus, G.B. (1988) The impact of personal and national economic conditions on
the presidential vote: a pooled cross-sectional analysis. *Am. J. Political Sci.*, **32**,
137–154.

McKelvey, R.D. and Ordeshook, P.C. (1986) Information, electoral equilibria, and the democratic ideal. *J. Politics*, **8**, 909–937.

Moseley, P. (1984) *The Making of Economic Policy*. Brighton: Harvester Wheatsheaf.

Mueller, D.C. (1989) *Public Choice II*. Cambridge: Cambridge University Press.

Pacek, A.C. and Radcliff, B. (1995) Economic voting and the welfare state: a cross-national analysis. *J. Politics*, **57**, 44–61.

Page, B.I. and Shapiro, R.Y. (1992) *The Rational Public: Fifty Years of Trends in Americans' Policy Preferences*. Chicago, IL: University of Chicago Press.

Popkin, S.L. (1991) *The Reasoning Voter*. Chicago, IL: University of Chicago Press.

Rivers, D. (1988) Heterogeneity in models of electoral choice. *Am. J. Political Sci.*, **32**, 737–757.

Sanders, D. (1991) Government popularity and the next general election. *Political Quar.*, **62**, 235–261.

Sanders, D. (1993) Why the Conservatives won – again. In A. King (ed.) *Britain at the Polls 1992*. Chatham: Chatham House Publishers.

Sniderman, P.M., Brody, R.A. and Tetlock, P. (1991) *Reasoning and Choice: Explorations in Political Psychology*. Cambridge: Cambridge University Press.

Weatherford, M.S. (1978) Economic conditions and electoral outcomes: class differences in the political response to recession. *Am. J. Political Sci.*, **22**, 917–938.

Whiteley, P. (1986) *Political Control of the Macroeconomy*. London: Sage Publications.

Whiteley, P. (1995) Rational choice and political participation – evaluating the debate. *Political Res. Quar.*, **48**, 211–234.

Whitten, G.D. and Palmer, H.D. (1999) Cross-national analyses of economic voting. *Electoral Stud.*, **18**, 49–67.

Zaller, J.R. (1992) *The Nature and Origins of Mass Opinion*. Cambridge: Cambridge University Press.

11 From class voting to economic voting

Patterns of individualization of electoral behavior in Italy, 1972–1996

Paolo Bellucci

Studies of Italian electoral behavior have generally devoted little attention to the relationship between economic conditions and voting choice. This has been due to the institutional characteristics of the Italian polity, which influenced mass electoral behavior in a direction quite far from the dimensions analyzed by comparative students of economic voting. The rational actor model – with its basic concepts of incumbency and policy voting, pocketbook and sociotropic electors – was found inadequate for a political system characterized by multiple parties, proportional representation, strong ideological and religious polarization at all levels, and class party allegiances. All of these are aspects that led to low electoral volatility and frequent cabinet crises, though counter-balanced by a basic continuity of government personnel, insured by the dominant role of the Christian Democratic Party (Dc) in every government up to 1994.[1] From a comparative perspective this was no novelty: it has been shown that economic voting appears stronger in Westminster models of democracies than in consensual polities (Alt and Chrystal, 1983; Paldam, 1991). In an effort to account for such differences, recent research has devoted attention to the very institutional aspects which mediate between economics and politics, such as clarity of responsibility with regard to government management of the economy, minority government, and ideological leanings (Powell and Whitten, 1993; Anderson, 1995, 2000; Whitten and Palmer, 1999; Lewis-Beck and Paldam, 2000).

   In this chapter, I argue that for economic voting to emerge in a consensual democracy like Italy, electors must be relatively free from traditional "anchors of partisanship" (Gunther and Montero, 1998) and, at the same time, be offered a more prominent role in the selection of the government. Traditional sources of electoral stabilization, class, ideology, and religion in the Italian case, have long inhibited issue and economic voting. At the same time, institutional factors – such as proportional representation and parliamentary selection of government – made elections more into an expressive than an instrumental act of political participation. In other words, elections became first of all an opportunity to restate partisan loyalty rather than a way to select the ruling parties.

The drastic change of the Italian political system in the 1990s offered the chance to alter this stable format. Political change has been brought about, even though the institutional change which would stabilize Italian ruling institutions is still lacking (Fabbrini, 2000). A new majoritarian electoral law forced old and new parties to form coalitions to contest elections. This actually opened the way to alternation of different parties in power and empowered the electorate, particularly at the subnational level (Fabbrini and Gilbert, 2000), but also nationally, with (the perception of) an unprecedented capacity. Unlike earlier elections, the 1994 and 1996 elections showed a clarity of available alternatives, a favorable condition both for economic voting and for electors choosing the government (Anderson, 2000). The religious cleavage, eroded by a long process of secularization which attenuated its influence on the vote (Segatti, 1999), received the final blow by the disappearance of the Christian Democratic Party, making a religion-driven vote politically even less relevant, as happened in the Netherlands (De Graaf *et al.*, 2001). Finally, in 1994 and 1996 economic issues were prominent in the campaign, so we must examine closely their impact on the vote, also compared to the past.

In Section 11.1, we review Italian political change in the 1990s and relate it to the literature on economic voting. In Section 11.2, the issue of class voting is addressed, since, unlike religion, it has attracted less attention for scholars who generally emphasize the interclass appeals of Italian parties and the homogeneity of their electoral base. Employing measures based on log-odd ratios, we find a stronger level of class voting than assumed in previous studies and relate it to the class-based appeal of the parties' policy proposals. In Section 11.4, we show there exists a greater impact of economic concerns on the vote compared to earlier periods.

11.1   ECONOMIC VOTING AND ITALIAN POLITICAL CHANGE IN THE 1990s

Past research on the Italian case has found some evidence, regarding the supply side of political-electoral cycles, of government electoral manipulation of the economy through increasing public expenditures (Santaganta, 1995). However, other research also discovered a weak response of the electorate (Lewis-Beck, 1988). This low response was limited to a narrow stratum of the electorate, mainly to the so-called opinion voters, which are people with no party identification and a high interest in politics (Bellucci, 1991). This was interpreted as due to system-specific aspects of Italian politics which – remarkably for a polity sharply divided along ideological lines (communism/anti-communism) and strong class organizations – did not attribute electoral importance to economic issues. Stated briefly, class interests, always present in political rhetoric, did not enter strongly into the calculus of voting, and economic issues were not central in electoral campaigns and party manifestoes. The real meaning of the left–right dimension was then less based on social and economic contents and more on religiosity and international alignment.

So for a long time, at least since the beginning of the 1970s, the mainstream interpretation of the relationship between social class and voting in Italy has portrayed a minor impact of social stratification on electoral behavior. Two explanations were put forth in the literature. On the one hand, since the early 1960s the social structure of the electoral bases of major parties appeared similar (Barnes, 1974, 1984; Sani, 1974). In addition, notwithstanding the strong ideological polarization between the Christian Democratic and Communist parties, their economic policies in the electoral programs were alike (Corbetta *et al.*, 1988; Bartolini and Mair, 1990). Moreover, the transformation of Italian social structures – i.e. the declining weight of the manual working class and growing employment in the tertiary sector – was seen as a factor, in Italy as elsewhere in Western countries (Franklin *et al.*, 1992), capable of further diminishing both the strength of the class-based partisan loyalties and the class appeal of parties. On the other hand, it was observed that the determinants of the vote were not to be found in the social stratification, but rather in the ideological and cultural identification of the electorate with either the Catholic or the Socialist–Communist subcultures (Mannheimer and Sani, 1987). Therefore, social and economic interests of different classes did not constitute the base of partisan identification. Quite the opposite, it was the party identification which would mold the electorate's perception of their class interests (Pizzorno, 1981). In other words, the major parties were able, through the diffusion and strengthening of their subcultural and organizational channels of communication with the electorate, to structure collective identities, which would comprise quite different societal groupings. As Mackie *et al.* wrote in their 1992 review of the class-vote association in Italy in the 1968–1988 period:

> ... in Italy social structure has never had more than limited ability to predict and explain voting choice. Indeed there are good reasons to suppose that class differences would have only a limited impact upon partisanship. Appeals based upon religiosity and religious tradition by the Christian Democrats (a party which has always stressed its inter-class appeal) have undercut the potential of class politics. A sizeable proportion of the Italian working class has always voted Christian Democrat. Conversely, the appeal of Pci and Psi has extended beyond the blue-collar population to include

by the 70s fairly large groups of white-collar workers and even professionals and managers.

(Mackie *et al.*, 1992: 242)

This could explain why, in the past, Italian parties' high ideological polarization was accompanied by a convergence in their economic policy programs. Bartolini and Mair's comparative study (1990) has shown that the distance among the parties' economic policies correlates inversely with their ideological polarization. This means that parties' competition over different economic policies is stronger, the broader the ideological consensus in the political system. Accordingly, given the past Italian ideological juxtaposition of left and center, electoral campaigns would not emphasize issues of economic policy. This was either because parties did not really divide themselves along these ideological lines or because élites would fear the risk of a strong programmatic competition, thinking that the ideological polarization would actually translate into a real economic polarization. They would rather limit economic policy discussions to their respective political subcultures.

At the beginning of the 1990s these three features of Italian politics – namely the strength of party identification, the weak class appeal for the vote, and the perception of a similarity in the parties' economic programs – underwent drastic changes. All of them relate to the dramatic transformation of the Italian political system, i.e. to the process of democratic change which, with the 1994 national elections, marks the end of the so-called Italian First Republic.

Several intertwined factors contributed to the decomposition of the political system established after World War II. In 1992, an anti-corruption campaign developed, called "Clean Hands", which eventually brought about the collapse of a large part of the political class and the disappearance of the two major parties in all government coalitions since the late 1960s: the Christian Democrats and the Socialists (PSI). In the same year, the Lira was devalued by 7 percent and Italy was forced to get out of the European monetary system. The burden of the huge public debt became highly visible and clearly perceived as a failure of the entire political class. The end of the East–West international polarization forced the Pci to reform itself and change its name in 1992 to Partito Democratico della Sinistra, or PDS (Bellucci *et al.*, 2000), followed by the Christian Democrats in 1993 (who became the Partito Popolare Italiano, PPI) and by the post-fascist Movimento Sociale Italiano (MSI), who called themselves since 1994 the Alleanza Nazionale (AN). More importantly, in August 1993 a new majoritarian electoral law (a mixed system which allocates three quarters of the seats in single-member district and the remaining quarter with a proportional formula) was approved by Parliament. The change of the electoral law was hailed as a decisive step towards both reducing the fragmentation of the Italian party system and empowering the voters to elect a government directly. Finally, in 1994, 3 months before the national elections, the media-tycoon Silvio Berlusconi launched a new party, Forza Italia (FI).[2]

This process deeply affected the strength of mass party identification. The disappearance of the major ruling parties, which had molded that subcultural identification known in Italy as vote of belonging (voto di appartenenza) – or in Barnes' (1977) definition, institutionalized traditions – represented the apex of a long-term process of political dealignment and demobilization of Italian voters. While in 1968 almost 90 percent of electors declared to feel close, to some degree, to a political party, in 1990 the corresponding figure was 55 percent. Also the intensity of identification lessened, and in 1990 only one out of eight voters felt "very close to a party" (Bellucci, 1995; Segatti *et al.*, 1999). Italian voters, then, faced the 1994 new majoritarian elections with the lowest feeling of political identity in decades.

The weakening of party identification and of the mobilizing capacity of political subcultures has interacted with the condition of the national economy, decreasing the inter-class appeal of the parties, letting a potential dividing conflict come afloat, and revealing problems associated with a compromise between divergent class interests inherent in a policy of economic stabilization sharpened by international constraints (the Maastricht Treaty). The policies implemented by the Amato and Ciampi governments (1992 and 1993, respectively), which increased seriously the tax burden in a strong effort to cut down the huge public debt, ignited tax protest and made it clear that the previous social compromise – putting the cost of welfare on devaluation and public debt – was no longer feasible (Bellucci, 1997).

This made the economic issue highly visible in the 1994 and 1996 electoral campaigns, when the different economic programs of the party coalitions demonstrated that the economy was no longer a matter of valence but had become a strong position issue. The decisive move came from Berlusconi, who chose to radicalize the issue of an alternative economic policy both on substantive economic grounds and in an effort to underline the difference from the past. Consequently, Forza Italia proposed a program of drastic reduction of state intervention in the economy and welfare, and dramatic tax cuts in favor of market forces. It was a radical program even before it was remarkably extended by the presence in the center–right electoral coalition of a traditionally statist party like the postfascist MSI/AN. In contrast, both the left (Progressisti) and the center (Patto per l'Italia) advocated only a rationalization of the functions of the state, which, however, was to keep full responsibility for welfare and a somewhat smaller role in the economy.

The economy, however, became also a kind of meta issue symbolizing a discontinuity from the past economic policies. In this respect economy became a component of the regeneration of political issues, especially in the personalized version proposed by Berlusconi. The economic issue was composed of two aspects: a retrospective one, meaning the attribution of responsibility for past poor economic performance (inflation, state deficit, heavy tax burden, etc.), and a prospective one, the proposals for future policies. The center–right coalition, especially Forza Italia, based its campaign on both dimensions. With regard to the retrospective component of the economic issue, the center–right imputed to both the DC and the left the responsibility for Italian economic and social problems, proposing for the future, the prospective dimension, a "new economic miracle" to be brought about by market forces liberated by state controls. The left and the center opposed such program, and presented themselves as capable of reforming the Italian socioeconomic structure without destroying the positive provisions of the welfare state.[3]

Also in the 1996 campaign the economic issue was prominent, showing a further polarization among the coalitions. The Ulivo (the center–left coalition headed by Prodi) economic and social program favored a system of mixed state regulation and market development, in which the reduction of the budget deficit was matched by a strong redistributive fiscal policy. The Polo (center–right) program, strongly based on economic liberalism, anchored Italian development to the promotion of market forces and a reduction of the tax burden (Sani and Segatti, 2000).[4]

11.2   ECONOMIC ISSUES, CLASS VOTING, AND PARTIES' POLICY DISTANCE

The literature on the declining electoral importance of traditional social cleavages, and of social class, in particular, is quite extensive. Yet there is no clear consensus on the actual diminishing impact on voting and the factors explaining the phenomenon (Manza *et al.*, 1995). The debate is lively also on the dependent variable: what is class voting? A useful distinction is the one proposed by Mair (1993, quoted in Hout *et al.*, 1995) between "class voting" and "class politics". Class voting refers to the extent to which social classes vote for different parties in a given election, while class politics implies that these social blocks persist over time. This distinction allows identifying different phenomena. For instance: (a) the decline of the structural relationship between class membership and vote; (b) the erosion of the traditional alignment of the working class with the left; (c) the emergence of new social coalitions. The decline of class voting means that social class loses its explanatory and predictive power of voting, as class membership is simply no longer associated with voting choice. When the relationship between class and vote does persist, two different outcomes are possible. The first one is that there is class voting but its direction is not stable and, in an unlikely extreme scenario, social coalitions could change at each new election. In other words, class voting does not institutionalize into class politics. The second possibility is that class voting is associated with a stability of the alignment between social coalitions and parties, which is when it becomes the case of class politics.

Hout *et al.* (1995) argue that the literature on the decline of class voting explicitly addresses the issue of the decline of the traditional alignment between working class and left voting but, at the same time, implicitly assumes the disappearance of any relationship between social structure and voting (i.e. the irrelevance of social class as explanatory variable). The existing studies further imply the disappearance of class politics in general. Literature reviews of available studies identify three different groups of factors capable of explaining the declining effect of class on voting (Dalton, 1988; Manza *et al.*, 1995; Nieuwbeerta and Ultee, 1999). The first two, on the one hand, base their analyses on the change of social structure in Western societies and on its impact on the political cleavages within polities. Their focus is on the decline of class voting interpreted as relationship between social class and voting. The third group, on the other hand, calls into question the conditions under which class politics develop and can persist overtime.

The first approach relies on the changing social composition of classes. Postwar economic development and the advent of postindustrial society make obsolete the traditional cleavage, which pitted bourgeois against proletariat. Working classes decline in absolute numbers and emerge as a new wide middle class, composed by professionalized upper sectors of the working class and employees in services and public administration. Their life-styles and consuming and voting patterns differ from both traditional working and middle classes. At the same time, economic development brings about intergenerational mobility which undercuts the demographic identity of classes, thus fostering voting choices intermediate between those of their class of origin and of arrival (Weakliem, 1992; De Graaf *et al.*, 1990).

A second line of reasoning points at the rise of new social divisions and at the development of a better educated and reasoning electorate, less willing to adhere to the traditional ideological appeals by parties. Accordingly, it is the very economic development, matched by higher income and a wider social welfare system, that undermines the electoral importance of economic issues in the traditional class-polarized fashion. Non-economic issues – from the environment to the quality of life to civic rights, all postmaterialist themes (Inglehart, 1990) – enter the political debate, giving rise to new parties which signal their distance from traditional cleavage parties by their emphasis on single issues. Slowly, the new political values penetrate the traditional working class parties but also a new left develops, with a social base in the middle class and among educated electors, thus weakening the overall association between left voting and working class (Lipset, 1981; Weakliem, 1991).

The third approach looks at the configuration of cleavages in the polity (Lipset and Rokkan, 1967), but shifts the attention from electorate to parties. Political élites and party leadership are the protagonists, the leading actors in strengthening, weakening, or changing the ideological contents historically linked to the social cleavages on which the parties themselves developed (Sartori, 1982; Bartolini and Mair, 1990). Clear and persistent cleavages, mostly associated with consensual polities, reinforce traditional political allegiances. Cross-cutting cleavages on the other hand, typical of majoritarian democracies, reduce the relative encapsulation of the parties' social bases. However, parties overtime can also choose, on different grounds, to reinforce or weaken the appeal, and the policies, based on the traditional political allegiances. In manifestoes and through policy making, leaders can reaffirm the importance of divergent socioeconomic class interests or they can de-emphasize them. A weakening of class appeals may allow to attract wider sectors of the electorate (may be to compensate for a shrinking working class) which in turn may lead to a convergence of the party programs. Accordingly, the decline in class voting would reflect both a "weakening of the voters' class identities and a narrowing of party positions on class-based issues" (Dalton 1988: 159).

We can ask whether this covariance between class identities and party positions could not actually mean causation, in the sense that for class politics to persist, class voting implies an appeal made by parties. If we interpret voting behavior as the electorate's answer to party proposals, then we have to turn to the way parties present themselves, to their programs and the policies pursued. Sartori presents the argument clearly:

> Party is not a consequence of social class; quite the opposite, it is class which receives its identity by the party. Class political behavior pre-supposes parties which not only feed incessantly their 'class image' but which also provide the structural concrete of a 'class reality'.[5]
>
> (Sartori, 1982: 152)

Of course one must be aware, with Sartori, that a class appeal in party programs is no warranty of a class proposal or of class policies. There might be no need for parties to appeal to class when the voters' class loyalty is strong or, in the opposite situation, class appeal may be explicit when the electorate's sense of identity is weak. On the whole, however, parties remain the key actors in activating a class reality and identity, building it through symbols, organization, and policies. Moreover, results from the Manifestoes Research Group show a strong congruence between party programs and policies enacted, thus pointing out the importance of these programs as a declaration of commitment to voters to adhere to promises about policies (Klingemann *et al.*, 1994).

The hypothesis we want to test in the Italian case is whether the past weak impact of class differences on partisanship we reviewed above, correlates with a similarity of party programs. That is, whether the Italian lower-class voting can be explained by similar economic stands (i.e. lower-class appeals) among the parties. Before moving to the analysis it is worthwhile to take a comparative perspective.

Nieuwbeerta and Ultee's (1999) comparative research shows a general European trend of declining class voting but also great variability in the level of class voting across countries. Variations are best explained by union density and structural cleavages (the higher the religious and linguistic heterogeneity in a country the lower its level of class voting), while sociological variables such as social mobility and income distribution exert no impact. They also tried to model the extent to which class issues manifest in the electoral competition explain class voting, with negative result. Interestingly, though, in their conclusion they call for further research exactly on this issue, maybe doubting their operationalization of the variable – expert judgments which, as they acknowledge themselves (133), show no variation overtime:

> It can be hypothesized that declines in class voting levels [...] were caused by the fact that left-wing and right-wing political parties became more similar in their policy preferences and images. Consequently, members of the different classes can be assumed to have become less able to draw clear distinctions between the parties, and levels of class voting decreased.
>
> (Nieuwbeerta and Ultee, 1999: 149)

To make a first test of this hypothesis a secondary analysis can be carried out, correlating Nieuwbeerta and Ultee's (1999) country average log-odd ratios of manual workers voting left-wing rather than right-wing, with Bartolini and Mair's (1990) average country index of economic polarization based on factor analyses of economic-policy content of European party programs.[6] As can be seen in Figure 11.1 there is a strong relationship between policy distance and class voting: 47 percent of the variance in class voting is explained by the policy distance, i.e. the mean interval between two extreme parties on the economic dimension. The wider the economic policy distance, which we interpret as an indicator of parties' economic class appeal, the stronger is the alignment between class and vote. Clearly, Italy's low level of class voting is associated with a restricted space of interparty policy competition, notwithstanding its strong ideological polarization, while the opposite is true for the Scandinavian countries. These results are, of course, only illustrative, since they are based on a cross-sectional analysis (being restricted to the period analyzed, they cannot account for trends overtime). Above all, they rely only on a bivariate relationship, which is potentially spurious. Yet they appear promising and quite remarkable, taken that they come from independent estimates produced by independent research.

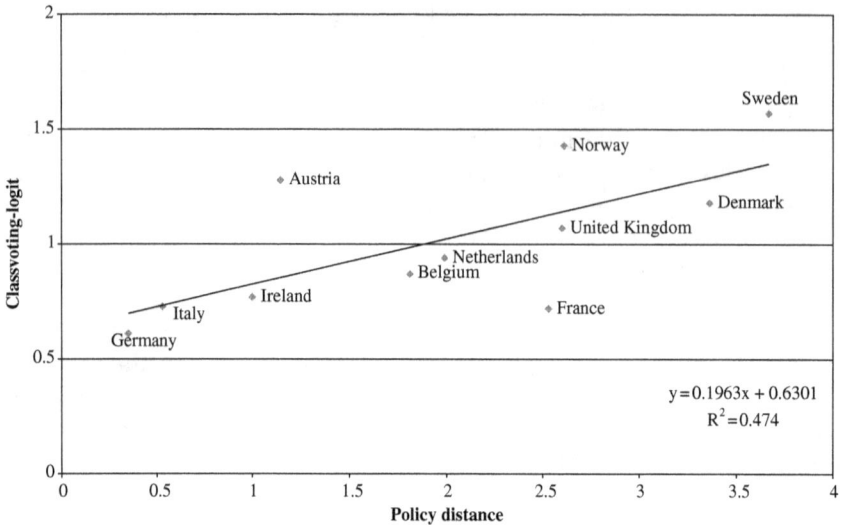

Figure 11.1 Relationship between policy distance (1976–1985 average) and class voting (1971–1980 average) in Western Europe.

The same research strategy has been applied to the Italian case in the following analysis. Class voting indexes, measured as log-odd ratios of manual workers versus upper middle-class voting left rather than center, have been computed from available Italian electoral surveys from 1953 to 1996.[7] Parties' class appeals are defined as the yearly policy distance between extreme parties on a forced one factor-analyzed dimension of the economic statements in Italian party programs since 1946.[8]

Before looking at the results from the entire postwar period, it is useful to look at the 1946–1992 years, focusing on the confrontation between the Communist Party (PCI) and the Christian Democratic Party (DC).[9] This period encompasses the long history of the so-called Italian First Republic, where leading political actors were the DC and the PCI, whose combined electoral strength averaged between half and two-thirds of the national vote.

As can be seen in Figure 11.2, DC–PCI confrontation on the economic policy issue appears rather weak in the earliest years, when ideological polarization was more on international alignment. But the policy distance increased significantly in the early 1950s, showing a slow decline over the following two decades. A new economic polarization is revealed in the 1983 election and declining rapidly in the following years. These data do not show a linear process of convergence in the PCI–DC economic programs, but up and down movements linked to the many political cycles Italy experienced.[10] So the notion that the ideologically polarized

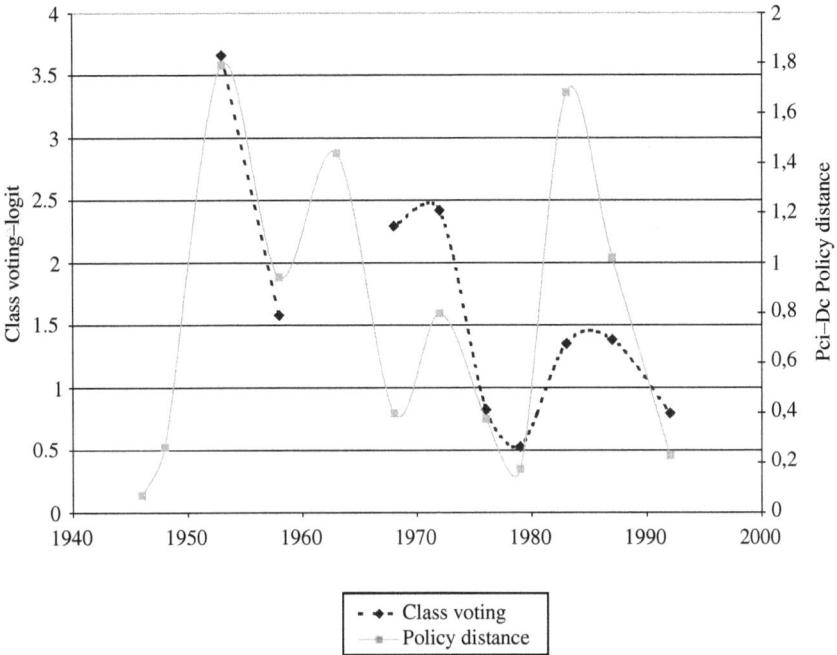

Figure 11.2 Relationship between class voting and policy distance: PCI and DC, Italy, 1946–1992.

Italian political system was characterized by a stable similarity in parties' economic appeals needs to be reconsidered, at least as observed from the perspective of the two (polarized) leading parties. It is true, however, that with the 1992 elections differences in policy (and class) appeals between the Communists and Christian Democrats have come to a full circle, being as low as in 1946.

The curve of the class voting index follows relatively close that of the policy distance, indicating that higher economic polarization is associated with a higher level of class vote alignment. Actually, regressing class voting on party distance yields a moderate fit, with an R^2 of 0.381.[11] The beta coefficient for policy distance is 0.617, indicating that classes' voting responses to a change in the parties' economic confrontation are less than proportional. Indeed, while there is no linear trend in policy distance, this appears more evident, and negative, in the class voting beta coefficient. However, deviation from linearity is explained by the policy competition.[12] At the same time, we can cast doubt on the past prevailing interpretation of the social structure similarity of the electoral bases of the DC and PCI. A better measurement of class voting, offered by the odd ratio

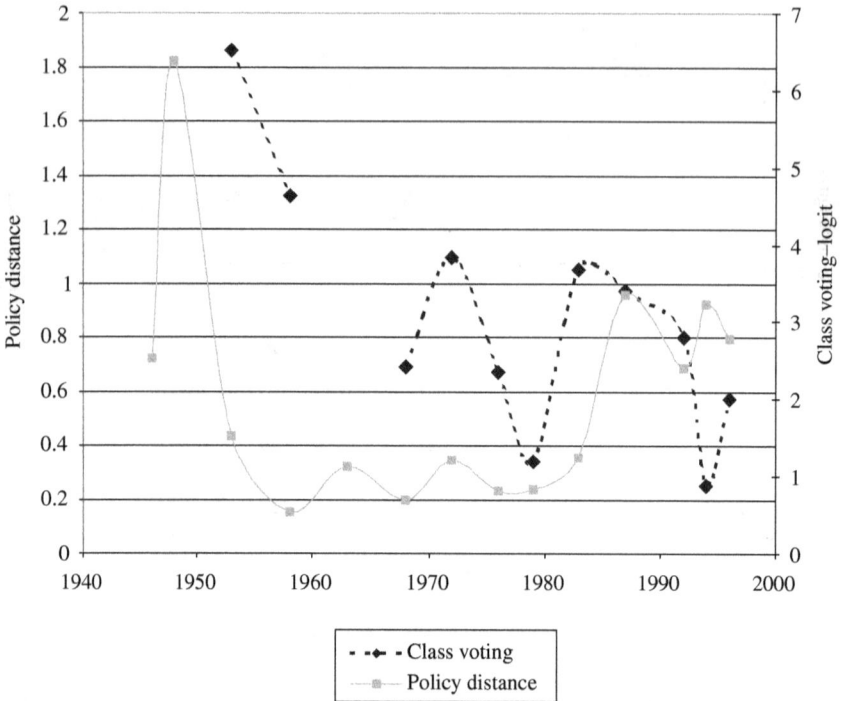

Figure 11.3 Relationship between class voting and policy distance: left versus center, Italy, 1946–1996.

coefficients, show that class differences in the vote, though declining, persisted over the entire 1946–1992 period.

Figure 11.3 replicates the analysis for the 1946–1996 period, but taking into account the full array of Italian parties and the political change after 1992. Class voting is measured as the logit (log-odd ratios) of working class versus upper middle-class voting left rather than center from yearly multinomial logistic regressions allowing all three voting options (left, center, right).[13] Policy distance is the interval between the factor score of the rightmost and leftmost parties on the left–right dimension, emerged from factor analyzing the economic policy statements of all parties in the period.

The graph is only apparently different from the previous one. As to the party-policy distance, it shows again a great polarization in the early years of the Republic followed by a net decline accompanied by up and down movements through the 1960s and 1970s. The 1987 elections mark a turning point, with a renewal of class appeal, followed by a new drop in 1992. The first 1994 majoritarian elections show, as anticipated, a new economic polarization which slightly declined in 1996. But the average 1994–1996 policy distance is greater than the one of 1983–1992, and even more so with respect to previous two decades. Overall, then, Italian parties' class-based economic polarization shows clear period differences: a high start in the 1940s, followed by a long phase of stabilization through the 1970s, and a strong renewal afterwards.

Is this policy trend reflected in the class–vote alignment, as hypothesized? The answer is positive, with a strong specification. The ups and down of the class voting curve follow those of the parties' appeals – at different levels, to be sure, as to suggest a priming effect on class loyalties which only slowly erode – in the years of the First Republic, but not so clearly afterwards. The critical election is the one of 1994, when party distances increase but class voting shows its lowest coefficient ever. Elsewhere (Segatti *et al.*, 1999) we explained this result in terms of a displacement effect on the electorate produced by the changing format of the party system and the disappearance of long established parties, which quickly vanished in 1996.[14] Overall, however, the post-1992 logit coefficients show a weaker impact of class on voting when compared to earlier years. This interpretation is confirmed by regressing class voting on policy distance and modeling both the trend and the 1994 displacement effect via a dummy.[15] There is an overtime decline of the class–vote alignment, and a 1994 displacement effect. Still, there is clear and significant impact of parties' policy distance on the level of class voting.

To summarize our findings so far, we found no evidence of party program convergence in Italy, which confirms for the Italian case the overall pattern of Western democracies (Klingemann *et al.*, 1994). On the contrary, parties' class-based economic polarization shows clear period movements, linked to different political cycles and patterns of party competition. We found a slowly overtime declining level of class voting, which can probably be attributed to sociological factors (such as the changing composition of social classes and conditions of life), although we have not empirically addressed this issue. But, linking the two sets of variables, we hypothesized and found supportive evidence that parties make the difference. Distinct parties' class appeals, measured by their distance in economic policy programs, elicit a class response in the electorate, counterbalancing opposite sociological drives. Further, even though the Italian level of class voting may appear weaker when compared to other European countries (Nieuwbeerta and Ultee, 1999), in contrast with the previous and prevailing interpretations we found class differences in the vote which, though declining, are evident over the 1946–1996 period. We can now assess the impact of economic conditions on the vote, and see how traditional anchors of partisanship, religion, and class, mediated by institutional factors, have changed the impact of the economy on the vote.

11.3   ITALIAN ECONOMIC VOTING: HOW AND WHY THE PAST WEAK RELEVANCE HAS CHANGED

In order to assess how the erosion of long-term factors (religion, class, party identification) and the introduction of a new institutional and political context (party system change, a new electoral law, prominence of the economy in the campaign) have changed the impact of economic concerns on Italian voting, we have modeled their relation to the vote in three different periods: the 1970s, 1980s, and 1990s. The surveys selected to represent each decade are the (unfortunately) only ones in which economic questions with the same format and wording had been inserted. By chance these election surveys correspond to the years in which class voting was strongest within each decade (see Figure 11.2). The same model has been estimated for each year: voting is a function of economic concerns, class membership, religion, party closeness, ideological identification, plus a series of conventional control variables.

Our primary interest lays in the relative impact of economic variables versus the traditional determinants of partisanship on the vote. Table 11.1 shows the MLE estimates from the multinomial logistic model. We can see that in 1972 traditional determinants of partisanship – religion, class, and ideological identification – were the dominant forces of electoral choice. The economic effect was weak and asymmetrical: the responsibility hypothesis works in the contrast between a vote for the (tiny) opposition right and one for the ruling center, but it does not when choosing between the opposition-left and ruling parties. In the latter situation, the perception of a worsening personal economic condition increases the likelihood of a vote for the ruling parties rather then for the left-wing opposition, an outcome traditionally explained in patron-client terms (Bellucci, 1984) and recently reframed as clientele-partisan effects (Carlsen, 2000). In 1983 as well, retrospective egocentric and sociotropic economic evaluations show no impact, while the traditional cleavage and ideological variables' impact remains strong. The situation changes significantly in 1996. Before seeing how, let us briefly review the political events that led to the election.

The center–right government which emerged from the 1994 elections – a coalition which included Forza Italia (holding the premiership with Berlusconi), Alleanza nazionale and Lega – lasted only a few months. The Lega abandoned the government and Berlusconi was forced to resign after an attempt to introduce a bill that would have severely cut the pension scheme of the employees, which prompted widespread demonstrations over a socially divisive issue, thus confirming the expectations of a class conflict over the stabilization of the Italian welfare state. At the refusal of the Italian president of the Republic Scalfaro to call new elections as requested by Forza Italia and Alleanza nazionale, a new

Table 11.1 Determinants of Italian electoral choice, 1972–1996 (multinomial logistic regression)

	1972		1983		1996	
	Left vs. center	Right vs. center	Left vs. center	Right vs. center	Ultivo (left) vs. right (Polo)	Lega (center) vs. right (Polo)
Satisfaction with family economic condition (yes)						
No	0.220 (0.285)	0.351 (0.456)				
Retrospective personal economic condition (same)						
Better	−0.511 (0.317)	−1.208 (0.489)**	−0.111 (0.395)	0.622 (0.530)	0.632 (0.4669)	0.432 (0.486)
Worse	−0.614 (0.375)*	0.238 (0.487)	−0.223 (0.343)	−0.071 (0.530)	0.162 (0.237)	−0.110 (0.284)
Retrospective national economic condition (same)						
Better			−0.091 (0.504)	0.137 (0.782)	1.043 (0.326)****	0.177 (0.419)
Worse			0.368 (0.396)	0.658 (0.659)	−0.562 (0.231)***	−0.449 (0.263)
Social class (upper middle class)						
Lower middle	0.819 (0.939)	−1.823 (0.740)**	0.571 (0.601)	−1.268 (0.474)***	0.661 (0.290)**	1.001 (0.388)***
Self-employed urban lower middle	1.397 (0.937)	−1.619 (0.690)**	0.646 (0.663)	−0.382 (0.735)	0.282 (0.365)	0.393 (0.462)
Self-employed agricultural lower middle	0.652 (1.016)	−2.132 (0.859)**	0.200 (1.08)	−1.838 (1.191)	0.865 (0.772)	0.218 (1.228)
Manual workers	1.968 (0.943)**	−1.475 (0.708)**	1.741 (0.66)***	−1.935 (0.836)**	0.506 (0.305)*	0.840 (0.388)*
Religion (practicing)						
Not practicing	1.651 (0.284)****	1.550 (0.426)****	1.125 (0.474)**	1.361 (0.667)**	−0.294 (0.216)	−0.006 (0.252)
Party identification (not close to any party)						
Close to party	−0.340 (0.336)	−0.640 (0.512)	0.133 (0.306)	0.162 (0.432)	−0.048 (0.383)	0.366 (0.359)
Left–right self-placement	−1.073 (0.105)****	0.525 (0.099)****	−1.179 (0.127)****	1.015 (0.151)****	−2.697 (0.124)****	−1.230 (0.121)****
Political interest (low)						
High	−0.225 (0.280)	0.619 (0.431)	0.516 (0.340)	−0.399 (0.533)	0.185 (0.201)	−0.473 (0.236)**

Table 11.1 (Continued)

	1972		1983		1996	
	Left vs. center	Right vs. center	Left vs. center	Right vs. center	Ultvo (left) vs. right (Polo)	Lega (center) vs. right (Polo)
Education (low)						
High	-0.167 (0.429)	1.094 (0.507)**	-0.073 (0.353)	0.474 (0.518)	0.012 (0.233)	-0.588 (0.269)**
Gender (male)						
Female	-0.372 (0.272)	-0.121 (0.401)	0.131 (0.309)	-1.268 (0.474)**	-0.151 (0.208)	-0.400 (0.242)*
Region (Northern)						
Center	0.381 (0.311)	-0.030 (0.603)	0.258 (0.366)	1.092 (0.574)*	0.641 (0.283)**	-1.683 (0.394)****
South	-0.309 (0.324)	1.039 (0.468)**	-0.214 (0.361)	0.618 (0.517)	-1.100 (0.232)	–
Constant	2.434 (1.15)**	-5.076 (1.195)****	4.385 (0.961)****	-7.774 (1.552)****	7.604 (.588)****	3.415 (0.709)****
N	628		463		1783	
χ^2 (DF) (P)	491.3 (30) (0.000)		436.9 (32) (0.000)		1880 (32) (0.000)	
Pseudo-R^2	0.448		0.488		0.593	

Notes
MLE estimates with standard errors in parentheses. * $p < 0.1$; ** $p < 0.05$; *** $p < 0.01$; **** $p < 0.001$ – two-tailed test.

government took office. It was headed by Dini, former Director of the Italian Central Bank and the very Treasury minister of the Berlusconi government who had drafted the aborted proposal of pension reform. It was, however, considered a technical government since the presence in cabinet of many non-partisan professionals ("experts") as ministers was the condition laid down by the right. This way, the latter allowed the birth, through abstention at the confidence vote in Parliament, of a government which was supported by Lega, the center (Partito popolare), and some of the leftist Progressisti parties (Pasquino, 1996). This mixed nature of the government, in a political as well as a technical sense, raises some problems as to both its political leaning and to the clarity of responsibility for the management of the country and its economic policy. The fact, however, that Dini joined the Ulivo coalition to contest elections, and that many of the policies enacted by the Cabinet – including a less radical pension reform – were backed by the Pds, the main leftist party, allowed the public opinion to assess the incumbent as a center–left government whose policy would continue if, as it actually happend, the Ulivo would result victorious. Its opponent was again the center–right coalition led by Berlusconi, while Lega contested elections running alone. Finally, as we have already indicated, the economic issue was central in the electoral campaign.

Against this background, we can see in Table 11.1 that the 1996 model tells a clear story. Retrospective evaluation of national economic conditions is significantly correlated to the vote and consistent with the responsibility theory. Discontent electors voted for the center–right opposition, while a positive evaluation elicited a vote for the Ulivo coalitions. On the other hand, pocketbook voting does not show. In explaining these results and to demonstrate that we are observing economic voting indeed, we have to look at the impact of traditional determinants of the vote, religion and social class, and check whether they have a diminished electoral impact. They have. As expected, religion does no longer exert any effect on the vote. Social class does, but its influence is weaker than before: compare the fourfold stronger logit coefficient of the 1972 manual workers (1.968) with that of 1996 (0.506). However, the social stratification of the vote appears coherent with the policy distinction of the coalitions' economic programs: the appeal to market forces by the Polo has elicited most support by the self-employed and entrepreneurs, while the left-wing defense of welfare is supported by manual workers and employees, especially by public sector workers. Last, the impact of the ideological identification – measured by the left–right self-placement – is strong in 1996, even stronger than in preceding years. This implies the permanence of a clear political division among the electorate. What has diminished, even though in the specification of our model this does not show as statistically significant, is the impact of party identification (closeness to party). The relative coefficient in 1972 (−0.340 for left versus center) is far greater than in 1996 (−0.048 for Ulivo versus Polo), tracking the long-term decline of subcultural party involvement of Italian electors. Moreover, while the former coefficient borders the conventional level of significance, the latter does not. In sum, the rise of economic voting in Italy seems to be explained by the decline of traditional cleavages and the development of individualized patterns of electoral behavior. Both factors are linked to crucial variables: clarity of government responsibility and actual available ruling alternatives.

11.4   SOME FINAL REMARKS

The transformation of the Italian party system which took place after 1992 has altered the pattern of party competition and the relationships between parties and voters. The three main cleavages that have in the past molded electors' party allegiances – religion, class, and ideological polarization (communism/anti-communism) – have declined, thus reducing the strong party identification that has for 40 years been the base of the Italian small electoral volatility. At the same time, and for the same reason, the new party coalitions that contested elections with a new majoritarian electoral system stressed economic issues during the electoral campaigns, also in response to the international constraint on the Italian public budget, due to the European monetary integration. So, class interests and retrospective economic evaluations entered in the ballot box, showing a relationship with the vote broadly coherent with findings in the comparative literature. These results point to the importance of political institutions in the relationship between economic conditions and electoral behavior: economic effects on the Italian vote appear once the electoral system changes from proportional to majoritarian; when party ideological polarization declines; when long-term party identification decreases; when alternative government coalitions appear feasible; when different issue positions become clearer. From the perspective of current comparative research, which calls for attention to the political contest in which economic voting takes place with clear demarcation between Westminster and consensual democracies, Italy's experience offers a longitudinal study in which overtime variation of the political and institutional context influences economic voting trends.

ACKNOWLEDGMENTS

This chapter originates from a larger research project on the transformation of Italian electoral behavior carried out with Marco Maraffi

(Università di Milano) and Paolo Segatti (Università di Pavia). I wish to thank them for allowing me to present some findings from a coauthored work in progress. This research has been funded by a 1997 Ministry of University and Research inter-university grant (No. 9714036484).

NOTES

1 For a discussion of the applicability of the economic voting paradigm to Italy see Bellucci (1990, 1991).
2 Analyses of the transformation of the Italian political system are offered by Bartolini and D'Alimonte (1995, 1996). See also the special issue of European Journal of Political Research on the 1996 elections (D'Alimonte, 1998).
3 The economy issue was highly visible in the television electoral campaign, which showed a remarkable change in how the news was framed and conveyed to the electorate. For the first time policy issues dominated over political questions. For example, in the 1987 elections television debates mainly rotated over political issues (party relations, government coalitions, etc.), which represented 37.5 percent of the total issues discussed, compared to 21 percent of policy issues, whereas in 1994 policy issues counted as much as 39 percent of all issues covered in the debates. And within the policy issues, those referring to the economy and welfare represented 56 percent of the total (Mancini and Mazzoleni, 1995). In the last 2 weeks of campaign the economy was then a central concern: the three issues which received most attention were the proposal for a tax-cut (which accounted for 9.7 percent of the time of total coverage), privatization of welfare (7.7 percent of the time), unemployment (6 percent). Justice and political corruption, as a comparison, ranked only 14th and 15th, accounting for only 2.3 and 2 percent of coverage time (Marinelli and Dolce, 1995, p. 123).
4 Analyses of the television electoral campaign show how policy issues further dominated the debate with respect to the 1994 campaign, summing in 1996 to 51 percent of all issues; fiscal policy and public debt alone counted for 9 percent of all issues debated (Marini, 1996).
5 Translation by the author. The original article was published in Sartori (1968).
6 1971–1980 Country average log-odd ratios come from Table 1 in Nieuwbeerta and Ultee (1999, p. 137). 1976–1985 Country mean policy distances are from Table 8.2 in Bartolini and Mair (1990, p. 199).
7 We employ a neo-weberian class definition, revising the one proposed by De Lillo (1988), which distinguishes five classes, based on the family provider's occupation for those outside the labor force (housewives, students) and on former occupation for retirees and unemployed: Upper middle class (entrepreneurs, executives, top management, professionals, university teachers); Lower middle class (employees, technical workers, teachers); Urban (i.e. non-agricultural) self-employed lower middle class (artisans, craftsmen, shopkeepers, self-employed owners of small businesses); Rural (i.e. agricultural) self-employed lower middle class (farm owners and tenants); Manual workers (blue-collar and unskilled white-collar workers, rural manual workers). We coded Left all parties on the left–right continuum up to the Socialist Party; Center the Christian Democratic Party and its heirs after 1994 plus minor center parties; Right the Liberal Party, Msi–An, Lega, and Forza Italia after 1994. Source of surveys: 1953, Doxa S-326; 1958, Doxa S-5010; 1969, S. Barnes study; 1972, S. Barnes and G. Sani study; 1975: Political Actions Study; 1979: Eurobarometer 11; 1983: Eurobarometer 20; 1985: Four Nations Study;

1990, 1992, 1994, 1996: Italian National Election Study (Itanes). The datasets have been made available by: 1953–1958, CirCap-University of Siena; 1968, 1972, 1975, 1985, ICPSR; Eurobarometer; ZA, University of Cologne; 1990, 1992, 1994, 1998, Itanes, Istituto Cattaneo.

8 The pooled factor-analyzed solution of the policy statements of the economy domain (as defined by the Manifesto Research Group) in the Italian party programs between 1946 and 1996 produces a clear left-planning/right-market ordering of the economic categories, broadly overlapping the programs of Bartolini and Mair (1990) and Çarkoglu (1995). The variance explained by this left–right dimension is 16 percent. The factor score for each party for each year identifies its position on the left–right dimension. The policy distance is computed, for each election year, as the interval between the factor scores of the most leftist and the most rightist parties. The Italian Manifesto Research Group dataset has been made available by the principal investigators through CirCap-Università di Siena. See for the UK (Evans *et al.*, 1999).

9 The 1946–1992 analysis has been carried out as described in notes 6 and 7, restricting factor analysis to the 1946–1992 period and computing odd ratios of the PCI–DC vote contrast. For each year, then, the PCI–DC policy distance equals the interval of their factor scores on the left–right dimension.

10 We can observe that the PCI–DC policy distance increased in concomitance with political turning points: in 1953, when the Dc tried to pass a majoritarian law, in 1963, when the Socialists first joined the government, and in 1983, when the Socialists were entering the government coalition again and obtained the premiership. By contrast, the low 1976 class appeal marks the Communist Party's joining of the government coalition.

11 The regression equation is: class voting PCI–DC $= 0.801(1.70)+1.02 \times$ policy distance (2.07). $R^2 = 0.381$; $N = 9$; t in parentheses.

12 Introducing the year to model the trend yields the following results: class voting PCI–DC $= 2.55(3.07) + 0.682 \times$ policy distance (1.81) $- 0.188 \times$ year (-2.38). $R^2 = 0.680$; $N = 9$; t in parentheses.

13 Parties have been recoded as explained in note 7.

14 In 1994, the prevalence of the working class–vote for the left stopped, and many of these votes were transferred to right-wing Forza Italia. In 1996, however, the usual pattern showed again.

15 The regression equation is: class voting left–center $= 1.636(7.42) + 0.339 \times$ policy distance (2.81) $- 0.145 \times$ year $(-4.32) - 0.588 \times$ year_1994 (-1.92). $R^2 = 0.783$; $N = 11$; $t -$ statistic in parentheses.

REFERENCES

Alt, J. and Chrystal, A. (1983) *Political Economics*. Berkeley, CA: University of California Press.

Anderson, C. (1995) *Blaming the Government. Citizens and the Economy in Five European Democracies*. Armonk, NY: Sharpe.

Anderson, C. (2000) Economic voting and political context: a comparative perspective. *Electoral Stud.*, **19**, 151–170.

Barnes, S.H. (1974) *Italy: Religion and Class in Electoral Behavior*. In R. Rose (ed.), *Electoral Behavior: A Comparative Handbook*. New York: Free Press, pp. 171–225.

Barnes, S.H. (1977) *Representation in Italy. Institutionalized Tradition and Electoral Choice*. Chicago, IL: University of Chicago Press.

Barnes, S.H. (1984) Secular trends and partisan realignment in Italy. In R.J. Dalton, S.C. Flanagan and P.A. Beck (eds), *Electoral Change in Advanced Industrial Democracies. Realignment or Dealignment?* Princeton, NJ: Princeton University Press.

Bartolini, S. and D'Alimonte, R. (eds) (1995) *Maggioritario ma non Troppo: le Elezioni Politiche del 1994*. Bologna: Il Mulino.

Bartolini, S. and D'Alimonte, R. (1996) Plurality competition and party realignment in Italy: the 1994 parliamentary elections. *Eur. J. Political Res.*, **29**, 105–142.

Bartolini, S. and Mair, P. (1990) *Identity, Competition and Electoral Availability. The Stabilisation of European Electorates 1885–1985*. Cambridge: Cambridge University Press.

Bellucci, P. (1984) The effect of aggregate economic conditions on the political preferences of the Italian electorate. *Eur. J. Political Res.*, **12**, 387–401.

Bellucci, P. (1990) Economia y voto: resena de los estudios sobre el ciclo politico de la economia en Itali. *Revista del Instituto de Estudios Economico*, **4**, 133–159.

Bellucci, P. (1991) Italian economic voting: a deviant case or making a case for a better theory? In H. Norpoth, M.S. Lewis-Beck and J. Lafay (eds), *Economics and Politics: The Calculus of Support*. Ann Arbor, MI: University of Michigan Press.

Bellucci, P. (1995) All' origine delle identità politiche. In A.M.L Parisi and H.M.A. Schadee (eds), *Sulla Soglia del Cambiamento. Elettori e Partiti alla Fine Della Prima Repubblica*. Bologna: Il Mulino.

Bellucci, P. (1997) Classi, identità politiche e interessi. In P. Corbetta and A.M.L. Parisi (eds), *A Domanda Risponde. Il Cambiamento di Voto degli Italiani nelle Elezioni del 1994 e 1996*. Bologna: Il Mulino.

Bellucci, P., Maraffi, M. and Segatti, P. (2000) *Pci, Pds, Ds. La Trasformazione dell'Identità Politica della Sinistra di Governo*. Roma: Donzelli.

Çarkoglu, A. (1995) Election manifestos and policy – oriented economic voting. *Eur. J. of Political Res.*, **27**, 293–317.

Carlsen, F. (2000) Unemployment, inflation and government popularity – are there partisan effects? *Electoral Stud.*, **19**, 141–150.

Corbetta, P., Parisi, A.M.L. and Schadee, H.M.A. (1988) *Elezioni in Italia. Struttura e Tipologia delle Consultazioni Politiche*. Bologna: Il Mulino.

D'Alimonte, R. (ed.) (1998) *The Italian Elections of 1996: Competition and Transition*. *Eur. J. Political Res.*, **34** [special issue], 1.

Dalton, R.J. (1988) *Citizens Politics in Western Democracies. Public Opinion and Political Parties in the United States, Great Britain, West Germany, France*. Chatam, NJ: Chatam House Publishers.

Dalton, R.J., Flanagan, S.C and Beck, P.A. (eds) (1984) *Electoral Change in Advanced Industrial Democracies. Realignment or Dealignment?* Princeton, NJ: Princeton University Press.

De Graaf, N.D., Nieuwbeerta, P. and Heath, A. (1990) Class mobility and political preference: individual and contextual effect. *Am. J. Sociol.*, **100**, 997–1027.

De Graaf, N.D., Heath, A. and Need, A. (2001) Decline cleavages and political choices: the interplay of social and political factors in the Netherlands. *Electoral Stud.*, **20**, 1–15.

De Lillo, A. (1988) La mobilità sociale assoluta. *Polis*, **2**, 19–51.

Evans, G., Heath, C. and Payne, C. (1999). Class: Labour as a Catch-all Party? In G. Evans and P. Dorris (eds), *Critical Elections, British Parties and Voters in Long Term Perspective*, London: Sage.

Fabbrini, S. (2000) Political change without institutional transformation: what can we learn from the Italian crisis of the 1990s? *Int. Political Sci. Rev.*, **21**(2), 173–96.

Fabbrini, S. and Gilbert, M. (2000) When cartel fails: the role of political class in the Italian democratic transition. *Government and Opposition*, **35**(1), 27–48.

Franklin, M.N., Mackie, T.T. and Valen, H. (eds) (1992) *Electoral Change. Responses to Evolving Social and Attitudinal Structures in Western Countries*. Cambridge: Cambridge University Press.

Gunther, R. and Montero, J.R. (1998) Electoral volatility and stability: a comparative analysis of the socio-structural and attitudinal bases of partisanship. Paper Delivered at the Istituto Cattaneo Conference Democrazia, Transizione Politica, Scelte Elettorali, Bologna.

Hout, M., Brooks, C. and Manza, J. (1995) The Democratic class struggle in the United States: 1948–1992. *Am. Sociol. Rev.*, **60**, 805–828.

Inglehart, R. (1990) *Culture Shift in Advanced Industrial Society*. Princeton, NJ: Princeton University Press.

Klingemann, H., Hofferbert, Budge, I. *et al.* (1994) *Parties, Policies, and Democracy*. Boulder: Westview Press.

Lewis-Beck, M.S. (1988) *Economics and Elections: The Major European Democracies*, Ann Arbor, MI: University of Michigan Press.

Lewis-Beck, M.S and Paldam, M. (2000) Economic voting: an introduction. *Electoral Stud.*, **19**, 113–121.

Lipset, S.M. (1981) *Political Man. The Social Bases of Politics*. Baltimore: Johns Hopkins University Press.

Lipset, S.M. and Rokkan, S. (1967) Cleavage structures, party systems and voter alignments: an introduction. In S.M. Lipset and S. Rokkan (eds), *Party Systems and Voter Alignments: Cross-national Perspectives*. New York: Free Press.

Mackie, T.T., Mannheimer, R. and Sani, G. (1992) Italy. In M.N. Franklin, T.T. Mackie and H. Valen (eds), *Electoral Change. Responses to Evolving Social and Attitudinal Structures in Western Countries*. Cambridge: Cambridge University Press.

Mair, P. (1993) Explaining the absence of class politics in Ireland. In J.H. Goldthorpe and C.T. Whelan (eds), *The Development of Industrial Society in Ireland*. Oxford: Oxford University Press.

Mancini, P. and Mazzoleni, G. (eds) (1995) *I Media Scendono in Campo. Le Elezioni Politiche 1994 in Televisione*. Roma: Nuova Eri.

Mannheimer, R. and Sani, G. (1987) *Il Mercato Elettorale. Identikit dell'Elettore Italiano*. Bologna: Il Mulino.

Marinelli, A. and Dolce, T. (1995) Le trasmissioni di telepolitica. Struttura tematica e stili comunicativi. In M. Morcellini (ed.), *Elezioni di TV. Televisione e Pubblico nella Campagna Elettorale'94*. Genova: Costa e Nolan.

Marini, R. (1996) *I Contenuti della Televisione Elettorale. Le Novità del 1996*. Paper Delivered at the Meeting of Ais-Sezione di Sociologia politica, Torino.

Manza, J., Hout, M. and Brooks, C. (1995) Class voting in capitalist democracies since World War II: dealignment, realignment, or trendless fluctuation? *Annu. Rev. Sociol.*, **21**, 137–162.

Nieuwbeerta, P. and Ultee, W. (1999) Class voting in western industrialized countries, 1945–1990: systematizing and testing explanations. *Eur. J. Political Res.*, **35**, 123–160.

Paldam, M. (1991) How robust is the vote function? A study of 17 nations over four decades. In H. Norpoth, M.S. Lewis-Beck and J. Lafay (eds), *Economics and Politics: The Calculus of Support*. Ann Arbor, MI: University of Michigan Press.

Pasquino, G. (1996) Il governo di lamberto dini. In M. Caciagli and D.I. Kertzer (eds), *Politica in Italia*. Istituto Carlo Cattaneo, Bologna: Il Mulino.

Pizzorno, A. (1981) Sulla razionalità della scelta democratica. *Stato e Mercato*, **7**, 3–45.

Powell, G.B. and Whitten, G.D. (1993) A cross-national analysis of economic voting: taking account of the political context. *Am. J. Political Sci.*, **37**(2), 391–414.

Sani, G. (1974) Determinants of party preference in Italy: toward the integration of complementary models. *Am. J. Political Sci.*, **18**, 315–329.

Sani, G. and Segatti, P. (2000) Platforms, media and voters. *Eur. J. Political Res.*, **34**, 105–119.

Santaganta, W. (1995) *Economia, Elezioni, Interessi. Una Analisi dei Cicli Economici Elettorali in Italia*. Bologna: il Mulino.

Sartori, G. (1968) Alla ricerca della sociologia politica. *Rassegna Italiana di Sociologia*, **4**, 597–639.

Sartori, G. (1982) *Teoria dei Partiti e Caso Italiano*. Sugarco.

Segatti, P. (1999) Religiosità e territorio nel voto alla democrazia cristiana dal 1948 al 1992. *Polis* XIII, **1**, 45–65.

Segatti, P., Bellucci, P. and Maraffi, M. (1999) *Stable voters in an unstable party environment. Continuity and change in Italian electoral behaviour*. Estudio/Working Paper 1999/139. Instituto Juan March de Estudios e Investigaciones.

Weakliem, D.L. (1991) The two lefts? Occupation and party choice in France, Italy and the Netherlands. *Am. J. Sociol.*, **96**, 1327–1361.

Weakliem, D.L. (1992) Does social mobility affect political behavior? *Eur. Sociol. Rev.*, **2**, 153–165.

Whitten, G.D. and Palmer, H.D. (1999) Cross-national analyses of economic voting. *Electoral Stud.*, **18**, 49–67.

12 The retrospective voter in Spain during the 1990s

Marta Fraile

12.1 INTRODUCTION

The fame of the Spanish Socialist Workers' Party (Partido Socialista Obrero Español, PSOE) rests, among other factors, on its unusually long period in government, which lasted for almost 14 years from 1982 until 1996. Among the various explanations for the PSOE capacity to retain power, this chapter focuses on those involving the impact of economic conditions on electoral outcomes.

The economic-voting approach seeks to measure the extent to which the electorate reacts to a government's economic performance. There exist very different empirical strategies to investigate how economic conditions shape voters' views of incumbent governments. The aim of this chapter is to provide a model of economic voting to investigate the relationship between elections and the economy for the last two mandates of the Socialists in Spain (in 1993 and 1996). I will provide an explanation of why the Socialists lost the elections in 1996 (a period of economic recovery) rather than in 1993 (a period of serious economic recession). In the research design, I pool data from 1993 and 1996 to directly compare the impact of the economy across elections. This analysis also offers a methodological contribution to the debate on how to compare the factors explaining individual determinants of the vote across elections.

This study evaluates the importance of the perception of a country's economic status relative to other determinants of voting intention such as ideological identification or socioeconomic characteristics. An investigation of the impact of voters' subjective views about the state of the economy is important for theoretical and practical reasons. Elections are the principal mechanism by which citizens control governments, but it is well known that politicians can escape the control of voters through various strategies. They enjoy an advantage of a high degree of available information compared to the information at the disposal of voters. They might also escape voters' control by alluding to their historical image or to the personal attraction of their party leaders. Common sense, however, suggests that the capacity of incumbent governments to escape the control of electors is limited, otherwise they would never lose an election.

However, political discourse that helps to avoid responsibility loses its effectiveness over time. For instance, the Spanish Socialists, in their first mandate, may have blamed the former conservative government for the economic crisis. They may also have alluded to Spain's entry into the European Community to avoid responsibility for severe economic programs, or even to appeal to the patience of the electors, promising a future of prosperity regardless of the present tough economic adjustments (Maravall and Przeworski, 2001). Yet, after three consecutive Socialist mandates, it is reasonable to assume that electors became more willing to base their vote on the achievements of the incumbent government rather than on promises. Hence, in the 1990s, the retrospective voting hypothesis should gain relevance for the Spanish case. First, the efficacy of the exonerative discourse decreases as time passes; second, the credibility of the principal opposition party (Partido Popular, PP) has grown. The hypothesis of the retrospective voter is in particular plausible to explain the defeat of the Spanish Socialist party in 1996.

The remainder of this chapter is organized as follows. I first explain in detail the theoretical reasons for the specification of the economic-voting model that I test for the case of Spain. Next, I will present the data and methods I have used to test the model. Finally, I summarize the principal findings of the analysis by providing a measure of the magnitude of the effect of the economy on elections and draw some tentative conclusions.

12.2   TESTING THE ECONOMIC VOTING IN SPAIN DURING THE 1990S: THE MODEL

In this section, I propose to test the existence of economic voting in Spain during the 1990s by systematically considering the political, economic, institutional, and sociological contexts in which elections are embedded. The model seeks to identify the different ways in which public opinion may be related to the state of the economy.[1]

Even though research has encountered difficulties in demonstrating the existence of a stable vote function, some main results have emerged (Lewis-Beck and Paldam, 2000). Other things being equal, a good economic performance is more likely than a poor economic performance to make voters support the incumbent. Thus, research generally supports the simplest form of the reward–punishment hypothesis. However, the existing literature on economic voting has also shown that there are many situations under which this simple hypothesis does not hold. Consider, for instance, a voter who is not satisfied with a government's performance, but who sees no alternative. It does not make a lot of sense to punish the incumbent under such circumstances. This does not mean, however, that under these circumstances there is no connection between public opinion, voting, and the state of the economy. To demonstrate the existence of such a connection, however, it has to be modeled properly.

12.2.1   Retrospective and prospective economic voting

Retrospective voting assumes that voters only look to the past (i.e. they focus on outcomes obtained by the incumbent) and not to the future. Nor do they consider the proposals that alternative candidates put forward in election campaigns. In this theory, elections become simple referenda of the incumbent's performance. But what about the opposition? It is necessary to take the electorate's expectations into account. After all, elections are undeniably future-oriented, since voters must choose between candidates who wish to govern in the future, and their alternative proposals and promises for that future. Hence, I include both retrospective and prospective evaluations of the state of the economy in the empirical model to be tested.

In addition, there are two empirical reasons for including voters' prospective economic evaluations in the specification of the voting model. First, previous studies of economic assessments in Spain have concluded that voters' retrospective and prospective evaluations for the period 1980–1995 are by no means equivalent, both at the aggregate and at the individual level. Moreover, citizens seem to adopt a more critical stance when looking back than when looking forward (Maravall and Przeworski, 2001). Second, if we seek to demonstrate that the voter was more likely to be retrospective in Spain during the 1990s, this might be done by comparing electors' retrospective and prospective considerations in the 1993 and 1996 elections.

12.2.2   The credibility of the main opposition party

If elections are not just referenda on the incumbent's performance, but also an opportunity for voters to choose among alternative candidates and proposals, then the potential effectiveness and credibility of the main opposition party should be another significant factor mediating economic conditions and voters' political attitudes. In other words, I test what has been referred to in the introductory chapter as the clarity-of-opposition hypothesis.

When voters do not perceive a credible alternative within the spectrum of alternative electoral candidates, then punishing the incumbent government becomes less likely, regardless of its past performance. Existing studies have shown the importance of public perceptions about the main opposition party's capacity to manage the economy (Sanders, 1996).

According to survey data, the Spanish electorate has put little trust in the conservatives, i.e. the main opposition force to the ruling social democrats, since the transition to democracy. Potential reasons for this include the fact that this party (first known as Alianza Popular, AP, and then as Partido Popular, PP) was formed by prominent political leaders of the previous authoritarian, Francoist regime. Moreover, the party has usually been perceived as organizationally weak (Montero, 1990). In fact, in spite of its increasing organizational cohesion, confidence in its capacity to govern remained relatively low during the first half of the 1990s.[2] Hence, the main opposition party's capacity or competence to handle the economy should be another mediating factor in the relationship between voting behavior and the state of the economy.

12.2.3 Attribution of responsibility to the incumbent

The retrospective voter is guided by outcomes rather than policies (Key, 1966). An incumbent government is re-elected if voters believe that it has provided a minimum standard of general welfare. Generally speaking, the incumbent will be rewarded for a strong economic performance, but punished when the economy performs poorly. According to the literature, however, how the incumbent has achieved the minimum standard of welfare seems to matter less.

How do voters define such a standard of general welfare? The easiest way, from the voters' point of view, is to use information that is freely available and at their immediate disposal. Therefore, it would be reasonable to assume that individuals determine the standard on the basis of their own experiences, or that of the people belonging to their reference group. This is called egocentric economic voting. There are, however, good reasons to believe that people in fact base their vote on the state of the national economy as a whole (Kinder and Kiewiet, 1981; Ferejohn, 1986). This is termed sociotropic economic voting. Economic voting is generally retrospective and also sociotropic.

It is not always clear whether voters actually hold governments responsible for the state of the national economy. Unfortunately, there is little direct evidence demonstrating that voters hold the incumbent responsible. This is partly due to the lack of explicit survey questions referring to this issue. One of the advantages of the Spanish case in this respect is precisely the existence of evidence showing that a large proportion of citizens attributes responsibility for the state of the economy to the incumbent. For example, in a survey carried out in 1992, 83 percent of all respondents thought that the state of the economy largely depends on the incumbent's policies and decisions (Center of Social Investigations: CIS2042).

This evidence does not fully resolve the problem of the attribution of responsibility. Governments might attempt to escape the blame for poor economic results by arguing that economic outcomes do not directly derive from their own policies, but rather from national or international pressures. It is generally acknowledged that many other factors, apart from governments' policy decisions, influence the state of the economy. To address the clarity-of-responsibility problem, I examine voters' direct evaluations of economic policies, which leaves much less room for blame avoidance strategies to distort the picture. As stated in Chapter 1, economic voting is a form of policy voting. If it can be established that citizens do attribute direct responsibility to the incumbent for its economic policies, then we have much more consistent proof of the attribution hypothesis.

12.2.4   A broader view of the economy: a look at social policies

Apart from specific economic policies (i.e. those directly targeted at economic growth, unemployment, inflation), other policies may prove crucial for the incumbent's survival. Governments can potentially influence the welfare/utility effects of economic conditions (see Chapter 1). In this respect, social policies (income maintenance, protection of the unemployed, education, and health care), which are inherently related to economic policies, but often even more salient than the latter in the public's eyes, should not be excluded from the picture (Pierson, 1996). In particular, a critical fact that models of economic voting often neglect is that social policies can be used as compensations in tough economic periods, in the same way side-payments are recognized in the study of the relationship between government policies and citizens' preferences within current welfare economics.

The economic-voting literature tends to employ a very narrow empirical definition when identifying the dimensions of the state of the economy that citizens consider important. Usually, analyses are limited to voters' reactions to unemployment, inflation, or economic growth levels. I argue that a more comprehensive view of the economy should be adopted. From a broader perspective, social policies can indeed be considered as part of a government's economic program. This is certainly the case for the Socialists' economic program in Spain. Hence, I will test the possible existence of social policy voting.

Previous research on the Spanish case has highlighted the importance of including voters' evaluations of social policies. It has been shown that, while the Socialists' economic policies were quite unpopular with the electorate, there was always support for their social policies, and this in fact increased over time. Moreover, social policies were used by Felipe González (Prime Minister from 1982 to 1996) to "defend his economic policy before public opinion. Furthermore, the political identity of the government depended, rather than on a distinct macroeconomic program, on its specific social policy choices" (Maravall, 1999: 187). Social policies were explicitly used as side payments to compensate for the short-term negative economic consequences of tough long-term economic policies that were perceived as being imposed by the international environment and the state of economic knowledge: "social policies tried to reduce hardship, avoid distributional opposition, and build support constituencies" (Maravall, 1999: 190).

Is it really true that social policies have important electoral consequences? Can positive assessments of social policies mitigate the negative effects of critical views of an incumbent's economic policies? There is already empirical evidence pointing in this direction. When the political consequences of high unemployment in Spain were studied, it was found that social policies (together with entrenched ideological beliefs inducing party loyalty) to a large extent mitigated the negative electoral effects (Maravall and Fraile, 2001).

12.2.5 The dynamic context of elections

There is one further important factor to be considered to properly account for the political context of economic voting in Spain. It is now well established in electoral studies that certain issues acquire particular importance in each election. The theory on issue voting suggests that particularly salient issues during a government legislature or in a political campaign may have a significant influence on voters' electoral decision (Campbell *et al.*, 1960). In the case of Spain, I argue that it is important to incorporate into the economic-voting model citizens' visions about corruption. There is little doubt that during the 1990s political scandals related to corruption became a particularly important political issue (Jiménez, 1998). From January 1990 onwards, the illegal financing of the Socialist party gave rise to a series of scandals that attracted a good deal of media coverage and popular attention.

12.2.6 From the basic to the extended EV model

The simple reward–punishment model states that an election is a two-actor game between the incumbent and electors. The party in government presents its past performance to voters, who in their turn decide whether or not to renew their support on the basis of their retrospective evaluations. In formal terms, this model can be summarized in the following equation:

$$Y = f(\text{retrospective assessments of the economy}, \text{control variables}, \varepsilon)$$

$$(12.1)$$

According to Eq (12.1), the voting intention for the incumbent is a function of (1) voters' retrospective evaluations of the state of the economy, (2) some individual characteristics of those voters (used as control variables), and (3) other unobservable factors that are assumed to be randomly distributed (the error term ε).

As discussed above, and given the concern of this volume for the proper identification and measurement of the different contexts of economic voting, I propose to test the following extended economic-voting model:

$$Y = f(\text{expectations, economic policies evaluations, social policies}$$
$$\text{evaluations, opposition, corruption, control variables, } \varepsilon) \quad (12.2)$$

In words, the intention to vote for the incumbent is a function of several factors: (1) electors' economic expectations, (2) voters' retrospective evaluations of both economic and social policies, (3) voters' views about the credibility of the main opposition party, (4) prevailing views about political corruption, (5) some individual characteristics of voters (used as control variables), and (6) other unobservable factors that are assumed to be randomly distributed (the error term ε).

This economic-voting model is tested for the 1993 and 1996 elections. Along with a test of economic voting in Spain for the two former elections, this chapter is concerned with the reasons that account for the Socialists' defeat in 1996, just when the economy started to recover. Aggregate electoral results cannot be explained with the analysis of individual survey data. However, by pooling the data of the 1993 and 1996 surveys, I provide stringent empirical evidence on how the individual determinants of the voting intention change across the two mentioned elections. These findings give clues towards understanding the reasons of the PSOE's electoral defeat in 1996 at the macro level. Below, I explain the data, methodology, and results of the empirical analysis.

12.3   DATA AND RESULTS

12.3.1   Description of the data and variables

The data used here have been drawn from two cross-sectional surveys carried out prior to each election.[3] The dependent variable is indicated as voting intention. More specifically, voting intention has been defined as 1 for the incumbent and 0 for the other parties. I include in the 0 category those respondents who declare that they are not going to vote, because this can be considered as a way of punishing the incumbent. Additionally, I excluded from the analysis those respondents who were undecided as to whether to vote or not, or about which party to vote for.

The independent variables of the economic-voting model are operationalized as follows. First, voters' economic expectations is a dummy variable coded as 1 when citizens' economic expectations were optimistic and 0 when voters' economic expectations were not optimistic, i.e. when they thought that the overall state of the economy in the future – within one year – would be either similar to or worse than at moment of the interview. Second, electors' retrospective judgments of both economic and social policies are recoded as 1 for the positive evaluations and 0 for the negative evaluations. Third, voters' views about the credibility of opposition are coded 0 if the opposition is given no credit and 1 if the opposition is considered credible. Finally, individual judgments about corruption are coded 1 for critical voters and 0 for non-critical voters regarding corruption. Positive and significant coefficients are expected for the retrospective and prospective judgments, and negative and significant coefficients are expected for views about both the opposition and corruption.

Further, the control variables comprise all the so-called socio-demographic variables which, according to the literature on electoral behavior, have influenced the voting intention. Voters' ideological self-placement is recoded as a continuum between 0 (left) and 1 (right). Thus, we control for the possibility that voters' retrospective judgments about both economic and social policies are more than just a rationalization of their ideological ascription. Previous research on electoral behavior has highlighted the extensive influence of ideology on the voting intention (Gunther and Montero, 1994) so that the specification of voters' ideology in the model becomes indispensable. In addition, we control for some individual characteristics: age (grouped in seven categories), level of education (from 0, no studies at all, to 1, university education), and socioeconomic position. The latter one is coded as a set of five dummy variables: (1) worker, (2) unemployed, (3) retired, (4) student, and (5) housewife.[4] The socioeconomic variables are included not only to alleviate possible specification biases but also to capture the sociological determinants of the voting intentions in the 1990s. Descriptive statistics about the variables used in each election model are given in Appendix.

12.3.2 Methodology and results

Given the dichotomous nature of the dependent variable, Eq (12.2) has been estimated through logistic regression. The results for each election are given in Table 12.1. The first column shows the names of the independent variables in each model. The next two columns give the parameter estimates and associated standard errors as estimated by logit regressions for each election. Below I summarize the principal findings of the analysis.

As can be seen in Table 12.1, the model fits the data very well, correctly predicting at least 80 percent of the cases in the samples, and the χ^2-statistic for each election shows that the model performs far better than a null intercept-only model. Furthermore, the variables of interest (the ones regarding the extended economic-voting model) are all correctly signed and

Table 12.1 Voting for the incumbent party (PSOE), Spain, general elections of 1993 and 1996 (logistic regression)

Independent variables	1993	1996
Constant	1.42 (0.60)*	−0.91(0.33)*
Ideology	−2.51(0.45)**	−1.94(0.42)**
Age	−0.009(0.008)	0.009 (0.006)
Education	−2.98(0.53)**	−2.37(0.37)**
Unemployed[a]	0.05 (0.27)	0.45 (0.39)
Retired[a]	0.74 (0.32)*	0.36 (0.27)
Students[a]	−0.09(0.36)	−0.34(0.28)
Housewife[a]	0.27 (0.24)	0.63 (0.21)**
Optimistic economic expectations	0.63 (0.18)**	0.56 (15)**
Economic policies assessments	2.21 (0.23)**	1.04 (0.15)**
Social policies assessments	1.08 (0.26)**	1.30 (0.23)**
Opposition	−0.81(0.25)**	−3.61(0.38)**
Event: corruption	−0.82(0.20)**	−0.52(0.22)*
Number of cases	1015	1692
LR $\chi^2(11)$	455.53**	762.85**
Pseudo-R^2	0.35	0.37
Correct (%)	81	80

Notes
Entries are logit maximum likelihood estimates and their associated standard errors.
** significant at the level of 99%; * significant at the level of 95%, significant at the level of 90%; [a] These coefficients have been calculated with the employed as the category of reference.

statistically significant at the level of 99 percent. Table 12.1 demonstrates that Spanish voters in the 1990s are more retrospective than prospective, since the coefficients representing voters' retrospective control over the incumbent are higher than the coefficients corresponding to voters' economic expectations. Citizens' optimistic economic expectations increase the probabilities of rewarding the incumbent, but to a lesser extent than their positive judgments about both economic and social policies. In contrast, negative judgments about corruption decrease the probabilities of voting for the incumbent. The credibility of the main opposition party (PP) also exerts an important influence in the voting intention for the Socialists: the probability of voting for the incumbent decreases as the credibility of the PP increases. The empirical analysis presented here also confirms the ideological component of the vote so that the probability of voting for the Socialists decreases the more voters identify their political position as rightwing.

The coefficients of the model do not yet indicate the magnitude of the effect of each independent variable on the probability of voting for the Socialists. Table 12.2, however, provides this information. It translates the logit coefficients into real probabilities by way of simulations. The strategy is as follows. First, the values of all the independent variables

Table 12.2 Magnitude of the effects of the explanatory variables on probability of voting for the incumbent party (PSOE), Spain, general elections of 1993 and 1996 (logistic estimators)

Variables of interest	Probability of voting for the incumbent (PSOE) in	
	1993	*1996*
Voters' retrospective judgment about economic policies		
1 Positive	0.67 (0.58–0.75)	0.23 (0.17–0.29)
0 Negative	0.18 (0.15–0.21)	0.09 (0.7–0.12)
Difference	0.49	0.14
Voters' retrospective judgment about social policies		
1 Positive	0.36 (0.30–0.42)	0.17 (0.13–0.22)
0 Negative	0.16 (0.12–0.22)	0.05 (0.03–0.08)
Difference	0.20	0.12
Voters' economic expectations		
1 Optimistic	0.34 (0.28–0.40)	0.17 (0.12–0.21)
0 Non-optimistic	0.21 (0.17–0.25)	0.10 (0.07–0.13)
Difference	0.13	0.07
Voters' views about PP		
1 Positive	0.16 (0.11–0.23)	0.02 (0.00–0.03)
0 Negative	0.30 (0.26–0.34)	0.35 (0.31–0.39)
Difference	0.14	0.33
Voters' views about corruption		
0.77 Not a lot	0.40 (0.32–0.48)	0.13 (0.09–0.16)
0.77 Too much	0.23 (0.19–0.26)	0.08 (0.05–0.12)
Difference	0.17	0.05
Ideology		
0 left	0.35 (0.32–0.44)	0.17 (0.12–0.21)
1 right	0.12 (0.09–0.14)	0.06 (0.03–0.07)
Difference	0.23	0.11
Baseline probability	0.26 (0.22–0.29)	0.12 (0.09–0.15)

Notes
Estimated probabilities were calculated with the other variables set to their sample mean values. Numbers in parentheses correspond to 95% confidence interval for each simulation. To calculate the simulations, I used the program CLARIFY (Tomz *et al.*, 1999).

included in the model are set to their sample mean values and the predicted probability of voting for the incumbent is computed, which gives the baseline probability. Then, the predicted probability of voting is computed for the incumbent for each of the independent variables of interest. This means that from the baseline probability, only the value of the independent variable we are looking at has been changed; for example, retrospective evaluations of economic policies. I give the

predicted probability of voting for the incumbent both for the highest
value of the variable in question (e.g. 1 for economic retrospective
judgments) and for the lowest value of the same variable (in this case: 0).
I give the raw difference between these two probability estimates
(presented in bold in Table 12.2). The so-called "first difference" then
equals: $\hat{E}(Y_{max}) - \hat{E}(Y_{min})$ (King, 1989).

Column 2 of Table 12.2, 1993, gives a measure of the influence of
electors' judgments of economic policies upon the probability of voting for
the incumbent. A voter with positive retrospective judgment of economic
policies (and holding the rest of variables constant at their means) would
have a probability of voting for the incumbent in 1993 of 67 percent.
However, a voter with negative assessments of economic policies would have
a probability of voting for PSOE in 1993 of 18 percent. This represents a
difference of 49 percent. The influence of retrospective assessments of
economic policies seems to be especially strong in 1993 when compared to
1996. If we look at column 3, the difference between having positive and
negative evaluations of economic policies in the probability of voting for the
incumbent is 14 percent. And the same applies with respect to voters'
judgments about social policies: the positive effect seems to be stronger in
1993 than in 1996. More specifically, the difference between having positive
and negative evaluations of social policies with regard to the probability of
voting for the Socialists is 20 and 12 percent, respectively, in 1993 and 1996.

In contrast, the effect of voters' expectations about the economic future
of the country is smaller than that of voters' retrospective evaluations
of both economic and social policies for both elections. As Table 12.2
indicates, the difference between a voter having optimistic economic
expectations and a voter being pessimistic concerning the probability of
rewarding the Socialists is 13 and 7 percent, respectively, in 1993 and
1996 elections. This is further evidence demonstrating that Spanish
voters were more likely to vote retrospectively rather than prospectively
during the 1990s, after four consecutive PSOE mandates.

Table 12.2 also indicates that the credit of the main opposition party
must be taken into account when modeling the relationship between
elections and the economy. The difference between a voter giving credit
to the PP and one giving them no credit at all is 14 and 33 percent,
respectively, in 1993 and 1996. Finally, critical views of voters regarding
corruption of politicians have also an effect on the probability of voting for
the Socialists. More specifically, in 1993, the view that the degree of
corruption of Spanish politicians is very high in contrast with the view that
corruption is not so high produces a difference on the probability of voting
for the incumbent of 17 percent. The magnitude of the effect of public
opinion about corruption is expected to increase in the 1996 elections. The
empirical evidence, however, does not support this expectation, as the
difference for the 1996 model is only 5 percent. This may be an empirical
problem. The variable used for the 1996 model is not measuring directly

the elector opinion about the degree of corruption of the incumbent party. It simply asks electors to say which is the most important problem of the country to be solved. Thus, the corruption issue is mixed up with unemployment, terrorism, and poverty. There was no better variable available with which to specify the model. It is reasonable to assume, however, that with a variable equal to the one that has been used for the 1993 model, stronger coefficients would have been found.[5]

In addition, the effect of ideology, when compared to the effect of the other variables, is not especially strong. For example, comparing the probabilities of voting for the Socialists for a self-positioned leftwing voter (position 3 on an ideology continuum from 1 to 10) and a self-positioned rightwing voter (position 8) – holding the rest of the variables constant at their mean – the difference is 23 and 11 percent, respectively, in 1993 and 1996. From this, it can be concluded that voters resort to their ideological conviction when deciding how to vote, but only to a certain extent. This evidence casts some doubts on the conclusions coming from previous research on electoral behavior in Spain that highlight the ideological and stable component of the vote (Gunther and Montero, 1994).

The empirical evidence so far verifies the hypothesis of the retrospective economic voter in Spain both for the 1993 and 1996 elections. However, we must still explore the specific factors explaining the defeat of the Spanish Socialist party in 1996. A formal test is needed to be able to confirm that the differences in the effects of the independent variables upon the voting intention in 1993 and 1996 are statistically significant. In other words, a statistical test pointing out that the effect of certain variables on the probability of voting for the incumbent changes over time (or across elections).

The empirical strategy is pooling both surveys as a first step in adopting a dynamic approach regarding voting behavior analysis. To test for changes in the importance of each independent variable between 1993 and 1996, I employ interaction terms between the year (a dummy variable identifying the cases corresponding to 1996 with value 1 and the cases of 1993 with value 0) and each independent variable. This is a formal test that examines whether the differences in the effect of the independent variables upon the voting intention in 1993 and 1996 are statistically significant (Firebaugh, 1997).

The results of this second analysis are given in Table 12.3. The model presented here has been obtained after dropping all the interactions that did not turn out to be significant in the saturated model, which included interaction terms of all the independent variables with the dummy year variable.[6] In comparison with the saturated model, the model in Table 12.3 has passed the likelihood ratio test. The results of this test are as follows: likelihood-ratio test = $\chi^2(10) = 10.65$. Prob $(\chi^2) = 0.38$ (>0.05). Thus it can be concluded that the nonsignificant interactions of the saturated model can be dropped. Additionally, when comparing the model of Table 12.3 with the simplest one (that has only the dummy year

Table 12.3 Reanalysis of incumbent (PSOE) vote, Spain, general elections of 1993 and 1996 (logistic regression)

Independent variables	Both elections
Constant	0.34 (0.34)
Ideology	−2.22(0.30)**
Age	0.002 (0.004)
Education	−2.49(0.30)**
Unemployed[a]	0.32 (0.26)
Retired[a]	0.52 (0.20)*
Students[a]	−0.24(0.22)
Housewife[a]	0.48 (0.16)**
Optimistic economic expectations	0.60 (0.12)**
Economic policies assessments	2.22 (0.22)**
Social policies assessments	1.22 (0.17)**
Opposition	−0.88(0.24)**
Event: corruption	−0.69(0.15)**
96 Year × economic policies assessment	−1.19(0.26)**
96 Year × opposition	−2.66(0.43)**
96 Year	−0.78(0.18)**
Number of cases	2707
LR χ^2 (15)	1211.25**
Pseudo-R^2	0.36
% Correct (%)	81

Notes
Entries are logit maximum likelihood estimates and their associated standard errors. ** Significant at the level of 99%; * significant at the level of 95%; significant at the level of 90%. [a] These coefficients have been calculated with the employed as the category of reference.

variable), we may conclude that the introduction of the two significant interaction terms improves the fit of the model. The results of the likelihood-ratio test are the following: likelihood-ratio test = $\chi^2(2)$= 69.64. Prob (χ^2) = 0.000 (< 0.05).

Table 12.3 can be read in the same way as Table 12.1. The first column shows the names of the independent variables, included the interactions that turned out to be significant. The next column gives the parameter estimates and associated standard errors as estimated by logit regressions for both elections together. Table 12.3 provides evidence that the effect of voters' retrospective judgments about economic policies upon the probability of voting for the Socialists is weaker in 1996 than in 1993. Table 12.3 also indicates that the effect of the credibility of the main opposition party on the probability of voting for the incumbent is stronger in 1996 than in 1993. This was already suggested by the previous simulations of Table 12.2 where the largest change in the effects of the independent variables is found in voters' economic evaluations, and voters' views about the PP (first and fourth rows).[7] The former simulations, however, suggest that there are also changes in the effect of voters' evaluations of social policies, their economic expectations, and their ideology on the probability of rewarding the Socialists in 1993 and 1996.

None of these changes proved to be statistically significant in the pooled cross-sectional analysis carried out here.[8]

Table 12.3 also demonstrates that time matters when explaining how the individual determinants of the vote change across elections. Furthermore, the coefficient corresponding to the effect of time (i.e. the dummy variable that contrasts the individuals belonging to the 1996 survey with those of the 1993 survey) turns out to be significant. This means, basically, that in the 1996 model there is a higher propensity to punish the PSOE. We should hereby note that the coefficient is negative, and that the value 1 of the dummy year variable corresponds to all the individuals in the 1996 survey. This implies that there might be additional factors explaining the electoral defeat of the Socialists that the model is not able to capture in 1996 when compared to 1993. As I noted before, a proper corruption variable for the 1996 election would in all likelihood have clarified an important aspect of the defeat.

I shall now focus on the explanation of the two interaction terms that turned out to be statistically significant in the analysis presented in Table 12.3. How does the effect of voters' views on economic policies and the main opposition party (PP) upon the probability of voting for the PSOE change between 1993 and 1996? Results are presented in Table 12.4.

Following the same logic as before, I calculated the baseline probability of the average voter.[9] I then compared the effect of citizens' positive and negative evaluations of economic policies with this baseline probability in both elections.[10] I did the same for citizens' views about PP credibility.

Table 12.4 Differences in the effects of voters' assessment of economic policies and credibility of the opposition on probability of voting for the incumbent party, Spain, general elections of 1993 and 1996 (logistic estimators)

Variables of interest	Probability of voting for the incumbent (PSOE) in	
	1993	*1996*
Voters' assessments of economic policies		
1 Positive	0.51 (0.41–0.60)	0.19 (0.16–0.22)
0 Negative	0.10 (0.08–0.11)	0.07 (0.05–0.09)
Difference	0.41	0.12
Views about PP's credibility		
1 Yes	0.09 (0.07–0.13)	0.02 (0.01–0.05)
0 No	0.21 (0.18–0.24)	0.26 (0.20–0.29)
Difference	0.12	0.24
Baseline probability	0.16 (0.14–0.19)	0.16 (0.14–0.19)

Notes
Estimated probabilities were calculated with the other variables set to their sample mean values. Numbers in parentheses correspond to a 95% confidence interval for each simulation. To calculate the simulations, I used the program CLARIFY (Tomz *et al.*, 1999).

These results illustrate that the effects of economic policies upon the probability of rewarding the incumbent diminished in the 1996 elections. For instance, the difference between a voter with positive judgments about economic policies and a voter with negative evaluations is 41 percent in 1993, while the difference decreases in 1996 to 12 percent. Thus the effects of voters' evaluations of the incumbent's economic program decreases in the 1996 election.

In practical terms this means that, in the event of positive evaluations of the Socialists' economic program, they would have benefited more in the 1993 than in the 1996 elections.[11] The economic measures taken by the Socialists in their last legislature to tackle the economic crisis were not so much to their advantage in the 1996 elections as the same economic measures would have been in the 1993 elections.

The credibility of the PP also helps to explain the Socialist defeat in 1996. The difference between a voter who considers the PP a credible alternative ready to govern and a voter who does not deem the PP to be credible in the 1993 election is 12 percent, while this difference is higher in the 1996 elections, namely 24 percent.

Finally, time matters and it seems that there are additional factors in the 1996 elections that the extended economic-voting model is not able to capture in 1996 when compared to 1993. The hypothesis is that corruption is the other factor explaining the electoral defeat of the Socialists in the 1996 elections. A number of tentative conclusions can be drawn from these findings.

12.4   CONCLUSION

In this chapter, I have investigated the hypothesis of the retrospective voter in Spain during the 1990s. I have first justified, in theoretical terms, the economic-voting model that I test for the 1993 and 1996 elections. Starting from the simplest reward–punishment hypothesis, I give reasons for the introduction of additional factors in order to better account for the political, institutional, and sociological contexts of economic voting.

The empirical results verify the hypothesis of the retrospective economic voter since the coefficients corresponding to voters' retrospective economic assessments are higher than voters' economic expectations. Hence, it can be argued that in the 1990s, after the Socialists had been in power for three consecutive legislatures, Spanish electors retrospectively controlled them by judging their economic and social program. This implies the existence of both social and economic policy voting in Spain during the 1990s.

It is worthwhile to lay bare the mechanism explaining the defeat of the Socialists in 1996, just when the economy started to recover, rather than in 1993, which was during a period of serious economic recession. Following an economic-voting logic and using the empirical strategy of pooling the data of 1993 and 1996 elections, I provide statistical evidence showing that some of the advantages that the Socialists enjoyed for a long period of time came to an end in 1996. Particularly, the positive effect of voters' retrospective judgments about economic policies is weaker in 1996 than in 1993. This decrease in the electoral importance of the economic program helps to explain why the Socialists finally did lose the elections in 1996. The growing effect of the heightened credibility of the main opposition party together with the issue of corruption complete the puzzle of the Socialist defeat in 1996, just when the economy stared to recover.

ACKNOWLEDGMENTS

I wish to thank Fabrizio Bernardi, Richard Breen, and Jose M. Maravall for invaluable comments on previous versions of this chapter.

APPENDIX A

Table 12.A1 Descriptive statistics of the variables used in the incumbent vote model, 1993

Variables	Number of observations	Mean	Standard deviation	Minimum	Maximum
PSOE	1775	0.32	0.47	0	1
Ideology	2045	0.41	0.24	0	1
Education	2491	0.30	0.23	0	1
Age	2502	45.5	18.4	18	99
Labor market position	2490	2.63	1.55	1	5
Optimistic expectations	1908	0.33	0.47	0	1
Evaluations of economic policies	2210	0.16	0.36	0	1
Evaluations of social policies	2260	0.53	0.34	0	1
Views about the opposition	2182	0.25	0.43	0	1
Views about corruption	2315	0.77	0.42	0	1

Notes
Data from CIS2048: this is a survey collected in February 1993, with a number of cases of 2502.

Table 12.A2 Descriptive statistics of the variables used in the incumbent vote model, 1996

Variables	Number of observations	Mean	Standard deviation	Minimum	Maximum
PSOE	4979	0.34	0.47	0	1
Ideology	4926	0.40	0.21	0	1
Education	5831	0.26	0.19	0	1
Age	6639	44.7	18.1	18	99
Labor market position	6569	2.62	1.55	1	5
Optimistic expectations	4360	0.32	0.46	0	1
Evaluations of economic policies	5633	0.25	0.43	0	1

Table 12.A2 (Continued)

Evaluations of social policies	5470	0.68	0.35	0	1
Views about the opposition	5200	0.31	0.46	0	1
Views about corruption	5373	0.14	0.35	0	1

Notes
Data from CIS2207: this is a pre-electoral survey collected in February 1996. The number
of cases is 6642.

NOTES

1 A detailed explanation of the extended economic-voting model being tested in this chapter for the Spanish case can be found in Fraile (2000).
2 For example, in 1993, 40 percent of those interviewed thought that things in Spain would have been much worse if the AP/PP had been in power. Moreover, only 42 percent of respondents thought that any other party apart from the ruling Socialists could solve Spain's unemployment problem, while the equivalent figures for solving the country's economic problems in general, and handling education were 36 and 30 percent respectively (DATA S.A., May 1993).
3 Further information about the data used can be seen in Appendix A.
4 I take the dummy variable of the workers as the category of reference when estimating the other four dummy variables' coefficients.
5 Preliminary empirical research indicates that such is the case (Barreiro and Sánchez Cuenca, 2000). Even the variable I am using for the 1993 model is not the most adequate for measuring properly the electoral impact of voters' opinion about corruption. It shows that voters are more likely to react to the government's response against corruption, than to the corruption itself. The reason is simple: the government accepts no direct responsibility for the scandals involving leading members of the PSOE. However, the government does feel it has a responsibility to express its opinion about such scandals. Unfortunately, there were no questions asking individuals directly about their views on the government's response to corruption.
6 By including the significant interactions only, the filtered model presented in Table 12.3 is more adequate in terms of parsimony as well as goodness of fit.
7 The change in the effect of voters' retrospective evaluations between 1993 and 1996 is, according to the simulations presented in Table 12.2, 35 percent $(0.49 - 0.14 = 0.35)$. The change in the effect of voters' views about the PP between 1993 and 1996 is nineteen percent $(0.33 - 0.14 = 0.19)$.
8 The change in the effect of voters' ideology between 1993 and 1996 is, according to the simulations presented in Table 12.3, 12 percent $(0.23 - 0.11 = 0.12)$. The change in the effect of voters' evaluations of social policies between 1993 and 1996 is 8 percent $(0.20 - 0.12 = 0.08)$. The change in the effect of voters' economic expectations between 1993 and 1996 is 6 percent $(0.13 - 0.07 = 0.06)$, and the change in the effect of voters' views about corruption is 12 percent $(0.17 - 0.05 = 0.12)$. All of these changes are smaller than the changes of the other two variables, that did prove to be statistically significant (see previous note).
9 That is, setting the values of all independent variables included in the model to their sample mean values.
10 For computing these simulations, I use the equation of the pooled cross-sectional model presented in Table 12.3. This explains that the baseline probability is equal for the two elections. I also artificially maintain constant

the dummy year variable at its mean value, for the sake of simplicity in the comparison exercise presented in Table 12.4.

11 This can be read from Table 12.4 where positive evaluations of economic policies increase the probability of rewarding the Socialists with 35 percent in 1993 (0.51 − 0.16), and with only 3 percent in 1996 (0.19 − 0.16).

REFERENCES

Barreiro, B. and Sánchez Cuenca, I. (2000) Las consecuencias electorales de la corrupción, unpublished.

Campell, A., Converse, P., Miller, W. and Stokes, D. (1960) *The American Voter*. New York: Wiley.

Ferejohn, J. (1986) Incumbent performance and electoral control. *Public Choice*, **30**, 5–25.

Firebaugh, G. (1997) *Analyzing Repeated Surveys*. Sage University Paper Series on Quantitative Applications in the Social Sciences Series/Number 07-115. Thousand Oaks: Sage.

Fraile, M. (2000) *Does the economy enter the ballot-box? A study of the Spanish voters' decisions*. Unpublished Ph.D. dissertation. European University Institute.

Gunther, R. and Montero, J.R. (1994) Los anclajes del partidismo: un análisis comparado del comportamiento electoral en cuatro democracias del Sur de Europa. In P. del Castillo (ed.) *Comportamiento Electoral y Político*. Madrid: Centro de Investigaciones Sociológicas, pp. 467–548.

Jiménez, F. (1998) Political scandals and political responsibility in democratic Spain. *West Eur. Politics*, **21**, 80–99.

Key Jr., V.O. (1966) *The Responsible Electorate: Rationality in Presidential Voting, 1936–1960*. Cambridge: Harvard University Press.

Kinder, D.R. and Kiewiet, R. (1981) Sociotropic politics. *Brit. J. Political Sci.*, **11**, 129–161.

King, G. (1989) *Unifying Political Methodology*. Cambridge: Cambridge University Press.

Lewis-Beck, M.S. and Paldam, M. (2000) Economic voting: an introduction. *Electoral Stud.*, **19**, 113–121.

Maravall, J.M. (1999) Accountability and manipulation. In B. Manin, A. Przeworski and S. Stokes (eds), *Democracy, Accountability and Representation*. New York: Cambridge University Press.

Maravall, J.M. and M. Fraile (2001) The politics of unemployment: the Spanish case in comparative perspective. In N. Bermeo (ed.) *Unemployment in the New Europe*. Cambridge: Cambridge University Press.

Maravall, J.M. and Przeworski, A. (2001) Political reactions to the economy: the Spanish experience. In S. Stokes (ed.) *Public Opinions and Economic Reforms in New Democracies*. New York: Cambridge University Press.

Montero, J.R. (1990) Los fracasos politicos y electorales de la derecha española: alianza popular, 1976–1987. In J.F. Tezanos, R. Cotarelo and A. De Blas (eds), *La Transicion Democratica Española*. Madrid: Sistema.

Pierson, P. (1996) The new politics of the welfare state. *World Politics*, **48**, 143–179.

Sanders, D. (1996) Economic performance, management competence and the outcome of the next general election. *Political Stud.*, **44**, 203–231.

Tomz M., Wittenberg, J. and King, G. (1999) *CLARIFY: Software for Interpreting and Presenting Statistical Results*, Version 1.2.1. Cambridge, MA: Harvard University Press. http://gking.harvard.edu

13 Conclusions

Han Dorussen

If one would meet a group of economic voters, what would they look like? If we are to go along with either common political wisdom, or most scholars working on economic voting, they should look pretty much like normal people, more or less a random selection of society. The point here is not so much that economic conditions determine for a lot of people what parties they are going to support. Rather, the *model* of the "economic voter" claims to be less of a theoretical abstraction than its rational choice cousins "economic" or "political (wo)man". At the same time, the economic voter still exhibits a lot of the defining characteristics of a rational choice actor. To quote Lewis-Beck (1988: 33–34): "Voters are not blind subjects of sociological forces. Nor are they *tabulae rasae*, waiting to be filled with campaign promises. Rather, voters weigh how things have been and act accordingly." Economic voting is an instrumental act.

The model of the economic voter, at least in the political science literature, may thus find itself between a rock and a hard place. On the one hand, the psychology of the economic voter is clearly underdeveloped. On the other hand, the claim that the model of economic voting as a rational-instrumental act applies fairly directly to reality raises several serious questions. It should come as no surprise that these questions have actually become the main controversies in the literature on economic voting.

A good illustration is the debate about whether the economic voter is mainly retrospective or prospective. The retrospective voter looks at past and current economic conditions and, at best, extrapolates from these conditions into the near future. If, in addition, such a voter only considers the most readily available information, we are looking at the "peasant" economic voter. Add some beer and a smoky bar, and the peasant easily becomes a real life character, but one that hardly fits the rational choice interpretation of economic voting. The prospective voter, or "banker," considers all available information and responds to events the moment that they are anticipated, rather than waiting until they occur. MacKuen *et al.* (1992: 598) argue that economic voters actually behave accordingly: "In the aggregate, we can imagine an electorate guided by the same intelligence as the economic forecasters." The banker fits more closely the rational-expectation models of economic behavior, but the evidence is still out on whether it describes actual economic voting. Moreover, the portrayal of economic voters as economic forecasters is remarkable by itself. I doubt that economists ever conceive of "economic men" as persons with the same intelligence as themselves.

The decision to study economic voting as an instrumental act that actually occurs in real life forces us to deal with several other questions as well. To what information about the economy do voters pay attention? Are there specific biases in how they deal with this information causing them to systematically misperceive the actual state of the economy? How much do they care? Or, in other words, how much time and energy are they willing to invest in gathering and processing information? Who do they blame? A recurrent theme in this book has been that institutions are especially relevant when considering the last question, because they make it more or less difficult to attribute responsibility for economic conditions. However, institutions are likely to affect the answers to the other questions as well. Moreover, the same answers do probably not apply to all voters. It is not a bold claim that any electorate most likely consists of some mixture of bankers and peasants, more and less sophisticated voters, or partisan and non-partisan voters. Again nearly all contributions also pay attention to the effects of voter heterogeneity.

From an empirical point of view, these questions strengthen the need for comparative research, because only in this way are we likely to get sufficient variation to actually observe the effects of institutions and voter heterogeneity. They also demonstrate why the instability problem or the comparative puzzle has become so central to research on economic voting. It would be extremely unsatisfactory theoretically, if we would be left with a multitude of models of the economic voter, each applying only to specific institutions or subsets of the electorate. It is appropriate to quote Paldam at this point:

> The question of model generality is, as usual, the toughest one: obviously it is highly desirable if models are general and institution free, so that the same model works across countries and over time. This does not necessarily mean that the model takes no account of country differences and institutions; but only that any relevant difference is explicitly modeled.
>
> (Paldam, 1991: 11)

In Chapter 2, Nannestad and Paldam report a remarkably stable cost of ruling which leads them to look for a "deep parameter" to explain the stability. They argue that the loss/risk aversion complex provides the most parsimonious explanation. In other words, regardless of most institutional and contextual factors, sensitivity to losses and aversion to risks causes a constant subset of the electorate to withdraw its support from the incumbent government. A similar approach may be valid more generally. *A priori*, nothing precludes the effect of a "deep" variable from being conditional on contextual factors. To provide an obvious example: the rational actor is also a fundamental model, but we know that rationality leads to different behavioral predictions depending on the context to which it is applied. In other words, the rules of the game determine the equilibrium outcome. Institutions and economic conditions may thus very well matter for VP functions.

What would be the main advantage of developing the psychological model of the economic voter beyond the basic rational actor framework? First of all, it would help to identify institutional, group, and country factors that need to be modeled explicitly. The model would tell us which differences should matter for economic voting and which not. Second, it would allow us to derive and formulate more precise hypotheses. Finally, the model in itself would become an important area of research. For example, Lewis-Beck and Paldam (2000: 114) observe that "little is known about the macroeconomic knowledge of voters and how it is obtained." Clearly, this should become a core research area for any psychological model that relies on learning or perceptions. The hope is, of course, that the VP functions will turn out to be mainly stable given appropriate control variables, accurate measurements, and proper understanding of the link between economics and voting.

What psychological models are likely candidates? The literature suggests basically three avenues: (i) the loss/risk aversion complex, (ii) limited-information rationality models, and (iii) models emphasizing emotional and affective factors. The chapters in this volume actually use all of these possible explanations, but also reveal a slight preference for the loss/risk aversion complex.

The use of the concept of risk aversion is widespread in economics and, more general, in formal social scientific models. Several important propositions actually only hold under the assumption of risk aversion, for example, the general existence of a bargaining solution. There is plenty of evidence, from experimental as well as less structured observations, that most people are risk averse. In contrast to risk aversion, which is future-oriented, loss aversion refers to past events. Kahneman and Tversky use loss aversion to develop the notion of "framing," for which they find strong experimental evidence (Kahneman and Tversky, 1979; Kahneman, 1994). Loss aversion and possible framing effects remain, however, less widely accepted. In the context of economic voting, risk and loss aversion is primarily used in the grievance-asymmetry hypothesis: the expectation that voters more readily punish governments for bad economic conditions than reward them for good economic conditions.

Apart from Nannestad and Paldam, several other studies also either observe that risk/loss aversion best explains the observed pattern of results or find support for the grievance-asymmetry hypothesis. In Chapter 8, Riba and Díaz provide evidence for the existence of grievance asymmetry in the case of Catalan politics. In Chapter 4, Palmer and Whitten find that the electoral importance of unemployment is greater in political systems in which unemployment insurance has a high policy priority. The finding suggests that politicians anticipate the risk aversion of voters, in particular, their sensitivity to unemployment. Partially in contrast to Nannestad and Paldam, Palmer and Whitten find that voter volatility, economic voting, and the cost of ruling are stronger in systems with higher clarity of responsibility. Such findings do not necessarily conflict with risk or loss aversion. They suggest, however, that the effects of the "deep parameter" may vary depending on institutional context. In Chapter 7, Norpoth also reports that only non-incumbent presidential candidates suffer from the cost of ruling, but to a much larger degree than the 2.5 percent reported by Nannestad and Paldam. Finally, in Chapter 9, Sanders and Carey suggest that cross-national variation in the strength of the clarity-of-responsibility effect is best explained as due to variation in voters' risk orientations.

Dorussen and Taylor, in Chapter 5, observe that groups more exposed to the risk of unemployment are more loyal to social-democratic parties. Risk aversion thus explains a preference for parties with unemployment as their clear issue priority. These findings are based on disaggregated, individual-level data and suggest that variation in risk aversion is a source of voter heterogeneity. The aggregate-level analyses of Stevenson (Chapter 3) would at first appear to present a contradictory picture. He finds the strongest support for the luxury-goods model, i.e. voters prefer economic conservatism during downturns and are willing to "buy" more public services during economic good times. By itself, the luxury-goods model is easily reconcilable with the notion of risk aversion. The main difference lies in the perception of the issue priorities of left and right parties. Groups of voters may very well differ systematically in their perception of issue priorities. Stevenson acknowledges that analyses of aggregate data are insufficient to expose more subtle contextual effects of the economy on economic voting.

Limited information rationality is the second main way in which the research presented in this volume aims at extending the psychological model of the economic voter. Several scholars have argued that the assumptions of rational-expectations models have little relevance given the political and economic sophistication of the average voter. Instead of the rational-voter model, Popkin (1991) suggests a model of the *reasoning* voter. It would seem reasonable to expect voters to differ in their levels of sophistication. Recent research has demonstrated that the media influences political discussion, public opinion, and voting behavior (Bartels, 1993; Hetherington, 1996). Political sophistication may thus depend on the distribution and reception of information. Education and better access to mass media increase levels of political sophistication. There is, however, uncertainty about the importance of variation in media exposure and cognitive ability (Kinder, 1998). The cost of acquiring and processing all necessary information to make a fully rational evaluation is enormous but the individual-level payoff is extremely small. Consequently, it would be unreasonable if voters were to invest heavily in the process of information seeking. We should expect them to process readily available information with the help of a "schema" such as party identification (Conover and Feldman, 1984; Lau, 1986). Voters can also rely on simple heuristics to guide their decisions in complex situations. Finally, uninformed voters can behave in a relatively sophisticated manner using cues from informed voters (Ferejohn and Kuklinski, 1990; Lupia, 1994).

The clarity-of-responsibility hypothesis, originally formulated by Powell and Whitten (1993), definitely receives the most attention in this volume. Institutions may display or hide the political responsibility for prevailing economic conditions and thus affect the ability of voters to engage in economic voting. Of course, institutional smoke screens should not impress fully rational voters. The clarity-of-responsibility hypothesis thus assumes less than full voter rationality. In Chapter 11, Bellucci argues that a change of electoral laws in Italy has facilitated the emergence of economic voting in Italy. In a majoritarian system, clarity of responsibility makes economic (dis)content a more powerful force. The system also induces parties to provide more distinct party programs, or visions for the future, thus enhancing clarity of available alternatives, or opposition. Dorussen and Taylor argue that economic voting may still be feasible in proportional systems with coalition governments. In multi-party systems, coalitions not only increase the amount of required information, but also provide a context helping voters to process information. Moreover, instead of trying to form rational expectations about coalitions formation, voters will rely on a simple heuristic: the impact of their vote on the creation or removal of the main alternative to the incumbent government. More generally, Palmer and Whitten (Chapter 4) provide further evidence that economic voters respond in a rather sophisticated manner to their political and economic contexts. Although generally in support of the clarity-of-responsibility hypothesis, their findings amend the hypothesis by suggesting more subtle effects of political institutions on economic voting.

In Chapter 7, Duch and Palmer extend their earlier work on voter heterogeneity to a cross-national perspective. Systematic variation in subjective evaluation of economic conditions causes serious problems for VP functions based on aggregate data. The same is true when the sources of systematic bias are left unaccounted for. Duch and Palmer demonstrate that subjective perception of the economy is shaped by political predisposition, personal socioeconomic experience, and level of understanding about the political economy. Moreover, the impact of these subjective factors varies considerably from one country to another; for example, the effects of partisanship and media influences are country-specific. The intriguing implication is that institutions may not only influence how voters use available information, but that they may be among the factors that directly shape the manner in which individuals acquire information about the economy.

Intuitively, it would seem unreasonable to entirely dispense with emotions in a model of the economic voter. Nevertheless, emotional reactions have traditionally been neglected in models of the economic voter emphasizing instead a rational cost–benefits calculus. Relatively few researchers have given a central place to the impact of emotional reactions to the economy (Peffley, 1984; Conover and Feldman, 1986; Conover *et al.*, 1986, 1987; Marcus and MacKuen, 1993; Clarke *et al.*, 1998). The relation between affective factors and voter heterogeneity and political institutions has hardly been explored.

The salience hypothesis asserts that economic factors need to be sufficiently strong before they will actually affect vote choice. In Chapter 10, Clarke, Stewart, and Whiteley propose that emotions thus matter for economic voting. An interesting aspect of their research is that they integrate affective and cognitive accounts of the formation of economic expectations. To put it more simply, voters start reacting when they are angry or worried about the economy, but the specific reaction differs depending on the voter's level of sophistication. Since emotional reactions are partial substitute for cognitive judgments, they both can become sources for heterogeneity of subjective economic evaluations among subgroups in the electorate.

Emotional factors also provide a likely explanation for how some institutional features appear to matter for economic voting. In Chapter 12, Fraile observes that the Spanish electorate did put little *trust* in the conservatives, i.e. the main opposition force to the ruling social democrats since the transition to democracy. Potential reasons for this include the fact that this party was formed by prominent political leaders of the previous authoritarian, Francoist regime. In effect, emotional factors are an important part of an institutional feature, namely a lack of clarity of opposition. Norpoth elaborates on the inability of candidates to run for a third term in office, an important institutional feature of the US presidential elections. Identification with the incumbent party was insufficient to secure the election of Vice President Al Gore even during good economic times. Clearly, an incumbent *party* does not strike the same emotional resonance with the electorate as an incumbent *candidate*. Finally, Riba and Díaz report another intriguing finding: even lacking important competencies for economic policy, the popularity function of the subnational Catalonian government relies to a significant degree on economic variables. In this particular instance, economic voting may very well represent a "feel good" factor or an expressive act voicing *pride* in one's regional identity.

The political and personal contexts of economic voting has been a recurrent theme in this volume. In various ways, the contributors all agree that the specification of VP functions needs to be done with attention to their context. In this respect, country-specific studies remain clearly important. Expert knowledge may be required to identify the important institutional features. Further, there remain important gaps in our information about the (macroeconomic) knowledge of voters. Data are often not (or not yet) available to allow for a cross-country comparative research design with individual-level data encompassing information on political and macroeconomic knowledge. However, the comparative perspective holds a lot of promise. The instability problem may be frustrating to some; actually, it represents a fascinating research puzzle, forcing us to identify what factors matter for economic voting and how they matter. Political institutions and voter heterogeneity present additional pieces of the puzzle. There are, however, important differences. Information about political institutions is often readily available, and their effects can mainly be dealt with at the aggregate level. Information about relevant sources of voter heterogeneity is much more sparse, basically only available for a few countries and measured at irregular intervals. Voter heterogeneity, however, requires the use of disaggregated, individual-level data. Unfortunately, these data are much more costly – in terms of time and money – to collect, administer, and analyze. From a practical point of view, it is clear that international cooperation is crucial. The development of theory, however, also has practical implications: future research on economic voting will have to choose between emphasizing risk-assessment, cognitive, or affective variables.

REFERENCES

Bartels, L.M. (1993) Messages received: the political impact of media exposure. *Am. Political Sci. Rev.*, **87**, 267–286.

Clarke, H.D., Stewart, M.C. and Whiteley, P. (1998) New models for New Labour: the political economy of Labour Party support, January 1992–April 1997. *Am. Political Sci. Rev.*, **92**, 559–575.

Conover, P.J. and Feldman, S. (1984) How people organize the political world. *Am. J. Political Sci.*, **28**, 95–126.

Conover, P.J. and Feldman, S. (1986) Emotional reactions to the economy: I'm mad as Hall and I'm not going to take it anymore. *Am. J. Political Sci.*, **30**, 50–76.

Conover, P.J., Feldman, S. and Knight, K. (1986) Judging inflation and unemployment: the origin of retrospective evaluations. *J. Politics*, **48**, 565–588.

Conover, P.J., Feldman, S. and Knight, K. (1987) The personal and political underpinnings of economic forecasts. *Am. J. Political Sci.*, **31**, 559–832.

Ferejohn, J.A. and Kuklinski, J.H. (eds) (1990) *Information and Democratic Processes*. Urbana, IL: University of Illinois Press.

Hetherington, M.J. (1996) The media's role in forming voters' national economic evaluations in 1992. *Am. J. Political Sci.*, **40**, 372–395.

Kahneman, D. (1994) New challenges to the rationality assumption. *J. Inst. Theoret. Economics*, **150**(1), 18–36.

Kahneman, D. and Tversky, A. (1979) Prospect theory: an analysis of decision under risk. *Econometrica*, **47**, 263–291.

Kinder, D.R. (1998) Communication and opinion. *Annu. Rev. Political Sci.*, **1**, 167–197.

Lau, R. (1986) Political schemata, candidate evaluation, and voting behavior. In R. Lau and D.O. Sears (eds), *Political Cognition*. Hillsdale: Lawrence Erlbaum.

Lewis-Beck, M.S. (1988) *Economics and Elections*. Ann Arbor, MI: The University of Michigan Press.

Lewis-Beck, M.S. and Paldam, M. (2000) Economic voting: an introduction. *Electoral Stud.*, **19**(2/3), 113–123.

Lupia, A. (1994) Shortcuts versus encyclopedias: information and voting behavior in California insurance reform elections. *Am. Political Sci. Rev.*, **88**, 63–76.

MacKuen, M.B., Erikson, R.S. and Stimson, J.A. (1992) Peasants or bankers? The American electorate and the US economy. *Am. Political Sci. Rev.*, **86**, 597–611.

Marcus, G.B. and MacKuen, M.B. (1993) Anxiety, enthusiasm and the vote: the emotional underpinnings of learning and involvement during presidential campaigns. *Am. Political Sci. Rev.*, **87**, 672–685.

Paldam, M. (1991) How robust is the vote function? A study of 17 nations over four decades. In H. Norpoth, M.S. Lewis-Beck and J.-D. Lafay (eds), *Economics and Politics: The Calculus Of Support*. Ann Arbor, MI: University of Michigan Press, pp. 9–32.

Peffley, M. (1984) The voter as juror: attributing responsibility for economic conditions. *Political Behav.*, **6**(3), 275–294.

Popkin, S.L. (1991) *The Reasoning Voter*. Chicago, IL: University of Chicago Press.

Powell, G.B. and Whitten, G.D. (1993) A cross-national analysis of economic voting: taking account of political context. *Am. J. Political Sci.*, **37**, 391–414.

Index

Alesina, A. 37, 69
Anderson, C.J. 4, 45, 53, 57, 113, 140, 174, 204
asymmetry hypotheses 45–6, 60, 62
attribution of responsibility 56–7, 173, 176, 277, 287–8; model of 178–81; political institutions 307; autoregressive model 129, 134

"banker" economic voter
  see prospective economic voter
Bartels, L.M. 139, 144
Bartolini, S. 264, 269
Beck-Katz panel-robust standard errors 75, 78–9
Berlusconi, Silvio 265, 274
Brooks, C. 264
Butler, D. 173

Catalan politics 177–8; differential abstention 178; dual vote 178
Chappell, H.W. 69
clarity of opposition 9, 174; Italy 278; Spain 286, 292, 297–8
clarity of responsibility 94, 122, 124, 174, 288; cross-national variation 200, 217, 224–5; divided government 125; Italy 277–8; Lib-Lab pact 203, 210; measurement 76; temporal variation 200–1, 210, 217–23; and term limits 125; UK 203; cost of ruling 83–4; hypothesis 4, 8, 45
class voting 266–73; and class politics 266–7; party policy positions 268–73
Clinton, Bill 121
coalition complexity 93, 95–7, 99–100
coalition government 92, 95–7, 174
cognitive engagement 235, 239

comparative puzzle 1, 3;
  see also instability problem
conditional responsibility 92, 94, 101; Germany 109–13; Netherlands 104–7
Conover, P.J. 235, 243, 397, 308
consensual democracy 261
constant "sucker-fraction" 29
corruption; Italy 264; Spain 289, 292, 294
cost of ruling 11, 17, 67, 126; relation with VP functions 18; term limits, 126–7; see also constant "sucker-fraction"; grievance asymmetry 19, 31–2; macroeconomic performance 73–4; clarity of responsibility 74–5; median gap theory 19, 29–31, 39; stability of 26–8; coalition of minorities theory 19, 28–9
credibility of opposition 201, 202, 204–5, 209, 286; cross-national comparison 224–5; measurement 212; Spain 285
devolution 175

Duch, R.M. 140
Durr, R. 49–50

economic context 45, 47, 67
economic expectations; Spain 290, 292, 294; see also prospective economic voter
economic growth; US presidential vote 123–4; see also unexpected growth
economic perceptions 201, 202–4; versus objective economic indicators 209, 225

For Product Safety Concerns and Information please contact our EU
representative GPSR@taylorandfrancis.com
Taylor & Francis Verlag GmbH, Kaufingerstraße 24, 80331 München, Germany

www.ingramcontent.com/pod-product-compliance
Lightning Source LLC
Chambersburg PA
CBHW070552270326
41926CB00013B/2288